"For the most complete overall picture of what genuine wilderness camping entails, the Sierra Club's *Walking Softly in the Wilderness* is the ultimate manual."

HOUSTON CHRONICLE

"*Walking Softly in the Wilderness* is crowded with information on gearing up, on food and fuel, finding your way, making and breaking camp, and advice on trouble. A common-sense and literate approach."

LOS ANGELES TIMES

"Author Hart is a thorough and fluid writer [and] *Walking Softly in the Wilderness* ranks with the best basic guides to backpacking."

CAMPING JOURNAL

K

WALKING SOFTLY

IN THE WILDERNESS

The Sierra Club Guide to Backpacking

COMPLETELY REVISED
AND UPDATED

——————— JOHN HART ———

SIERRA CLUB BOOKS • SAN FRANCISCO

The Sierra Club, founded in 1892 by John Muir, has devoted itself to the study and protection of the Earth's scenic and ecological resources—mountains, wetlands, woodlands, wild shores and rivers, deserts and plains. The publishing program of the Sierra Club offers books to the public as a nonprofit educational service in the hope that they may enlarge the public's understanding of the Club's basic concerns. The point of view expressed in each book, however, does not necessarily represent that of the Club. The Sierra Club has some sixty chapters coast to coast, in Canada, Hawaii, and Alaska. For information about how you may participate in its programs to preserve wilderness and the quality of life, please address inquiries to Sierra Club, 85 Second Street, San Francisco, CA 94105.

www.sierraclub.org/books

Copyright © 1998 by John Hart.

Library of Congress Cataloging in Publication Data
Hart, John, 1948–
Walking softly in the wilderness.
Includes index.
1. Backpacking. I. Sierra Club. II. Title.
GV199.6.H37 796.5 76–21260
ISBN 0-87156-392-4

Book design, production, and composition by BookMatters.
Cover design by Amy Evans McClure.
Illustrations by Joyce Jonté and Bonnie Laurie Russell. Maps by Amy Mazza.
Front cover photo by Markham Johnson/Robert Holmes Photography.

Printed in the United States on acid-free paper containing a minimum of 50% recovered waste paper of which at least 10% of the fiber content is post-consumer waste.

Third edition: 1998.

10 9 8 7 6 5 4 3 2 1

CONTENTS

ACKNOWLEDGMENTS

The author of a book of this kind is less creator than compiler, assembling the knowledge of an unthanked many; but I must thank a few.

On the always ticklish medical side, I'm grateful for the advice of Drs. Gordon Benner, Sierra Club Medical Officer; William Epstein; Michael J. Franzblau; and Eric Weiss, as well as the very knowledgeable Oscar V. Lopp of the Mountain Medicine Institute.

On wilderness impact and management questions, I've gleaned from researchers like David N. Cole of the Aldo Leopold Institute, bear expert Stephen Herrero of the University of Calgary, impact researcher John Stanley, and long-time Sierra Club national outings leader Jim Watters. Thanks also to Laurel Boyers of Yosemite National Park, Jim Papevo of the New York Department of Environmental Conservation, Elizabeth Rieben of the Environmental Education Office, Bureau of Land Management, and Marit Sawyer of the Leave No Trace Program, National Outdoor Leadership School.

For help in understanding the status of various wilderness conservation battles, my thanks to Bruce Hamilton of the Sierra Club; Fran Hunt of the Wilderness Society; Michael McCloskey of the Sierra Club; Alice Chambers of the Sierra Club of Canada, Prairies Chapter; Steve Gatewood of the Wildlands Project; Mary Granskow of the Canadian Parks and Wilderness Society; Elizabeth May of the Sierra Club of Canada; Ray Payne of the Smoky Mountains Hiking Club; Juri Peepre of the Canadian Parks and Wilderness Society; conservation biologist Reed Noss; Will Skelton of the Tennessee Chapter, Sierra Club; Rob Smith of the Sierra Club's Southwest Regional Office; and very especially to Alaska crusaders Peggy and Ed Wayburn.

When it comes to the ins and outs of gear, I've taken my questions to helpful people like Mary Abbott of A&H Enterprises; Rich Davies of Recreational Equipment, Inc.; Maria Frederiksen of Sun Precautions; Richard J. and Beverly Garcia of Garcia Machine; Chard Lowden and Mark McCartney of Marin Outdoors; Mark Randall of Yosemite Concession Services; Jim Reid of Peak 1; Mike Scherer of Kelty; Buck Smith of Marmot Mountain Works; and Bob and Ted Wallace of Polar Equipment.

I've learned much from fellow wilderness travelers such as Eric Brand; Susan Drayne of the Sierra Club Outings Committee; Lew Gardner of the Boy Scouts of America, Bay Area Council; Jon and Gail Hall of the Boy Scouts of Canada, Northern Region; John Harlin of *Backpacker* magazine; Lelia Loban Lee; John Lewis; Linda MacMillan; Julie Manson; Gordon Peterson of the Sierra Club's Knapsack Subcommittee; Steve Roper; Allen Steck; Mary Anne Stewart; Nicholas Van Pelt; Carol Vellutini and her cohorts in the Redwood Chapter, Sierra Club; and Gene White.

I've had the assistance of numerous folk at the agencies who manage public land, federal, state, and provincial. I must mention specifically Richard Fenton and Henry Savory of the New York State Department of Environmental Conservation; Barbara Garcia of Coconino National Forest; Mark Mandenberg of the Michigan Department of Natural Resources; Marty Roberts of the British Columbia Ministry of Environment; and Jean-Robert Gautier, Per Nilson, and D. B. Yurick of Parks Canada. Thanks also to Michel Cardinal and Steve Westley of Geomatics Canada.

Thanks far beyond the customary go to my copyeditor, Mary Anne Stewart.

—JH

NOTE TO THE READER

Welcome to the third edition of *Walking Softly in the Wilderness*. Much has changed, especially in the area of gear, since the second edition of 1982. Hardly a paragraph has escaped revision; indeed, most of the book has been rewritten from scratch.

The changes in the backpacker's world, and the revisions they entail, are hardly likely to stop now. I would like to invite your help in keeping this book accurate. Does something in these pages seem wrong to you, or inefficient, or outdated? I would very much appreciate your letting me know about it, care of the Sierra Club. Reader feedback is invaluable. My thanks to those who have responded in the past.

Of course, no book of manageable length and decent clarity can explore all the possible choices in wilderness gear and methods. Instead, a book must simplify. It must select. Often it must present only one way of doing things when there may be others just as good. Every backpacker works out a personal style; your style in the wilderness will be your own.

However, I hope that you will be slow to discount what this book has to say about low-impact methods in the wild places: about the skills of using but not injuring the vulnerable land. For these are not merely points of backcountry manners or wilderness etiquette. Not afterthoughts. Not optional finishing touches. Low-impact methods are the new necessities. And while there are legitimate disagreements about some of the details, the outlines are clear enough. There is little doubt about the things each hiker needs to know and do. I hope you will help.

THE LAND BEYOND THE ROADHEAD

Where do the six trails go?
What are the mountains named
That are colored like Iroquois?

Jeanne McGahey, "Journey"

1 THE LAND BEYOND THE ROADHEAD

There is in Idaho a cold sky-colored lake, untroubled in an airy scoop of stone. And from the nearest road it's two days' walk to be here.

In South Carolina there is a waterlogged forest, an American jungle of vines and trailing moss and cypress trunks 10 feet through.

In Utah there is a canyon in red rock, a path so narrow that with either hand you sometimes brush the wall.

In Washington a vast volcanic mountain seems as untouchable as a cloud. But you can wander to its ice and alpine flowers on miles of shady trail, up one of the greenest valleys in the world.

And off the Michigan shore, on a primitive island that is 50 miles long, the timber wolves still hunt, and moose are still the hunted.

These are a few of the places we call wilderness. These and a thousand more are the unoccupied landscapes of America, the places we have not reshaped to our busy purposes, not stamped with our straight lines. They are survivals of the untamed land beyond the old frontiers: the wildness that once was a continent wide.

We value these places for being what they are. We value them for the wildlife they shelter, for the clean water they yield. We value them as zones where the webs of life are more or less intact, not torn and rearranged by our own overwhelming, needy presence. We recognize wilderness areas as refuges for natural things, from us.

And yet they are also refuges *for* us. If we enter them with a certain humbleness, leaving behind our more aggressive tools and attitudes, we find in these regions a strange and utterly addictive joy. Quite early in our history, before we understood much else about the value of wild places, we began to feel that joy. It remains an excellent reason for wanting wilderness saved, and the best of all possible reasons for wanting to go into it.

THE DOOR

Wilderness belongs to everyone: it is a cultural possession. We can use it without going near it. But wild country does inevitably have a particular meaning, a further meaning, to those who make the effort to travel in it. For these people, the wild places are not a heritage only, but also something like a home.

You can visit the wilderness by water, say in a canoe; you can visit it on horse- or muleback, or with the help of pack animals. This book is for those who do it all on their own two feet: that very large yet very distinctive group, the backpackers.

Today there are millions of them, heading out from the roadheads. They are the people who don't mind a long day's walk, who are willing to carry moderate loads on their backs, who find a luxury in self-sufficiency. The backpackers earn their pleasure and would not find it so pleasant if it were not earned.

And yet the entry to the world of the trails is not hard. There are rather few Americans who are physically prevented from making the effort that the entry to the wilderness requires. There are many—indeed, the large majority—who have so far not tried. Some just aren't attracted, find the idea foreign. Others are quite genuinely content to have their wilderness secondhand, in books and photographs. But still others—who knows how many?—stay away because they simply don't know how to start, or have an exaggerated idea of the difficulties, the discomforts, the expense.

Wilderness travel is not free—but it is still among the cheaper things we can do with our leisure time.

Wilderness travel is not effortless—but it is, if you choose to make it so, quite easy.

Wilderness travel is not entirely without discomforts—but these seem slight enough once you have experienced the rewards.

Wilderness travel is certainly not for everyone. But it may be for a good number of people who have not yet found it out. There seems to be in many people a kind of hunger for wild places that, once aroused, is never to be satisfied by any substitute.

During the 1960s, backpacking became established as one of the major American outdoor pursuits. Just how major is unclear—the statistics are fuzzy and often at odds. But *Backpacker* magazine, drawing on various sources, estimates the count of backpackers at 13 million, of whom something like 4 million hit the trails frequently. There are indications that this audience, after leveling off in the 1980s, is once again vigorously growing.

For those who love and worry for the wilderness, who fight to defend it from logging, mining, destructive livestock grazing, and the endless thrusting-forward of the roads, an expanding audience for the wild places is an encouraging thing. The more people know those places, after all, the more may be moved to join the effort to preserve what can still be preserved.

THE IMPACT PROBLEM

But the popularity of wilderness has brought some problems as well. Some of that wilderness is unmistakably, jarringly *crowded*. And some of it is trampled: certain especially accessible or scenic places are getting the worked-over look of run-down city parks.

In the Appalachians from the Smokies to the Catskills, the woods around popular campsites have been stripped of dead branches and young growth by hikers hunting fuel.

At popular lakes in any western range, you may find shorelines beaten bare and spotted all around with blackened fire rings.

On the famous High Peaks of the Adirondacks, the trampling of thousands of boots is destroying the moist alpine tundra that makes these peaks so much of another world. In Colorado, the flanks of 14,000-foot peaks are webbed with eroding paths. In Rocky Mountain National Park, damage may take hundreds of years to reverse itself.

Such signs of wear and tear are most frequently seen in wild areas near cities, or in remoter landscapes so celebrated that they draw travelers from around the world; yet hardly a wilderness anywhere is free of recreational scars.

This kind of physical damage, disturbing as it is, is in fact just one of three dimensions of the impact problem. It may not even be the most important one.

A second type of damage, which may accompany the first, is ecological rather than esthetic. It is long-term disruption of natural systems. It may be invisible. Unlike the eroded trail, the overfertilized, subtly polluted lake may still look good. Nor is it obvious when little-noticed species disappear from a well-used area, or when a grizzly bear, tempted into aggression by backpackers careless with their food, becomes a menace that must be destroyed.

A third type of damage overlaps both of the others. It is the effect of people on people, what we do to one another's enjoyment of places.

When backpackers are asked what they desire most of all from wild places, the answer comes back: solitude. Not, to be sure, the total solitude of the single traveler; most backpackers move in groups of two, three, or four, and like it that way. "Solitude," for them, means that they should meet few other groups; that they should meet no large parties at all; and that they should have no company at camp. Four or five meetings a day, for many, begins to cheapen the experience. There are exceptions. Climbers bound for popular routes of ascent are philosophical about company, and the participants in large groups obviously value it. Yet by and large we backpackers, while we are backpacking, are antisocial, or anyway anticrowd.

Physical damage to the land, subtler damage to the ecosystem, the diminution of solitude: these are the three dimensions of "impact." All are controllable. If every hiker were scrupulously careful to make no mark on the country, to do no harm to its creatures, and to intrude on other people as little as possible, the threefold problem would be far less difficult to solve. Unfortunately, too many backpackers are still relying on old methods, still acting like lonely pioneers in an empty world. Too many more believe they are up-to-date and careful but, in reality, are not. Their weight on the land is heavy. It takes only a few of them to make a crowd.

A WILDERNESS OF RULES

It is not only the backpackers who are troubled by the changes they see in the backcountry. Government agencies manage most of our protected wilderness, and it is their charge to keep it authentically wild. But that means that the door to the wilderness cannot be endlessly, unconditionally open. In the 1970s, the authorities moved to regulate use as never before. Visitors to popular regions are now commonly required to secure "wilderness permits" for their trips, and in some well-used areas and seasons they are subject to daily quotas. If you head for the hills without inquiring first, you may find yourself forced, when you get there, to revise a cherished plan.

It is hard to be comfortable with such restrictions. One of the chief pleasures of the land beyond the roadhead has always been the independence of the traveler there, the freedom from formal rules. Quotas, certainly, should be a last resort. There is reason to complain, in some instances, that other, less intrusive methods have not been properly tried. But for all that, there seems little chance that formal controls will vanish from the scene.

One thing is unmistakable. Restriction will come soonest, and in the most annoying form, in the places where hikers themselves have dropped the ball. As an official at Yosemite National Park put it, "We have to plan everything with the *worst* backcountry user in mind." Others can study and scold, comment and cajole, lay down the law and try sporadically to enforce it, but the job of protecting wilderness belongs primarily to just one group: to us who enjoy it.

Each backpacker must make certain that his or her own way in the wilderness is a gentle and a thoughtful way. Each of us must make a game, an ethic, a matter of pride, of walking softly in the wilderness world. Each of us must develop a personal, knowledgeable code, subtler and perhaps stricter than any set of standardized rules can possibly be. We have to grasp the fact that no change we inflict on the wilderness is trivial: each of us now is a thousand.

In addition to watching our own ways, we can serve as eyes and ears for the deskbound people who work, in one way or another, for the wilderness cause. We can call the managers' attention to the gullied trail, the misleading sign, the cattle grazing where they aren't supposed to be. We can praise and blame, suggest, kibitz, and have a real influence on what is done.

There is another contribution that some may want to make. We each have the chance to speak out for the preservation of wilderness, and of near-natural areas in general. Each can lend some individual weight— small, but not so small as you might think—to the cause of defending lands that are now protected; of extending protection where it is now lacking; and of encouraging the restoration of key regions that are not wild now but could be wild again. If every second or third backpacker did so, the future of the wilderness would be considerably brighter. For more on this, see Chapter 31.

What we hope to experience, when we go to the wild places, is wideness, freedom, *room*. The more wilderness we manage to preserve, the roomier it will be.

GOING LIGHT: FIRST POINTS

A generation ago, when you spoke of "going light," you were probably thinking of the poundage in your pack. "Going light" was the skill of paring down the load, of leaving at home every ounce that could be spared. And that is still an excellent thing to do.

But today "going light" has an additional meaning. Today you go light to spare the land and the sensibilities of other people. You choose your gear, your route, your schedule with the welfare of the wilderness in mind. You camp and travel by the rules of "low impact."

Those principles are not complex. There are, indeed, varying problems from region to region, from landscape to contrasting landscape. There are questions different experts answer differently. There are subtleties to wander in. Yet certain major points are clear.

The go-light backpacker rarely camps on vegetation. This is a hard one; it seems to run against some instinct out of the Stone Age. The novice hurries to camp on the grass at the edge of the water or—a second choice —on the grass at the edge of the forest. Most experienced hikers have gotten the word that lush meadows are fragile (also damp, cold, and full of mosquitoes). It's not so widely recognized that some other types of vegetation are even more vulnerable. Short of learning a lot of botany, you can fall back on a simple principle: don't camp on green things at all. You can almost always find bare ground to settle on. Even in steep terrain, three or four people can usually locate a flat, pleasant, unvegetated spot.

Go-lighters take the landscape as they find it. The perfect camp is found, not made. If you want a developed campsite, choose an established one. If you pitch a tent, find a site with natural drainage. Don't cut limbs, dig ditches, pound nails, pile stones. The game is preservation, not pioneering.

Responsible backpackers carry out all their trash, including uneaten food. Hikers are pretty conscientious these days about outright litter, but some still think it good practice to bury or scatter food they cannot consume. *Don't do it.* Whatever isn't readily, completely burned must go out the same way it arrived—in your pack.

The go-lighter carries a stove and is sparing with fire. This is one of the more complicated matters: see Chapter 18. But note that in many wild areas, fires are allowed only at certain sites or in certain zones or in certain seasons. A light, portable stove gives you much more freedom to camp where you like.

The modern backpacker goes along with agency rules. All land management agencies have lists of recommended practices and are anxious to promote them. Whether or not you need to secure a "wilderness permit" (see Chapter 11), make it your business to get the official guidelines. Comply with these, even when their rationale is less than clear. The agency workers aren't just hassling you: they are the people who watch the country from year to year; they see it changing. Some of their rules are experimental, but the experiments have to be made. Play along—or go them one better in your efforts to spare the land. If you have a bone to pick, express your opinion not by action but by courteous letter.

There is now an educational program with a name that is also a slogan: Leave No Trace (LNT). LNT is headquartered at the private National Outdoor Leadership School but involves researchers and managers from all the land agencies. You'll see LNT guidelines, and often the organization's distinctive spiraling logo, in all kinds of wilderness information these days. Advice from this source is to be trusted. It is thorough, subtle, based on very current research, and inflected for conditions in each separate region. LNT maintains an excellent website (see the Resources appendix).

Backpackers are anxious to do the right thing. In fact, as studies show, it would be hard to find another group of people so conscientious. It is misinformation, not any vandalistic instinct, that keeps bad habits going. To change those habits, the friends and users of North American wilderness need only to know what to do and why. That is the most hopeful fact of all.

THE FREEDOM OF THE WILDERNESS

We look back now with something like sorrow to the days of the Great Wild, when a John Muir could set out into the unknown Sierra of California, sleeping on beds of cut boughs, with no further provisions than a loaf of bread, a warm coat, and a billycan. That condition of the world could not last. Now we find that we have gone too far in the other direction—that we have pushed well beyond what might have been a better balance point of civilized and wild.

Yet the wilderness we have—even that shrunken wilderness—is grand and welcoming beyond description. And if it is no longer large enough to absorb and nullify whatever abuses we pour into it, it can be large enough for the delight of everyone who comes to visit it. It can be—if we can learn the self-restraint that makes it possible, in this our crowded world, to be free.

2 BREAKING IN

The way is open.

Wilderness travel is not for the experts only, nor just for the well-to-do, nor just for the young. It is not only for the people who love to travel hard and count the miles behind them. It is not a competition. It is not a proving ground.

The way is open; yet it can be hard to know just where and how to begin. How do you find out where to go? How do you learn just how much you can do? How do you make sure of choosing the right gear?

Fortunately, you don't have to tackle the whole job in one season. Though some people hurry themselves, the thing can be taken in very manageable stages.

The easy first step: *start hiking close to home.* You need not walk far at first, nor seek out rugged terrain: just start taking short walks, as easy as you like, on any available parkland trail. You will need no special gear at the beginning, and later only a light daypack and a pair of boots or hiking shoes. If you would like to go with a group, get in touch with a local hiking club. These are found all over the country: the Appalachian Mountain Club, the Mazamas, the Mountaineers, the Carolina Mountain Club, the Colorado Mountain Club, and endless others. The Federation of Western Outdoor Clubs and the Appalachian Trail Conference (see addresses in the Resources appendix) can give you information on their member organizations. The Sierra Club has chapters all over the United States and Canada; most of these run local outings. Inquire also at gear stores. If you have a computer and modem, you can check out numerous "websites" containing such information and tap into "newsgroups," ongoing electronic mail discussions full of good (and bad) advice. (See the Resources appendix for a few electronic starting points.)

There are advantages to hiking with a group. For one thing, it hooks you into a grapevine, with the constant chatter about gear, experiences, places to go, problems encountered and solved. For another, you can watch how experienced hikers handle themselves. And though most backpackers eventually choose to travel in family-sized parties, larger groups are good social fun.

Now, as gradually as you like, begin building up your stock of gear and the skills that go with it. A good pair of boots or trail shoes will be about the first on your list (see Chapter 4). As soon as you have these, set out to break them in. Wear them for short distances, then for long, until boot and foot have adapted each to the other. Try out the combinations of clothes you have in mind to wear on later overnight trips (see Chapter 5). When you buy your first full-sized pack (see Chapter 6), get accustomed to it by carrying it on day hikes with increasingly realistic loads.

Spend time working with a compass and a topographic map on local, familiar ground; learn to translate from map to land and from land to map. This is important: even if you never plan to step off plain trails, you are bound to find places where you need to do a little navigation, and you might conceivably find yourself someday in a situation in which map and compass could save your life.

If day hiking is step one, step two (which many skip) is the organized, overnight backpacking trip. Most hiking clubs run these; in national parks and some other wild areas, you will find trips run by concessioners as well. In such a group you have the support of experienced people, and if you've arrived without some small, crucial object, you can just about count on the party having a spare.

These sizable organized groups have a very special function. Many people never need them; some frankly detest them; but for many hikers they are the indispensable bridge into a wilderness that seems at first a bit strange and incalculable. Organized groups, some studies suggest, have more middle aged people than you find elsewhere in the wilds and more children; unlike smaller parties, where males still predominate, they are made up about equally of men and women.

Step three, for those who wish to make it, is the first independent trip with family or friends. The first time you head out, you may want to choose a well-known corner of the wilderness; inquire around the grapevine, seek information on-line, or check one of the thousands of trail guides sold in backpacking stores and in general bookstores (see also Chapter 30). With that first trip behind you, you have known real self-sufficiency; you are no longer "breaking in." You are on your way.

GETTING OR STAYING IN SHAPE

Hiking with a pack is not, of itself, very hard. Many people—especially young, or older but physically active ones—start backpacking without any kind of preliminary training. But not everyone is young or active. To people who have accustomed themselves to a life of physical leisure beyond the limits of what is healthy, backpacking can seem hard. To those who have spent years behind desks—even though they golf or ski on weekends —it can seem hard. To the muscular fellow who regards himself as strong, yet seldom walks or bicycles or swims, it may come harder than he expects. And when you have limited time, it's a pity to waste any of it on aches, pains, and breathlessness.

There are several ways in which one can be "fit." One kind of fitness matters most on the trail: the kind known variously as stamina, aerobic conditioning, or just plain wind. This is not a matter of bulging muscles but a matter of efficient heart and lungs. When you are fit in this way, your heart will beat relatively slowly, even when you are working hard; you will be taking deep, satisfying breaths; you won't feel pressed for air. You get this stamina from lots of walking, lots of cycling, or from briefer periods of running or swimming. Anything that makes the heart and lungs work will strengthen them. Peak effort isn't important. The long haul is. If you don't have such activity in your life already, you need to begin it at least a month before a backpack trip. Three bouts of such aerobic exercise a week are recommended.

The specific training for backpacking is backpacking; the second best preparation is hiking without a pack. Make sure that you can hike pretty vigorously with no ill effects before adding the stress of an overnight load. As a transitional stage, you can carry an empty or very lightly loaded pack on local hikes and build up to full weight. (Don't overload a little daypack for this purpose, though; a heavy pack without a hipbelt is hard on the shoulders: see Chapter 6.)

What about muscles? The important muscles for backpacking are those in the legs and, to some extent, in the arms, and those that support the back. The habit of picking things up by squatting and then straightening the legs, good because it does not stress the spinal column, also strengthens the big quadriceps muscles in the thighs. Bicycling is excellent training. So is climbing stairs.

If you already have a program of weight lifting or other muscle-building exercises, you can easily adjust it to support your backpacking. Focus on routines that work the abdominal muscles and quadriceps, and don't neglect stretches, notably of the hamstring muscles in back of the thighs. Where you're going, endurance matters more than peak strength and infinitely more than how you look in a mirror; do many repetitions with fairly light weights.

There's a less methodical, more typical, and perfectly reasonable approach to muscle conditioning: do it only as your body complains and tells you what your weak points are. You can think of each persistent ache as an order from some part of your anatomy: "Strengthen me." The older you are when you hit the trails, the more such messages you will receive. To interpret them correctly, you'll need the advice of a physical therapist, orthopedist, or family doctor with some understanding of sports medicine. If the first advice you get is to quit an activity you love, seek a second opinion.

Sore knees are a frequent problem with beginners of any age; knee braces, available in stores that sell athletic equipment, can be a temporary help. If the problem is at all persistent, you will need to work all the more diligently on the muscles that stabilize the knee.

It goes without saying that not *all* bodily complaints can be trained away. In particular, you need a doctor's advice if you suspect a heart problem or any other condition that might truly limit your backpacking; older people who have been sedentary should start very slowly and keep the doctor posted on what they're undertaking. But the chances are good that your physician will enthusiastically approve. The backpacker's kind of fitness is the kind that doctors most welcome in their patients, and nobody basically healthy needs to deny himself or herself the pleasure of the trails.

B
GEARING UP

Naturally, we also carried all the standard mountain climbing equipment: cleated shoes and nails of all kinds, ropes, screw rings, hammers, snap hooks, ice axes, crampons, snowshoes, skis and all accessories, as well as instruments for observation like compasses, clinometers, altimeters, barometers, thermometers, range-finders, alidades, and cameras. And arms: rifles, carbines, revolvers, short sabers, dynamite—in other words, enough to face any foreseeable obstacle.

René Daumal, *Mount Analogue*

No matter how gradually you begin, you will soon have to start locating gear—*objects*, and quite a few of them. Even the lightest pack will contain seventy or eighty separate items. The novice, looking at a list like the one on the next few pages, sees a sizable job ahead.

Take a moment to scan this list. Somewhat spartan and economical, it allows something more than minimum comfort on a trip in hospitable western mountains in a hospitable season, late summer. Humidity is low, water plentiful, weather mainly pleasant, trails plain. Such conditions are by no means the rule in the American wilderness. This list is *not* a model to go by, but only an illustration of the way one party packed for a particular, not especially challenging journey. It is meant to show something of the *logic of gear*.

What do you need in order to travel safely and in comfort?

You need *boots or shoes* sturdy enough, and heavy enough, to support and protect your feet—and not one bit heavier than that.

You need *clothing*: garments to protect you from sun, from wind and cold, from rain and snow, from scratching brush and irritant plants, from mosquitoes and stinging flies.

You need *sleeping gear* for warmth at night and *shelter* to keep you dry.

You need *water and food*, and the tools of eating and cooking (unless you choose to rely on no-cook meals).

You need a *knife, a flashlight or headlamp*, plenty of *matches*, and a good length of *cord*.

You need *navigation tools*—usually just maps and a compass.

You need *emergency, medical, and repair gear* for problems major and minor.

You need *personal items*—toilet paper and a toothbrush at the barest minimum.

And you need *containers*—mostly bags, big and little, and a pack to put it all in.

One of the minor pleasures of wilderness travel is the comfortable feeling of dealing with good gear. You come to know this collection of objects almost like a language: the uses of each item, its faults, its limitations, the location in which it should be packed to be most easily at hand when

An Economical Summer Packlist

For one person in a party of two. No prices shown for items found at home.

ITEM	WEIGHT IN PACK	COST
CLOTHING, WORN		
nylon pants with web belt	—	$43
underpants	—	—
undershirt	—	—
cotton shirt	—	—
sunhat	—	$21
sunglasses and keeper strap	—	$30
hiking socks, outer	—	$9
hiking socks, liner	—	$7
hiking boots	—	$115
watch	—	—
CLOTHING, PACKED		
spare socks, one set	4 oz.	$16
hiking shorts	10 oz.	$26
rainchaps, urethane-coated	8 oz.	$20
spare sunglasses and case	1 oz.	$18
balaclava	2 oz.	$8
polyester pile jacket	16 oz.	$55
Gore-Tex wind/rain parka	16 oz.	$125
SLEEPING GEAR		
mummy sleeping bag in stuffsack	43 oz.	$220
foam pad, short length	9 oz.	$11
groundcloth, 5½ ft. × 7½ ft.	15 oz.	$5
KITCHEN AND BASIC TOOLS (INDIVIDUAL)		
headlamp with batteries	5 oz.	$32
spare batteries, bulb	2 oz.	$3
matches	1 oz.	$1
cup (Lexan)	3 oz.	$3
spoon (Lexan)	trace	$1
pocketknife	2 oz.	$20
bandannas, two	trace	$3
nylon cord, 50 ft.	4 oz.	$5
candle	2 oz.	$1
iodine for water treatment	4 oz.	$9
OFFICE		
notebook, pencils	2 oz.	$1
topo maps, three	4 oz.	$12
compass	1 oz.	$10

ITEM	WEIGHT IN PACK	COST
PERSONAL		
tooth care items	1 oz.	—
lip balm	trace	$2
sunscreen	4 oz.	$5
soap	2 oz.	$1
other toiletries	1 oz.	—
toilet paper	1 oz.	—
toilet trowel	2 oz.	$2
MISCELLANEOUS		
first-aid kit	14 oz.	$30
sew/repair kit	3 oz.	$14
whistle, mirror	2 oz.	$11
HAULAGE		
pack	84 oz.	$100
stuffbags, 5 assorted	12 oz.	$30
plastic bags and closures	1 oz.	—
liter water bottles, 2	7 oz.	$8
SHELTER (GROUP)		
tarp, 12 ft. × 10 ft.	37 oz.	$41
KITCHEN (GROUP)		
white gas stove (burner, pump)	14 oz.	$50
fuel bottle	4 oz.	$8
windscreen	2 oz.	$9
two aluminum pots	21 oz.	$18
pot gripper	2 oz.	$4
soap and scouring pad	2 oz.	$1
CONSUMABLES (GROUP)		
food (2 people, 4 days)	192 oz.	$80
reserve food	32 oz.	$10
fuel, 1 pint plus 1 cup reserve	9 oz.	$1
water (average 2 quarts in packs at one time)	64 oz.	—
TOTAL PACK AND CONTENTS		
Personal gear	288 oz.	$1,033
One-half of group gear	41 oz.	$66
One-half of consumables	149 oz.	$91
Total weight in ounces	478 oz.	
Total weight and cost	**30 lb.**	**$1,190**

you require it. This familiarity *can* lead to a kind of obsessive fussiness. It can also produce the "gear freak," the zealot who is restless when lacking the very latest innovation in every department. But for all that, the pleasure of gear is a genuine pleasure.

In buying gear, there's a Rule Number One: *Go slowly.* There is no reason to purchase everything at once, and unless you are unusually sure of yourself you should not try to. Borrow and rent equipment whenever your can. Make do with what you have on hand. Some tricky items like stoves and tents are shared, so you may be able to rely at first on better-equipped companions; or you can begin with organization-sponsored trips where these items are part of the package. It is rarely a mistake to put off buying equipment. The longer you delay, the better chance you have to find out what truly suits you.

WHERE TO BUY

By all means get the help of a backpackers' specialty shop—or of several. There are now many of these nationwide. Department stores, surplus outlets, and general sporting goods stores also carry wilderness gear, some of it quite adequate; but salespeople there can rarely answer the questions you need to ask.

To find appropriate stores, take a look in phone company Yellow Pages or similar directories: first under "backpacking and mountaineering," then under such headings as "camping equipment," "ski equipment," and "sporting goods." You probably have several competing specialty shops in your area. Visit all of them. Consider. Shop around. No need to stay home while you're considering: many stores also rent packs, tents, and sleeping bags. And renting is not a waste of money—it's a valuable series of lessons in the merits of different brands and designs.

The salespeople in most of the specialty shops are knowledgeable, easy to talk to, and generous with their time. Don't feel you're imposing on them: the time they spend on you is reflected in the prices charged. They have opinions, and there is almost always disagreement from store to store; compare the versions, and you learn a good deal.

If you don't have access to specialty shops, there's always mail order. It's worthwhile to collect the catalogs of the major outfits, in any case, for the information they contain (see the Resources appendix for a very partial list). The "reader service cards" bound into outdoor magazines make it easy to order numerous sample catalogs. Some good, specialized gear is sold primarily by mail. Many makers' offerings can also be perused on-line—gear advertisements now include Internet addresses more often than not. At least one maker publishes its offerings *only* on the Net. But there is truly no substitute for seeing and handling the gear yourself.

This is doubly the case if you are very tall, very short, or otherwise hard to fit. If you've found the item you want but not in your size, stores are generally good about ordering what you need. Make sure in advance that you can return unsuitable items after testing them indoors. In very rare cases, people have gear made to order.

Women are still at a certain disadvantage in buying gear. Even today there are rather few firms that make gear sized and proportioned for the female body, rather than for smallish men. So-called "unisex" designs work for some women, not for all. Though the situation is improving, you, a woman, may have to look longer to find what's right for you.

THE LEARNING PROCESS

However you approach the gear-buying business, you face a long series of choices. For every type of equipment there are not just competing brands but competing, fundamentally different, designs. The days are gone when a mere backpacker can keep track of the changing technological scene, and the glossy ads of the makers are designed to sell, not to inform. (Do you really need a parka that went up K2? Maybe, maybe not.) This con-fusion makes the advice of the salespeople, opinionated though it natu-rally is, more important than ever.

For further help, you can turn to equipment-rating articles published in such magazines as *Backpacker, Outside,* and occasionally *Consumer Reports.* Such assessments are not beyond dispute. You must also keep in mind that a negative report on a product often causes the manufacturer to alter the design—thus all such studies tend to become rapidly dated. Nonetheless, reviews can help the buyer navigate the equipment laby-rinth.

In addition to its reviews, *Backpacker* devotes one issue a year to a "gear guide" that simply lists the specifications of boots, packs, sleeping bags, and so on—*as supplied by the manufacturers.* These useful compilations should not be confused with critical assessments. Even the simplest data may be measured, by different makers, in different, incompatible, and sometimes downright nonsensical ways; the makers' estimates of the uses to which their gear is suited may be wildly self-serving. The industry is working to rationalize assessments in a few areas—sleeping bag makers, for example, are trying to agree on a standard method for measuring the insulation value of their bags. But there's a long, long way to go.

Much comparative product information is available now on-line. A *Backpacker* website at www.gearfinder.com permits you to search out gear with particular characteristics, for instance packs of a certain price, weight, and capacity. Such services will be multiplying.

Although it's good to learn a lot and to take your time, it's also good to remind yourself frequently that gear is only a set of tools: a means to an end. The backpacker does the work, not the backpack. And when you get out into the field, you're likely to find that different, competing models, if well made and matched to your actual needs, do the job about equally well.

HOW MUCH WILL IT COST?

What about the first weekend trip? How *little* can you spend and still be safe and comfortable in the wild?

This depends, of course, on where you are going, how much useful junk you have around, and how many people you have with you to share common expenses. By renting some of the major pieces of gear and buying the cheapest adequate versions of other items, you can probably reduce the tab to under $400 the first time you go out. Lower than that it is difficult to go.

The cost of successive trips will depend on what new items of equipment you buy each time. The shopping never stops entirely; there are always minor objects to add or replace. Once you are past such major purchases as pack and boots, however, you will find yourself spending much less. In fact, the cost of gear, food, and fuel for the trail is typically overshadowed by the cost of transportation to the trailhead.

What about the total tab for building your permanent stock of good equipment? It can no longer be said that backpacking gear is cheap. A pretty complete set of well-made summer gear will set you back $1,000 to $2,000, in 1997 prices, before you are through. About half the price tag is likely to be for three major items—your *boots* (Chapter 4), your *pack* (Chapter 6), and your *sleeping bag* (Chapter 7). A *tent*, which not everyone needs, is another major purchase (Chapter 8). *Clothing* (Chapter 5) can be economical or very pricey indeed. *Kitchen gear* (Chapter 9) is relatively cheap.

There are ways of beating down the entry cost. By shrewd shopping, you can get perfectly good gear at a discount. What you lose out on is the advice that goes with "normal" pricing; you may also be foregoing standard guarantees, so be careful here.

- You may be able to find *seconds*—items that come from the factory with harmless imperfections and are sold at reduced prices, in the parent stores, at factory outlets, or in special "seconds shops."
- You can pick up excellent bargains at the end-of-season sales that gear stores hold.
- You can draw on large mail-order houses, which are likely to be cheaper than your local mountain store. Three to check out are Campmor, Recreational Equipment, Inc. (REI), and Mountain Equipment Coop (in Canada).
- You can buy used gear. A few stores handle secondhand items; many have bulletin boards where sellers advertise. Sound items may turn up at flea markets and in thrift stores. And shops that rent gear eventually sell those items at cut prices.

Whether you buy high or low, don't spend money needlessly on gear that's intended for heavier use than you plan to give it. Some shoppers look by reflex at the "top of the line." They buy the weightiest, costliest, most nearly "expeditionary" sleeping bags, packs, boots, tents, jackets. For almost all of them this is an error. The sleeping bag you could use in the winter in the Never Summer Range of Colorado is only hot and clammy in a normal wilderness July. And a Himalayan-scale backpack is a poor container for a weekend's worth of gear. Don't buy image!

Please bear in mind that all prices given in these pages are both approximate and liable to change. They reflect the situation in 1997 and, like EPA mileage estimates, are best used for comparative purposes. It isn't just possible that you will find higher price tags when you go out to buy: it is nearly certain.

Minimum Cost of First Weekend Trip

For party of two. Reflects search for bargains and near-maximum use of rentals.

INDIVIDUAL

rent external frame pack (3 days)	$34	
rent sleeping bag	$34	
buy cheapest good boots	$100	
hiking socks, 1 set (outer + liners)	$16	
spare socks (cotton from home)	—	
pad, groundcloth	$13	
poncho, chaps, hat	$63	
other items	$30	
food	$25	
Individual total	**$315**	*(plus any restaurant meals)*

GROUP

rent tent (?)	$34	
rent cartridge stove	$10	
fuel	$5	
pans (found at home)	—	
Group total	**$49**	*(plus shared auto costs)*

HOW MUCH WILL IT WEIGH?

Let's say you have a packload without too many extras: no paperback novels, no ropes, no cameras, no Monopoly games. Assume your load is for a lightweight summer trip. Forget for a moment about water, food, and fuel. And forget about shelter, stove, pots—the gear you will be sharing among companions.

Thus limited, the *basic dry weight* of your pack—including clothing, bedding, first-aid kit, various oddments, and the pack itself—should be somewhere between 16 and 18 pounds. This does not count your boots or the clothes you start out wearing, but it does include clothes for rain and moderate cold, which will, with luck, be stowed away much of the time.

To get a notion of what the rest of the packload will weigh, you can apply these rules of thumb:

- For food, figure on 2 pounds per person per day, tops. With expensive freeze-dried foods and an average appetite, you may find yourself happy with less. Women may eat somewhat less; teenagers may eat more.
- Add 1 pound for each pint of water you expect to be carrying during a typical hiking day. (You always want to have some water on board.)
- Add 6 ounces for each cup of white gas or kerosene you will start out with. An economical allowance is one-quarter cup, or 1.5 ounces, per person per day. It's a little harder to estimate fuel needs for the popular "cartridge" stoves burning gaseous fuel, because you can't carry a fraction of a cartridge, but approximately the same ratio applies; see Chapter 12.
- If your group will use a tent or tents, figure about 3 pounds per person. But allow just 1 pound per person if shelter is a tarp or tarps.
- Finally, a group of two or three hikers will carry 2 to 3 pounds of cookware and stove.

So, if two of you were heading out for five summer days, in, say, the Adirondacks; if you carried, as you should for that trip, both stove and tent; and if each of you had a pint of water in a canteen, your theoretical share of the load would be something like this:

17.5 lb. of personal kit
10 lb. of food
1 lb. of water
1.5 lb. of cooking gear
0.5 lb. of fuel (1.5 oz. per person per day)
3 lb. of shelter

for a theoretical total of 33.5 pounds.

This, like the detailed list a few pages back, is merely an illustration. But it makes the point—on a trip of less than a week in a place and month not extraordinarily hostile, you won't need a load of more than 35 pounds.

HOW MUCH CAN YOU COMFORTABLY CARRY?

An old rule of thumb said you could carry a third of your body weight. And indeed, if you have to, you can; climbers and winter campers may wind up toting that or more. But for most people on today's trails, such heroics are quite unnecessary. With light, modern gear, it should be possible to limit your pack to a fifth of your own weight on trips of a few days.

So a 120-pound woman might have a comfortable limit of 24 pounds; a 190-pound man, by this formula, would be limited to 38. (If you are seriously overweight, however, go by your target body weight, not your actual one.) With loads of this order, experienced hikers may almost forget that they have packs on their backs. If you hike with companions, as most people do, you can split up food, fuel, and community gear according to body weight. Lighter people often insist on toting an arithmetically equal share that puts them at a disadvantage; if this is you, reconsider. As to your purely personal gear, you're stuck with the weight of your choices. If you travel alone, your pack will include all "community" gear and ride a little heavier.

The one-fifth guideline is only a starting point. It is possible to cut down this standard load, easier still to build it up. Recommended pack weights seem to be creeping higher—I've seen 40-pound packs for a weekend trip described as "light." Every hiker makes an individual compromise between the advantages an easily carried pack and the advantages of extra gear. Older backpackers, in particular, may find themselves torn between comfort in camp, which implies more equipment, and comfort on the trail, which depends on toting less.

GOING LIGHT: OLD STYLE AND NEW

You will hear the most drastic advice about cutting the weight in your pack. People really do cut handles off toothbrushes. Whether or not this deadpan game makes a practical difference, it's true that the overloaded hiker gets ingenious at finding objects to leave home.

But "going light," that familiar slogan, has undergone a subtle change in meaning. Today it refers less to the load in your pack than to the weight —the impact—of your passage on the land. And in adopting this version of "going light," backpackers have learned to accept a few more ounces of weight on their own shoulders.

First among the new necessities is the stove. Nobody should travel in today's wilderness without one. Don't put yourself in the position of *having* to kindle a fire when conditions are wrong. (Sometimes there is no downed, dead wood to be had. Sometimes fires are not permitted, or permitted at certain sites only. In other cases your fire would leave unacceptable scars.) And a stove gives you a much wider choice of campsites—much more freedom to revise your plans.

Shelter, too, is always carried with you. You never plan to save weight at the expense of the land—by building, for instance, hutches of green branches. That was fine for the mountain men of the 1830s, but it has no place in the modern wilderness.

Extra water containers are carried more often now. If you have a hanging waterbag in camp, you will make fewer trips to lake, stream, or spring, and thus reduce trampling of fragile banks.

In regions with bears, bearproof food storage canisters are becoming more and more an essential. In an increasing number of areas, hanging food in bags in trees is no longer enough to protect your groceries—or the bears, which often must be killed once they have learned to scavenge human food.

And all, or very nearly all, of your food comes in with you. Natural foodstuffs are to be found, all right, but they are abundant precisely because not many people have yet thought of harvesting for them. Enjoy the trout, enjoy the huckleberries or wild onions, but count them as luxuries. "Living off the land" is a notion from a less crowded day.

The pattern in all this is ironic and yet quite logical: the stronger our wish to preserve the wild places, the less we can meet them on their own terms; the more plentiful, sophisticated, and complex becomes the gadgetry we must bring into them.

Like all consumer products, backpacking gear has a history before it ever reaches you. Its manufacture represents a greater or lesser amount of pollution and resource cost. The plastics used in modern clothing fibers and some pack frames, for instance, can be made of "virgin" petrochemicals—or recycled from soft-drink bottles. Companies that do the latter, a lengthening list, rightly pride themselves on it. There is increasing use of recycled materials in gear of all sorts, and the customer should reward it.

There may be a social cost, too, to the manufacture of gear. More backpacking products than not, especially items of clothing, are now assembled in what used to be called the Third World. Tags on gear usually tell you where. You may want to apply your own "screen" here and avoid buying goods made under regimes, or working conditions, of which you particularly disapprove.

THE WILDERNESS REGIONS AND THE GEAR YOU TAKE

From region to region and season to season, needs change. One list of gear won't serve for all landscapes, all weathers, all the different demands of the American wilderness.

Some places are pretty dry in summer; some are very wet. In the dry-summer mountains of the West, shelter and raingear can be simple and light; the occasional thunderstorm may be more an entertainment than a piece of serious weather. Quite a few people here rely on tarps and bivouac sacks for staying dry in the normal hiking season. But in the Smokies or the North Cascades, summer rain is serious, and real tents are the norm. Tents are also strongly recommended in grizzly bear country; see Chapter 29.

Humidity counts, too. If the air is dry between rains, cotton clothing and classic down sleeping bags can be efficient. But in the Catskills or the Blue Ridge, even a cool, clear night may be damp enough to chill you in cotton clothes and saturate your sleeping bag. In such places, wool or synthetic clothing is standard, and sleeping bags should be synthetic filled or equipped with water-resistant shells.

In the deserts, and on some ridge routes in less arid ranges, water is a problem in another way. Springs and convenient streams may be far apart and unreliable. In the Sonoran Desert of Arizona, for instance, two-thirds of your packload might be water. See Chapter 23.

In areas where winter brings snow, a whole new kind of wilderness, a white and challenging wilderness, appears with the first cold storm. Travelers in that world need considerably more gear; see Chapter 24.

HASSLES WITH GEAR

Catalogs often contrive to give you the impression that wilderness gear is perfect and indestructible. Of course (as you find out soon enough), this isn't so. Some items and some brands hold up better than others; none are trouble-free or immune to wear. Sleeping bags and tents get torn. Stoves balk and have to be tinkered with. Waterproofing wears off and has to be renewed. Zippers fail. Plastic buckles age and crack. Stitching frays. Flashlights let you down.

Backpacking equipment is certainly better made, on the average, than other consumer goods today. Yet some of it is made less well than it could be. When you shop for gear, pay special attention to the details of construction: durability is perhaps the greatest virtue of all. Look also for generous warranty policies. Some stores will take back and replace an item that has failed even after years of use.

When gear goes bad on the trail, minor repairs, of a rough-and-ready sort, can often be made on the spot. More substantial work can be done at home, with a certain amount of instruction and patience. A superb guide for the fix-it-yourselfer is Annie Getchell's *The Essential Outdoor Gear Manual* (Ragged Mountain Press, 1995).

For problems that surpass the home workshop, you can turn to the general repair services at many gear stores, not restricted to items sold or under warranty there. Shoemakers are also very helpful: they will sew on leather patches, replace grommets, and handle many other problems with leather and heavy fabric.

About the first thing you'll have to acquire for backpacking is a good pair of boots. A few stores do rent them; if there's such a source near you, $10 to $12 a day will get you some initial experience of the breed. Soon, however, you will want to choose your own clodhoppers. At $100 to $300, this is big-ticket-item number one.

The choice is wide. About three dozen manufacturers make boots and specialized shoes, and every one of them claims special virtue for its product. You can get lost in the clamor of competing features and learned arguments for this or that cunning design.

And yet there are just two things you require from a backpacking boot or shoe. The first is comfort: the footgear should be as light, well fitting, and easy on the flesh as it possibly can be. The second is protection: it must shield the foot from incessant jarring, bruising stones, encroaching water, and the coldness of the ground, and it must support the ankle against twisting. Comfort and protection compete, and every boot or shoe is a compromise between them.

The trick is to choose footgear that is heavy enough for the kind of hiking you will do—and not one ounce heavier. Only experience will tell you just where that balance point lies for you. For years, people wandered around the wilderness wearing vastly excessive amounts of leather, simply because it was the expected thing. Then ultralightweight footgear had a vogue. What you actually need will depend on the type of hiking you do, the kind of loads you carry, and your personal steadiness of ankle.

KINDS OF BOOTS

The lightest boots weigh less than 2 pounds the pair in a man's size 9, still the conventional basis of comparison (see Shopping and Fitting, below). But the boots suitable for backpacking start at about 2 pounds and run up to almost 5 pounds.

General trail boots are relatively light and flexible. Their uppers often incorporate materials other than leather: nylon cloth, nylon mesh, and even canvas. They are fine for travel on smooth trails when the weather is not too cold, and some backpackers find them adequate for rougher terrain as well. Typical weights, for a middle-range size, lie between 2 pounds and 3½ pounds the pair. Prices presently run from about $100 to well over $200. I'd think twice before choosing anything lighter or cheaper for backpacking use.

All-terrain boots are heavier and stiffer. Although constructions vary, you'll see predominantly leather. These are suitable for cross-country travel, for heavy loads, and for cold weather. But there's a penalty in off-the-shelf comfort and in weight: these boots run 3 to 5 pounds the pair. Prices run from $125 to more than double that. Lighter is not necessarily cheaper: the harder the maker has worked to create a boot both light and strong, the higher the cost is liable to be.

All-terrain boots overlap with another category, *light mountaineering boots*. These are defined by excellent waterproofing, a rather rigid shell, and a groove where the sole meets the upper, which permits the wearing of crampons. Most are made of leather, some of tough plastic. You can also recognize them by their cost, up to $400. Boots heavier than 5 pounds —no longer "light" by any standard—can safely be left out of your backpacking calculations.

Let's mention here some other types of boots you may see in stores but can rule out for basic travel. *Rock-climbing shoes* are light, tight, fragile, and completely unsuited for plain walking. *Approach shoes* also come out of the rock-climbing world; they are like ultralight backpacking boots but equipped with soles of "sticky," carbon-impregnated rubber. They don't offer much ankle support and may lack the normal protective flaps or bellows at the tongue. *Shoepacs* are high boots with waterproof rubber around the foot and leather rising up the ankle; they are much used for winter travel in the East. *Cross-country ski boots* are built to attach to skis with light, simple three-pin bindings. *Ski-mountaineering boots* are heavier models for much more rugged skiing. For more about winter footwear, see Chapter 24.

So: how heavy should your first pair of general-purpose boots be? The decision depends partly on your experience and partly on your ambitions.

Day hiking should already have given you some ideas. If you've hiked in sneakers, running shoes, or other light footgear, what do your feet tell you? Do you find that you keep your balance easily, or do your ankles tend to turn under you? At the end of the day, are your soles bruised and sore from the hardness of the ground? If you've felt comfortable in soft shoes, you can reasonably consider boots toward the lighter end of the range. If you have felt tentative and vulnerable in light shoes, then a somewhat heavier boot, probably all leather, makes sense for you.

As for ambitions, do you expect, for the time being, to hike well-maintained trails in warm climates? Or do you plan to branch out soon into cross-country travel and cold-weather hiking? Lighter boots fit the first case, somewhat heavier boots the second.

Still undecided? Then start with a boot in the middle of the spectrum, within a few ounces on either side of 3 pounds the pair. Choose one of the lighter and more pliable of all-leather boots. Or go with one of the stouter of the models that mix leather and fabric, with a good stiff heel counter, a good stiff toe, and a high top that supports the ankle well. Such boots can hardly fail to be useful in quite a range of conditions, and you won't have to take out a loan to buy them. After a season or two, you will know much better what your real requirements are. Then you can replace your starter pair or add other, more specialized gear to your collection. Many backpackers wind up owning (and using) a whole row of diverse clodhoppers.

ANATOMY AND FEATURES

Boot soles today may look like those of traditional running shoes, like those of traditional hiking boots, or like something in between. Always there is the tread layer, or *outsole*, next to the ground; one or several *midsoles*; and the *insole* next to the foot. Hard-rubber outsoles have various patterns but are more or less toothy; some are made of "sticky" rubber for good gripping on (dry) rock. Midsoles may be of various materials, including nylon, rubber, and urethane. Ethyl vinyl acetate (EVA), found in

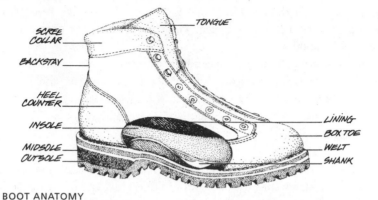

SCREE COLLAR
BACKSTAY
HEEL COUNTER
INSOLE
MIDSOLE
OUTSOLE
TONGUE
LINING
BOX TOE
WELT
SHANK

BOOT ANATOMY

some cheaper boots, is not very durable. The midsole layer may contain a *shank*—a flexible band of metal, plastic, or carbon fiber—to add support and springiness. Some midsoles incorporate air-filled pockets.

The *insole* is what your foot actually rests on. In boots of the most traditional design, it may be just a piece of thin, smooth leather; more often it is a "footbed," a curvy piece that can be removed for washing or replaced with a thinner or thicker version to refine the fit (see Shopping and Fitting, below).

The margin where the sole joins the *upper* is called the *welt*. Uppers are fastened to soles in various ways. Traditional leather boots have stitching here; not-so-traditional boots of any weight are cemented. In cemented boots, the joint between sole and upper will be protected by a waterproof rubber *rand* that overlaps the latter. One odd-looking boot (the Asolo Globaline) has a sole that curves well up around the foot, joining the almost vestigial upper several inches from the ground.

Uppers, as noted, are made of various materials. You will see boots built of nylon packcloth or the textured nylon called Cordura; of cloth with leather reinforcements; of leather, with cloth "cutouts"; and of leather throughout.

The advantages of the lighter materials are clear. Lightness. Lower price. Coolness on the feet. Instant comfort (if the fit is good). There is a cost, however, in support, and also in durability: an active cross-country hiker can demolish a pair of ultralight boots in a season. I would rule out as a primary pair any "boot" that does not contain considerable leather.

LIGHT BOOTS OF MIXED CONSTRUCTION

On a rack of leather boots, one cosmetic difference will jump at you. Some models have a rough, feltlike surface; others are smooth and shiny. This really doesn't matter, and all finishes give way to the same battered look after a few journeys. More important is the distinction between top-grain, split-grain, and full-grain leather. Full-grain leather, the heaviest and toughest, uses the full thickness of the tanned cowhide, including the rugged, pliable, naturally oily, water-repellent surface that was next to the hair. (The currently popular "Nubuk" is full-grain leather with a suedelike finish.) Commonly, however, the hide is split into several layers. Off the outer surface comes top-grain leather, including the weather-resistant epidermis. The lower regions of the hide yield split-grain leathers, more permeable and not so strong. Fine for trail hiking, they do stretch and get a lumpy look, and they wear out more quickly than boots of top-grain or full-grain leather. Not surprisingly, they are also cheaper.

There are other differences among leathers. Some pieces are tougher and cost more. Large chunks also cost more. Some boots are made from several pieces of hide and have many seams; some are made of few pieces or even just one, with a single seam down the heel. These one-piece boots are the most expensive, the most durable, the easiest to waterproof, and the hardest to break in.

Many boots of all weights now incorporate linings or layers of special materials designed to block the penetration of water from the world to the foot while still permitting the evaporation of moisture from the foot to the world. See Chapter 5 for generalities about these waterproof breathable fabrics. Gore-Tex and Sympatex are two brands used in boots. By and large, they work as advertised, and boots so equipped are nice to have in mud, shallow snow, and sodden grass.

Whatever material makes up the body of the upper, both heel and toe must be quite rigid for protection and proper fit. Some models have rubber toecaps. Some have a molded plastic heel cup that is actually an extension of the midsole.

The collarlike opening around the ankle should be soft where it touches the skin but stiff enough to provide at least some support when a foot threatens to turn. Some boots have leather or plastic *scree collars* here, designed to keep the tiny rocks of "scree" from bouncing into your boots, but perhaps more functional as padding. A nice feature on heavier boots is a well-anchored finger loop at the back of the heel opening: hauling on this makes it easier to insert the foot in the morning.

Boot interiors are lined with thin leather or with cloth, sometimes treated with antimicrobial agents to discourage mildew and the buildup of odor. Between the lining and the main wall of the boot, most makers put at least some areas of protective closed-cell foam. Such padding makes boots comfortable sooner.

Lacing hardware varies but should be of metal, perhaps plastic-coated, but not plastic throughout. There may be grommeted *eyelets, D-rings* that rivet onto the upper, or *hooks.* Most often there is some combination. Eyelets break less frequently than the other fittings but are a little harder to lace, especially with cold hands. Rings and hooks tend to break off, but any cobbler can repair them for a small charge. Sometimes, midway in a row of hooks, one pair of normal hooks is replaced by a pair of "lace hooks" or similar friction devices that grip the laces and prevent them from sliding through. Using these, you can tighten the laces firmly on one side of the clinch while leaving them loose on the other. You can get much the same effect, however, by tricks of lacing (see Chapter 15). The laces themselves should be nylon.

Beneath the lacing is the *tongue* (sometimes two tongues). It is more or less padded, to protect the top of the foot from bruising under the pressure of the laces. On either side of the tongue are spaces that, in a backpacking boot, must be closed off in one way or another. Some boots have overlapping flaps; others use fanlike, flexible bellows or gussets. Light mountaineering boots may have a set of inner laces on the tongue itself.

SOCKS

Before choosing boots, you need to know what else you'll be wearing on your feet. Most people these days wear a single thick sock (per foot!) and perhaps a very thin, smooth liner. The main sock can be synthetic, wool, or a mix, but not cotton. Merino wool is a luxurious component; wool and synthetic fleece are the best at "wicking," or pulling sweat away from the skin. Avoid coarse weaves and bulky seams, especially at the toe. Socks made especially for hiking ($10–$15) may offer extra cushioning at various points: underfoot, around the toes, and along the upper surface, where the laces press. The thin liner sock ($3–$10)should be of slick fabric, often polypropylene.

SHOPPING AND FITTING

Except as a last resort, buy your boots in person in the specialty outlets. With the proliferation of gear stores, mail purchase is no longer really worth discussing. What can hardly be discussed enough is the challenge of getting the right fit. Make up your mind to insist on something near perfection.

Before you head for the stores, trim your nails as they will be for the trail: short, but not so short that they fail to protrude past the surrounding skin. Take along the combination of socks you plan to wear when you hike (see Socks, above). Veterans recommend shopping for boots in the afternoon or later, when your feet will have expanded a bit with the day's activity.

Before you enter a store, you should already have an idea of the type and weight of boot you want, or at least of the conditions you want to hike in soon. Will you be going on-trail or off? Under what loads? In what likely weather? Tell the salesperson these things, along with your street shoe size, and let him or her take it from there. You'll soon be standing on a "Brannock device," the familiar tool that measures total foot length, heel-to-ball length, foot width, and height of arch. Then come the boxes of boots.

Slide on your first candidate pair. They will feel a bit roomier than your street shoes, especially in front. They should be at least ½ inch longer than your stockinged foot, but less than 1 inch. Before you lace up, push your foot forward inside the boot as far as it will go. You should just barely be able to fit an index finger all the way down between your heel and the back of the boot. (Two fingers is too much room.)

Now kick back in the boot to settle the heel into the socket and lace up firmly. In the final tightening, it is natural to pull the lace ends across the boot, so that the topmost hook or eyelet is pulled toward the midline. This is hard on the fittings, however. Instead, pull the laces outward, on each side, away from the boot, until you've pulled out all possible slack; only then cross the laces to begin your actual knot. If the laces draw the sides of the closure so close together that they almost touch, the boot is too loose.

Have the salesperson hold your heel to the floor and do your best to lift the back of your foot. The heel should rise no more than ¼ inch inside the boot. (That's not much. It should feel very firm.)

To check the fit of the toe, hook your heel over a rock, a wooden shoe-rack, or a street curb, so that your toe points sharply downhill. Kick forward inside the boot. If your toes feel stubbed against the tip, the boot is too short. (You can also kick against something hard, if the store will let you.) You must be able to wriggle your toes freely when you wear the boot, or you risk cutting off blood circulation. On the other hand, if a boot is too long, the normal flexing of the front end will occur too far forward, over your toes rather than over the ball of your foot, and give you blisters.

Besides length, the overall volume of the boot is important; your foot should feel snugly contained but not compressed or pinched. In traditional sizing, width is the indicator of volume; some makers have recently substituted explicit volume sizing. To make sure the boot is not too sloppy, have someone hold it to the floor while you try to rotate your foot inside it. The ball of your foot shouldn't have room to shift noticeably sideways, and your heel should shift no more than ¼ inch. In some lines of boots, volume is adjusted, within an overall size, by choosing among thicker and thinner footbeds.

You may hear it said that it is better to have a boot too large than too small, on the theory that you can always add socks or correct the fit with padding. Don't count too much on this. Although a slightly too narrow leather boot will adapt to your foot, a boot that is sloppy in the store will only get sloppier. And a loose fit is almost bound to give you blisters.

If the boots or shoes seem to pass these various initial tests, make sure you have them laced up firmly and spend ten or fifteen minutes "hiking" around the store. Don't just stroll: speed up, slow down, go up and down stairs, swivel, do knee bends. Watch again for a feeling of tightness in the toes or of sloppiness in the heels. As foot and boot warm up, the fit may change.

Do you like the stiffness or flexibility of the sole? Boots vary. Generally, heavier people need soles that are stiffer to start with; lighter people will be more comfortable on somewhat softer soles. Some makers take account of this difference, some don't.

Undecided between two sizes or models? Try wearing one of each. In a few minutes, one foot should start feeling markedly better than the other. Double-check by repeating the experiment with the two types on opposite feet. If you have a third model on your final list, compare it with the survivor of your first elimination round, using the same method. It's time consuming, but the time spent is worthwhile. No competent salesperson will try to hurry your decision. If you feel pressured, leave the store.

If you're almost but not quite sure of the fit, you can go ahead and make the purchase—but confirm that it's okay to return the boots after further indoor trial. At home, live in them a little. Walk around indoors, perhaps up and down stairs in a city building, until you have a clear opinion. Then, if necessary, take them back and try again.

If you find nothing that fits you properly in the stock of a particular store, go elsewhere. Keep looking. Different brands of boots can be quite different in configuration. Boots are built on standardized patterns called lasts. A last is nothing but a model foot—a hypothetical, average foot. Somewhere out there, somebody is probably building boots on a last that matches your foot shape reasonably well.

Women's feet are different from men's. They tend to be narrower, especially at the heel, and less well padded with flesh. Arches tend to be higher and toes longer. There is now, finally, a good range of boots designed to respect this anatomy. If female, be sure to try at least one. If male and hard to fit, consider that "women's" boots may provide the variation you are looking for. The only thing that matters is what fits *you*.

If you don't find the right fit in reasonably local stores, you may have to turn, after all, to mail order houses. Call, get their catalogs (or look them up on line), and ask their advice. You may be asked to send an outline of both your feet (or the larger, if there is an obvious difference).If working by mail order, be sure that each supplier will cheerfully take back boots tried out indoors.

Boots can be modified, in fact or in effect, to deal with stubborn fitting problems. You can add off-the-shelf insoles, or swap one insole thickness for another. (Even without a specific fitting problem, added insoles may be nice to reduce jarring.) Heel liners can help with a loose heel. The inner soles or footbeds that came with your boots can be cautiously trimmed. For extremely nonstandard feet, a podiatrist can prepare orthotics, customized footbed inserts (for a price not far less than that of the boots themselves). If your boots are all leather, a cobbler may be able to make certain adjustments.

But in my experience, a boot that doesn't fit doesn't fit, and after-the-fact adjustments are a losing game. For the truly hard to fit, the best, though expensive, option may be the custom boot maker.

BREAKING IN

Whatever sort of boots you buy, you want to be well acquainted with them before the Big Trip starts. With boots that are largely of fabric, the fit and feeling won't change much with wear. Leather boots are another matter. They do indeed adjust to your feet—with time. Light split-leather boots, especially those with generous inside padding, settle in fairly soon; heavier leather boots need deliberate, rather lengthy breaking in. It may take 10 miles for the first stiffness to disappear and 50 before the adjustment is complete.

Allow several weeks for this process. Start with easy walks and short distances. Don't be discouraged if you get a blister or two—better now than later. You may find that you can help tender skin to toughen by massaging it with rubbing alcohol every day. Some people use tincture of benzoin for the same purpose. Walking barefoot when you can helps also. If you know you blister easily at the heel, try leaving the upper hooks or eyelets in the lacing pattern unused for the first 5 miles or so; this may help.

Water softens leather and can help it adjust at this stage. The old advice to fill your boots with water, empty them, and "hike them dry" is overdrastic, but you needn't be shy of walking in the rain.

You can also take some corrective action on the boot. A slightly rough spot on the lining can be taped over or rubbed smooth with something like a knife handle. A dose of silicone spray can make an older boot lining slippery and easier on your skin. A change of insole or footbed may help.

When you first start wearing leather boots, make sure that the tongue lies straight under the lacing. If it gets twisted or lopsided at this stage, it will have a tendency to stay that way—forever.

If you're heading out on a long trail with blisters already started, or with leather boots that aren't really broken in, bring along some tennis or running shoes. They will be worth their weight many times over.

BOOT CARE

A top-grain leather boot should last five years or more and carry you across some 1,500 miles of the world. Light fabric boots wear out much faster, as do lightweight leather boots made of split leathers. Whatever kind of boot you have, you can get more wear out of it with a little care and the application of some protective compounds.

Except for cleaning, don't do anything much to your boots until they are somewhat broken in. For one thing, they may have been coated in the factory with short-lived polishes that could interfere with what you are applying.

Then treat external seams with beads of urethane sealant (available under various brand names at outdoor and shoe stores). The best application tool is a blunt-tipped plastic syringe. Before sealing, scrub the seams with water and something like a toothbrush; let them dry completely; and clean again with rubbing alcohol. When this has evaporated, use the syringe to lay a thin bead of sealant. Seal also the welt, or the upper margin of the rand. Let the treatment dry overnight.

Next, treat leather surfaces, whether these are just strips and patches or make up the entire boot. Just what to treat them with is a matter of some controversy. Most boot makers advise you to steer clear of pure greases, fats, and oils, which soften leather unduly. Some widely used preparations are Sno-Seal and Bee-Seal, which are based on beeswax; Ultra-Seal by REI; Biwell; and Nikwax. If care instructions accompany the boot, by all means use the treatment they suggest. Leather takes treatment best when warm (not hot!), and two thin applications are better than one. Some preparations are applied to wet leather. When done, thoroughly wipe to remove the excess.

The fabric portions of mixed-construction boots can be treated with spray-on water repellents like those used on clothing. Nikwax is one brand.

Some ultralight boots can be resoled; some can't. This is a good thing to find out and consider when you shop. In the very lightest models, the uppers are unlikely to outlast soles in any case.

ON THE TRAIL

Moisture, whether it comes inward from the outside world or outward from your own feet, is bad for boot materials. Keep boots as dry as you can. Take them off when you have an opportunity. Keep them under cover at night. If your pair has removable footbeds or insoles, remove these in the evening and wring water from any absorbent materials. When boots are seriously wet, the quickest way of drying them is to wipe them inside and then wear them with several successive pairs of dry socks. In winter, try to keep damp boots from freezing. Often that means taking them inside your sleeping bag with you (in a plastic bag).

Heat and ultraviolet rays are bad for boots. *Never* dry them at the edges of a campfire. Don't even leave them in the hot sun any longer than you can help. Leather, for all its ruggedness, is as burnable as skin. Cemented soles are vulnerable to heat as well. Cooked boots fall apart like cooked meat. Don't chance it.

Dirt and grit are bad for boots. The cleaner you can keep them, the better. Wipe off surface grime each evening. Don't leave mud caked on a boot: it draws natural oils out of leather, and can also damage glues. If you expect mud on a trip, carry a small, stiff wire brush.

Make sure that the laces continue to run smoothly through hardware, and file off any snags. Broken laces? Substitute your nylon utility cord.

Especially in light boots, soles will sometimes begin splitting apart layer from layer. These delaminations can be fixed temporarily with one of the superstrong instant-hardening glues, or with duct tape wrapped around sole and upper.

BETWEEN TRIPS

When you get home, brush crusted dirt from your boots. Clean leather boots with a sponge and a little cool water; saddlesoap is nice for leather surfaces. Fabric may be cleaned with nondetergent soap and water. Let the boots dry gradually but completely. (You can stuff them with newspaper to draw dampness out, and stuff again for storage.) Finally, treat the leather portions once more with whatever product you have been using.

REPAIRS AND RESOLING

A cobbler will make minor repairs on your boots—restitch a fraying seam, replace a grommet or a hook, reglue a separating sole—for a small charge.

Regardless of construction, most boots can be resoled. The price is currently $30 to $40—probably a fraction of the cost of your boot and very much worth it. All but the lightest boots are likely to make it through two soles. Take this step before the soles wear so thin that the midsole— the second layer up—is exposed, which makes the process much more difficult. Thinned soles are also hard on the feet, reducing cushioning and insulation.

One brand, Vibram, dominates the market in neoprene rubber lug soles; a sole that's not Vibram is probably "proprietary," made by one maker for the boots of its own line. There are several large mail order resoling and repair operations, including Vibram's Fix By Mail (see the Resources appendix).

ACCESSORIES

Gaiters ($15–$40) are fabric coverings that fasten around the tops of your boots when you slog through snowbanks or shallow water, wade through ankle-deep scree, or simply walk in the rain. They protect your feet and prolong the life of the boot. They are also of safety value in rattlesnake country. For summer use, a short, relatively inexpensive gaiter is the most you might need.

Other extras go directly on your feet. A real necessity is some sort of *protective layer* to stick on at need; it may be "moleskin," "molefoam," adhesive tape, or duct tape. Apply the appropriate patch whenever you suspect an irritation that could lead to a blister. Spenco's 2nd Skin is an excellent patching material when it's too late for prevention (see Chapters 12 and 15). A few hikers take *foot powder to* fight both blisters and athlete's foot.

Camp shoes—tennis shoes, river sandals, moccasins, or whatever—are sometimes taken for use around camp, especially if the trail boots are heavy; besides being comfortable, these may reduce wear and tear on the local environment (see end of chapter). Light and cheap will do, but you can spend up to $80 for specialized models. A practical question is whether you want a thong-type sandal that can only be worn barefoot, or a slipper-type arrangement into which you can thrust your stockinged foot. Light shoes are also sometimes useful for crossing streams.

Booties ($20 and up) are loose, high-topped slippers stuffed with insulation. A luxury in summer, they can make the difference between achingly cold feet and pleasantly warm ones on a cold winter night. Booties with heavy fabric soles cost more. These grade into *mukluks,* constructions of fleece and felt that are unmatched for living in extremely cold temperatures (see Chapter 24).

LUG SOLES: A QUESTION OF IMPACT

There is really only one impact question when it comes to boots: are lug soles bad for the land?

Common sense suggests they might be. The lugs of the typical boot sole, projecting like so many rows of teeth, dig in and grip. That's what they're for. It seems reasonable to suspect that they break up the soil surface, leaving fragments that runoff can carry away. Critics of lug soles have stated this suspicion as fact; and in earlier editions of this book, I urged backpackers to ask themselves whether they really needed lug soles for surefootedness, and to consider replacing deeply lugged soles with flatter versions when the time came to resole.

But these commonsensical ideas may be wrong, or at least not demonstrably right. The few controlled trampling studies so far done have shown no significant difference between the effect of toothy soles and flat ones.

Common sense still suggests that lighter boots (which tend also to have less ferocious soles) may produce a gentler stride, simply because the people who wear them have to place their feet a bit more carefully: they are less likely to plow through a bog, for instance, or to drive their weight down hard on their heels when descending a slope. On the other hand, this same caution may encourage them to step off an unpleasantly muddy trail and establish a damaging new track alongside it. For trail travel, then, the balance of evidence seems most unclear.

What about in camp? There are certainly anecdotes to suggest that heavy boots can cause more damage there than light shoes do. But conscientious behavior—determination not to expand the total trampled zone within the wilderness—would seem to be the real key.

The wild country can be thought of as a green expanse webbed with brown lines and patches: trails and campsites where the ground has been compacted, probably eroded, and effectively sterilized by human traffic. The first goal of low-impact travel is to avoid expanding the brown territory, to leave the enveloping green intact.

Until some more solid data replace the conflicting impressions, I'm just not convinced that footwear has much to do with it, either way.

CLOTHING

Clothing is the fundamental wilderness gear. You can survive in remote places without a pack, a tent, a stove, a sleeping bag, a compass, a flashlight. You can even do without specialized boots. Naked, in typical hiking climates, you wouldn't last long.

There is no such thing as a standard list of clothing for the wilderness. Metabolisms vary. Tastes vary. The wilderness itself—from hot to cold, from wet to dry, from calm to battering wind—varies most of all. Each backpacker learns what works for him or for her—place by place, trip by trip, season by season.

Broadly speaking, wilderness hikers have two sets of clothing. First, there is a basic fair-weather outfit: underwear, boots and socks, pants or hiking shorts, light shirt, hat and sunglasses, and a few other items. Second, there is a set of *reserve* clothing, more often in the pack than on the back, for dealing with cold, wind, rain, and snow. In spring, summer, and fall hiking, this reserve may be rather small, but it is always there. In winter travel, the basic outfit gets thicker, and the reserves are more formidable.

THE BASIC OUTFIT

The first question to ask, as you gather clothes for the wilderness, is whether you dare wear cotton.

Cotton is the cheapest fabric for the trail; if you rely on it, chances are you can find the basic garments you need at home. And they will serve you well—until the day when they get wet. Wet cotton fabric ceases to insulate; in fact, it becomes a conductor, taking heat away from the skin. The annals of rescue and mountain medicine are full of stories of people who wore cotton to snow country, or in cool mountains where it rains a lot, and got into serious trouble. The fabric is also uncomfortable, though not so dangerous, when conditions are wet but warm.

So cotton is out of favor; yet there are regions and seasons where it still makes sense. In desert travel, it would be silly to avoid it. Even in the mountains, in the summer-dry Southwest, you will see a lot of veterans in jeans. If you're unsure what you're facing, better go with the noncotton options. But if you're better equipped with knowledge—consider, and choose.

The alternatives to cotton are wool, sometimes silk, nylon, and a variety of other synthetic fabrics that dry quickly and don't turn into heat sinks when wet. Many of these synthetics now have a very cottonlike "hand" and feel nice against the skin. And though such clothes cost more than cotton garments, the difference need not be huge.

Even if they avoid cotton in their outer garments, many hikers stick with it for summer underwear. Cotton bikini briefs for both sexes have the advantage of being very packable and quick to wash and dry. Briefs and boxer-style shorts are also available in synthetic fabrics. Undershirts, if worn, can be cotton T-shirts or singlets; synthetics are more comfortable, though, in humid places. Prices per noncotton item run $7 to $20 and up. Brassieres designed for life outdoors cost $22 to $30.

I'm fond of the old-fashioned "Swedish net" undershirt, now available in nylon; it's an openwork construction that looks like "holes knotted together with string." It insulates well when covered by the outer shirt but lets the breeze get right to your skin when you unbutton the upper garment. Net shirts must have ordinary solid fabric over the shoulders; otherwise the pack straps will drive the netting painfully into your flesh. Less drastic versions of the open-weave concept are available, too.

If it's chilly enough, long johns and long-sleeved tops feel good. Some people wear "longies" in mountain summers routinely and even as the basic garment, with shorts worn on top for modesty's sake. The fabrics most used are polyester and polyester-wool mixes (no cotton here). Polypropylene, which accumulates odors and is prone to shrink, is less often used. Despite the dirt factor, light colors are best to prevent too much solar heating in warm conditions, when the outer layers may be off. For more about these underwear options, see Winter, below.

Spare underclothing? If you're wearing cotton, you must have at least one set of spares. If you've got synthetic garments, it's up to you. Some people do laundry on the trip. Some just don't worry about it.

Trousers can be simple or elaborate. Denims are tough and cheap, and they're fine for "cotton weather" if you don't find they chafe you in steady walking. (Wash them once, if they are new, to soften the fabric.) Jeans should be loose fitting and not close to the point of disintegration. Avoid wide bottoms and dirt-catching cuffs. Old nylon slacks are also sometimes seen on the trail.

Specialized hiking trousers come in various fabrics, including cotton—but there seems little point in paying extra for the same old disaster-prone fabric. A better choice is ripstop nylon, alone or blended with other synthetic fibers. There is also now a polypropylene/cotton mix that lacks the usual drawbacks of the latter. The inner surface may be a different fabric or a different weave, softer against the skin.

Some trail pants are loose, and some—mostly designed for cooler conditions—fit snugly; pants must in any case be generous enough to wear over long johns if you like and trim enough to wear under raingear. The typical loose-fitting type will have lots of pockets, including some mounted low enough so that the pack belt doesn't block access. There may be gussets, added panels of fabric set into the basic tube shapes, at the crotch and perhaps down the leg to knee or ankle; these make movement freer. For the same purpose, there may be "articulated knees" tailored in a

slight bend. Instead of conventional beltloops, which are awkward under the hipbelt of your pack, specialty pants have elastic gathers, built-in belts of flat, wide webbing, or both. I find a belt essential; elastic waistbands alone get dragged up and down when you put on or take off your pack. Ankles are tapered, to avoid snagging and flapping, but should be wide enough to fit over the top of your boot. Some models have inner, elasticized ankle-sleeves. Some have zippers up the leg, permitting you to put them on over boots. Prices of specialty pants, depending on fabric and construction, range from $35 to $80 and can even push $160.

Hiking shorts are a nice luxury; in hot, wet places, everybody wears them, but sun exposure is a concern. You should always have a pair of long pants along as well. You'll need these at least when the sun is highest, for any hiking off the trail, and wherever irritant plants are a problem. Mosquitoes, too, can make bare-legged walking unappealing. Shorts can cost from zero (your old cotton cutoffs) to $40 or so; some specialty pants, equipped with zip-off legs, can shrink into shorts at need. (Give such models a good walking trial in the store to be sure the zippers don't bother your skin.) For shorts, too, a webbing belt is nice.

Shirts are less specialized. They must have long sleeves, high collars, and pockets that button, zip, or close with hook-and-loop patches (Velcro is the familiar brand). The cotton wearer may find suitable work shirts at the department store. Some people use stout chamois shirts, also cotton, but in a thick, feltlike weave. For the cotton avoider, a light wool shirt is hard to beat. Hiking shirts are also made in ripstop nylon; these may have inset mesh panels for ventilation. There are also now shirts designed specifically for maximum sun protection (see Chapter 28). All things considered, you can spend as little as $20 or as much as $65 for a trail shirt.

You need a broad-brimmed hat to protect your face and neck from the sun, your head from heat, and your eyes from glare. The best protection is the type that has a long front visor and protects the back of the neck with a sort of curtain (called a "havelock"): a Lawrence of Arabia look. There must be a drawstring "keeper" that snugs up under your chin. A suitable hat will cost $20 to $40. You also need effective sunglasses ($12–$40), with their own keeper strap or cord to prevent loss. On snow and at high altitudes, carry not just one pair but two, in case you lose or break your primary pair. For more about the hazards of ultraviolet radiation, see Chapter 28.

There are places where mosquitoes are so tormenting that some hikers add to the basic outfit a head net: a veil of mosquito netting (under $10). Most people make do with insect repellent and netted tents.

Bathing suit for swimming? Sure, depending largely on the company you're hiking with.

INTO THE RESERVES

So much for the dry, pleasant day. Now suppose the temperature begins to drop: from 70 to 50 to 40 degrees Fahrenheit or lower. Clouds move across the sun; a cold air is stirring. Or maybe it has been cool all along. You were warm when you were walking, but when you sit down to eat lunch, you feel a chill.

Or maybe the mists of a temperate morning are congealing into rain. What do you pull out for what conditions?

It is useful to split the problem into parts. One environmental challenge is *cold,* and you respond to that by adding one or more layers of *insulation.* Another set of problems is posed by *wind and rain* (or snow), and you deal with that by adding *shells.* Some garments usefully combine insulation with a wind-resistant layer, but insulation and rain protection are best kept separate.

INSULATING GARMENTS

The first essential for warmth is a wool or polyester *stocking cap* ($5–$25). More than a third of the heat the body loses into the air is radiated from the head. Conserve some of that, and you'll feel warmer all over. Some stocking caps are thick and fuzzy; others are thinner and less formidable looking; others contain wind-blocking layers. For most purposes, the simplest will do. For colder places and times, get a longer cap that rolls down to cover the neck, with a gap left for the face, helmet-fashion (called a *balaclava*). Hands also radiate a lot of heat; on chilly summer evenings, gloves or mittens ($7–$25) can be nice.

For the torso, the simplest armament is one or two wool sweaters, or an extra wool shirt and a sweater. In sweaters you have a choice between the pullover type and the type that opens at the front. The pullover is simpler and lighter, but a front closure lets you cool off without taking off the garment. For closures, zippers, not buttons, are standard.

A good substitute for wool is polyester fabric, woven in nappy textures known as pile, fleece, and microfleece. Polyester garments can be thought of as heavy sweaters or light jackets; $35 to $70 is typical. Like wool, polyester has the great virtue of retaining its insulating power when it gets wet; of the two, polyester absorbs even less moisture and dries more readily. Pile garments now account for most of the insulating outerwear you see.

Still available, however, are *insulated jackets and vests,* incorporating either waterfowl down or synthetic insulations. Down is the luxurious choice for dry cold conditions but loses its warming power when wet, so synthetics are more generally used. A versatile alternative to the full-scale jacket is the insulated vest or armless jacket, with or without collar. You can expect to pay $115 to almost $200 for a good insulated jacket; a vest may cost as little as $65.

SHELL TECHNOLOGY

If the human body didn't sweat, or need to dissipate heat, rainproofing it would be a cinch: just wrap it in plastic. Unfortunately, we do sweat, and when we hike we sweat a lot. If we feel more or less dry, it's because evaporation whips the water away as fast as we produce it. If this doesn't happen, we get hot and sticky. Thus the shell maker's problem: how do you protect the hiker from moisture coming in while still allowing moisture to get out? Despite recent advances, the perfect garment—completely waterproof against the storm, completely open to evaporation from the skin —does not exist. What we have instead is a range of cunning compromises, ranging from very waterproof (but clammy) garments at one end of the spectrum to very permeable (but only briefly waterproof) garments at the other.

At the waterproof end of the scale are garments coated inside with an *impermeable* layer (of urethane). These waterproofs are simple, effective, and fairly cheap. But it is never fully comfortable to hike in such clothing. Even if the air is cold, you're likely to find it hot and damp inside. A partial solution is to design garments with just as much ventilation as possible. There's a dissenting approach, though. A few people swear by what are called vapor barrier (VB) garments, in which the impermeable layer is placed quite close to the skin. In theory, the air next to the body becomes moist, causing sweating to shut down and preventing the loss of both moisture and heat. VB garments seem to work well when the environment is very cold and when the wearer is not active, say for ice fishing. But in my view they're nonsense for temperate hiking.

That's the waterproof end of the spectrum. At the opposite, permeable end are garments that make little claim to block rain but are effective against wind. They do resist water to some extent because they are treated with a chemical called durable water repellent (DWR), as indeed all foul-weather gear is treated. Of course, such garments are very comfortable when it's not raining.

The rest of the spectrum of raingear, the great middle, uses what are called microporous fabrics. These contain a layer peppered with extremely tiny openings. Liquid water, which sticks together in bulky droplets, can't get through the microscopic holes. But water vapor, which travels in separate molecules, can pass. Wrap a microporous layer around a human body, and sweat will tend to evaporate and escape outwards; rain will tend not to get in.

There are rival ways of achieving microporosity. The longest-established technology uses Gore-Tex, a thin, fragile Teflon film originally developed for kidney dialysis. To make a strong fabric with Gore-Tex, the film is bonded to a layer of ordinary cloth, which faces the weather, and protected on the body side by a lining (which may be bonded or loose). After some early disappointments, these Gore-Tex laminates have proven themselves. Numerous variations on the same idea—Stormshed and Klimate are two—have meanwhile appeared. Alternatively, the micropores can be created directly in shells made of urethane, the same stuff used in fully waterproof rainwear; Ultrex and Helly-Tech are two brands that use this technology.

The microporous fabrics have many applications. They are used in tents, sleeping bags, and boots. However, their most significant use, by far, is in clothing. Never before has it been this comfortable to wear water-resistant garments while actually hiking.

The modern fabrics are not magical. They neither exclude water nor pass vapor perfectly, let alone both. There is still an unavoidable tradeoff between water resistance and breathability: the more of one you achieve, the less you have of the other. Different products now offer different compromises. There are even microporous garments "calibrated" for maximum breathability and designed to be used only against wind and the occasional light drizzle.

If you don't choose the expensive microporous garments, an old solution is still very practical: take a set of light waterproofs and a separate set of coverings to block a dry but chilling wind (if that's a kind of weather you expect to encounter).

STYLES OF SHELL GARMENTS

The simplest, cheapest, and best-ventilated piece of raingear is certainly the *poncho*. This is simply a big rectangle of urethane-coated nylon with a hole for the neck and a hood. The short-tailed or regular poncho is really just a loose, untailored raincoat. More versatile is the *backpack poncho*, so long in back that it hangs over the pack and protects the load as well as the porter. Generous ponchos can double as tarps for shelter if the rain is not too serious (see Chapter 8). Because the pack is inside with you, so to speak, a packboard poncho isn't pinched in around your body by shoulder straps and hipbelt. Thus ventilation is excellent. Good nylon ponchos cost $25 or more. To be practical, they must be worn with rainpants or rainchaps, or possibly long gaiters.

But if the rain is heavy, especially if there is wind, no poncho will be protection enough. Rain always works its way in at the sides. When the mist comes down in the hills and the sky closes over in a slow-arriving, slow-departing storm, you need a regular raincoat and a separate cover for your pack.

Next up the line in cost are coats of urethane-treated nylon. These usually come with full front openings and hoods, the *jacket* style. A longer jacket is a *parka*. But you may also see the *anorak*, a short, hooded nylon jacket that has a short zipper at the neck opening and pulls on over your head. Perhaps the most total protection possible is the full-length anorak, or *cagoule*, which covers you down to the knees. The more vents to help you deal with the body moisture problem, the better. Urethane raincoats cost from $30 to $65.

Light wind-protection jackets, mainly intended for runners, can also serve the backpacker ($40–$50). There are also wind jackets of "calibrated" Gore-Tex. Like the simpler wind garments, they don't weigh much or take up much room; unlike them, they cost a bundle.

The typical weather protection today is the much heavier, bulkier parka that uses microporous fabrics. It has a hood with a drawstring; a rugged front zipper protected by a storm flap that locks down with snaps or hook-and-loop closures; and usually several enormous pockets, which should be arranged so that pack straps don't block access to them. The coat should be long enough so that you can sit down on the tail. A drawstring in the lower hem allows you to tighten the coat down below when it's cold and windy. Parkas intended for winter use will also have a "powder skirt" inside at waist level, an elasticized strip that clings to the body and keeps you drier if you take a tumble in a snowdrift. Most hoods are integral, but some are detachable. (Having once had the detachable kind blow off my head in a snowstorm, I greatly prefer built-in.)

Ventilation is achieved by various means. The main front zipper should open from the bottom as well as from the top so that you can crack it either way. Most parkas have zippers under the armpits, which you can open to let some unwanted heat and body moisture escape. Some have instead "gill" zippers, which angle from chest to lower back. Pockets may also be floored with mesh, providing another exit for warm, moist air.

Some microporous parkas are made of two-layer laminate, with a loose inner lining; others of three-layer laminate, with the lining bonded in place. Loose linings make a softer fabric that drapes better, but bonded liners make the coat tougher, more packable, quicker to dry, and indeed more water-resistant; these are to be preferred.

Whatever style of raincoat you carry, it must be cut generously, to fit over inner clothing. Too tight an outer garment inhibits air circulation and evaporation. It should be long enough to cover your buttocks so it won't creep up under the pack's hipbelt and give you a wet spot.

You'll pay $125 to $365 for a heavy-duty microporous parka.

What about your legs? In warm country, many hikers wear shorts and let their legs get wet. In cooler climates, you'll need waterproofing all the way down. Many people who wear waterproof breathable garments on their torsos find that they can wear simpler coated coverings on their legs without discomfort. Urethane-coated *rainchaps* come in literal pairs, a separate tube for each leg, and tie on to the belt at the top. Full *rainpants* protect the crotch and waistline better. There may be zippers up the leg so that the garment can be put on over boots, or even full-length zippers allowing it to be put on over skis. Whatever combination of coat and leg protection you work out, make sure there is a generous overlap at the waist. Pant cuffs should be loose, not elasticized, as the latter design channels rain into your boots. Chaps cost $12 or so the pair; urethane-coated rainpants cost $27 to $40; and rainpants with microporous fabrics run anywhere from $50 to $275. Simple wind-pants for dry conditions have all but disappeared, except for "calibrated" microporous shells that cost about the same as their more water-resistant cousins.

There was a time when you had to finish the manufacture of your own foul-weather gear by sealing the seams with urethane, a tedious, messy job. Today just about all seams are sealed in the factory with melt-on plastic strips. These are shiny and recognizable on the inside, unless concealed by a lining; you can also see the strips, on some garments, by holding them up against the light. If in doubt, confirm with the store before you buy.

WINTER

If you are going into seriously cold conditions, clothing changes and becomes still more critical.

Here, long underwear is essential. You have a wide choice of fabrics, all of which retain their warmth (or more accurately, your warmth) when damp. Wool has the desirable tendency to wick sweat away from your skin; it also makes many people itch and, once wet, dries slowly. Silk feels lovely and wicks well but is also slow to dry and can accumulate quite an odor. Polypropylene does not wick; it is woven loosely enough to permit evaporation directly from the skin, but you may get moist when exercising hard. Polypro also has a famous odor problem and will shrink to a fraction of its proper size if machine-dried at too high a temperature. Polyester also does not wick but can be induced to do so by chemical treatment (which only lasts a year), or by a kind of mashing that changes the fibers' shape, or by tricks of weaving. Many makers use combinations of fabrics in blends or layers. Wool-polyester combinations seem to have the advantages of both and the drawbacks of neither. Nylon may be added to resist pilling and Lycra or Spandex for stretch. Some garments are built of meshy fabrics with lots of tiny holes for ventilation. Some incorporate odor-fighting substances. The variations continue to accumulate, and most are pretty good.

Underwear comes in various weights. Lightweight garments are best for year-round use or in very energetic pursuits like cross-country skiing. Middle weights, thicker and more tightly woven, are the winter basics. Heavyweight garments work best for situations in which you won't be working terribly hard and need to conserve all possible body heat.

Underwear bottoms should be simple, snugly fitting tights with wide waistbelts and elasticized cuffs that can be rolled up. They should have smooth outer surfaces that resist snagging, slide easily under outer layers, and look presentable when the outer layers are missing. Seams should be flat and smooth. A gusseted crotch is good for freedom of movement. Men's versions will have a fly opening; at least one maker offers a model

that allows women to relieve themselves without pulling the inner garment down.

Underwear tops are more variable. You can get plain round crew necks; turtlenecks with short zippers; or three-button "henley" models. Sleeves should push up when you want them to (but not creep up when you don't). Tails should be long, for ready tucking in. One-piece "union suits" are also to be had.

Depending on fabric and features, you can expect to pay $18 to $70 per piece for light or middleweight underwear and as much as $120 for heavier models.

Some people use medium or heavy long johns as their basic pants, skipping the usual trouser layer and adding only pile pants or weather shells as needed. Indeed, some heavier underwear is designed to be used this way, with such outerwear features as pockets.

More commonly, actual pants are worn. Differently tailored from downhill ski wear, these may be of polyester pile or of wool. Gear stores sometimes sell full-length wool trousers, but you can find these at lower prices in surplus stores and thrift shops. Another option is knickers, loose-cut pants that stop at the knee; they are worn with correspondingly elongated socks. Though very comfortable, this combination seems to be disappearing. Expect to pay $40 to $80 for legwear.

Shirts, insulating layers, and shells are not much different in winter from the cotton-free basic outfit. Insulation, however, is going to be thicker, a result achieved best by adding several separate layers of wool or polyester fleece, none too thick by itself. Some people carry light woolen mufflers to further protect the neck.

For weather protection, snow travelers are likely to favor shells somewhat toward the permeable end of the waterproof-to-breathable spectrum. In cold conditions, you're more likely to get wet from the inside out than from the outside in. It's in this situation that the expensive microporous windcoat makes best sense.

Gloves and mittens are essential for winter. People wear different combinations. A typical one in very cold places is a light, five-fingered wool or polyester glove liner inside a heavier mitten with a water-repellent (probably microporous) mitten shell on top of that: a combination costing $30 to $60.

Another winter essential is a pair of *gaiters*. These tough nylon sheaths fasten around the ankle, closing off the gap at the top of the boot where snow would otherwise get in. Some gaiters, for wading occasional snowbanks, are simple and collarlike. For real snow travel you need the fitted or spat type that covers the upper half of the boot and rises well up the leg. For best convenience, the closure should be in front; it may be a zipper (backed up with snaps or hook-and-loop fabric) or consist simply of a wide hook-and-loop overlap. A cord or strap, running under the boot, keeps the gaiter from creeping up out of place. Gaiters may be waterproof or not, waterproof only in the lower part, or of waterproof breathable fabric; some wearers find that completely waterproof ones are clammy. Prices range from $15 to $50.

ADJUSTABILITY: WHY LESS IS SOMETIMES MORE

When you hike, whether in summer or winter, you burn a lot of fuel and produce a lot of heat. At the same time, you're losing that heat, mostly to the air. To stay comfortable, you have to maintain a rough balance between the heat you generate and the heat you give away. Retain too much, and you'll be hot; lose too much, and you'll be miserably cold. Not too far beyond misery, in either direction, is danger. See Chapter 28 for more about these problems.

Every moment you spend on the trail, something happens to shift the heat balance a little. Maybe at first you are walking along a flat, shaded valley, feeling comfortable. Then the trail climbs a ridgeline in the sun, and you are hot and sweating. Later, a chill takes you as you reach the windy height above. Wind, sunlight, temperature, terrain, your own metabolism—everything is constantly changing.

The body has certain built-in ways of managing heat, but the adjustments it can make are limited. Beyond that narrow range, what you adjust is your clothing. The change may be as simple as rolling your sleeves up or down or as complex as putting on a jacket and a stocking cap; the purpose is always the same.

The easier it is to make these adjustments, the more likely you are to make them at the proper time. In choosing clothes for the wilderness, look for garments that allow you to change your protection exactly as required when the heat balance shifts from too much to too little and back again.

To this end, most hikers prefer several *thin* garments to one thicker layer. If you have two light shirts along, you can wear neither, or one, or both, for three levels of warmth. If you have only a single, heavier shirt, it's either on you or in your pack; you've lost an intermediate choice.

In the same way, backpackers tend to favor *single-purpose* garments over those that try to do several jobs at once. If you have both a light insulated jacket and a shell, you can wear the jacket alone when it's cool and still, the shell alone when it is not so cold but blowing, and both together when you need the greatest protection. But if you brought a monstrous down-stuffed parka that is shell and jacket in one, you have no choice. You either wear the thing or you don't.

A third principle: it's nice if each piece of clothing is ad*justable* in itself. Thus most people prefer an open-front raincoat or sweater to a pullover style. If the pullover gets too hot for you, you can simply suffer. Or you can stop, take off your pack, take off the pullover, put it away, hoist your pack again, and go. By that time you may be chilled again anyway. But with a front closure, you can let a cool breeze in any time.

All of this matters, in typical summer weather, only to a degree. It is in really bad weather, and especially in winter, that ease of adjustment can make a striking difference. When you are traveling in a bitterly cold wind, you don't want to work up too much of a sweat; evaporation will chill you the moment you stop. The world you are in, wonderful though it may be, is also hostile. You have to keep the balance to survive.

PUTTING IT TOGETHER

How, then, do you choose the clothes for a particular trip? Whether you're heading for the local woodland in June or for a 12,000-foot peak in December, the approach is the same. Start with the basic outfit appropriate to the place and season, and then ask yourself, What insulators, if any, do I need to add for *cold*? What shell or shells should I add for *wind and wet*?

There are three or four typical climates that backpackers encounter in North America, and three or four typical lists of clothing that result.

First, there's the comfortable weather of the southwestern hiking season. In the wilderness lands of California and the mountain states to the east, temperatures may be hot or cool in summer, depending on month and elevation, but the air will seldom be wet for more than a day at a time. Humidity is almost always low; if rain comes, it is likely to be in brief, torrential thundershowers. Under these circumstances, the hiker is likely to wear and carry a pretty minimal assortment.

SOUTHWESTERN CLOTHING LIST

boots
socks
briefs (cotton okay)
pants (cotton okay)
hiking shorts (cotton okay)
undershirt (cotton okay)
shirt (cotton okay)
sunglasses (and spares in alpine and desert areas)
hat
bandanna
one or two sweaters or light insulated jacket
light urethane-coated raincoat
rainchaps
stocking cap

At lower elevations, and in areas that are almost totally free of summer rain, this short list can be shortened still further.

Less hospitable, in some ways, is the moister, cooler summer landscape of Maine or western Washington or Minnesota, not to mention Canada or Alaska. Really hot days are not common; storms can develop at any time and last for several days; the temperature can drop sharply and quickly. Here, cotton almost disappears from the wardrobe.

NORTHERN CLOTHING LIST

boots
socks
synthetic briefs or long johns
hiking shorts (possibly cotton)
pants
undershirt
shirt
sunglasses (and spares in alpine and desert areas)
hat
bandanna
one or two sweaters or light insulated jacket (not unprotected
    down)
microporous raincoat

rainchaps or rainpants (possibly microporous)
stocking cap

Different again are the regions where the normal hiking season is both humid and either warm or hot, with perhaps the relief of cool nights at higher elevations. Here the usual hiking uniform is boots and shorts and as little else as possible. The clothing pack list grows shorter. Cotton may be worn, but other fabrics are more comfortable.

SOUTHEASTERN CLOTHING LIST

hiking shorts
pants
light shirt
sunglasses
hat
bandanna
sweater or light jacket for higher elevations
microporous raincoat
stocking cap

These lists could be varied—there are a thousand personal preferences, legitimate arguments for adding this, deleting that—but I hope they make the point: trail clothing, for most wilderness conditions, need not be complex. It is only in winter (or in places that are permanently wintry) that the whole range of wilderness clothing may have to be drawn on at once.

WINTER CLOTHING LIST

polyester long johns
polyester undershirt
polyester pants or knickers
socks or knee socks
microporous rainpants
insulated jacket
microporous parka
wool cap
ordinary hat
goggles and spares

high microporous gaiters
polypropylene gloves
wool mittens
microporous overmitts

CLOTHING CARE

Specialty wilderness clothing, for all its toughness, needs a little special care. Washing instructions vary—check labels—but hand-washing and hang-drying are frequently preferred. Use gentle soaps that contain neither detergents nor surfactants. Dreft and Ivory Flakes are two familiar brands in powder form; Nikwax makes an expensive liquid cleanser for gear. Bleach should never be used.

If you do use a washing machine (sometimes appropriate), it must be the front-loading, drum type; top-loading, agitator-type machines are to be avoided. You will rarely use the "hot" setting. Some items can be tumble-dried at low heat; some can't. No wilderness clothing gets dry-cleaned, period.

Noncotton underwear, whatever its composition, is best laundered by hand. Polypropylene fabric can't stand even minimal dryer heat. Polyester can, but don't overdo it. If you do use a dryer, leave out the dryer sheets. Silk never goes in machines.

Noncotton pants and shirts have varying requirements, but again you can't go wrong with hand-washing. Wool should be washed as little as possible, even by hand. If there are especially grimy spots, attack them first with a toothbrush and a paste of your laundry soap in warm water. Make sure pockets are free of crumbs. Immerse the garment in warm water, knead it thoroughly (but don't twist or wring), and let it soak for half an hour. Drain, press out the water, refill your basin with warm rinse water, soak the piece fifteen minutes, and knead again. Repeat this rinsing step at least once.

Insulated garments, whether they contain down or synthetics, are best hand-washed and air-dried, with one exception: down garments actually need a warm-air tumble to fluff up properly. Let them drain well first. Throw into the dryer with them a clean, dry towel—maybe several, and maybe several towels in succession—to absorb water and hasten drying. The old advice to toss in a tennis ball or a clean sneaker, however, seems to be out of favor: intended to break up clumps of down, this treatment is now thought too rough for these rather fragile garments.

Polyester fleeces machine-wash perfectly in cold water and emerge almost dry. Zip zippers (as you always do when you put a garment in a machine) and turn items inside out to reduce pilling.

The care of shells is a little more complex. Coated-nylon garments (including some waterproof breathables) should be rinsed off, inside and out, to remove sweat residue that can attack the coating. If further cleaning seems necessary, follow the manufacturer's suggestions. Never wash in a top-loading, spindle-type washer.

For garments incorporating Gore-Tex or similar membranes, machine-washing is usually okay or even preferred. Again, zip zippers and mate pieces of hook-and-loop tape: if unattached, these rasp at fabric and pick up mats of threads and lint. To keep sleeves from twisting or turning inside out, link opposite cuffs with their hook-and-loop tabs or snaps.

Tumble-drying at low or even medium heat (check your label) is actually beneficial for some shells because it rejuvenates the chemical coating known as durable water repellent, or DWR.

Just about any shell garment, whether nominally waterproof or not, comes from the factory impregnated with this fluoropolymer, a kind of dispersed Teflon. DWR causes water to bead up and prevents the outermost layer from becoming saturated. This makes a difference: water-logged outer fabric impedes the evaporation of sweat and can make a garment *feel* like it's leaking even when it's not.

DWR loses effectiveness over time. Moderate heat, as in a drier, freshens it up. You can also iron the outer surface of the garment with a steam iron at moderate setting.

There comes a time when DWR needs a more thorough renewal. The chemical is available in spray and liquid forms. A widely distributed brand, essentially the same stuff used in manufacture, is TX-Direct by Nikwax. DWR is best applied in liquid form, to a freshly cleaned garment, in a washing machine whose cycle can be interrupted for a long soak. After the drum has filled with water, pour in the DWR; after about five minutes, stop the action for a quarter of an hour, then let the machine finish its routine. Complete the process with a thorough tumble-drying.

Although the liquid treatment ordinarily is the best, spray-on DWR treatments (not to be confused with silicone sprays) are also available. In one situation, they are required: Gore-Tex or similar garments with loose-hanging inner linings should not get wash-in DWR treatment, as the lining is supposed to wick sweat, and you don't want that action interfered with.

There is also a wash-in DWR treatment specifically for down; this helps the plumules stay springy in humid (but not too humid!) conditions. For a manageably small garment, the washing-in is best done by hand, with the usual finish in a commercial dryer.

When the main waterproof layer of urethane-coated raingear starts peeling, most people write the garment off. It can, however, be given a second life by painting the outer surface—not the inner one that is peeling—with any of several liquid, water-based polymers. Any factory-sealed seams that peel are defective; return such a garment to the manufacturer.

In the field, fabric tears are usually repaired with sticky tape designed for the purpose (and possibly even matched by color). The area around the rip should be cleaned thoroughly (use an alcohol-soaked towelette). Before applying the patch, trim off square corners, which tend to lift. Duct tape is much used, too, but leaves a stubborn, gummy residue.

6   THE PACK

The pack makes the backpacker. Without it you remain a hiker, confined to a circle with a car at its center and a radius as long as you can walk in half a day. But with your pack on your back, you are a *traveler on foot*, you can go for a week or longer and cover, if you wish, several hundred wilderness miles. There is something formal, almost ceremonial, in the way an experienced packer hoists the load on the first morning of a trip.

And that moment should be a pleasant one. A properly fitted pack is comfortable. Nobody, on a wilderness trip of normal length and difficulty, should have to feel like a pack animal, struggling forward under a painful burden. Although any pack is likely to seem heavy at the end of a long day, no pack should make you groan sincerely when you put it on (some people groan for show). If it does, something is wrong. Either you've filled the pack too full, or you have it wrongly adjusted, or—just possibly—you have the wrong pack in the first place.

BUYING A FULL-SIZED PACK

There are several hundred different models of full-sized packs on the market, and new variations are turning up each year. You needn't rush to choose among them. This is a large and important purchase, and the chances are you'll be traveling with the thing for many years.

Many gear stores have packs for rent. Take advantage of this if you can. Only experimenting on the trail permits you to know for sure what you like best, especially if you are deciding among fundamentally different designs. A typical three-day rental fee is $35 to $55. Since there are acceptable packs as cheap as $100, that may seem hefty; but I think this first hundred is better spent renting than buying what may turn out to be "disposable" gear. If you do buy cheap, Camp Trails, Coleman, Outbound, and Peak 1 are creditable low-end brands.

Now, more on the anatomy of backpacks, and the choices to be made.

INTERNAL AND EXTERNAL FRAMES

Modern full-sized backpacks are a genus with two species. First, there are *internal-frame packs*, which appear to be one-piece towers of fabric. Second, and now rather less commonly seen, are *external-frame packs*, with obvious rigid frameworks to which separate packbags are attached.

Both types can be traced back to designs in use before World War II. But all the packs of that period had the same fault: they were supported entirely by the shoulders. The upper body carried the whole load. In fact, the upper body is not well adapted to supporting weight. No pack that hangs off the shoulders, without any other point of support, is comfortable with a load of more than 15 to 20 pounds; and the packs of that period—compressing the spine and dragging at the back—were uncomfortable indeed by current standards.

Modern full-sized packs solve this problem. All contain rigid members that transmit the weight of the load down to a padded hipbelt; the pressure comes to bear, not on the weak shoulders and back, but on the robust joints and powerful muscles of the hips, buttocks, and thighs. When you wear a properly adjusted backpack, your shoulders take only a small share of the burden. More than any other innovation, this change in pack design made wilderness hiking appealing to a wide public, and made the wilderness a place where almost anyone could go.

Do you want a pack with an external frame, or an internal-frame design?

Internal-frame packs are general-purpose packs, useful both on and off the trail. Their frames are somewhat flexible, and their outline is narrow. They fit closely against the back. Thus they tend to move with you, not to shift around like independent beings. They also tend to be warm on the back in hot weather.

External-frame packs are the most comfortable tools for carrying massive loads on trails. Their packbags are wider and flatter, with a higher center of gravity and less inclination to bulge out behind; thus they permit a more upright posture than do internal-frame packs. And they have a considerable advantage in warm weather: standing well out from the back, except at shoulder and hip, they give sweat plenty of chance to evaporate. Finally, exoskeletal packs (often known simply as frame packs) are considerably cheaper than the internal-frame variety.

On the negative side, rigid frames tend to bounce and swing whenever the wearer makes a quick motion. When the hips swivel and dip, as they do when you hike downhill, the frame pack does the same—but in its own competing rhythm. Externals are miserable to carry when, for instance, you stride and leap across the boulder fields called talus. They may also creak and squeak in a manner that some people find annoying.

You might relate the choice to your ambitions like this:

- If you plan to spend much time off the trail, going cross-country, especially over rugged ground; if you want to use the pack for scrambling or for climbing; or if you want a pack that you can carry when skiing, there's really no choice: the internal-frame pack, with its flexibility and closer fit, is almost certainly for you. (For snowshoeing, too, an endoskeleton is preferable, though a frame can be managed.)
- If you plan to carry oversized loads, as for very long trips—and if you will do nearly all your travel on the trail, or in very easy cross-country—then a frame pack is a reliable choice.
- If you expect to carry moderate loads and to do most of your hiking on-trail—a description that fits most backpackers, most of the time—then either an external-frame or internal-frame pack will make sense. All you can do is rent differing kinds for a trial, and trust your experience.

Consult also your wallet. Two hundred dollars is quite expensive for an external-frame pack, but just middling for an internal frame. A few very elaborate internals cost more than $500.

INTERNAL-FRAME PACKS: FRAME AND SUSPENSION

These apparently "soft" packs get their rigidity from long bars of aluminum, graphite, or polycarbonate. The bars may be arranged parallel, one on either side of the spine; in an X design, in which case the pack must stand out a little farther from the back; in a U, with a crossbar at the bottom; in a V; or in still other variations. There may also be a wider piece of molded plastic called a framesheet, which adds some support and prevents items in the pack from poking into your back. A pack with a framesheet may have just one vertical bar.

These weight-bearing members connect with, and transmit weight to, the hipbelt. The key connection may take several forms, each a compromise between the rigid linkage that would transmit the pressure best and the soft linkage that would allow the pack to follow best the movements of the torso. Some belts are solidly pinned to the frame at a point behind the lumbar pad; at the other end extreme are models in which adjustable webbing loops form the entire connection.

The hipbelt itself is an elaborate padded structure, more or less sculptured to grip and cradle the hips. Typically you have soft open-cell foam against the body and firmer closed-cell foam behind, backed up again, in some models, with a plastic stiffener. Softer isn't better for everyone: some people prefer a firmer feel. Open-cell foam has the drawback of soaking up the rain. Some makers use a "slow memory" foam that's supposed to adapt itself to the shape of a particular wearer. Others build in cunning adjustments that let you tilt the belt to match your anatomy, or change the angle at which the essential webbing belt emerges from the enclosing pads. Hipbelts adjust for length with buckles and close in front with heavy plastic snap-in clamps.

From either side of the hips, straps rise to the shoulders, over them, and down to an attachment point or points just back of your shoulders. As with all packs suitable for backpacking, the shoulder straps function

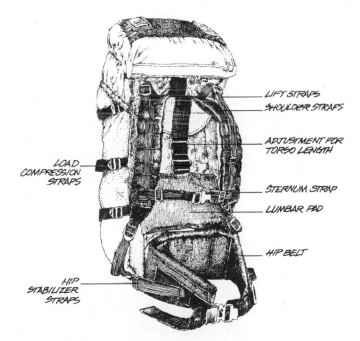

LIFT STRAPS
SHOULDER STRAPS
ADJUSTMENT FOR TORSO LENGTH
LOAD COMPRESSION STRAPS
STERNUM STRAP
LUMBAR PAD
HIP BELT
HIP STABILIZER STRAPS

ANATOMY OF AN INTERNAL FRAME PACK

more to keep the load upright and steady than to support its weight. Their design can be quite elaborate, however, with plenty of padding and sculpting, a skin-sparing lining on the underside, and perhaps as many as four possible adjustments for each shoulder. Where the straps go down the back, they may converge in what is called a yoke or remain separate; to allow variations of fit, strap origins can usually be shifted up or down.

To add to stability, most packs will have *sternum straps* and *lift straps*. Sternum straps buckle across the chest, linking the two shoulder straps. *Lift straps* rise from a point just in front of the shoulders to the upper corners of the packbag, about at ear level; when tightened, they press the load closer to your body, thus permitting you to stand more nearly upright as you carry it.

The part of the pack that lies against the back will be padded. Some makers build in slots or channels designed to increase ventilation and keep things cooler back there. Usually there is a thick *lumbar pad* where the weight of the pack comes to bear on the sloping base of the spine.

At the bottom corners of the pack, short *load stabilizer straps* may be provided; these tug the packbag firmly against the belt, in hopes of reducing sideways sway.

INTERNAL-FRAME PACKS: PACKBAG

Most packbags are made of a smooth, tightly woven nylon duck. Others have a rougher nylon called Cordura or an ultrastrong fabric known as ballistics cloth. Almost all manufacturers now make their bags of urethane-coated fabric, though the glossy inner surface may be concealed by a lining. This water repellency, by itself, won't keep your gear dry in heavy rain or wet snow, but every little bit helps. On better packs, seams will be factory sealed. A few expensive packs have two layers of waterproofing.

The space within the internal-frame pack can be variously organized. There may be a single major compartment, or an upper and a lower one. Some packs open only at the top, others at the front of the pack (that is, on the side away from your back), others in both places. Frontal zippers may be horizontal, vertical, diagonal, or shaped like an upside-down U, allowing you to lay the whole compartment open like a suitcase. If there are upper and lower compartments, the divider between them may be a solid floor or a sleevelike arrangement that closes with a drawstring. There may be smaller internal pockets: possibly a slab pocket, inside next to the back, for the stowing of heavy gear, or a netting pocket for small, losable objects. Little pockets for wallets and lanyards for keys are likely to appear somewhere.

Top-opening packs usually have drawstrings at the mouth. Often they have *extension sleeves*, tubes of lighter fabric that, once pulled out, rise well above the original top of the pack and increase its capacity. The vulnerable opening is protected by a *storm flap*, a long tongue of fabric that arches over it, runs part way down the front of the pack, and cinches securely there.

You'll see *compression straps* arranged on the outer surface of the pack. Tightening these, you draw the center of gravity closer to the back and take pressure off bulging zippers. If you're carrying an undersized load, the same straps will neaten it by cinching up unused volume. And they will hold your pack together if a panel-loading zipper has failed. The larger the pack, the more of these tighteners it is likely to have.

For storage on the outer surface of the pack there is always a large top pocket; in top-opening packs, this rides on the storm flap. Frequently this pouch can be detached and used as a fanny pack for day trips (see below). There may or may not be some smaller outside pockets, either built in or strapped on and detachable. The typical packbag is also fairly decorated with attachment points for tying things on: slotted plastic patches through which straps can be passed, built-in belts or elastic bungee cords, ice ax loops, "daisy chains" of webbing with many openings. "Ski sleeves" may be formed by the space behind side pockets. There may be a shovel flap, a long tongue of tough fabric on the packfront that can be secured around a snow shovel, wet clothing, or anything else that's awkward to store inside.

Various gimmicks go in and out of fashion. Currently popular is the "hydration system," a water bladder housed in the pack, with a hose you can suck on as you walk. The setup may be built in or just provided for. Accessible water bottle holders may also be built into hipbelt, shoulder strap, or anyplace on the pack that you can reach while wearing it. All such refinements, of course, add to the weight of the pack itself.

EXTERNAL-FRAME PACKS: FRAME AND SUSPENSION

The exoskeletal pack is a simpler creature than its internal-frame counterpart. Its two basic components—the suspension system and the packbag—are distinct. The classic frame is a structure of metal tubing shaped like an H with several crossbars, to which hipbelt and shoulder straps are attached. The packbag itself—tall, wide, flat, and boxlike—is attached to the frame in any of several ways, most often with metal skewers called clevis pins. Though you buy packbag and frame as a unit, you may be able to exchange components by one maker, and to some extent between brands.

Frame materials vary. The traditional stuff is tubular aluminum, but plastics are increasingly used, in addition to metal or in place of it. Any joints are usually welded. All frames are curved from top to bottom and from side to side to match the shape of the body.

Not all frames are of the basic H pattern. Some close off the H at top or bottom. Some frames rise extra high, creating a sort of shelf above the packbag where things can be strapped on. Some curve backwards at the bottom in a sort of curl, creating a shelflike space down there. Some have an hourglass shape, like a rectangle pinched in at the sides. Some frames will stand up unsupported; most won't. There are other variations.

One striking variant is the so-called wraparound design in which the sides of the frame curve sharply forward at the bottom. The result is that the two vertical tubes end right beside the hipbones (rather than on your back well behind the hip). Thus the shoulder straps and the hipbelt attach to the frame much farther forward than with the standard H. This arrangement is intended to bring a still larger proportion of the total load onto the hips, and also to reduce the lurching effect on a rough trail. Reports are mixed, but the variation seems to work well for people with broad hips; I have found it comfortable myself.

When you wear a properly fitted frame, none of the rigid structure touches your body. The three parts of the pack that actually touch you are the hipbelt, the shoulder straps, and the backbands or lumbar pad.

The hipbelt attaches at the bottom tips of the H and runs around the body just below the waist, buckling securely at the front. Some belts are heavily padded, like those on internal-frame packs, and some aren't—experiment to find out which you like best. Compared with an internal-frame pack, which puts quite a bit of its weight on the lumbar spine, the external frame rides more definitely on the hips.

Shoulder straps rise from the same bottom points of the H, cross your shoulders, and converge to join the frame at a point near the back of your neck. A buckle in front of each shoulder adjusts for length. Straps are more or less elaborately padded where they rest on the body.

Belts and straps are usually attached to the frame with clevis pins that run through grommets in fabric and holes in metal, and lock in place with retaining rings.

The packbag touches your back toward the rump, at the lumbar spine. Here you may find a mesh *backband* or a thick, soft *lumbar pad* like those found on internal frames. The pad is cushier and keeps the load a bit more stable, but backbands are cooler.

EXTERNAL-FRAME PACKS: PACKBAG

Packbags can be attached to external frames in several ways but are most often joined with clevis pins like those used elsewhere in the design. A few bags clip or strap to plastic frames.

Most frame packbags are *three-quarter length*—shorter than the frames on which they are mounted. The sleeping bag, stuffed in a storage sack and strapped to the lower crossbars of the frame, fills the remaining space. Some packbags are so designed that you can shift them up or down to change the center of gravity (a low-slung load helps in cross-country scrambling). In packs with extra-tall frames, a second slot for tying things on exists at the top.

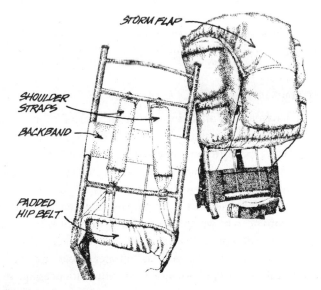

CLASSIC EXTERNAL-FRAME PACK

External-frame packbags lend themselves to subdivision. In the most common design, there is a large upper compartment held open at the top by a light metal framework and protected by a storm flap (with the usual big top pocket mounted on it). There may be an extension sleeve that adds height to the pack for bulky loads. Underneath the upper compartment there is commonly a smaller bottom chamber, with its own zippered opening to the world.

Some bags aren't divided at all but have a single deep compartment. This is less convenient for getting at things, easier for packing bulky or odd-shaped items. Some packs have zip-out dividers so that you can have it either way. Some have permanent dividers but leave corner gaps so that you can stick long objects down through.

As with internal-frame packs, the panel-loading suitcaselike alternative is also found, with the same advantage—convenience—and the same disadvantage—that gravity isn't helping you keep the contents in place if a zipper fails.

Frame packs, much more than internal-frame models, lend themselves to a multiplication of outside pockets. It's a luxury to have so many places to put objects you may need during the hiking day. Pocket zippers, like the heavier zippers on the major compartments, may run straight across the tops of the spaces they open; or they may be vertical; or they may be arc shaped or inverted-U shaped (opening around three sides). Though I personally prefer straight-across zippers, there's no advice to give but to suit yourself.

SELECTING A PACK

Once you have decided on an internal or an external frame, some other questions arise.

How much *capacity* to do you want? If you expect most of your trips to be weekend affairs, you can get by with as little as 3,000 cubic inches, or about two standard brown supermarket bags' worth (the bag holds about 1,400 cubic inches). In metric terms, that's about 23 liters. More flexibility is provided by what might be called three-brown-bag and four-brown-bag packs, holding between 4,500 and 6,000 cubic inches; that's plenty for a week's worth of gear in summer. Packs over 6,000 cubic inches are really for expeditions or winter mountaineering. If you are buying one of these load monsters, look for extra padding on the shoulder straps and for a hipbelt engineered with a very soft exterior and a very stiff, supportive layer somewhere in its makeup.

Bear in mind that capacity figures include only the inside space of a pack and its pockets; thus they understate the volume of frame packs, which lend themselves to strapping things on the outside, and especially of packs with three-quarter-length frames, where the sleeping bag *always* rides outside. Bear in mind too that manufacturers compute volume in different ways and have been known to overstate it.

The pack's own *weight* needs consideration. It is, after all, part of the load you carry! The tradeoff isn't really between weight and volume, nor is it always between weight and durability. Rather, it's between weight and convenience: every added pocket, strap, zipper, and gizmo adds its ounce or two. Packs large enough for a week-long trip vary all the way from 4 pounds to almost 9 pounds when empty, which is way too much; many solidly built ones can be found below 5 pounds. Not surprisingly, very light packs that are also rugged are among the most expensive.

When you've zeroed in on a pack and features, take time to examine some of its *workmanship*. You can always get a faulty specimen of a generally excellent brand. And a quality check can help you decide whether a given model is worth its price.

If you're considering an external-frame pack, examine that frame. Some are built so strongly that you could use them for ladders. For normal purposes you don't need such high technology, and most frames, except suspiciously cheap ones, will be strong enough. To check, set the pack up with one "foot" on the floor, one raised, and press down diagonally from the upper opposite corner. This pressure catches the frame at its weakest. If you see the frame even beginning to distort as you push, let up quickly and find another store.

Don't fail to examine sewing on packbags. Though some brands are certainly more consistent than others, price and prestige don't guarantee good work. Stitches should be small and not too widely spaced; ten to twelve stitches to the inch is standard. Rows should be straight and neat. If you see much double or triple stitching, you know standards are high. Check the end of each row of stitches. It should be bar-tacked—the line should finish in a dense band of stitches, one almost on top of another. Look at the sewing at the bottom of the pack and around the pockets. In the best packs there will be multiple stitching at these points and possibly thicker or doubled fabric in places that take extra stress, like the ends of zippers and the "root" of the storm flap. Fabric edges at seams should either be heat sealed or bound like the edge of a rug. Cloth that is simply cut will fray.

Internal-frame packs need to be built like crazy. Load-bearing straps and belts usually attach with hardware to the internal frame; on a few good packs, connections may be cloth to cloth, in which case stitching must be copious and reinforcement obvious. Look for leather pads, rivets, extra fabric, or other strengtheners at critical points.

FITTING A PACK

Fitting a pack correctly is less exacting than fitting a pair of shoes, but only just.

You know how tall you are, but do you know how tall your back is? More accurately, do you know the length of your torso? Before venturing to the pack store, better find out. You need a fabric tape measure and a friend. Stand with your feet in a natural position, about shoulder width apart. At the sides of your body, locate the tops of your hipbones and have your friend imagine (or even draw) a line connecting them across your back, close to the small. Tilt your head forward and find, at the back of your neck, the obvious bony protuberance (the seventh vertebra). Now have your friend measure between these markers, following the actual contour of your back. As a general rule, if the measurement is less than 18 inches, your size in packs will be "small"; if it's 18 to 20 inches, you want a "medium"; if you're longer of torso than that, you need a "large."

Not all packs have sizes as such. Some makers achieve good fit by offering a range of interchangeable belts and harnesses for the same pack-bag. And some packs, highly adjustable, are supposed to be "one-size-fits-all." (Be skeptical if you are very short or tall.) On adjustable packs, the anchor point or points behind your back, where the shoulder straps attach, can be shifted up or down. The hipbelt may slide up or down as well. But there are limits to adjustability, and a very adaptable pack adjusted to your body will feel a little sloppier than a pack that adjusts in a narrower range—if the latter is sized correctly for you.

In the store, a salesperson can help you locate the right size and harness, show you how to shift movable harness anchor points, and make obvious adjustments to the hipbelt and shoulder straps. In preparation for the next step, load the pack with 20 or 30 pounds. Most stores offer you sandbags or climbing ropes for weights; bringing gear of your own in stuffsacks will make a more realistic test—and also give you a practical idea of pack capacity.

Get the pack on your back, close the hipbelt, and tighten it firmly. It should lie just below the upper edge of the hipbone, not so high that the belt is really around your waist, but not so low that it slips off below the widest part of the bone. The lumbar pad or backband should fit snugly just beneath the small of your back, where your body starts to swell toward the rump. As you tighten the hipbelt, the whole pack should shift upward on your back. If this doesn't happen, the pack is probably too short for you.

Now for the shoulder straps. Tighten them to feel the load come onto the shoulders, then ease off to feel it settle back onto the hips. Adjust lift straps so that they rise at about a 45-degree angle on their way back to their attachment points on the packbag. On the rare frame pack that lacks lift straps, the main shoulder straps should run straight back from shoulder to attachment point, or even slightly upward. In front, the padded portion of the shoulder strap should end 1 or 2 inches below your armpit.

If there is a sternum strap across your chest, it should be a couple of inches below your collarbone; on most packs, it can be adjusted up or down.

Continue tinkering until you have reached the point of maximum comfort: a state in which the weight is plainly on your hips, but the upper part of the pack seems pleasantly firm.

Now, take an indoor hike with your load. Climb stairs, bend, sit down, stride. Make sure that the hipbelt is comfortable and that it shows no sign of slipping down, or up, from its proper position. (Exception: with some frame packs, the belt always shifts when you sit down.) Satisfy yourself that the hard parts of a frame don't touch your back at any point. Check that the buckles on straps and belts do not slip (on some cheap models they may). If anything seems inclined to loosen in the store, it will be far worse on the trail.

Also try tilting your head back, as though you were tracking a bird or reaching for a hold. Does the back of your head bump the frame or top pocket? Better look for another model.

The more adjustments your model allows, the longer you need to spend working out the arrangement most comfortable for you. When in doubt between sizes, go to the larger one. As with boots, keep going until you are very satisfied.

Internal-frame packs, with their flexible, close-fitting supports, allow and occasionally require a special type of adjustment: actually bending metal stays to match your back's own shape. A knowledgeable salesperson will be willing to spend some time helping you tweak the supports just right. If price is no object, a few companies even custom-build internal-frame packs to your measurements.

Women should try on at least one pack designed specifically for female proportions. Packs used to be regarded as unisex, but, as with other kinds of gear, they were really designed for the male body; sometimes they suited women just fine, sometimes they didn't. One common problem: shoulder straps too wide. But now there are many packs engineered specifically for shorter and narrower torsos, slimmer shoulders, narrower waists, and wider hips. Check that shoulder straps stay put on your shoulders, and that overwide pads do not pinch at your armpits or encroach on your breasts.

The question of fit is only part of the larger question of comfort. Makers are constantly trying new variations in hipbelts, shoulder straps, and lumbar pads. The design that works for somebody else, even somebody else with similar proportions, won't necessarily work for you. For example, some people like straps and pads quite soft, whereas others prefer a harder feel. (On a few internal-frame models, lumbar pads or hipbelts contain air bladders and can be pumped to different degrees of firmness.) Don't let yourself be talked into somebody else's idea of comfort.

Although packs don't need "breaking in" in the sense some boots do, a basically acceptable pack will probably grow a little more comfortable with time. Some hipbelts, for instance, use a foam that adapts to your hips —but not right away. Your hips will get a little tougher, too; if you don't have much natural padding, you may want to apply tape or moleskin there at first. And you'll learn by experience how to adjust all those straps.

CARE OF THE PACK

The best packs are pretty reliable objects, designed and built to endure years of hard use. Some are more fragile, though; accidents do happen; and even good gear gets old.

Besides the usual sewkit and duct tape, your repair kit should include a few items for the pack: a clevis pin, if it's a frame pack; a spare slider or two for the most important zippers; maybe a spare buckle (see below). On a long trip, you may want to supplement your ordinary sewing things with an awl and a few squares of packcloth.

When packing, avoid overstuffing, which stresses both seams and zippers. On the trail, avoid fuel spills on pack fabric and clean them up promptly if they happen; insect repellents containing DEET (see Chapter 10) also attack nylon. Keep your pack free of food crumbs and don't leave food in it at night. On a long trip, it's a good idea now and then to rinse the part of the pack that adjoins your back, and also the shoulder pads, to wash away the salty residue that can attract gnawing animals. For more about defending your food, your gear, and yourself from scavenging wildlife, see Chapters 18 and 29.

If your pack fabric gets holed in the woods, you can patch it initially with duct tape or sticky repair tape. But the likeliest thing to fail is one of the large molded-nylon buckles, especially the big one that closes the hipbelt in front. The hollow "female" side is especially prone to crack if walked on. It helps to leave buckles joined when the pack is off. Some people carry a spare buckle set; there are many incompatible makes, so you need both halves. You can usually do a temporary repair by wrapping the split area with duct tape.

The second familiar trouble area is zippers. Keep them free of grit and don't force them if they catch fabric; rather, back off gently. If fraying threads are caught, tug these out with pliers. If a zipper slider moves freely but doesn't close the tracks behind it, it is probably worn. It's a little tricky but quite possible to replace it in the field; if your pack is so designed that a major zipper failure would spill your stuff all over the landscape, carry a spare slider and learn how to install it. In a pinch, safety pins can make a temporary closure.

Frame packs have some specific weak points. The lock-ring that holds a clevis pin in place can get broken or lost; replace it with a spare or with a piece of wire. If a lock-ring goes missing, its clevis pin may follow it; replace this, also, with a spare. Grommets can sometimes pull out of straps, leaving a ragged hole; you can make a neat substitute hole with a hot stick or a heated awl. A bent or broken frame can be splinted with a stick and cord, or more elegantly with a section of split tubing and hose clamps from a well-stocked repair kit (see Chapter 10).

After the trip, give your pack a good shake and a good wipe and check it over before stashing it till next time. Stains in general don't matter, but foodstains should be scrubbed away, and any sticky spots, as from pitch, need to be removed. Any grit in seams or zippers should be chased out by brushing or with the pressure nozzle of a garden hose. Check for any fraying fabric along seams and especially near zippers; trim loose threads, and neaten the edge by melting with something like a lighter flame. If the stitches that actually hold a seam together seem to be getting abraded, you can protect them with a bead of urethane; any cut threads need to be oversewn with an awl. Tiny punctures can be sealed with dots of polyurethane; slightly larger ones can be patched, if you're handy with thread and awl; gaps larger than 3 or 4 inches need professional care. In frame packs, check if any grommets are tearing out of the straps they are set in. Replacement straps and backbands are available. If any field repairs need to be replaced with permanent ones, do this, or have it done, now. When the pack is thoroughly dry, store it in a cool, dry place. Humidity breeds mildew.

DAYPACKS, RUCKSACKS, AND TRAVEL PACKS

Even before you buy a full-sized pack, you will need a *daypack*—a small, uncomplicated bag just big enough to carry a lunch, a camera, a canteen, and the essential safety items you should never leave behind (see list,

Chapter 15). You'll use such a pack, of course, for trips near home, but also on long wilderness trips if you want to be able to shuck your main pack and take off on a side excursion. Some large packs are designed to shrink to this purpose, but you still have the problem of stowing all gear that isn't coming along for the afternoon.

The traditional daypack is simple. A tough fabric bag and a couple of wide shoulder straps, and you've about got it. Slightly more luxurious models will have padded shoulder straps, padding against the back, leather-reinforced bottoms, and stabilizer straps across the belly. Though desirable in themselves, these features make the auxiliary pack a heavier, bulkier item. Whatever you buy, look carefully at the points where the straps attach to the basic bag: reject any pack that lacks good sewing and some kind of reinforcement here.

The packbag is usually nylon, coated inside with urethane. Typical dimensions might be 12 inches wide and 6 inches front-to-back, with a depth of 1 foot or more. Since a loosely loaded bag fits more comfortably to the back than one stuffed to the limit, be generous. Some bags open and close with zippers, variously placed; others use drawcords. Some have outside pockets; some don't. Basic shoulder-hung daypacks will cost $20 to $60, weigh a pound or a little over, and handle loads of 15 pounds or so. A daypack can also serve as a backpack for a child. (For more on packs for kids and baby carriers, see Chapter 24.)

Larger and more elaborate daypacks are known as *rucksacks* or *summit packs*. Still lacking hipbelts, these have well-padded shoulder belts, padding against the back, and sometimes rigid framesheets like those in internal-frame packs. They may have compressor straps to snug up an undersized load. Such features make it possible to use a rucksack for an overnight trip with minimal gear. They also make the unit too heavy and bulky to bring along as a mere accessory, as a true daypack can be. Such packs cost $85 to $150.

Not all daypacks hang from the shoulders. There's also the *fanny pack*, essentially a big belt with a pouch in the back. When a pocket of a large pack detaches for daypack use, it usually takes the fanny pack form. Capacity is markedly less than in a standard daypack. Skiers like these rigs on short trips because they don't bounce so much. Another variant, the *lumbar pack*, rides a little higher. Some packs are amphibian: they start as fanny packs but unfold into full-size daypacks with shoulder straps, if you need the room. Prices $15 to $50.

Yet another corner of the backpack warehouse contains "travel packs." These are compromises between packs and suitcases. Some are really just luggage with hipbelt and shoulder straps; at the other extreme are a few quite credible packs modified for urban travel convenience. All variations provide a way of stowing the harness out of harm's way, usually behind a zippered panel, while airport personnel are doing their worst. Features vary widely, and so do prices, from $50 to $300.

A better option for travel is to place your no-nonsense wilderness pack in a duffel bag. Duffels come in all sizes. Some have rugged linings and generous padding and can be used to carry vulnerable external-frame packs or sharp-edged climbing gear. Prices run from under $30 to $180. For more about taking gear on aircraft, see Chapter 13.

ACCESSORIES, BAGS, AND CARRIERS

If your basic pack is on the small side, you may find yourself cramped for space when you take a trip of unusual length or difficulty. Several things can be done to make a minimal pack carry a big load.

Most packs come equipped with *tie-on patches,* squares or strips of tough plastic with slits. Running thin nylon webbing through the slits, you can fasten various objects securely outside. If your pack doesn't have patches where you need them, you can buy them cheaply and sew them on (with an awl); but a cobbler does a neater job for a small price. Whenever objects have to be tied on, elastic *shock cords* are invaluable to keep things stable. Extra *pack pockets* may also be purchased for some models and either strapped or sewn on.

To a frame pack you can add a *frame extension:* a U of metal tubing that rounds off the top of the original H to give you more stowing room. You can tie objects to the tubing, or store them under the storm flap, supported by the extension.

Although most packs are made of urethane-coated, water-resistant fabric, this built-in protection isn't enough for hiking in the rain. For short summer storms, a multipurpose *poncho* may serve ($25 or so). For extended rain or snow, you just about have to have a waterproof *packcover* ($20), a coated-nylon shell that snaps on over the pack. Once on, it's a nuisance because it blocks access to the outer pockets, but items inside stay dry.

For storage inside the main pack, the common containers are nylon stuffbags, usually urethane coated, that close with drawstrings and cordlocks. Netting stuffsacks, which allow you to see at a glance what's in them, are fun (and can double as food coolers in a stream or lake). Zippered pouches may also come in handy. Depending on size and features, cloth container prices run anywhere from $3 to $24. Zipper-locking plastic bags in various sizes are indispensable. So are large plastic garbage bags —always carry a couple. Except possibly for a few food items, rigid boxes are not used.

A useful accessory is the *beltbag*—a zippered rectangular cloth pouch that rides on the pack's belt or your own. You can use it for ski paraphernalia; for film and small camera accessories; for pencil and paper; for lunch; for anything you need close at hand and don't want to shift from pocket to pocket every time you add or subtract a layer of clothing. A belt-hung *map case* can be handy, too. Then there's the *bottle carrier,* which can turn any water bottle into an accessible canteen attached to pack or belt ($12 or so). You can even get a waterbag that sits high in your pack and sprouts a feeder tube for easy sucking ($15–25).

If you use a camera and don't want to shed your main pack to reach it, you can try to carry it on your chest. Strap arrangements are available, but I have yet to encounter one that keeps a full-sized camera from bouncing around unpleasantly. A padded camera pack, like a small daypack built backwards, seems a better choice (around $50). Any way you cut it, you will feel awfully festooned with straps when you wear a big pack and a camera rig at the same time.

PACKS AND LOW IMPACT

When you buy your pack, you encounter the troublesome question of *color*. Wilderness gear is sold today in every shade, aggressive or subdued: various blues; reds and yellows and explosive iridescent oranges; leaf greens and olive greens, rust browns and earth browns, and compound colors in between. Color is part of the pleasure of handling good gear, and one of the things that gives a stack of fine equipment that curiously valuable look.

But there's more than personal taste to consider when you choose a color. There's a question of impact as well. Simply put, do you want to stand out or blend in? Unless you're hiking in the eastern woodlands in October, a bright pack makes you highly visible. Indeed, it makes you *too* visible: the more fellow hikers you see and are seen by, the more crowded the wilderness landscape must appear. This is a problem everywhere but doubly so above timberline. A dozen hikers in an alpine basin, carrying gear in muted colors, may give you no hint of their presence—three with packs in blaze or "international" orange can make the same place seem busy. For low impact, then, you choose the soft shades.

There is a counterargument, however, and that is safety. Maybe you do a lot of traveling in popular hunting areas at just the wrong time of year and *want* to be seen. Or maybe you're thinking about a time when you could conceivably need to be rescued. Standing out as it does, bright gear can draw searchers to a lost or injured hiker.

Every backpacker must weigh the arguments of safety against the pleasures of unobtrusiveness. If you're very concerned about the rescue angle, I would suggest this compromise: carry something brightly colored in your pack—raingear, perhaps, or a groundcloth. This you can spread on the ground, or drape on your pack, or wear on your back, if you badly need to be seen. But a pack made of a vivid fabric is like a light you can never turn off.

7 THE BEDROLL

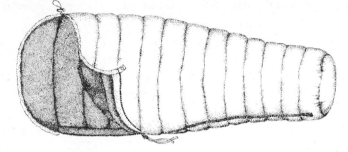

MUMMY-STYLE SLEEPING BAG

Being out in the wilderness is one thing. *Sleeping* out in the wilderness, and on the ground, and with the lightest equipment, is quite another. For people unaccustomed to it, it can take some getting used to. For anybody, it takes some pretty good gear: groundcloth, pad, and above all, sleeping bag.

How do you set about choosing the right bag? As with every major item of gear, there are certain distinct questions to ask yourself. In buying a sleeping bag, you need to know *how warm* a bag you need; *what kind of insulating material* you want in it; and *what shape and design* are best suited to your use. Then there are certain features you should look for in any bag.

HOW MUCH BAG DO YOU NEED?

First things first. How cold will it get where you plan to go? People tend to buy heavier and costlier sleeping bags than they actually need. The bag you choose should be about right for the temperatures you expect to encounter frequently during the next few years. Don't think in terms of an eventual dream trip to the high Arctic. Don't even buy for the coldest possible night in the place and season you will visit; rather, think of a night somewhat below the average. You can make a light bag do very nicely for the occasional chillier time, and you won't be carrying needless weight when it's warm.

On summer trips in temperate North America, you are unlikely to see many nights below freezing, even in the high country, and in some regions, summer nights are in the fifties and above. Even three-season backpacking—spring, summer, and fall—is unlikely to take you below the twenties Fahrenheit. If you have an idea where you will go most often—New England mountains, say, or the Sierra Nevada—you might check trail guidebooks or talk to experienced hikers about the conditions they have found. On-line newsgroups are good sources of information.

How warm-blooded are you? People vary a good deal. Some are obvious cold-sleepers—they shiver in sleeping bags that look like they belong on the Greenland ice. Others find it unusually easy to keep warm. It depends pretty much on your metabolic rate. Women on average seem to sleep a little colder than men.

GRADES OF BAGS

Sleeping bags of a sort can be gotten very cheap. Department stores everywhere sell rectangular bags that look like thick zippered blankets. They have quilted seams and use the cheapest synthetics for fill. At $30 to $60, these bags are cheap, but they are either too cool for most wilderness camping, or too heavy and bulky to tote, or both.

Look instead to the well-made *summer sleeping bags* sold in many gear shops. These may be made of polyester fleece; if they use a puffy insulation, it will probably be packaged in the simplest way, with sewn-through seams. In some models, one surface is quilted, the other just a sheet; depending on which side you put upwards, you have two variants in warmth. Target temperatures vary—some summer bags get chilly below 55 degrees Fahrenheit, others are rated down to 40 degrees or so; but the latter have the same construction as the more serious sleeping bags discussed below. Cost varies widely, but you won't find many products under $100—pretty expensive for a sort of glorified blanket.

Most hikers will be out in more than a few nippy nights. For this majority, the medium-weight *three-season bag*, good to about 20 degrees Fahrenheit, is the standard. Such bags have no sewn-through seams; there is insulation all around you. No three-season bag needs more than 2 pounds of fill if the filler is waterfowl down, nor much over 3 pounds if good synthetic filler is used. A three-season down bag should weigh no more than about 3½ pounds total, a synthetic-filled model 5 pounds at the very most. Prices range from under $100 to over $400, depending largely on the fill material used. The archetypal three-season bag is a mummy bag filled with down (see below), weighing about 2½ pounds, and costing about $200. As the amount of fill increases, three-season bags grade into *winter* sleeping bags, marvelous constructions intended only for conditions down toward zero degrees Fahrenheit and below.

JUDGING THE WARMTH OF A SLEEPING BAG

How do you tell how warm a given bag will keep you? The answer is not so simple as you might expect. How warm you are on a particular night depends on half a dozen things besides your sleeping bag itself: the padding under you, wind, humidity, protection from the open sky, how much you ate for dinner, and of course your own warm-bloodedness. Even if we forget all these variations and speak of an "average" sleeper in "ideal" conditions, it can be hard to judge the insulating power of a bag.

You have three things to go by: manufacturer's temperature ratings, weight and kind of fill, and visible loft.

Manufacturers make predictions for their bags: this one is supposed to be comfortable to freezing, that one perhaps to 10 degrees above zero. Unfortunately, these ratings are variable and subjective. Better makers are cautious, afraid to claim too much, but some assertions are still out of line. No guarantee is ever implied. Manufacturers' assessments are best used to compare bags within one brand: a maker's bag rated to 20 degrees may or may not deliver, but it will certainly be warmer than the same maker's 30-degree bag.

The second consideration is fill. Every sleeping bag has a fabric label attached that states the type and weight of the insulating material used. Now if the same material is used in bags of the same design, more fill means a warmer bag. But seldom is the comparison so straightforward. More often you are looking at bags of different shapes filled with different substances, or with waterfowl down of different grades (some insulate twice as well as others). So weight is not the key.

The third factor is one you can check for yourself: *loft.* Loft is the height to which a sleeping bag puffs up when it is nicely shaken out. It used to be said that loft was the sole determinant of warmth, but the cleverness of the designers has overtaken that statement. Certain insulations have credible claims to be warmer, inch for inch, than their competitors;

shell materials and other components can change the picture, too. All you can really say is that, of two bags with the same fill material and the same shell fabric, the loftier bag is going to be the warmer. Some manufacturers provide loft figures for their bags, but you can make your own estimate with a couple of rulers. Lay one ruler on top of the bag, to compress it just slightly and give you a reference point; use the second ruler to measure the distance from the floor to the first ruler. Again, the best use is comparative: other things being equal, each added inch of loft adds about ten degrees of warmth.

With the demise of loft as a reliable sole criterion, we badly need a new method of comparing bag warmth. The tools, in fact, exist. Using a metal mannequin, researchers can measure exactly how well a sleeping bag retains heat. Manufacturers, though, have been unable to agree on the details of converting such test results to standardized ratings. The goal keeps receding; bag buyers hope on.

In the end, of course, your comfort is the only accurate measure. Once more, it may be a good investment to rent several bags (though these are harder to locate than other rentals). Each time you try a bag, make a note of its materials, its loft, and of the temperatures you encounter. When you find out how comfortable you are in a particular bag on a particular night, you will have more than theory to go on. You can extrapolate, at least, to others of similar construction.

WHAT KIND OF INSULATION?

What is it that keeps you warm outdoors in a sleeping bag? Nothing but your own body heat, trapped by the material around you. Heat escapes by traveling through solids (conduction), through space (radiation), and most importantly through moving air (convection). Insulation creates a layer of still air, blocks convection, and holds heat in. The thicker the barrier, the less heat will escape. Thus the importance of insulation thickness: loft.

There are now just two filling materials in wide use that are light enough and lofty enough for wilderness sleeping bags. These are *waterfowl down* and *polyester* in half a dozen cunningly crafted forms.

Top-quality goose down is the gold standard of sleeping bag insulation. Nothing else gives so much warmth for so little weight. Nothing else compresses into such a tiny volume in your pack. Nothing else lasts so long. Nothing else costs so much. The nearest competitor, not often seen currently, is down from ducks.

What counts is the down's springiness or ability to loft. "Lofting power" can be measured precisely in cubic inches filled by a single ounce of puffed-up material. Grades vary; 750 cubic inches per ounce is about tops.

All synthetic insulations are attempts to imitate and ultimately to catch up with down. Progress is being made, but even the newest synthetics insulate less well than any decent down. The synthetic bags are not only heavier but also clumsier—they won't compress as well. And they are less durable.

They have, however, two powerful selling points. First, they are very much cheaper. Second, synthetic bags are safer when it's wet and cold. It would be difficult to overstate how important this can be.

Down, like cotton, turns on you when it gets wet, losing nearly all its loft. A waterlogged down bag is not just a nuisance, it's a horror. Anyone who has ever spent a night in a wet snowstorm, two days' walk from a roadhead, with a couple of hundred dollars worth of wringing-wet goose down, can make the case for a synthetic bag. A synthetic bag loses only part of its loft when wet. You won't be exactly happy in a wet synthetic bag, but you'll make it through the night. You can squeeze the bag out like a sponge and dry it completely, once good weather returns, in a few hours.

As noted, all synthetic fills are forms of polyester. Most are made in short fibers, in emulation of down; current competitors are LiteLoft by 3M; Thermolite Extreme and Micro-Loft by DuPont (the latter with ultrafine fibers); and two versions of Primaloft by Albany International. Several claim to have rendered obsolete the old rule of thumb that warmth depends simply on loft. Two fills that were standard a few years ago, Hollofil and Quallofil by DuPont, are now the economy products. The short-fiber fills are fairly light and compressible but tend to break down quickly, losing their loft after several years of use. There seems as yet to be no compelling case for preferring one to another.

Polarguard 3D by Hoechst-Celanese, the latest version of one of the oldest good synthetic fills, is different: it is a continuous hollow filament spun like cotton candy. This quite new material seems at present to be down's closest competitor (and is priced to match). Its predecessors, Polarguard HV and plain Polarguard, are cheaper, but, by bulk and weight, a little less efficient. The older Polarguards retain their lofting power a good deal longer than short-fiber synthetic fills; Polarguard 3D may do the same.

Some bag makers have developed their own in-house insulations, which may be either short-filament type or long.

Different fills are arranged in different ways.

In a down bag, the fill is loose. There are internal netting walls, called baffles, to keep the down from shifting and opening up cold spots. These walls run horizontally around the bag inside, leaving the outside seams that give all down bags the familiar caterpillar look. In square-box baffling, now seldom used, the internal walls make right angles with the shell. More often the walls are slanted; this slant-box baffling allows fewer cold spots. A third design adds more walls and makes small triangular compartments. This overlapping V-tube construction, heavy, expensive, and warm, is found only in expeditionary sleeping bags. Synthetic fills come in blocks, called *battings;* these are usually arranged to overlap like shingles, slanting from outer to inner shell like the slant-box down compartments, and leaving the same outside seams.

WHAT KIND OF SHELL?

Sleeping bag shells are made of nylon or polyester. Ripstop nylon is the old standard. Nylon taffeta is the same fiber woven to be softer and more flexible, but not quite as resistant to tearing. Polyester also comes in ripstop and taffeta weaves; it deteriorates more slowly in sunlight than does nylon, which can prolong bag life if you virtually live outdoors; it also

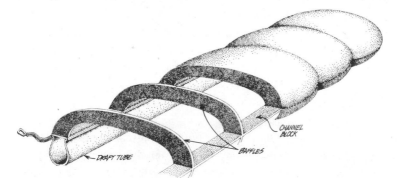

A DOWN BAG IN CUTAWAY VIEW

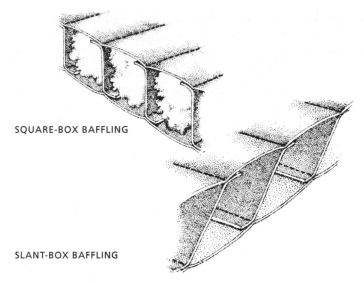

SQUARE-BOX BAFFLING

SLANT-BOX BAFFLING

tends to shed water. "Microfiber" shells are extremely tightly woven, which helps water repellency and wind resistance. Shells that include cotton threads, even combined with synthetic materials, should be avoided.

Then there are shells built of water-resistant "breathable" fabrics. The makers of Gore-Tex have developed a material called DryLoft specifically for sleeping bag use; some makers use their own proprietary fabrics. Such shells make excellent sense when the stuff inside them is vulnerable down; they are also used widely with synthetic insulations, to which they add some warmth. Some users complain that high-tech shells ice up and grow ineffective in cold conditions.

A third possibility is to sheathe a bag, inside and out, in simply waterproof fabric. See The Vapor Barrier Idea, below.

Whatever the fabric, a dark-colored shell is best, because it helps a damp bag dry faster in the sun.

DESIGN AND CONSTRUCTION

When you know how much warmth you want, and what kind of filler and shell you prefer, you are halfway along toward buying the right bag. What's left to consider is shape, design, size, and the finer points that show that the maker has done a good job.

Shape. The standard is the mummy bag, a close-cut design that starts wide at the shoulders but narrows with the body to the toes. The snuggest mummies are more like sleeping garments than portable beds: when you roll, they roll with you. Mummies give the greatest warmth for the least fill. At the head there is typically a hood that can be closed around the face to leave only the tiniest of openings.

Some people find mummies unpleasantly confining. Other designs give you more room: modified mummies with and without hoods; barrel-shaped bags; semirectangular and fully rectangular models. In general, it's good to choose the narrowest bag you can tolerate. The wider the bag, the more massive it must be to provide the same uniform loft, and the more air your body has to keep warm in order to maintain its local comfort zone.

Length and proportions. Most models come in three sizes: short, regular, and long, for people over six feet. When you lie in the bag with the hood (if there is one) tightened over your face, you should be able to stretch your neck and point your toes without compressing the insulation at head or foot.

There are now some sleeping bags designed specifically for women. These are built a bit narrower at the shoulders and a bit wider at the hips. They also have a little extra insulation, especially for the torso and at the feet.

Channel block. In most down bags an internal partition runs the length of the bag, on the side opposite the zipper, to prevent the fill from shifting between the topside and the underside. Some makers leave out the barrier, arguing that you can shift the down yourself to make the bag warmer or cooler. I prefer the stability of the channel block.

The foot end. A good bag won't simply pinch out at the foot. Instead, it has an elaborately constructed bulge, a sort of a box, with room for your toes and a good thickness of insulation beyond.

Zipper. Most bags have them, typically down the sleeper's right side to about the ankle. Some near-rectangular bags zip all the way to the foot and along the bottom. A few lightweight bags have just a short zipper down the middle of the top. The zipper should work in both directions, so that you can open the lower end while leaving the upper end closed. Massive nylon sliders are standard and pretty reliable. In better bags, each track of the zipper is set in a strip of stiffer fabric, to discourage snagging.

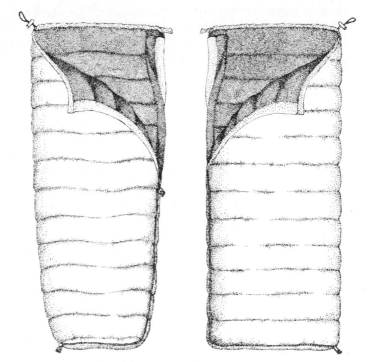

SEMIRECTANGULAR AND RECTANGULAR SLEEPING BAGS (MUMMY STYLE IS
SHOWN AT THE BEGINNING OF THE CHAPTER)

Another nice feature is a snap or hook-and-loop fastener at the zipper's
top, to discourage its working its way open. Bags of the same or compatible models can be zipped together to form a single, larger bed (but one
of them must have its zipper on the *left*).

Draft tube. The zipper must have an extra flap of insulation along its
inner side, or heat will escape. In a three-season or winter bag, be sure
that this draft tube is not attached with a sewn-through seam; it must
provide an unbroken thickness of insulation. The draft tube should be attached to the topside of the bag, so that gravity will tend to keep it hanging in place. It should also be longer than the zipper so that no cold gap
is left at the lower end.

Draft collars. Bags intended for very cold conditions will also have an
insulated collar or sill that clings to the body at neck or chest level to pre-

vent warm air from escaping. This may be a simple ruff, or may be elasticized or adjustable.

Pockets. Some sleeping bags have pockets built into their shells: a little one for stashing the stuff you may need at night; a larger one for a pillow; even a full-length pocket underneath into which you can slide a sleeping pad.

BUYING A SLEEPING BAG

In the store, spend some time with the available sleeping bags that fit your general specifications. Lay them out and crawl in. Thrash around a bit. Does the bag seem long enough when you are stretched out inside with the hood closed up around your face? Is it roomy enough for your personal taste? If you plan cold-weather camping, is there room at the foot to tuck in a water bottle or anything else you want to keep warm? When in doubt, favor the longer size.

Consider the hood. Different makers tailor these differently. Do you like the way your model drapes around your face when you snug it up? Does the hood opening stay put in front of your face when you change position—for instance, to lie on your side?

Consider the shells. The fabric next to your skin should be pleasant to the touch, not chilly and slick. If the fill is of down, shells must be woven very densely, or down particles will work their way out between the threads. (If you can blow through a fold of shell fabric, feeling your breath on the other side, the cloth is too coarse.) A few plumules always escape from a new down bag, especially at the seams—no cause for alarm unless the leakage continues.

Work the zipper up and down to see that it doesn't tend to snag, and that its draft tube is generous.

Even in a costly bag, check detailing. How good is the stitching? Examine a lot of it, especially where stress comes on the seams: along the zipper and around the hood where the drawstring runs in its sleeve. Double stitching, and of course strong bar-tacking, are important at these places. Turn the bag inside out and examine the foot end, the hardest part of the bag to sew. You can't get at everything, but a bag well made where you can see it is probably sound clear through.

Finally, stuff the bag into the stuffsack it comes with. Don't roll it but mash it in, handful by handful, starting with the foot end. Consider how much room the resulting package will take in your pack. If you will be wearing a traditional three-quarter-length external-frame pack, which carries the sleeping bag outside and below, the bulk of the bag hardly matters. If you're working with an internal-frame pack of modest capacity, it matters a great deal. If the bag is bulky, you may want to buy a *compression stuffsack* with straps that squeeze it down farther. If by any chance the original stuffsack isn't waterproof, get one that is.

ADDING LAYERS

Lately, the concept of the "sleeping system" has attained a certain vogue. Essentially, the idea is to supplement the insulating power of the basic bag with an assortment of shells and layers that act, in one way or another, to increase warmth and protection. The result is a layer system like the one applied to clothing. There is an element of hype in all this (when a heretofore simple piece of gear is redefined as a "system," watch out: the price has just gone up). Nonetheless, there is value in the concept.

Here are some of the possible added layers:

Bivouac sacks. Some bags, as noted above, have waterproof breathable outer shells. You can also carry a separate bivouac sack of the same high-tech fabric, perhaps in place of a tent. These "bivy sacks" cost $125 and up and weigh something over a pound. In very cold conditions, however, these separate shells have some tendency to ice up, losing the breathability that makes them different from ordinary urethane-coated cloth; they are more likely to suffer this effect than are microporous fabrics built into the sleeping bags themselves.

Overbags and liner bags. You can beef up your basic bag for a colder trip by adding to it a second light sleeping bag, inserted inside or wrapped without. You'll gain ten or twenty degrees of warmth. Some makers offer two compatible bags as a tailored package: depending on the temperatures to be faced, you can use either section or both.

Bag liners. Cleanliness, not warmth, is the reason for using a simple inner sheath of cotton, flannel, or silk. The readily washable liner intercepts the grime that otherwise winds up on your not-so-readily washable sleeping bag (see Storage, Cleaning, and Care, below). This addition strikes most people as inordinate fussiness, but a liner can add years to the life of a down bag that is frequently used. Liners weigh as little as 4 ounces and cost $25 to $75.

Radiant heat barriers. Ordinary sleeping bag insulation is not very good at blocking heat loss due to radiation: the infrared waves that pour from your body pass right through. A radiant barrier is a piece of reflective fabric designed to turn back these rays. Backpackers first came to know of this tool in the form of the "space blanket," a rectangle of fragile reflective cloth for use as cloak, shelter, or groundsheet. A few manufacturers now build radiant barriers into sleeping bags. Tailored reflective liners are also available, and can add ten or fifteen degrees of warmth to an existing bag. Some, but not all, reflective barriers are vapor barriers as well.

THE VAPOR BARRIER IDEA

Of all the types of layers that can be added to a bag, the most controversial is the vapor barrier liner, or VBL. A vapor barrier is, simply, a waterproof layer, deep inside the bag, which prevents body moisture from migrating outwards through the insulation and evaporating into the night air. Since this evaporation takes away a good deal of heat, you will sleep warmer if the process is blocked.

Fair enough, but won't you also get uncomfortably wet? No, say the advocates. If the vapor barrier liner is next to the skin, the thin layer of air between skin and VBL will quickly become humid. The body will respond by shutting its sweat glands down. You won't get wet, the argument goes: you'll just get nice and warm.

Only one maker, Jack Stephenson's Warmlite Equipment, builds bags with impermeable shells inside. Since there is no need for moisture to percolate out from within, these bags can also have waterproof outer shells. They are packaged in elaborate multipart systems that include, among other features, air mattresses filled with down.

Short of buying one of these radical and costly bags, you can make your own experiment with a vapor barrier liner. A big plastic bag or even a groundcloth will do. The impermeable layer, however, must be close to your skin, just outside your long johns. Never put a waterproof *outside* your sleeping bag, or you will wake up in a swamp.

But is a vapor barrier, in normal conditions, either practical or necessary? For most people, the answer appears to be no. At temperatures above about zero Fahrenheit, many users report that they feel clammy in their waterproof sheaths—whether the theory calls for it or not. Results depend, apparently, on how much you naturally sweat. Vapor barriers begin to make sense at deeply subzero temperatures, or when you are testing the limits of a bag too light for the weather you are camping in. Otherwise, they seem at best an unnecessary refinement.

BETWEEN YOU AND THE GROUND

Ground is hard. Ground is cold. Ground is often moist. To deal with these things, you need some defenses beneath you.

Undermost goes a groundcloth—just a rectangle of coated nylon or vinyl, available for a few dollars in any store that handles sporting goods. The more expensive ones last longer. Reflective "space blankets" are popular but awfully fragile. When you use a tent, you will want the same sort of sheet next to the ground under that, to protect the waterproof floor.

On top of the groundcloth you need a mattress or pad. This cushions, which is important; it insulates, which is vital. If your bag is down filled, the part beneath you will collapse almost to nothing under your weight. Bags with synthetic fills do not compress so totally, but a pad underneath is still part of what keeps you warm.

The ideal wilderness mattress would be simultaneously comfortable, durable, and compact. It doesn't exist. In the real world, you have to choose two virtues out of three.

Compact and durable (but not especially comfortable) are pads of closed-cell foam (Evazote and Ensolite are brands). These are rugged, impervious to water, and unaffected by all but the coldest temperatures. The sheets, sold in most sporting goods stores, are 18 to 22 inches wide and come in varied lengths. Many summer backpackers choose a length of less than 4 feet or cut a longer rectangle down. Thickness varies from ¼ inch to ¾ inch; the thinner style will do (for warmth at least) in summer, but snow campers buy the longest and thickest sheets they can find, and often carry two. Although the classic pad is smooth and rather slippery, some have cloth covers or textured surfaces, which make it easier to stay in touch with your insulation during the night.

Compact and comfortable (but not especially durable) is the foam-filled, self-inflating air mattress. In this arrangement, originally developed by Cascade Designs, an airtight shell encloses a piece of open-cell foam: when the valve is opened, the foam expands and sucks air in by itself. When the air is pressed out, the mattress reduces to a small package. It's tidy, elegant, and sort of magical. These are the most popular pads today.

Self-inflaters do have some drawbacks. Like any air mattress, they are vulnerable to puncture. And, although they were first adopted by winter campers, they in fact present some problems for cold-weather use. The foam within them loses resilience below the freezing point; you will be tempted to put mouth to valve and blow them up a little tighter than they naturally go. But this introduces moisture into the foam, which then can freeze, causing the foam and even the shell to crack.

Comfortable and durable (but not very compact) are pads made of open-cell foam, without airtight covers. One maker, Wiggy's, uses instead the polyester insulation found in futons, which is a little less bulky. Other makers are combining closed-cell and open-cell foam in laminates, with the cushier material on top. Especially if you wear a frame pack, with plenty of strap-on room outside, these options may be worth considering.

Me? Unless I'm camping on snow, I like plain old closed-cell foam.

The prices of pads vary widely, according to length, thickness, and construction. The cheapest good pad is still a closed-cell slab, ⅜ inch thick; even full-length ones can be gotten for less than $10. The most expensive might be a self-inflating mattress, full length and 2½ inches thick: over $100. Weights vary from ½ pound for a short, closed-cell pad to over 3 pounds for a maximum self-inflatable.

With the addition of a few straps, a self-inflatable pad can be made to serve as a camp chair, luxurious sometimes for the older back. Made-to-order rigs of this sort cost $40 to $50 and weigh little more than sleeping pads alone. Another useful accessory is the yokelike arrangement that joins pads side by side into a sort of double bed.

The ultimate air mattress is a *hammock*. Since most hammocks for wilderness use are set up as tents, with rainflies and netting, these are discussed in the next chapter.

What about a *pillow?* Most people use clothing, stuffed perhaps into a cloth bag. Air mattresses may have built-in pillow segments. Separate inflatable pillows can also be had.

STORAGE, CLEANING, AND CARE

A down bag should last ten or twelve years, a synthetic bag perhaps a third that long. But all sleeping bags have enemies: rough handling, compression, moisture, heat and sunlight, certain chemicals, and body oils.

The baffles of down bags and the battings of synthetic bags are fragile structures. Avoid twisting them or yanking on them. You have to be much gentler in pulling a bag out of its stuffsack than in pushing it in.

No matter what kind of fill your bag contains, do not store it compressed between trips. Stuffed for weeks or months, down loses part of its springiness and thus its all-important loft. Synthetic fill collapses even more dramatically. Bags that have built-in loops for the purpose, at the foot end, may be hung. Any bag can be stored safely in a very large cotton sack. The ideal storage area is dry, cool, and dark. In the wilderness, too, it's good to leave a bag unstuffed as much as you can. (Depending on humidity: when the air is very moist, a loose bag with nobody in it will just get damp.)

Dampness is the third enemy, though not of all bags equally. Synthetics don't mind water, but down that is continually damp will disintegrate, and any bag can mildew. Make sure your stuffsack is waterproof. On the trail, if a bag is moist and bedraggled when you put it away in the morning, you can dry it out, weather permitting, at lunch. After the trip, air your bag thoroughly. A seriously wet bag should be treated as though it had been washed (see below).

Don't, however, leave a sleeping bag lying in the sun for more than the minimum time necessary—sunlight eventually damages nylon shell material. Heat attacks both shells and fills, including synthetic fills; a synthetic bag locked in a very hot car trunk can be ruined. And campfire sparks can give you a pox of melted holes in a hurry.

Certain chemicals are bad for down, or for synthetic materials, or both. Insect repellents containing DEET are death on nylon. And sleeping bags should not be dry-cleaned, period.

Which brings us to the question: how *should* they be cleaned, when the time comes?

The best way, clearly, is by hand, with the help perhaps of a big tumble dryer. Do the washing in a tub with Ivory Snow soap flakes or a similarly gentle soap (never detergent or bleach). The water should be copious and warm, not hot. Ease the bag into the soup gradually (some like to submerge it first in its cotton storage sack, sack and all). Once the bag is saturated, work the suds through it by pressing. Don't twist. Don't wring. When the suds have turned dark, drain the tub and start over. Do this as often as you need to until the suds are white. Then rinse again several times, making sure to get all the soap out of the material. Let gravity drain most of the water from the bag; press gently to extract a little more.

The drying process can be started outdoors. You can hang the bag on a clothesline, but lengthwise, so that the dividers run vertical. To finish the job, you can tumble it in a laundromat dryer—the bigger, the better—at very low heat or no heat at all. (Down is very sensitive to heat; the resins that hold polyester battings in place are even more so.) If there's lots of room, throw in a couple of dry towels to help absorb water (you might replace these once along the way). Forget the once-traditional tennis ball or shoe. Every 15 minutes, check that the fabric is not too hot, and if you feel any clumping in the fill, work it out. You can pull gently across clots of down; synthetic batts that seem to be sticking together can be teased cautiously apart.

If you can't stand this lengthy process, you can shorten the job somewhat by using a front-loading washing machine (never a machine with an agitator) set on the coolest, gentlest cycle and using the usual gentle soap. The machine must be one you can shut down, once the soap is dispersed, for a good, long soak. Wash a second time soapless to get a thorough rinse.

When you wash a bag, should you take the opportunity to wash in a specialized water repellency treatment? There are variations on durable water repellent (DWR) meant specifically for down. But Annie Getchell, gear care guru, recommends against this treatment, except for a very old bag, or one that has suffered dry cleaning. Reason: the treatment can hamper the breathability of the shell.

Plainly, washing your sleeping bag is no joke. You don't want to do it more often than you have to, and in the case of down, you shouldn't. Down loses a certain amount of insulating power every time it is laundered.

Mattresses, too, need to relax between trips. Closed-cell pads are all but indestructible but lose thickness eventually; prolong their usefulness by storing them flat or loosely rolled. Self-inflating pads must be stored flat with valves open. Self-inflaters are also puncture-prone. You fix them like raingear, with a dab of urethane sealant for a pinprick and sealant plus a coated-nylon patch from your repair bag for a slightly larger opening. Specialty mattress repair kits are also available. A major rip requires professional attention.

LOW IMPACT AND THE BEDROLL

With sleeping bags, as with packs, there is just one impact question: what color? A bright-colored sleeping bag is not so obtrusive as a gaudy pack, because it will be stowed away much of the time (and may be in a tent when exposed). Even so, do you want to stand out in the wilderness like a spot of fire wherever you throw down your bag? Or do you choose rather to blend in? In the busy wildlands of the later twentieth century, the arguments seem heavy on the side of blending in. Also, a dark-colored bag can more quickly be dried in the sun. If the sleeping bag is carried outside the pack, the stuffsack, at least, should not be brightly colored.

8 SHELTER

When you head into the wilderness—no matter how fine the weather at the roadhead—you must have some plan for *shelter*. And that means something carried in your pack. Don't count on improvising a lean-to, or making a hut of green boughs (unless in extreme emergency). These methods were elegant when the wilderness was vast and the population small. Frontiersman Jim Bridger used them, and so did early conservationist John Muir, but now it is the wilderness that is tiny, the human pressure that is great. Don't count too heavily on trailside huts or lean-tos, either; some regions have them, but they afford little privacy, and when they are empty you may find them dirty or in disrepair. In another category are full-service backcountry hostels, like those in Yosemite or the White Mountains of New Hampshire: delightful, but not part of what this book is about.

What should your shelter be? In the eastern United States, in the coastal Pacific Northwest, and in the northern U.S. Rockies, the case is good for carrying a full-scale tent at any time of year. So too for Canada and Alaska. In the southwestern third of the United States, by contrast, a regular tent is more shelter than you really require in summer, at least past the peak of mosquito season. Consider it a luxury and suit yourself.

LESS THAN A TENT

The first requirement, of course, is a roof to shed rain. It will incidentally keep dew off your sleeping bag and keep you a little warmer. It can also protect you from hot, bright sunlight, which, in treeless landscapes, can itself be a problem.

The simplest possible roof is also an item of clothing: the *poncho*, a rectangular piece of waterproof fabric with neck hole and hood. Although some ponchos are made just large enough to cover the hiker's body, others are long enough in back to drape over the pack as well; these, called backpack ponchos, can be pitched as minimal one-person shelters. A poncho intended for such use should have several metal grommets along the sides and at the corners for the attachment of cords. Cheap ponchos are made of fragile plastic and are too flimsy to make workable shelters; $25 is the minimum for an adequate coated-nylon poncho. Dimensions will be about 5 feet by 9 feet; weight is 1 pound or a little over.

A much more versatile shelter, my favorite, is the *tarp*. A tarp is simply a rectangle of water-repellent cloth. A skillful handler—it takes a little practice—can make it through a severe rain, at least below treeline, under a tarp. Good tarps are made of urethane-coated nylon, tough and grommeted. Useful sizes are 10 by 10 feet and 10 by 12 feet (really a shade less because of hemming). Weights range from 2 to 3 pounds. Prices run $40 to $60. Tarps of polyethylene cost much less but lack the durability. The fly of a standard tent (see below) can also be used alone as a tarp. Because they are open at the sides, tarp shelters avoid any serious condensation problem.

Ponchos and tarps can in theory be pitched with nothing but cord. Actually, you may be glad if you have one or two tentpoles and several stakes along; natural anchors don't necessarily come just where you'd like them. For more about pitching and living in shelters, see Chapter 19.

In pitching a tarp you may wish for a grommet where one is lacking, even in the middle of the sheet. You can improvise an attachment by bunching the fabric around a small, smooth stone and looping a noose of cord around it. There are commercial gimmicks that do the same thing with a plastic or rubber "rock" and a plastic or metal "noose."

Finally, there are a number of solo shelters, not quite tents, to be had.

A WELL-PITCHED TARP

Some are essentially bivouac sacks with mosquito netting and one or two short poles that lift the fabric off the head. Others are better thought of as miniature tents. One variant is the specialized *bug shelter*, a netting enclosure that lacks a waterproof roof and may even lack a floor. Prices for these various subtents vary from $70 to $230; most expensive are versions using waterproof breathable (microporous) fabrics.

THE STANDARD COMBINATION: TENT PLUS FLY

When is waterproof not waterproof?

How can you build a tent that lets body moisture out—as it has to, or you will get very damp—without letting the rain get in?

One method is to build the tent roof or canopy of one of the waterproof breathable fabrics, like Gore-Tex. A second solution is to use simply waterproof materials, relying on sophisticated ventilation to keep interior moisture under control. Tents of either type are light in weight, hellishly expensive, and somewhat controversial. For more about these options, see Alternative Tents, below.

Most tent makers, however, hold to a traditional, more complicated solution. Their tents come in two parts: an inner shelter built largely of permeable nylon, not waterproofed, so that moisture can escape; and an additional, fully waterproof *rainfly* that is stretched just above the vulnerable structure underneath. Somewhat confusingly, this arrangement is called the double-walled design.

TENT ANATOMY

Tents for backpacking could once be grouped by shape into three or four basic types. This is no longer the case. You can now choose among the most diverse geometries, configurations, and canopy arrangements. Some basics, however, remain.

Though tents are built in many sizes, the one you take backpacking won't be a palace. Anything offering less than 27 square feet of floor space, a space about 4 feet wide by 7 feet long, is strictly a one-person model; 32 square feet is a snug fit for two. At about 40 square feet, two-person tents grade into lodgings for three. Though shapes vary widely, the smallest tents tend, like people, to be oblong; larger ones are more likely to have square or hexagonal floors. Roofs rise 2 or 3 feet in shelters intended for one, 3 or 4 feet in most two-person models, and almost 6 feet in the largest family-sized backpacking tents.

Tents vary widely in weight and ruggedness. At the light end of the scale are what might be called *southwestern* tents, built largely of netting and designed mainly to exclude bugs, but equipped with (sometimes rather scanty) rainflies. *Three-season* models, the norm for backpacking, can fend off serious rain; they vary in their ability to handle high winds. *Winter* tents are stoutly supported, carefully tailored, and strong. A winter tent may have to resist 80-mile-an-hour gusts or bear a weight of several hundred pounds of wet, clinging snow. A subclass of winter tents holds *mountaineering* tents, small, strong, and low in profile, designed for the most heroic conditions of all.

Another option seems to be emerging: the *convertible* tent, which allows adjustment for differing conditions. For instance, poles can be added or subtracted depending on the weather expected; or netting windows can be hidden under zip-on, solid-fabric shutters.

A three-season backpacking tent for two shouldn't weigh more than about 7 pounds; you can get that down toward 4 pounds with clever design and at some cost in roominess. As space for additional people is added, weight climbs too, but more slowly; a three-person, three-season model weighing more than 9 pounds is distinctly heavy.

Prices vary even more widely: you may pay as little as $50 or as much as $200 per person sheltered. REI and Camp Trails are about the cheapest specialty makers; Bibler and Stephenson, both makers of alternative, single-wall tents, are about the most expensive.

Most backpacking tents are made of nylon, either ripstop or nylon taffeta. Some use polyester, which holds up better against the ultraviolet radiation in sunlight, or nylon-polyester blends. There may be larger or smaller areas of mesh. Tent floors are always waterproof (with the urethane-coated side up), and the waterproofing extends 4 inches or more up the sides of the walls and up the door or doors. This "tub floor" cannot be built without seams, but the fewer there are, the better.

Above the upper edge of the tub floor, the canopy is made of ordinary permeable nylon, *not* waterproofed. This allows moisture to escape from the inside. To prevent water from invading from the outside, the tent has its second roof: the waterproof rainfly.

The rainfly is usually a separate piece of material. It drapes over the tent's supporting framework in such a way that it never touches the inner, permeable wall. It should overhang the sides enough to prevent slanting, wind-driven rain from reaching uncoated fabric. At the edges, this upper roof is held tautly in place by any of several means. For instance, straps with grommets may fit under the spiked lower tips of the poles (see below). For added stability, the fly may also attach to other points along the poles, to clips attached to the inner tent, or to outlying stakes in the ground.

The flies of many tents are designed to create a patch of rain-sheltered ground, a *vestibule*, just outside the entrance. This is a sort of porch area where you can park some gear or even cook. Some vestibules are walled and quite weatherproof, though floorless.

At one end or facet of the tent is a triangular or hemispherical *door*. Doors on the end are more convenient for two people, but side doors can be larger, helping ventilation. Doors sometimes hinge at the bottom, sometimes at the side. Each arrangement has advantages. If a door is bottom hinged, with zippers running up to the apex on either side, the top can be opened easily for ventilation; but the loose flap of a fully opened door is prone to get trampled and dirty. If the door hinges at one side and opens along the bottom, it must zip to a raised, waterproof sill. Many tents have two doors, on opposite ends or sides; when both are open, this may give you a cooling breeze.

Any tent to be used in warm weather needs *mosquito netting* over every opening. Doors are commonly split-level, with netting above and a solid panel below. Complete inner doors of netting are also still occasionally found.

Ventilation is exceedingly important in a tent. Besides the entrances, there must be at least one opening high up near the ridgeline. Two vents are better. Some tents have large areas of mesh, protected by the rainfly or by zip-on shutters of cloth.

Two or more *netting pockets*, hanging from the sidewalls, are essential for keeping track of small, losable objects. A few tents have *gear lofts*, netting attics of a sort, convenient but at the cost of some headroom. In long, narrow tents, you can dry damp gear, in a pinch, on a *ridge seam clothesline* strung between tabs at either end.

For the vital connection to the ground, all tents are equipped with *stakeout loops* at the corners and perhaps other points around the floor. You will also find attachment points for added cords called *guylines*, and perhaps the lines themselves. In some tents of the tunnel variety, the lines at either end must be staked to the ground to hold the tent erect. More commonly, guylines are insurance features, adding stability in wind.

HOLDING UP THE ROOF

Tent canopies are supported by poles of aluminum or, increasingly, a variant called tempered aluminum; both are found in excellent tents. Distinctly a second choice is tubular fiberglass. Poles come in sections, each 12 to 18 inches long, linked by elastic shock cord running inside. When the pole is set up, the base of each section nests in a socket in the end of the one below. Fiberglass segments are linked by metal sleeves. For packing, the sections pull apart, and the pole folds into a manageable bundle.

Poles are seated in grommets or pockets at the margins of the tent floor and pass through fabric sleeves on the outside of the canopy; or they may be attached to the canopy only by elastic cords and clips; or they may even run inside the canopy.

In the old days, most poles were straight; today, most are curved (when pitched) and form tensioned arcs. Rounded shapes and tension combine to pull the fabric tight, making surfaces that don't flap much in the wind.

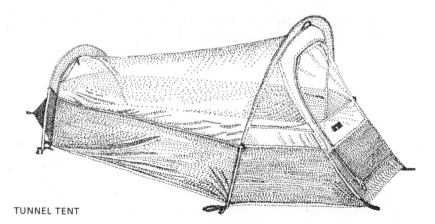

TUNNEL TENT

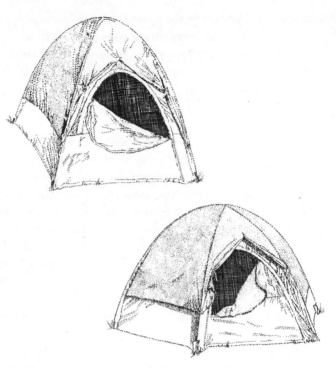

DOME TENTS

The simplest layout to visualize is the hoop or *tunnel tent,* with a long, rounded roof held up by two or more half circles of tensioned poles. The effect is a little like a Conestoga wagon. Some tunnel tents slope sharply down from head to foot; some hump up in the middle. The poles do not intersect, and in almost all versions, the tent must be pulled taut between ground anchors at either end before it is self-supporting. A two-pole tunnel tent is a pleasantly light design (under 5 pounds for two), and several enormously popular tents use this arrangement. At the other end of the spectrum, rugged tents are also built on this plan.

Another design is the *modified A-frame.* At each end of such a tent, a pair of poles forms a rounded A with no crossbar. There may be a third A or arc amidships. Linking these supports from end to end is a ridgepole. This arrangement is a hybrid between a tunnel tent and an older, almost vanished design, the basic A-frame (which is all straight lines and lacks the ridgepole). Unlike either of its parents, the modified A-frame will stand up by itself, without guylines.

The majority of tents today, however, are of *dome* or *modified dome* design. They rely on arcing poles that cross each other, intersecting in sometimes ingenious ways. In one simple variation, poles connect the diagonally opposite corners of a rectangular floor, forming an X. A popular refinement adds a third arc, like a cap on one end of the X, at the front door. Again, the poles may lean toward one another without actually crossing, like a pair of parentheses turned wrong way around. The combinations multiply from there. Generally speaking, added poles bring greater stability at a cost in higher weight. All tents of the extended family of domes are freestanding.

TENTS FOR WIND AND WINTER

Winter or "all-season" tents tend to be a good deal heavier than three-season models. They are often built of thicker material, with extra reinforcements at stress points. They have more and stronger poles; there may be a means of locking poles together where they cross. Also, they typically have somewhat more room than comparable three-season tents. All this gives winter tents an average weight per person of over 3 pounds—unless they are made of waterproof breathable fabric, in which case they can be much lighter.

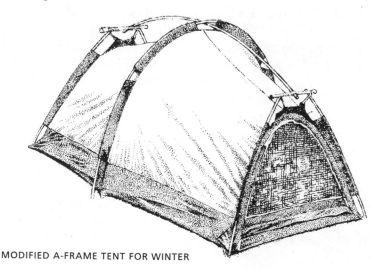

MODIFIED A-FRAME TENT FOR WINTER

Many winter tents have two entrances. A very few have *ground access holes,* zippered openings in the floor. Older names for this once-popular feature—"cookhole" and "relief hole"—give you an idea what it might be used for.

A winter tent, with its more solid construction, is by nature less airy than a summer one that may be half netting—yet ventilation remains absolutely vital. There must be several vents, and a door or doors that can be cracked at the top.

With all these requirements and options, it's no wonder that winter tents are more expensive than three-season types—the midrange is about $450 for a two-person model.

Tents designed specifically for mountaineering are different again. They are built small, light, and tough; most are rectangular, the better to fit on narrow sites. Many are single walled or unitary (see Alternative Tents, below). And they are the most expensive shelters made; you can rather easily spend $700 on such a mountain house for two.

ALTERNATIVE TENTS

Although the vast majority of tents have canopies with removable flies above, other arrangements are found.

In some few tents, the waterproof fly and the permeable tent wall are joined by sills, with a dead-air space between them. Instead of having tent and fly, either of which you may use alone, you have a single tent with a literally double wall. These all-in-one tents are warm, very easy to pitch, and exceedingly expensive.

Then there are tents with a single wall built of some waterproof breathable fabric. The makers of mountaineering tents favor this solution because it saves so much weight. I have been comfortable under a microporous canopy, but many users report that condensation is more a problem than in conventional tents.

A more radical solution uses simply waterproof fabrics. Jack Stephenson of Warmlite Equipment, the sole exponent of this design, argues that ordinary canopies don't breathe well, anyhow; it is really moving air that carries most of the tent dweller's body moisture away. So Stephenson designs his tents with "chimney" ventilation, taking in outside air at floor level and discharging warmed tent air near the high point. (Other makers now also employ this commonsensical plan.) In another Warmlite design, double-walled but unitary, Stephenson adds an inner canopy with a reflective coating; this surface, though impermeable, supposedly grows warm enough to discourage condensation.

How well do these designs work? Fabulously, say Stephenson and his numerous converts. But others are not so sure. The consensus seems to be that these radical tents, like those made of microporous fabrics, are indeed somewhat damper quarters than the traditional tent-plus-fly combination. They are, in addition, quite fragile.

Unfortunately, these specialty products are far too expensive to buy for experiment's sake; few models lie under $400. You also won't find them in rental departments. Most are in the winter or mountaineering classes. The general backpacker, especially the novice backpacker, can safely leave them off the list.

NARROWING THE FIELD

The decision to buy a tent is a good decision to delay. Rental tents are easy to find (about $25 a weekend), and there are questions you need to ask yourself before you spend perhaps ten times that amount on a purchase. First, do you really need a tent at all, or will a simple, versatile tarp give you protection enough? If you do need a tent, where will you use it most often—in rainy, mosquito-ridden woods? On summer treks above timberline? On ski or snowshoe trips? How many people should it be able to sleep? How long might you need to spend in it at a time? And, of course, how much are you willing to pay?

Sort out in your mind what your ideal shelter would be like. Every tent is a compromise. The roomiest tent won't be the lightest, nor the most stable in a wind. The cheapest tent won't be the most durable, nor the easiest to pitch. And the harder the tentmaker has worked to combine different practical advantages in a single model, the higher the price is likely to be.

Size. You have a choice of shelters for one person, for two, for three or more. If your tent will be only a now-and-then shelter, it need only be large enough to stretch out in. But if you expect to spend days in it, during long rains or snowstorms, with much of your gear inside, you need a good deal more room. A generous vestibule—the area under the fly but not under the main canopy—helps house your stuff.

Height. A related yet separate question. Some tents are high enough so that you can sit up in them without brushing the roof; some aren't. In grizzly bear country, it may be a good idea to have some extra room between you and the canopy (see Chapter 29). Lower profiles, though, tend to be more stable in high wind.

Wind stability. If you will be camping mostly in sheltered woods, high stability may not be worth the extra money it will cost. For typical backpacking, especially in the West, you need a tent that is at least moderately wind-stable.

Ventilation. Is there plenty? Make sure there is at least one vent high up.

Ease of pitching. Some tents are easy to put up, some harder, and the difference can matter. When you consider a tent, make a list of the jobs that have to be done. (How easily could you do them with cold hands, or in the dark?)

- How many poles must be slid into sleeves? If they are different lengths, can you quickly tell which is which? Must they be inserted under tension? Is it easy to see which path each pole is to follow? Is there risk of misthreading? How hard is push to get the last pole seated? With some tents, you have to crawl inside to set the poles.
- How many different anchors must be set before the tent is minimally self-supporting? With a dome design, there are none; most tunnel-type tents require two.
- What about the rainfly—how much extra and separate rigging does it require? Most vestibules require staking.

Durability. An obvious value. Durability comes from heavy materials, lots of reinforcement, and very careful workmanship (see below). For example, some poles are thicker than others; some urethane coatings are thicker than others. Such desirable extras cost you something in weight and something in money.

Light weight. The ultimate good—or is it? Most of the other things you value in a tent mean added weight. Tent innovations are mainly aimed at getting more advantages from fewer pounds, but you can pay a great deal to shed just a handful of ounces.

BUYING A TENT

Tents are different from other gear. You can usually get a good look at a boot, or a pack, or a sleeping bag, and see it as it is. But a tent, taken off the shelf, is a shapeless bundle of cloth and hardware. Only when you see it tightly pitched can you guess how windproof it is, how large it effectively is, how well sewn.

So the ideal place to shop for a tent is one of those barnlike stores where many different designs can be pitched side by side. If you have access to such a display, spend some time crawling in and out of tents, stretching out experimentally inside, and getting to know their features. Then go away and mull the choices, returning another day to make the purchase.

If you must buy a tent you can't look at first, reserve the right to bring it back after setting it up indoors for a closer look. Most stores and suppliers are good about this. A tent that doesn't please, like a boot that doesn't fit, will be taken back with no hassle.

Before or after purchase, take a look at the seams. Most of them should be what the industry calls "lap felled." In a lap-felled seam, the two pieces of fabric are folded, each over the other; stitching goes through all four layers. In any seam that is not of this type, make sure that stitching is not too close to the edge of any piece of fabric (such spots are likely to fray). In any seam in the fly, or in a single-layer Gore-Tex canopy, make sure that the joining is stable, not tending to gape when you pull on either side.

Stitching is crucial. The more places with double or triple rows, the better. There should be no holes without thread in them, no loose, hanging thread ends, and no puckered effect where some stitches, out of line with the others, are taking extra strain. Tent makers almost always use a *lockstitch*, so designed that the seam cannot unravel even if the thread is broken. The simpler chainstitch is to be avoided.

There should be plenty of reinforcement. Look for it wherever there is a grommet; a loop where a tent peg will seat or a cord attach; a sewn-on strap; and wherever guylines attach to the tent. At a minimum, each stress point should have a heavy, doubled hem. In better tents, an extra piece of material may be added, especially at the peg loops. Grommets and other metal parts should be rust-free aluminum or brass. All points of quality become doubly important in a tent intended for winter use.

Seams in the fly and in the tent floor may or may not have been sealed in the factory with melted-on tape. Even if they have been, the conservative thing to do is to add another layer of sealant yourself (see Seam Sealing, below). In fact, a container of urethane may be part of the package you buy.

Pay attention to the poles as well. If metal, are they smooth and free of burrs and sharp edges? Do the segments join easily and securely? Is the shock cord elastic and firm?

STAKES, LINES, ACCESSORIES

A set of stakes may or may not come with the tent. Even if one does, you'll want to own a larger assortment for different conditions. You have a choice of materials and of shapes. Of the materials, steel is the strongest (also the heaviest), followed by aluminum and then by plastic (though plastics vary). The simplest design is the slender, pointed skewer with an eye at one end—good for very hard ground, most insecure in softer soil. Better grip is provided by stakes that are T shaped in cross-section. Channeled stakes are C shaped in cross-section and work well in soft ground or consolidated snow. For winter there's the snow stake, a light aluminum angle, V shaped in section. Some stakes can be pounded in, some can't; there are even stakes that screw into the ground. Test for strength in the store: you don't want to buy a stake you can even begin to deform by hand. Weight is generally about an ounce per stake, and prices run from $.50 to $4.00 apiece. If you camp in a variety of places and seasons, you may find yourself choosing a different set of anchors every time you pack.

Your tent may or may not come with a guyline for each attachment point. If not, add these, using stout parachute cord.

When you rig a tent, you need a way of tightening or loosening the lines without shifting the stakes. Grip-slip knots (see Chapter 19) will serve; plastic gadgets are available to do the same thing. Some tents have tension adjusters built in.

Depending on your tent, you may be able to buy a "footprint" ground-cloth tailored to its dimensions: $10 to $25. Important tools in any tent that gets lived in much are a sponge for wiping up spills and condensation and a whisk broom for brushing out dirt or loose snow; you can even get a tiny broom-and-dustpan set.

Tents come with stuffsacks. Make sure that the tent and anything you want to travel with it—poles, stakes, repair items, groundcloth, whisk broom, sponge?—will fit into this bag with a little room to spare; if it's tight in there, buy a bigger stuffsack.

SEAM SEALING

Now the hard part. The tent, your ultimate refuge against the rain, is one item of gear that still needs to be seam-sealed. It's no small task.

Urethane—the same stuff the manufacturer uses—is the sealant. You can get it suspended in water or in chemical solvent; the latter, though environmentally questionable, makes a better bond, lasts longer, and is simply necessary for cold weather tenting. The most useful application tools are a small paintbrush and a blunt-nosed plastic syringe.

Start the job by tautly pitching the tent outside, or in an extremely well ventilated indoor space. You don't want wind, however, because of the dust it can carry. Though it's good to have the fabric warm, you don't want to work in sunlight, because it generates toluene fumes. Even with a brand new tent, wipe seams with rubbing alcohol. (You may see a "pre-cleaner" in stores: it's rubbing alcohol at several times the cost.)

What areas do you need to seal? At a minimum, treat all seams in the fly (both sides) and all seams in the waterproof floor (at least inside). Don't miss the lines of stitching where grommets or zippers penetrate these coated surfaces. Where seams have been factory taped, seal the nontaped side and apply a very thin bead of sealant along each edge of the tape on the taped side. In flyless single-wall tents, seal all seams in the canopy. Where seams are lap felled—each edge folded over the other—seal along the one exposed edge. Generally speaking, you want a thin but very continuous coat, no wider than it needs to be. For best control, use brush rather than syringe as much as you can. If there are snaps in the critical areas, put a dab of sealant in the middle of each. When your first coat is done, let it dry to the tacky stage and apply a second. To get at the inside of the fly, you may have to pitch it upside down or hang it on a line; you'll have to flip the tent, of course, to reach the underside of the floor.

Before you put the tent away, let it cure thoroughly—48 hours is not too much. (This is a good moment to attach appropriate lengths of cord to any loops on the tent or fly that are supposed to have guylines and don't.) Then dust the treated surfaces with cornstarch or talcum powder to keep them from sticking together in storage.

Altogether, a messy, stinky, protracted business—but it pays.

LATER HANDLING AND CARE

Few pieces of gear take as much punishment from the elements as a tent. After all, that's what it's for. But by the way you use your tent, you can prolong its life—or shorten it.

You're going to load your tent into its stuffsack. Is it better for the fabric to fold and roll it around its poles, or should it be stuffed, handful by handful like a sleeping bag, with the poles on the side? It's a surprisingly big and technical argument. If the manufacturer has a preference, you might follow that. Gear care specialist Annie Getchell recommends rolling when dry and stuffing only when wet. If you do fold and roll, try to avoid creasing fabric at the same places every time.

Ultraviolet light is hard on tent materials, so pitch the tent in shade as much as you can. Look for a piece of ground without sharp rocks, sticks, or anything else that could puncture or abrade the water-resistant floor. Under the tent, spread out a groundcloth, tailored or folded so that it doesn't extend beyond the tent edges, funneling rainwater inwards. If you are going to be lighting a fire, don't pitch the tent too close to the fire ring —the canopy won't go up in flames, but sparks melt nasty holes.

In assembling shock-corded poles, be slow and gentle. Start with the middle sections and work toward the ends. Check for grit and incipient damage as you go. A tent should be pitched firmly but need not be "drum-tight." A flapping shelter deteriorates faster than it should, but so does a hypertaut one.

Keep the inside of the tent as clean as possible. Boots stay outside in the vestibule, or in plastic bags. Cooking inside a tent, or even under its vestibule roof, is a risky business and not recommended. Nevertheless, winter campers routinely do it. Spilled stove fuel can damage the water-proofing on your floor. Citrus drinks are bad for nylon, and so are bug repellents containing DEET (see Chapter 10).

When you break camp, remove the fly first and spread it to dry, weather permitting, with the wetter side up. (After a clear night, that will be the condensation-soaked underside.) Take time to rub off any droplets of pitch or bird droppings. (Cooking oil, peanut butter, or kerosene will help.) Unstake the tent, shake out all grit and debris, and tip it on its side to air and dry. When you ease the poles out of their sleeves, use a pushing motion, not a pulling one: pulled segments will separate and nip the fabric. If the fabric is very wet and the weather fine, you can tie the tent on the outside of your pack in a loose bundle. Nylon is treated to resist mildew up to a point, but the drier you can keep it, the better.

If you get a minor puncture during a trip, wax from a candle, or even lip balm, will caulk it for a while. For a multiday temporary patch, use duct or adhesive tape, applied to the outer surface. Appropriately colored and textured nylon patches are also available; they look nicer but (in my experience) are a little harder to make stick. Be sure the surface is clean and dry; wipe it with an alcohol towelette from your repair or first-aid kit. Cut a patch a little larger than the problem. Trim it into a rounded shape (corners will peel) and smooth it on. To get a better bond, put something firm inside the canopy and a piece of paper outside, over the patch, and rub the edges of the tape with something like a knife handle. A little urethane sealant, if you have it, should go on the inside of the trouble spot. A dab of urethane can also close a small tear in mosquito netting.

A broken pole can be fixed temporarily with duct tape and the metal splint that may have come with the tent. A C-shaped stake can also be used.

After a trip, set the tent up and police it. Check for abrasions, bad zippers, pulling threads, overlooked tears—the usual items to fix yourself or delegate to a shop, depending on your time and skill. Sponge off any especially dirty spots with mild soap and water. Rubbing alcohol is the first home remedy for pitch; nail polish remover will lift it in a pinch. If a tent has been stored wet and has developed mildew, you can stop the damage, but not remove the stain, with baking soda or borax. Never wash a tent in a machine: too hard on coatings, membranes, and netting. If the thing is really filthy, you can take a garden hose to it. Let it dry standing briefly in the sun and for a longer time in the shade.

Check the poles, too, at this point. Make sure they're clean; wipe them thoroughly, especially if you have been camping near salt water. Pay special attention to the joints. Burrs can be gently filed off; flattened circumferences can be gently squeezed back to round. You may notice that once-straight poles are starting to reflect the arc shapes they are pitched in; that's all right. If there are breaks or kinks, you'll have to replace a segment. Weakened shock cords need shortening or replacement as well.

Tent waterproofing is not forever. In time you may have to repaint large areas with waterproof coating. For this you can use liquid, water-based polymers like AquaSeal, Poly Coat, Kenyon Recoat 3, or Thompson's Water Seal. As with urethane-coated raingear, the treatment is applied to the outer, formerly uncoated side.

TENTS AND LOW IMPACT

The improper placement of bedsites is one of the principal causes of damage to wilderness lands. *Where* you pitch your tent is much more important than *how*. Avoid vegetation and moist ground. For much more on impact considerations in camping, see Section E.

In cross-country travel, away from established campsites, very low-impact sites may be tricky to find. It helps to have a shelter that will fit in narrow spots. Tarps are the most flexible, because only the actual sleeping area needs to be level and clear. Where trees and stakable ground are scarce, freestanding tents may have the advantage over those that require guylines to be self-supporting.

Is the driving of stakes a significant impact on wilderness ground? Probably not very, but the matter is worth considering. When you select stakes for a trip, choose the thinnest style the area and season make practical: in summer, the thin metal-eyelet stakes work fine. It is often possible to use natural anchors instead of stakes. See also Chapter 18.

We come too (for the third time in these chapters) to the issue of color. Do you make your campsite obvious with a tent in yellow, orange, or a light, bright shade of blue—or do you blend into the landscape with green or rust or brown? Even more strongly than in the cases of pack and sleeping bag, I recommend here the unobtrusive colors. Nothing makes a wild landscape seem so populous as a scatter of highly visible tents—a whole seeming village where you would prefer to see no human presence at all.

Two arguments are often raised in favor of "standing out." One is convenience in choosing a camp. If you look up an open valley and see the bright blotches of tents, you know better than to plan your own camp in that area. This argument is valid but—so I believe—inadequate: the virtues of blending in are still the greater. (And what of the hiking party that passes these campsites during the day? They aren't yet ready to stop —and meanwhile their pleasure is diminished by these too obvious signs of population.)

More pressing is the claim of safety—the thought that a visible tent could more easily be spotted by searchers from the air. How much weight you give to this consideration must depend largely on the kind of travel you plan to do. There are places and times when a bright-colored tent seems not only prudent but also psychologically right. On the immense white back of a glacier, or in the middle of a violent cold storm, a blazing canopy seems somehow in scale. The greater the force and genuine danger in the environment, the less you need to be concerned about somehow asserting yourself too much.

In summer, though, or below timberline in any season, the same sense of proportion suggests tents in less arrogant colors.

THE HAMMOCK OPTION

Every few years there is a burst of publicity concerning a type of shelter we haven't discussed yet: the hammock.

By wrapping a hammock in netting and stretching a fly across it, you have a construction that combines in one the functions of ground-cloth, mattress, and tent. Such units—there aren't many makers—cost $100 to $140 and weigh 3 to 5 pounds; they may accommodate one or (rarely) two.

The hammock might seem the ultimate low-impact sleeping tool. Since your weight does not rest on the ground at all, you won't be damaging vegetation and compressing soil. In my view this is of interest in one situation only: if you are camping off-trail, away from regularly used campsites. There it is vital that you leave *no* trace, and a hammock may make the job easier—if you're in an area with trees.

Most wilderness camping, however, is done on sites that have been used for years. In such spots, the price in impact has already been paid. Research shows that a campsite is altered drastically by the first few uses; after that, there is comparatively little change. Your body weight on the ground is not going to damage anything that isn't damaged already.

If you are an inveterate cross-country hiker in wooded country, you might consider a hammock on low-impact grounds. (Be sure to pad the trunks of supporting trees if they are thin-barked or young.) Otherwise, let comfort be your guide.

Comfort suggests that the hammock is a fair-weather tool. Given much of a wind, it will rock, as one reviewer puts it, "not like a cradle."

9   STOVE AND KITCHEN

The stove, in the modern wilderness, is a necessity still sometimes regarded as an option or a luxury.

There is no denying the pleasures (or the uses) of the old-fashioned campfire. An evening fire is a presence: almost, strangely, a pet or a companion. It gives pleasant light, pleasant heat, pleasant noises. It is an event, an entertainment. It draws a group together around it. For many, it is a symbol of camping, a symbol of the wilderness even. "A campfire burns in the submerged memory of the Americans," writes Bernard De Voto, "all the way west from Plymouth Beach."

And yet the fire, in the wilderness today, has fallen out of favor. There are simply too many of us now and too little pristine land for old habits to hold. Fires near timberline, where wood is scarce and the growing season short, are not now defensible. Nor is there any excuse for the building of new fire rings where none has been before. In our more populous wilderness landscapes, firespots mark the ground like so many black sores, and these, more quickly than anything else we leave to mark our presence, make the land look used and overused.

Thus the managers of wilderness have found it increasingly necessary to close large areas to fire. And there are times and places where no rule intervenes, but where you nonetheless feel reluctant to make a mark. Maybe you are setting up camp on a ridgeline miles from the nearest traveled trail, a place so remote and changeless that you could imagine yourself the first human being to walk there. There is no one to object to one small fire scar. There may not even be a compelling "ecological" argument against leaving one. And yet you recoil.

The case against fire should not be overstated. There are locations where a fire cannot, by the longest reach of conscience, be accused of doing harm: a sea beach tangled with drifted logs for fuel; a sandbar or a gravelly river bank (below the winter high-water line); an established fire ring in a moist forest littered with down wood. And even in a pristine landscape there are ways of handling a fire so that nothing visible remains.

But this is the point: if you have a stove, you simply don't have to weigh these things. You take nothing from the land and leave nothing behind. No ashes. No rings. No blackened stones to clean or conceal. Being self-sufficient, you are also much more free to camp where you will.

There are other practical advantages as well. Simplicity is the main one. The next few pages will inevitably make stoves sound like complicated, rather tricky gadgets. But once you have your stove and have grown used to it, you'll find its operation quick and easy. You'll be boiling water while the wood burner is still gathering kindling. You'll be working with a steady, controllable flame. Your pots won't even get sooty. No question about it: pleasant associations aside, stove cooking has campfire cooking beat all hollow.

And whether you choose a stove for conscience or convenience, you may in time discover something more. You may find that the stove brings with it pleasures of its own, equal, arguably, to the pleasures of a fire. A stove, too, becomes a kind of companion. It has its own rituals. If of the most serviceable type, it burns with a comfortable, reassuring roar. It calls to your mind, each time you light it, the other places you have used it: other camps, other journeys, other times.

But most important is that curious moment, after dark, when at last you turn the valve and bring the stove to instant quiet. There are no embers, of course, to sit by and watch fade. What happens instead is rather hard to explain. The wilderness, kept at a certain distance for a while by your lively kitchen, appears all at once around you. The night sky comes into being over you as if its black and its brilliance had just then been invented. The colors of the night, the movements, the slight noises, become instantly present. Against all these things the wood-burning fire is a defense—but a defense (you may come to feel) no more to be desired than it is needed.

On some trips in some regions you can have it both ways. If you carry a stove and fuel, you can leave them in the pack when conditions are right for a fire. Maybe your first night will be spent in the rain in a low-lying forest, where wood is plentiful, a fire a real comfort. But the next night you are at timberline in a no-fire zone. Or maybe, arriving at a place where you planned to build a fire, you find there is no dead, down wood within scavenging range. Far better to carry the stove and leave it unused than to carry none and find yourself forced to choose between eating cold food and lighting a fire where no fire should be.

Stoves suitable for backpacking are small and light. Most of the thirty or so available models fall into two groups. There are *bottled-gas* stoves, which draw fuel from canisters containing compressed gases that, when released, stream out under pressure. More widely useful are *liquid-fueled stoves*, burning white gas, kerosene, and sometimes other fuels.

BOTTLED-GAS STOVES

These are also called "cartridge stoves" because their fuel comes in self-contained tanks that you plug in, use up, detach, and discard (by recycling: see below). They are attractively simple and very popular. The stove is composed of a *stem* that plugs into the fuel cartridge, a *valve* that controls the rate of flow, and a *burner*. The burners of cartridge stoves are much like the ones you see on kitchen ranges, with many tiny openings, or "ports." The fuel, typically a mixture of propane and butane, would be gaseous at room temperature if unconfined; it is kept liquid, under pressure, in its rigid-walled container. Open the valve, and the fuel instantly streams out as vapor, ready to burn. There's no monkey business about lighting a cartridge stove under good conditions: a touch of a match, or a flick of a lighter, and you're there. The flame can be adjusted high or low and is silent.

The three basic components—cartridge, stem, and burner—can be arranged in different ways. Traditionally the cartridge sits upright and supports the burner on top. On some models, burner and cartridge are separate but linked by a flexible fuel line. Other variations are seen.

Cartridges differ. Some work only with a particular stove; others are widely interchangeable. Some must be left attached to the stove once the seal is broken; others can be removed between uses. In some models you can even unplug the burner and substitute a very effective lantern.

For all their elegance under good conditions, cartridge stoves have limitations.

The gas streams out so nicely because the pressure inside is greater than the atmospheric pressure outside. But the more fuel is used, the less the inside pressure. After about the halfway point, the flame begins to weaken. It may take twice as long to boil water with a fading cartridge as with a fresh one.

The problem becomes much worse under cold conditions. When the pressurized gas gets chilled, it pushes outward less strongly. To complicate matters, the stove cools itself as it operates—because the evaporation of a liquid consumes energy, the surface of the cartridge actually loses heat as

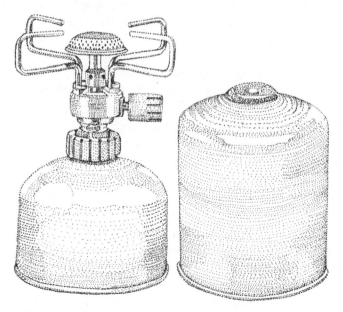

CAMPING GAZ MICRO BLEUET 270

the contents empty. When fuel temperature drops far enough, the stove will simply refuse to work.

Not all fuels are affected equally, however. Ordinary butane, the one-time standard, quits vaporizing at 30 degrees Fahrenheit. Most makers now use a mixture of propane and butane, which remains volatile to 20 degrees. Then there are cartridges filled with a special form of butane, *isobutane*, which has a still lower vaporization point, 12 degrees Fahrenheit. In all cases, though, the action gets sluggish well above the absolute cutoff point. I wouldn't count on ordinary butane below 40 degrees, on butane/propane mixes below freezing, or on isobutane below about 20 degrees.

Oddly enough, this advice must be modified for high altitudes. As you gain elevation, there's less competing pressure from outside to block the exit of fuel from the cartridge. At 10,000 feet, even a stove burning ordinary butane should work below freezing; above 15,000 feet, bottled-gas stoves are reliable standard equipment.

Cartridge stove weights vary widely, from as little as 8 ounces (without cartridge) to as much as 22 ounces; most are under 1 pound. One very specialized and expensive climber's stove weighs just 4 ounces! Prices range from $20 to $85, with the most common models midrange.

LIQUID-FUELED STOVES: BASIC ARCHITECTURE

At $42 to $100, a liquid-fuel stove costs a bit more than a bottled-gas type. It also has a good deal more anatomy. There is a *fuel tank*. There is a *fuel*

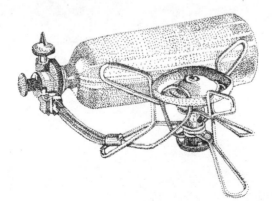

MSR WHISPERLITE

line linking the tank to the business end of the stove. Next comes a *generator* or *vaporizing tube,* in which the fuel is preheated and mixed with air to form a vapor suitable for ignition at the *burner* itself. In some burner designs, a single jet of gaseous fuel emerges from a tiny orifice and strikes a *burner plate;* in others, the vapor issues from many openings in a *ported burner* like those on cartridge stoves. Fuel flow is controlled by an adjustment knob and also by a *pump* that forces air into the fuel tank to maintain pressure there.

As with cartridge stoves, the basic components of liquid-fuel stoves can be arranged in different ways.

In one widely used design, the burner and the fuel bottle are separate, with a fuel line connecting them; the pump screws into the bottle. Stoves of this type are made by Mountain Safety Research (MSR), which invented them, and also now by Optimus, Sigg, and Peak 1 (a Coleman brand).

The second major option is the unitary stove, with the burner above a built-in tank. Here, today's dominant brand is Peak 1. Also in the second

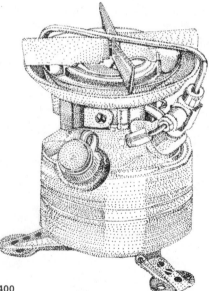

PEAK 1 FEATHER 400

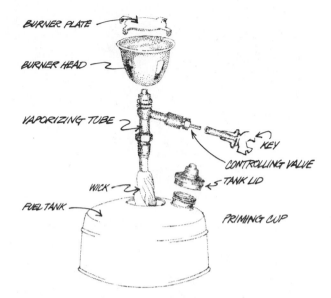

BURNER PLATE

BURNER HEAD

VAPORIZING TUBE

KEY

CONTROLLING VALVE

TANK LID

WICK

FUEL TANK

PRIMING CUP

WORKING PARTS OF A CLASSIC WHITE GAS STOVE

group are the classic Svea and Primus stoves that so many backpackers grew up with. The names have disappeared—look instead for Optimus—but the stoves are still being made. These models have built-in fuel tanks that may be under the burner or offset to one side (but not unpluggable as in the true separate-tank design). Also, unlike newer stoves, these classics lack built-in pumps (though add-ons are available).

When a stove is running, its own heat keeps the vaporizing tube hot enough to do its work. (In some models, the tube actually loops through the flame.) To get things started, however, you have to supply some initial heat, a process called priming. Typically, a trickle of cold stove fuel is released from the pressurized fuel tank through the burner into a *priming cup* and is simply ignited with a match or built-in sparker. Once this starter dose has flamed away, the works should be hot enough to vaporize fuel for normal operation.

The Peak 1 white-gas stoves are different. When you pressurize them and open a valve, the fuel emerges as a spray of droplets, ready to ignite; once it does, actual vaporization ensues. Under less-than-ideal condi-

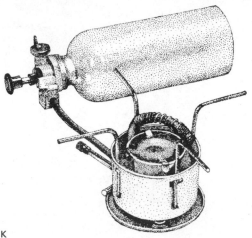

MSR X-GK

tions, however, you may still need to intervene. For much more about priming and lighting liquid-fuel stoves, see Chapter 18.

Almost any stove that uses liquid fuel will burn white gas, the standard backpacker's fuel in the United States and Canada. Once the term denoted a variant of automobile gasoline, available at many service stations. But today that product has disappeared, and "white gas" is a casual name for the highly refined camp stove fuels found in sporting goods and hardware stores. White gas burns very cleanly and leaves less residue than other fuels.

MULTIFUEL AND KEROSENE STOVES

White gas, however, is a rather specialized product; there are wide parts of the world where it is not available. A number of stoves are built to accept one or more other fuels, including ordinary automobile gasoline, kerosene, diesel oil, and methyl alcohol. Among other refinements, dual-fuel or multifuel units tend to have thicker-bored fuel lines. Be warned, though: some multifuel stoves require work on your part, like swapping one jet or vaporizing tube for another, before they will burn products other than white gas.

Fuel terms naturally differ around the world. The United States and English-speaking Canada use the same vocabulary, but Québec prefers the French words: "kérosène" for kerosene, "essence" for gasoline. Butane

OPTIMUS 111 HIKER MULTIFUEL STOVE

and propane are "gaz de butane," "gaz de propane." Overseas travelers must learn local terms.

Even the North American traveler may choose multifuel stoves for either of two reasons. When they burn white gas, their generous bores make clogging unlikely; when they burn kerosene, they are safer.

Kerosene, a far less volatile fuel than gasoline, is slower to evaporate and slower to ignite. It has a greasy feel, disappears slowly if spilled, tends to leave deposits in fuel lines, and likes to produce smoke and soot. But this very sluggishness is where the safety comes from. Though kerosene burns fiercely once lit—actually yielding more heat per volume of fuel than does white gas—it must be almost persuaded to ignite. Spilled fuel won't flare up in a flash fire, as can happen with spilled white gas. Nor is a kerosene-burning stove at all liable to dangerous overheating. It's no wonder that large organized groups of hikers often favor this fuel.

There is just one stove now that burns kerosene and nothing else: the charmingly traditional Optimus 00 Camper. It has no valve to control the height of the flame. Rather, you raise the flame by pumping and lower it by letting pressure out of a manual valve in the fuel cap.

Kerosene is found at a few gas stations and in hardware and sporting goods stores. Though the raw form has an odor that some find unpleasant, most kerosene now sold is nearly odorless. It costs a bit more than white gas, weighs slightly more, and stretches slightly further.

As for auto gas, it tends to contain nasty additives and should be used in a stove only as a last resort.

OTHER KINDS OF STOVES

Just as there is one classic stove that consumes kerosene only, there is one that uses only alcohol: the Optimus Trapper. The fuel simply burns in a cup under a housing that is windscreen and pot support in one. The package is elegant but slow to boil water, taking at least half an hour. Such a stove can't be considered for anything but mild conditions, or perhaps for cooking in a tent, where the fuel is very safe indeed.

Then there are *solid-fuel stoves.* These are mostly just housings over a can of Sterno (jellied alcohol) or a fuel pellet. These units are cheap and simple but lack the heating power to be of much use in wilderness cooking. Sterno is found most readily in hardware stores, and pellet fuel (Hexamine, Esbit, Heat Tabs) is available in sporting goods outlets.

Of special interest is the curious Sierra solid fuel stove by ZZ Manufacturing, a cross between a stove and a miniature fireplace. Priced like the cheapest white-gas stove, it burns twigs, pine cones, or any small dry wood, with the help of a battery-operated fan. It has a limited but enthusiastic following.

CHOOSING A STOVE

What stove is best for you? Start by asking yourself when, where, and for whom you will be cooking. Summer? Winter? High elevations or low? Large or small parties? Then consider these points.

Kind of fuel. Do you want to burn bottled gas or liquid fuel? Cartridge stoves are temptingly compact for short trips, but when you start packing extra cartridges, the weight adds up quickly. And cartridges cost between five and ten times as much as white gas per hour of burning. If you plan to camp in chilly weather, better go for liquid fuel (or for isobutane). If it's to be liquid fuel, do you want the ability to burn kerosene and maybe other products? Child safety can be a large consideration here and might even steer you toward an underpowered but relatively kidproof alcohol-burner.

Boiling power. How long does it take the stove to boil a quart of water from room temperature? Under good conditions at sea level, average boiling times range from 3 to 8 minutes. Most stoves boil more slowly in the cold and still more slowly in wind. In bad weather, you want the highest possible boiling power. MSR liquid-fuel stoves are famously good for winter camping.

Simmering ability. If you plan to prepare many dishes that require slow cooking, look for a bottled-gas stove or for a white-gas/multifuel stove with a ported burner and a valve mounted near the burner, not far off near the tank. Coleman's integral-tank models are especially good simmerers and can even be throttled down between courses.

Time between refills. The smaller your fuel tank or cartridge and the faster fuel is consumed, the more time you will have to spend fiddling with fuel. Most stoves burn between 2 and 4 hours. Liquid-fuel stoves with built-in tanks keep it up for shorter periods, even less than an hour. The same is true of butane/propane stoves that use small canisters, or burn very hot, or both.

If your fuel tank is of a piece with your stove, you must periodically recharge it from a larger storage container. You plan operations to avoid refueling in midmeal. With a separate fuel tank, you only rarely have to change supplies, and then it's a simple matter of unscrewing one bottle from the pump (or vice versa) and screwing on another.

Stability. Some stoves give very good support to the pot on the burner and have low centers of gravity. Others are quite tippy. Look at each model and ask yourself how easy it might be to lose a pot of goulash. Flexible fuel lines between burner and bottle help here; so do adjustable legs found on some stoves.

Ease of use. Can you see and reach the controls while the stove is running? Do they get hot? Are there any small parts that can fall off and go missing?

Reliability and ease of maintenance. Bottled-gas stoves are the most reliable; but if something goes wrong, there's little you can do about it. Multifuel stoves burning white gas are markedly trouble-free. Straight white-gas stoves are the most finicky. MSR stoves are notably field-maintainable, other brands far less so. If you should need help from the manufacturer, the North American firms (MSR and Peak 1) are reportedly easier to work with than European ones (Optimus and Sigg).

Weight. Always a consideration for the backpacker. Without fuel, suitable stoves range from about 8 ounces to something under 2 pounds.

The package. Some stoves come more or less naked, others in packages including cooksets and windscreens. There's no need to buy a combination deal, but you should consider how neatly your stove will pack, how well it will fit your pots, and how it will be screened from the wind.

FUEL AND ACCESSORIES

How much fuel you need depends on your stove, your cooking style, and your trip. It also depends on altitude; cooking times increase as air pressure drops. For a closer look at fuel planning, see Chapter 12.

Butane/propane, of course, is purchased by the cartridge. These typically weigh about 10 ounces and contain 6 to 8 ounces of fuel. Half-size units are also available. Cartridges cost $4 to $6 and, since each is good for 3 hours at most, get pretty expensive over time. Used containers, which are aluminum, can be recycled easily once every trace of fuel has been burned away; the recycling of partially emptied bottles, however, requires special equipment.

A gallon of white gas or kerosene now costs $3 to $5. It will cook thirty meals or more for two or three campers. If you purchase fuel by the quart instead, you will pay about double yet the smaller size may make sense for the occasional backpacker. Because fuels may deteriorate with time, you don't want to have more than a year's supply on hand. Even if you buy by the gallon, it's better to store liquid fuel in smaller, airtight bottles such as you might carry on the trail. After a year, pour any unused white gas into your car's gas tank. (A dissenting view should be noted here. For every knowledgeable person who repeats this conventional wisdom, an equally knowledgeable person scoffs, insisting that fuel lasts essentially forever. Being neither a chemist nor a stove technician, though, I take the more conservative advice and start each season with a fresh supply.)

If you choose a stove of the detachable-tank variety, which plugs right into its fuel, the choice of container is made for you. MSR, Optimus, and Sigg stoves of this type use interchangeable cylindrical aluminum bottles made under all three names. Depending mainly on size, these cost $7 to $12. Peak 1 uses its own, differently threaded bottles.

Bottles come in several capacities. If you need more fuel on a trip than one bottle will hold (see Chapter 12), you might as well carry the excess in the same kind of container: when the first gives out you can simply plug in the spare, with no fuss.

If your stove has its own built-in tank, this will probably not accommodate a trip's worth of fuel, so extra cans must be carried and fuel transferred to the stove from time to time. Aluminum bottles are fine, but in this case you have a wider choice of plastic or metal containers. Your fuel cans should in any case be prominently marked or otherwise strikingly different from those containing drinkables.

For filling a built-in fuel tank you will need a small plastic or metal *funnel* with a replaceable filter. (The filter is doubly important if you are burning something other than white gas.) Some funnels have a convenient shut-off feature: they stop accepting fuel when the tank they are feeding approaches full. Several convenient *pouring spouts* and *caps* are

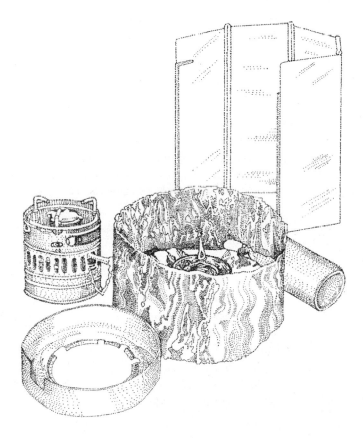

available for use with Sigg-type bottles. With white-gas stoves that lack pumps, you may also want an *eyedropper* to use in priming.

A substantial *windscreen* is essential and may be sold as part of a stove-and-cookset package. If not, buy wind protection separately. Mountain Safety Research makes a two-piece screen of thick aluminum foil—ugly but highly effective—that can be trimmed and restapled for use with models other than MSR's. You can also start from scratch with metal flashing. Don't be satisfied with the little wind barriers built into some stove burners: they help, but you want more protection when it really blows.

Whenever you use or improvise a windscreen, you must take care that the screen doesn't lead to overheating of fuel tank or fuel line. In the now-rare case of a white-gas stove without a pump, the tank needs to be quite warm, but it should not be too hot to touch. Make sure that flame doesn't tend to blow toward a tank. Butane cartridges should never become more than warm.

What you wish for with many stoves is a solid cylindrical windscreen on adjustable stilts, elevated so that it surrounds the burner without blocking air circulation to the fuel tank below. Sierra Club trip leader Gordon Peterson invented this elegant item decades ago and still builds it for use on club trips; but nothing like it has been available commercially for years.

If you are camping on snow, you will need a *stove pad:* a small piece of wood or closed-cell foam (wrapped in duct tape) about 6 inches across. This insulates the base of the stove, which otherwise would melt a well into the snow, or be chilled too badly to function. For separate-tank stoves, you can get a *stove stand* to which burner and fuel tank clip, making it all nicely stable ($25 and a few ounces).

Instead of MSR's likably primitive aluminum sleeve, you can install its cunningly fluted *heat exchanger* ($30), which wraps around the pot and captures heat ordinarily lost to the air. It weighs about 6 ounces but earns back its weight, in fuel conserved, after four meals for two.

Some stoves come with cases, or disappear into cookset pots. Others are pretty vulnerable in the pack. For these, a variety of padded stuffsacks and cases are available separately.

Many white-gas stove users, and all kerosene users, bring along a separate fuel to prime with. This may be some form of solid fuel, or it may be liquid alcohol (the denatured solvent form, not rubbing alcohol, which has high water content and burns poorly). Whatever you use, take plenty of it, especially the first time out with a new stove.

A small *butane lighter* can be handy, but also carry several sets of *matches*. Put them in your kitchen gear, in your first-aid or emergency kit, and in at least one other place—perhaps tucked in with some reserve food. Some stoves have built-in sparkers; they're nice when they work, but not cause to leave your matches home.

There are several sorts of matches to choose from. Cheapest, of course, are ordinary folder matches. They have to be dry to ignite, and must be struck on their own sandpapery striker pad. Then there are wooden kitchen matches, which you can strike on any dry, rough surface. Third are waterproof matches, which may or may not require their own striker; but both match and striking surface can, in theory at least, be soaking wet. (You can also waterproof ordinary kitchen matches by dipping them in wax.) Finally, there are waterproof/windproof matches. These burn like sparklers and cannot be blown out. Though they will actually burn under water, they must be dry to ignite.

In dry summer climates, many people favor the strike-anywhere kitchen type, or a mixture of strike-anywheres and waterproofs. If you plan to camp in rainy country or on snow, your matches should certainly be waterproof, and you should have perhaps a handful of the more expensive windproof ones as well.

"Waterproof" or not, protect your matches: in doubled plastic bags, foil envelopes, or (wooden matches) in a plastic or metal *matchsafe*. The best safe will be brightly colored and also distinctively textured for the groping hand. Some have built-in strikers. Carry, regardless, several extra striker pads for matches that require them.

Auxiliary firestarters must be on your list. In very wet weather, it takes more than matches to light a wood fire—and even a devout stove-user may someday desperately need to. The simplest thing you can take is a segment of plumber's *candle*. Some people make little logs of wax-soaked newspaper. A piece of *cork* works well. Various fibrous and woody incendiary products are found in gear stores. (The old standard, the paste called fire ribbon, is off the market because of toxicity concerns.) Spectacular but heavy is the *magnesium-block* firestarter: you shave it into tinder, strike a spark, and get a truly impressive flame.

BREAKING IN A STOVE

When you've purchased your stove, settle down and read the manufacturer's instructions, then read them again. Practice the lighting routine. Burn a full tank or pint bottle of white gas, or a full cartridge of butane/propane, to get an idea of how the stove behaves. Cook some meals while you're at it. Just how long will the stove run between fuelings? If it's a bottled-gas model, when in the life of the cartridge does the fall-off in heating power begin?

A bottled-gas stove needs hardly any maintenance, but a liquid-fuel stove is a notoriously tricky item. Before you fire it up the first time, it's a good idea to rinse out the built-in tank or detachable fuel bottle with a little clean white gas. Discard this into your automobile fuel tank. Then make it a habit to pour fuel through a filter-equipped funnel whenever you fill your stove.

Review what's in the parts kit you may have gotten with the purchase. If the stove boasts of "field-maintainability," take it apart and put it back together again. Identify the parts that are likely to need replacing somewhere along the line, especially the jet, the several O-rings, and the pump leather. Parts and instructions, of course, should go with you on the trail.

For more about the care and feeding of stoves in action, see Chapter 18.

Back home again, take a close look at the stove before forgetting it until next time. Check the jet: has it become enlarged from cleaning? Maybe it's time to replace it. To head off trouble, O-rings should be replaced about once a year. Check the flexibility of the piece of leather at the business end of your pump; if it's sound but a little dry, you can lubricate it with light machine oil (or lip salve). You can test for leaks by submerging the fuel bottle, pump in place, in water. If there's more than a trace of bubbles, quickly dissipated, you have a bad seal.

If you need more help, own a tinker-resistant stove, or would just rather not mess with the thing, many gear stores do stove overhauls: cost $10 to $15.

After a trip, white gas should not be stored for long in a stove or in the detachable tank you use with the stove. Pour off the dregs into your car. Once the last trace has evaporated, check the tank for grit or water droplets and, if you find any residues, rinse with a little more fuel. When the tank is completely dry, store with the lid on loosely.

COOKWARE

Backpack cookery is mostly boiling things in pots. A single hiker can get along with a single small pot (or none, if you choose to eat cold food). In a small group you need a couple of cooking vessels. Common sizes are 1.5 and 2.5 liters; nothing smaller is useful, and larger is often welcome.

Backpacking pots are made of aluminum, stainless steel, steel masking an aluminum core, or titanium; they may have nonstick surfaces within. Uncoated aluminum is simple, light, cheap, and easily dented. Stainless steel is more durable and more handsome but also heavier, 12 ounces or so per piece. Titanium, very light and strong, is the deluxe material.

Most pots are wider than they are tall; a few are deep and cylindrical. The tall, narrow pots are inefficient for cooking on most stoves. Top edges should be "lapped," folded over to make a rigid rim that resists distortion and is easily gripped. Inside, the bottom should merge with the sides in an easily scrubbable curve. Pots should nest, and it is nice if they work together as a double boiler. As for support, most backpacking pots are "naked," but some have strip or wire bails (very useful if you cook much over fire).

A nonstick inner surface is handy for quick cleaning. Materials now in use are less vulnerable to scratching than earlier versions, but care is still required. A black outer surface makes for faster heat absorption. Few makers coat their ware in the factory, but you can paint pot bottoms yourself with flat black stove paint (available at any hardware store). In the days of campfire cookery, many chefs just let their gear get sooty and stored it proudly in a special, spectacularly grubby bag.

Snugly fitting lids will shorten cooking time. If you want to go really light, you can substitute aluminum foil.

You'll need a light aluminum *pot lifter*. A bandanna or glove will do in a pinch. When it's very cold, a pair of light cloth gloves will take some of the sting out of the touch of freezing metal or spilled fuel.

Many people buy *cooksets*. The typical package includes one smaller and one larger pot, one or two lids (typically usable as frying pans), and a gripper. Some include windscreens and are matched to particular stoves. Tailored or no, it's handy if your stove can fit inside your largest pot.

Bought as a unit or assembled from scratch, your basic cookset will probably cost $15 to $35 and weigh under 2 pounds—under 1 pound if you go light and cheap. If you go light and expensive, with titanium, you'll pay more like $80 for a pair of pots alone.

What about other cooking tools? Some people like bacon and eggs enough to carry *frying pans* (some pots come with lids designed to double as fry pans). Separate pans weigh 12 to 15 ounces in steel or Teflon-coated aluminum and cost $10 and up. With a pan, you need an appropriate *spatula.*

Baking isn't any too easy on the trail, but it is possible. By placing a piece of metal on the flame of a not-too-vigorous stove, you can spread the heat enough to bake after a fashion. You can also produce a reasonable facsimile by boiling dough in a plastic bag—the Boston brown bread method—though of course you don't get a crisp top. To produce that top crust, you can light a tiny fire on the lid of a pot that is simultaneously being heated from below by your stove. One maker offers a specially indented lid for this purpose. More elaborate rigs are essentially little ovens that mount on top of the burner. For larger groups that build fires, there are full-size reflector ovens (3 pounds and $15). Campfire users may carry light *grills* ($3–$35; cheap cake racks will serve). A grate with legs is a low-impact tool. Besides its convenience, it improves ventilation, prevents spills, and encourages complete combustion of the wood below.

As you gain in altitude, cooking takes longer. For one thing, most stoves become less efficient in thinner air; for another, the boiling point of water declines. At 10,000 feet, the boiling point is about 192 degrees Fahrenheit, 20 degrees below the normal 212 degrees, and it takes more than 6 minutes to cook a "3-minute" egg. Instant and just-add-water foods are less affected.

One way of speeding up mountain cooking is to use a *pressure cooker:* a 4-quart cooker weighs 3 pounds and costs about $75. But in normal backpacking you needn't consider such a thing; cookers are mainly taken to very high altitudes or on trips so long that the saving in fuel makes up for the weight of the appliance many times over. Meanwhile, tight lids help a bit.

For the simple cooking that most backpackers do, about the only other important utensil is a ladle or s*erving spoon.* For pastas and such, a light substitute for a *colander* can be useful; a piece of cheesecloth works. Some people take *coffee filters.* Some take little *teapots,* which can also serve as colanders because of the screen in the spout. For that matter, tiny *espresso makers* are now seen on the trail . . .

Your personal mess kit can be minimal. Most people carry nothing more than a plastic or metal *cup* and a *spoon*; others like a plastic or aluminum *plate*, or *bowl*, or both. An *insulated mug* with lid is nice when it's cool. A very deep cup, however, is awkward to eat out of.

For dishwashing you need a wire or Teflon *pot scrubber*, and perhaps some biodegradable liquid soap. A small party may dispense with soap, but not unthinkingly: see Chapter 9. Detergents are never used, and washwater is dumped far away from any lake or stream (except in one or two special cases). You need some sort of *strainer* to pour the water through, so that solids can be added to your garbage. You can get along without a separate *washbasin*, though light ones of foldable plastic are available. Dish towel? Let things dry in the air.

CONTAINERS FOR FOOD AND LIQUIDS

Bottles are made of various plastics, including food-grade polyethylene and Lexan; Nalgene is the prevalent brand. Most containers are cylindrical, a few squarish. There are narrow-mouthed or nipple-nosed versions for liquids and large-mouthed ones for liquids and bulk solids; I find wide mouths more generally useful. An alternative to the rigid bottle is the soft bottle, or bladder, made of plastic or other synthetic material; it has the

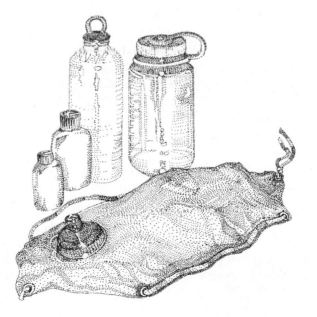

advantage of shrinking when empty, and the disadvantage, in most incarnations, of stinking after being filled with anything but water. Bottle prices run from $4 to $10 for a liter size, depending on materials and features, and weights run to 4 ounces. Bottles set up as canteens or "hydration systems" may cost a good deal more. You might also check with a local clinic or hospital, where tough liter-sized bottles, originally filled with sterile water, may be available free.

Large collapsible w*ater carriers* are often useful. In camp, hanging on a tree or rock, they can reduce the number of trips you have to make to the local watering hole, thus reducing trampling: a virtuous thing, especially if you're camping at an unmarked site. They also permit you to camp where there is no waterhole. Carriers hold from 1 to 5 gallons; they cost from $5 to $30. Not all types are leakproof in the pack, so be sure what you're getting. A light and effective in-camp substitute is three large plastic grocery bags, nested one inside the other.

In most wilderness situations, hikers now disinfect the water they find on the land. Boiling will do it, but filters or chemical treatments are often more convenient. For a discussion of the options, see Chapter 20.

Most solid food goes into larger or smaller *zippered plastic bags*. Oversized, very tough bags can be found in gear stores. There are also square plastic *boxes* with snap-on tops; flat, round, screw-top *butter dishes*; and plastic *egg carriers*. *Squeeze tubes*, with backs you can open for filling, are handy for things like peanut butter so long as the weather stays warm. Avoid containers with tops that snap on rather than screwing on: they always open and spill. Cheap two-part *shakers* are commonly taken for pepper and salt (or use film containers; just make sure the lids won't come off in your kit!). More ambitious cooks carry miniature *spice kits*. If you have steel cans to open, you can use a minuscule GI-style *can opener* or simply a knife blade. Multibladed knives (see Chapter 10) may include a serviceable can opener.

At home, all food and water containers should be washed and stored open with lids off.

BEAR PROTECTION

In many North American wilderness areas you have to protect your food from scavenging bears. The traditional method is to hoist it into a tree at night and whenever you leave an established camp unoccupied. So your kitchen gear must include, along with plenty of *cord*, one or more stout *containers* for the hoisting. Sometimes you can use an empty pack, a tarp gathered into a sack shape, or a hammock. The recommended counterbalance method of bearbagging works best with two large stuffsacks, the size you would pack a sleeping bag in. Laundry bags will also serve. Carabiners are handy for attachment. For rain protection, you can wrap plastic garbage bags around the cache; if you're headed for really soggy country, you might look for a light backpacker's version of the rafter's drybag, which rolls over itself at the top and fastens shut. For more on bear protection, see Chapters 18 and 29.

Another option is the *bearproof canister*, a rugged plastic cylinder that can be opened only with a coin or other tool. These can be rented at several national parks, ordered from the manufacturer, Garcia Machine (see Resources appendix), or, increasingly, purchased in specialty shops. The unit is 1 foot long and 8 to 9 inches in diameter. It holds about six person-days of compact food, weighs 2.7 pounds, and costs about $75.

Obviously, you won't want to carry such heavy defenses if you don't have to. These canisters must be regarded as essential, however, in certain areas. One such is the Arctic tundra, where there are voracious grizzly bears and no trees; the canister was developed for, and first tested at, Alaska's Denali National Park. Canisters are also required in certain more temperate areas where the bears seem always to be one step ahead of the rope-slinging camper.

The protection of your edibles is really only the secondary reason for toting these containers. The primary purpose is to protect the bears themselves. Once the animals become habituated to human food, they all too often have to be destroyed.

10   THE REST OF THE LOAD

Clothing; sleeping gear; shelter; cooking gear. With these we have covered the bulk of what goes in the pack (for food, see Chapter 12). What remains, though, is important: medical and emergency supplies, personal items, and some tools so essential and so useful that they demand a category of their own.

HEALTH AND SAFETY I: THE MEDICAL KIT

Every wilderness traveler needs a personal medical kit. How much is in it depends mainly on the place and season of your travel. In U.S. wilderness areas south of Canada, where it's pretty hard to get more than 20 miles away from a road, your kit is mainly for minor problems and first or second aid for major ones.

In other situations, a more extensive kit or a second, better-stocked group kit should be carried. Expeditions (especially with doctors aboard) tote quite sophisticated medical supplies. Hikers in the great wilderness regions of the far north need to be equipped for more than first aid; this book has little to tell them. In a party with children, the adults are the expedition leaders and have to plan for all contingencies.

What about prepackaged, commercial first-aid kits? There are many on the market; prices range from $30 on up. Good ones are the work of M.D.'s experienced in wilderness medicine. Yet these kits have drawbacks. For one thing, the selection of items is never quite the choice you would make; second, and more important, there's nothing like putting your supplies together from scratch to teach you exactly what you've got. If you do buy a packaged kit, don't just toss it in and forget it; study it, learn from it, and add or subtract items as your own experience grows.

Let's run down some of the common and not-so-common components of wilderness medical kits. Many of these are available separately, in suitable sizes, at gear stores. Items marked with an asterisk are of special importance.

The container. This can be a rigid box or a stout zippered pouch but should in any case be waterproof. A fairly generous kit should fit in a container of about 50 cubic inches—say 3 inches by 3 by 6, though almost any shape will do.

First-aid manual. A mechanical step-by-step routine for dealing with emergencies can be useful. There are various portable manuals, from densely printed cram cards to James A. Wilkerson's hefty *Medicine for Mountaineering*. One good packable book is Steve Bezruchka's *Pocket Doctor*. See the Resources appendix.

Bandage compresses. (Band-Aids is a brand.) Several sizes. Three or more of each. You can get all kinds of variants: knuckle bandages, fingertip bandages, butterfly bandages; but most odd shapes can be improvised.

Gauze pads. Three or four pads, 4 inches square, in sterile envelopes.

Gauze bandage. One inch wide. Not less than 15 feet. Not required to be sterile. Handiest is the self-clinging kind.

Porous adhesive tape. Also 1 inch wide and plentiful—take 10 yards.

Moleskin or equivalent. Stick-on pads to cushion feet when blisters threaten. Moleskin is thin, molefoam thicker. A newer product, Spyroflex, is flexible and less likely to peel. Some people find adhesive tape or duct tape works just as well for prevention. Spenco's 2nd Skin, a clear film developed for burn treatment, is good if you do get a blister. See Chapter 15.

Triangular bandage. An item with many uses; the classic arm sling. Bulky (about 11 square feet) and often missing from the small kits. Improvised substitutes are usually possible.

Elastic bandage. Three inches wide. Reduces swelling in joint injuries.

Antiseptic soap. Betadine (povidone-iodine) is the standard.

Antibiotic ointment. Three-in-one antibiotic cream, available in small foil envelopes.

Cotton swabs. Various possible uses.

Needle. For draining blisters.

Tweezers. Mainly for splinters. They must be very sharp and not unmanageably small.

Scissors. Mainly for cutting dressings, moleskin, repair tape. May be on knife.

Safety pins. You think of these as sew/repair items, but they have uses in first aid too, as for fastening arm slings and bandages.

Razor blade or disposable razor. Various uses. Blade can substitute for scissors. Also used to shave skin before applying tape, or the suction cup of the next item.

Venom extractor. A suction device that can reduce the effect of a bite by a venomous snake (see Chapter 29) and also of lesser encounters like bee stings.

Sting-killing lotion. Various ingredients to counter pain, itching, and swelling from insect bites or stinging nettles. Sting Eze is a brand.

Tick remover. Several little devices are available to help you remove an attached tick most efficiently.

Analgesic of choice. Aspirin, acetaminophen, ibuprofen, naproxen. Aspirin is cheapest. Ibuprofen is very popular for muscle and joint pain. Naproxen is a cousin. These three are related: all are anti-inflammatories, and if you're allergic to aspirin, you should avoid the others, too. Acetaminophen is easy on the stomach but less effective for after-exercise pain.

Prescription painkiller. Many hikers carry half a dozen 30-milligram tablets of codeine/empirin, or some other mild prescription medicine for pain. Consult your doctor. Watch the expiration date and replace as needed. Pills can be stored in little vials or, perhaps better, in tiny zip-lock bags with instructions inside.

Salt tablets. Skip this once-traditional item (see Chapter 28).

Digestive remedies. Antacid or acid-blocker tablets for indigestion; antidiarrheal tablets for a problem that is rare but miserable on the trail.

Personal medicines. Anything you know you're likely to need: Toothache drops . . . laxatives . . . antihistamines . . . your own prescription drugs. If you have a known medical problem, consult your doctor before you head into wild country.

Other drugs. Many are possible, but few are needed for ordinary travel. Doctors hesitate to prescribe except for immediate need. However, on very remote trips it may make sense to carry a broad-spectrum antibiotic like tetracycline and a heavy-duty narcotic painkiller (oral forms are now available). Drugs should be replaced as required.

Syringe. Not a needle for injections, but a blunt-nosed plastic model that can produce a stream of water under pressure, as for flushing out a wound. A plastic bag with a pinhole can serve the same purpose.

Latex gloves and CPR mask. If you find yourself giving first aid, you may wonder about AIDS and other diseases that may be transferred in body fluids. The danger of AIDS transmission in blood is real, and you should wear latex gloves when pressing on a wound to stop bleeding. There is, by contrast, very little danger of catching a disease when doing cardiopulmonary resuscitation (CPR); some like to carry a protective surgical mask, but this is not essential. See Chapter 26 for more about these matters.

HEALTH AND SAFETY II: SKIN PROTECTION

These items will be used too often to be packed away in a kit.

Insect repellent. At certain times of the year, in certain places, this will seem more like a survival item than a mere convenience. The most effective preparations are those that contain the chemical n,n-diethyl-meta-toluamide (abbreviated DEET). DEET is pretty powerful stuff; it will eat away at plastics and even at glass. Though it actually seems pretty harmless to flesh and blood, you don't want to overuse it. Choose one of the lower concentrations (they vary from 25 percent to nearly 100 percent) and apply sparingly. The major alternative to DEET is citronella, a lemony substance derived from an Asian grass. A surprising number of people swear by Avon's Skin-So-Soft lotion, which is mostly mineral oil. But nothing now available comes close to the effectiveness of DEET. For more about bug problems and solutions, see Chapter 29.

Suncream/sunblocker. Suncreams vary. Almost all preparations, however, are marked with a *sun protection factor (SPF)*, a number from 1 to 50. This indicates how long you can be exposed without burning: a cream with protection factor 5, for instance, would theoretically allow you to stay in sunlight five times as long as you could without protection. For outdoor recreation, use SPF 15 or higher. Above 8,000 feet or so, and on light-colored rock or snow or near open water, most people need the highest SPF they can buy. For more about sun hazards and protections, see Chapter 28. Combination creams combining SPF 15 sunscreen and low-concentration DEET are available.

Lip balm. Most hikers will need this to prevent and treat cracked, burned lips. The best preparations contain sunscreen. Unflavored ones won't get licked off so fast.

Poison oak/ivy/sumac lotion. Good blocking creams are coming on the market and may be worth buying if you're highly allergic, especially for off-trail travel where these irritant plants grow thick. For more about this problem see Chapter 29.

HEALTH AND SAFETY III: EMERGENCY AND SURVIVAL

In this third group are some special items you might want to have with you if you were lost, if you had to spend an unexpected night out without normal equipment, or if you hoped to attract the attention of rescuers. Prefabricated emergency kits ($16 or so) contain some of these.

Whistle. You blow it to summon help (three signals of any kind indicate distress, two indicate response). A whistle is most useful when there are other hikers in the vicinity; though better than a shout, the sound doesn't carry that far. Whistles may also help in keeping a large party together, and parents often give them to their kids. Cost runs $2 to $6, weight not much.

Mirror. A longer-range rescue signal, especially useful in the desert. Doubles as a first-aid item. Cost $3, weight not much. You may already have a mirror on your compass (see Chapter 16).

Signal cloth. A piece of bright-colored cloth—an item of clothing, a groundcloth, whatever—that you could spread out to attract the attention of aerial searchers.

Phone change. For an emergency phone call if you must hike out to a road for assistance. Though most phones now permit an emergency call without a coin deposit, better not count on it.

Waterproof/windproof matches. A special supply in your first-aid kit or emergency kit so that you will never be caught without.

Candle stub or other firestarter.

Emergency shelter. There are several possibilities, but the idea is simply to have something to wrap up in on a cold, wet night. Some people carry reflective "space blankets"; fragile, one-use models sell for $4 or so, and somewhat stouter ones go for around $12. Another type of shelter is essentially a large, tough plastic bag. If you have a hooded waterproof raincoat of some sort, a shorter plastic bag, into which you thrust your legs, will serve. This is one function of the old-fashioned long raincoat called the *cagoule* (see Chapter 5). You can pull your legs up inside it, tighten the drawstring at the hem, and make yourself almost weatherproof.

Snares, fishhooks, and such. Sometimes packaged with commercial survival kits, these are scarcely necessary in most travel. If you're lost for a short time in wild country, food is by no means your first need: warmth and water are primary. Still, it can be entertaining to learn a few skills for living off the land: how to build a "figure-4" snare or a noose of thread or hair, how to recognize edible and poisonous wild plants, and so on. Many books give instruction in these skills, which seem to fascinate people out of proportion to their practical importance.

Manual. Prepackaged kits may contain manuals on how to stay alive. Though these may be useful, it's far better to have done your reading and thinking in advance. Ask yourself, as a mind game, just how you would conduct yourself if you had to ride out a night, or several nights, with less than the usual gear.

Whenever you leave your main pack behind, as on a side trip, you want to make sure you have with you the basic items, including some of the above, that are often referred to as the "ten essentials." Your personal list is likely to include more like twenty essentials, and will vary with circumstances: see Chapter 15.

ESSENTIAL TOOLS

Map and compass. Each member of a party should carry both (see Chapter 16).

Knife. Any folding pocketknife will serve. Stainless steel is nice and widely used; plain carbon-steel sharpens more readily. One valuable feature is a lock for the main blade so that it won't suddenly shut and slice a finger. Basic knives cost $10 to $20.

Then there are "multitools," which offer a number of blades or tools in one. The traditional version is the Swiss Army knife, familiar with its imprinted cross and red rubbery handle (though other colors and textures can be had). These knives come with as few as three and as many as seventeen different blades and accessories. Other companies are now making multitools, some a good deal heftier than the Swiss version. It can be handy to have a number of basic items together like this; on the other hand, you may not find exactly what you want on one tool, or may choose to carry separate and more robust versions. Things you may get in a multitool are a second knife blade, a pair of needlenose pliers, one or several screwdrivers, a wire cutter, bottle and can openers, a pair of scissors, and ruler markings. You can probably do without saws, magnifiers, plastic scrapers, and files. Prices run from $40 to $80, depending mainly on blades, and weights are 4 to 9 ounces. Beware of cheaper Chinese-made knives that mimic exactly the Swiss Army knife, even to the name, but fall far short of it in workmanship and durability.

A folding knife or multitool needs to be sharp, and it needs to be clean.

To remove dirt, make a "knife soup": open all blades and tools, and drop the knife into hot, but not boiling, water. In a few minutes, remove and scrub with an old toothbrush. Rinse it, fold and unfold the blades several times, apply a little light machine oil, work the blades again, and wipe dry.

For sharpening, the best tool is a whetstone. Though a small stone might be packed for a long trip, usually this job is done at home. Lubricate the stone with water or light oil. Place the blade on it, sharp edge away from you, at a slight angle (23 degrees, if you have a mathematical eye!). Now push the blade across the stone, with moderate downward pressure; depending on the composition, bluntness, and roughness of the blade, it may take just a few passes or several minutes to get a sharp edge. For the other side, use the same push-away stroke but work with the opposite hand. Relubricate the stone as needed.

Flashlight or headlamp. It is no easy thing to find a flashlight that works, all the time and without persuasion, when you need it most. (I, for one, have trouble with *all* flashlights.) But the picture here is improving.

Flashlights made for wilderness use usually omit the conventional on-off switch, a perennial problem spot; to turn on one of these lights, you simply twist the lens housing or a basal piece at the other end. Some lights allow you to widen or narrow the beam, or to hood it, producing a lamp-like "area light." Prices of better flashlights run from $10 to $20; AA cells are usually included, but C and D cells are not. Weights without batteries vary from a couple of ounces to a full pound.

For $20 to $65 you can get a battery-powered *headlamp*. The working

end of a headlamp straps to your forehead and shines wherever you are looking. The batteries may be right behind the bulb, in a case at the back of the head, or even in a shirt pocket, connected by a wire; your hands are free. Most headlamp beams can be adjusted from narrow and bright to broad but dim. You can also buy inexpensive headband rigs that convert an ordinary flash to a headlamp of sorts, but it isn't the same.

Along with the original batteries, take a couple of extras and a spare bulb (of the original type). Alkaline power cells are more or less standard. Another kind of battery, the expensive lithium cell, lasts somewhat longer and works better below 20 degrees Fahrenheit. How long any battery holds up in use depends largely on the output of the bulb it is feeding; brighter beams die sooner. Typical flashlights using two AA cells will stay bright for 5 or 6 hours when it's warm, considerably less in cold conditions, unless the batteries are lithium. Battery prices run from 75 cents for a pair of the cheapest alkaline AA cells to ten times that for lithium cells.

Since disposable batteries are a form of toxic waste, it would be nice to substitute nickel-cadmium rechargeables. Unfortunately, these don't last long enough for wilderness use. Solar rechargers exist, but they work too slowly to be practical. Let's hope for progress toward a compact sun-charged flashlight whose batteries would never need changing at all.

When a light is not in use, guard against it "turning itself on" and draining the batteries. The traditional advice, to reverse one battery, is not always a good idea. You can get the same protection by unscrewing the bulb partway, or using tape or a rubber band to keep a switch from moving.

Inside a tent (or snow cave or igloo) a candle can give you good light. For $10 to $15 you can get a candle lantern that protects the flame from drafts. Some lanterns are tall and slender, best suited for hanging; stubby ones with legs are better for setting on things.

Cord. One of the real necessities, anywhere at all. Carry more than you think you'll need and never less than 50 feet; bear-bagging may require 100 feet (see Chapter 18). Cord is also a repair item. It should be pretty strong; ⅛-inch or 3.5-millimeter parachute cord, 500-pound test or more, is fine. Hard-finished cord is best for bear-bagging (less likely to snag or tangle).

Sanitary trowel. Often recommended these days, to make sure you dig the perfect "cathole" for human waste (see Chapter 20). A stick or a boot will often do as well, but pack a light trowel unless you know by experience you won't need it where you're going. The Forest Service, in some regions, requires every party to carry a small shovel or trowel if fires are to be built. Plastic trowels cost a couple of bucks and weigh a couple of ounces; stainless steel trowels, recommended where soils are stony, cost $17 or so and weigh 6 ounces.

Ax, hatchet, shovel, saw. Not ordinarily needed, or even desirable.

Notebook and pencil. For anything you feel like writing down. Also useful in emergencies to leave word for possible rescuers or for other hikers. Some specialty notebooks have waterproof paper you can write on in the rain.

What about a *wristwatch*? Some people make a point of leaving this item behind, but you may need it if your plans involve very early starts or perhaps a closely timed rendezvous. If you really do need a watch, you probably need one you can read in the dark, with a loud alarm. If digital, large buttons are also nice. With microelectronics, very elaborate functions can now be built into a timepiece. Some watches double as fallback navigation aids (see Chapter 16).

Staff or trekking poles. If you hike for a lifetime, you'll sooner or later discover the usefulness of a stick or staff. Whether it's a found object or an elaborate "trekking pole," a staff shifts some of impact of the footfall from the lower body to the upper, an excellent thing for aging or substandard knees. Two poles are even better, because you alternate them in a matter that mimics the natural swinging of the arms. You'll spend $60 to $120 for a pair of adjustable telescoping trekking poles with spring-loaded tips that further dampen impact; singles cost less. Ski poles can also be used. Besides their primary purpose, poles and staffs have endless incidental uses.

TOOLS: REPAIR KIT

There are excellent prepackaged kits ($5–$25) for general gear repair or for special tasks like fixing zippers and patching self-inflatable pads. These can get you started. Your specific needs will vary with the trip, with your gear, and with your taste for tinkering. The repair kit is also a convenient stashing place for items not strictly used for repair, like extra flashlight batteries and bulb. Here's a pretty comprehensive list of components, some of which I've never actually taken:

Sewing materials. Some very stout "button-and-carpet" thread, and some medium-weight thread. (Dental floss will double for the former.) A couple of needles with large eyes for easy threading. A couple of buttons. A few large safety pins. Twist ties (which will do nicely to hold together an opening that has lost its button). Less often carried are thimbles and awls for work with leather and thick fabric.

Repair tape. You can use adhesive-backed nylon tape for neat patches on tents, sleeping bags, jackets, and such. Adhesive tape from your first-aid kit will work for temporary repairs. For heavier jobs, the tough, silvery stuff called duct tape is unbeatable, though it leaves a sticky, stubborn residue. Duct tape is best carried wrapped around something, like a screwdriver handle or a segment of pack frame.

Alcohol towelettes. Unless you carry alcohol for priming, throw in a couple of these for cleaning an area that is going to be taped.

Webbing straps and hook-and-loop (Velcro) tape. Mainly for good sewers who want their field fixes to be elegant.

Urethane sealant. For waterproofing and cementing patches. Comes in several consistencies. The thinnest version is most generally useful; the thick stuff can be used to fix sole problems on ultralight fabric boots. Products by McNett are often recommended.

Glue. Glue sticks get melted over a candle or butane lighter. Epoxy is stronger but, with its two components that you mix, a little finicky. Instant "superglues" are good in the cold and can also be used in first aid, as to stick down a cut flap of skin on a fingertip.

Wire. A foot or more. Stout enough to be strong, pliable enough to bend around corners. Braided steel is the best. A dozen uses in repair.

Pliers. Many uses, especially with zippers: as to tug out pinched fabric, or to gently compress a worn slider that is gaping too widely to do its job. May be on multitool.

Screwdriver and screws. A screwdriver tends to be used most as a pry bar for jobs like removing a zipper stop in order to replace a slider. But it sometimes drives a screw as well. Skiers always carry screws for the repair of pulled-out bindings; screws can also help to anchor loose boot soles. A tiny driver may be useful for eyeglasses, binoculars, or cameras. Notice any screws you have in your gear, and choose a small assortment to match.

Extra sliders for critical zippers. The two that matter most are on the sleeping bag and panel-loading pack. Replacing a slider on a "separating" zipper, where the two sides of the closure come completely apart, is relatively easy; the same job on a "coil" zipper, where one end is permanently bound together, is quite a chore. You have the second kind on your pack and the first kind (probably) on your sleeping bag.

Extra cordlocks. These handy gripping devices allow you to snug up cords without knots. Although it's no disaster if one breaks, a replacement is easily carried.

Spare pack buckles. A broken buckle on a shoulder strap or hipbelt can be a major problem. Duct tape can probably get you home, but on a long trip you might be glad to have spare hardware. Take both components of each buckle, and be sure they're right for your particular pack. You can't insert a sewn webbing loop into the typical "ladderlock" buckle without either unstitching the loop at the root or slipping it through a slot snipped in the buckle's crossbar; pre-slotted emergency buckles may be found in commercial repair kits or purchased separately. They are invaluable.

Frame pack fittings. On frame packs, packbags are commonly held to frames by clevis pins and lock-rings. Rings can break, and clevis pins occasionally get lost. A spare pin is good to have; stout wire can replace a ring.

Tentpole repair sleeve. This can be a custom item from the manufacturer, a C-shaped tent pole, or simply a slit-open can.

Hose clamps. Can also be useful in packframe or tentpole repair.

Stove tools and parts. Likely to include jet and O-rings. A spare fuel can gasket can be vital. A cork can replace a lost cap. Consult (and bring along) the instructions that come with your stove.

Small butane lighter. To melt glue sticks; to seal frayed nylon; to light a stove or start a fire.

Monofilament (leader) line. For things that need binding.

Rubber bands. Assorted, mostly heavy. You're always wanting one; may be in kitchen kit instead.

PERSONAL ITEMS

These can be few or many. Most people take a *toothbrush*; many take *floss*. You can skip the toothpaste, which leaves a white splotch when you spit it out, or substitute *baking soda*. Don't forget a reasonable supply of *toilet paper* (even if your use is sparing, you might get diarrhea). *Tampons* and *contraceptives* may be appropriate. Contact lens wearers should carry saline and antibiotic eyedrops, and backup spectacles just in case. You know what you need.

For personal cleanliness, you'll want a sliver or tube of *soap* and several *bandannas,* one of which serves as a washcloth. Moist, sealed *towelettes* can be nice; in grizzly country, you're advised to carry a good supply (see Chapter 29). Some hikers like a *towel,* which may be a piece of artificial chamois from an auto supply store. Hikers who do a lot of swimming may splurge and carry a square of terrycloth. Some like a light pocket *mirror.* Everybody takes a *comb;* some also a small *brush.* In larger parties, it can be nice to have a folding personal *washbasin.* A luxurious item is a *shower rig* consisting of a large waterbag and a showerhead: leave the bag in the sun for a couple of hours, and serve.

If you are traveling with very small children, you'll of course be carrying all sorts of added paraphernalia: see Chapter 25.

WINTER AND TECHNICAL GEAR

There are various items that you'll need only in snowy winter: snowshoes or skis, waxes and ski accessories, snow shovel and snow saw, avalanche rescue transceivers, and so on. Then there's the endless range of more technical gear for mountaineers: ropes, ice axes, crampons, helmets, protective anchors of various sorts, and such. For more about just a few of these extras, see Chapters 22 and 24.

LUXURIES AND SPECIALTIES

Although none can be called essential, there are many items that add comfort or pleasure to a trip, if you're willing to put up with the weight. Some luxuries frequently taken: camp shoes to put on when the boots come off; camp chairs (which may double as sleeping pads) to lounge in; cameras (and all the absorbing paraphernalia that goes with them); natural history guides; binoculars or monoculars; magnifying glasses; fishing gear; barometers; altimeters; thermometers; books and games; cards; chess sets; even elaborate board games. Some of these become near-necessities in certain situations—altimeters for some kinds of navigation, for instance, and binoculars in grizzly bear territory.

You name it, somebody has probably loaded it into a pack, somewhere, sometime. And everyone has a short list of personal "luxuries" that seem as necessary as boots and cooking gear.

COMMUNICATIONS GADGETS

It began quietly enough a few years ago when expeditionary climbers began relying on radios to keep their parties in touch. Then winter campers started bringing weather radios to receive the latest forecasts from the National Weather Service. Now there are cellular phones, which, in regions well provided with transmitters, allow the wilderness traveler to "phone home" without special gear. Another relative novelty is the portable Global Positioning System (GPS), a high-tech navigation aid that gets its data from orbiting satellites. And faxes have been sent from the summit of Everest.

All these pieces of electronic gear have obvious advantages to the wilderness traveler. In a genuine emergency, the ability to summon rescue quickly could be lifesaving; in less serious cases, it would be nice, for instance, to tell your family that you're coming out a day late but all is well. The weather forecast can certainly be helpful, and the GPS (see Chapter 16) is an engaging toy.

Some of these technologies are also being misused. Rescue workers complain, for instance, that people are summoning help for trivial causes. And managers worry that overeasy contact with the outside will make people more ready to blunder into dangerous situations they might otherwise shy away from.

All this easy communication and available information has another, and to my mind, more serious drawback. It lessens the demand for self-sufficiency. It tears away the veil of isolation that is one of the reasons for being in the wilderness in the first place. A distinction could be drawn between devices that only bring in information from outside (like weather radios) and devices that permit two-way communication; but all, it seems to me, amount to a significant cheapening of the wilderness experience.

Since no physical damage to the land is done, it is hard to see any basis on which the use of such devices could be (or should be) restricted. But personal choices can be made. I have carried a weather radio, and I have been in situations when radio or telephone contact would have been a godsend. Nevertheless, it seems to me now that these tools are out of place in the wild. I offer, for what it's worth, my revised opinion: all should be eschewed.

If you do use such items, by all means be inconspicuous about it.

C

PREPARING THE TRIP

Then find in the horizon-round
One spot, and hunger to be there.

Gerard Manley Hopkins,
"The Alchemist in the City"

11   DESIGNING THE TRIP

The easiest way to take your first longer trip is to sign on with an organized party (see Chapter 2). But it's when you start setting your own targets and making your own plans that the real fun begins. The whole ritual of preparation—the packing, the planning, the study of the maps that build a landscape in your mind—is not just the dull means to the pleasant end: it is the first part of the journey itself.

Experienced packers—some of them, anyway—can throw a trip together quickly. On a few hours' notice they are packed and gone, needing little time to prepack, prepackage, preplan. But at the beginning, at least, you will need to be a little more methodical.

FIRST STEP: PICK A PLACE AND A TIME

Most trips seem to start with gossip: "They say it's nice at Stonecup Basin . . . the Big Craggies . . . Silver Falls." But if you're not tied in yet to a grapevine, you may need to do some asking around.

For instance, you can consult some of the numerous area guidebooks now in print. You can also contact the government agencies that manage wild land. In the United States, you might start with the regional offices of the U.S. Forest Service, the National Park Service, the U.S. Fish and Wildlife Service, and (in western states) the Bureau of Land Management; state agencies, especially in California, Michigan, Maine, Pennsylvania, New York, and Wisconsin, also control some important wild destinations. In Canada, get in touch with Parks Canada and provincial governments. (See Resources appendix for these addresses.) The responses you get from agency offices will help you focus your interest on particular parks, forests, wildlife refuges, and so on, and give you the local contacts you need for more specific advice.

In some regions, the focus of backpacking is likely to be not the single large wild area, but the lengthy trail that threads landscapes both very wild and relatively tame. Such trails as the Appalachian are more celebrated than the individual parks and preserves they traverse, with copious maps and guidebooks.

Computer users have additional ways of getting information. Guide-

Use of Desolation Wilderness, California

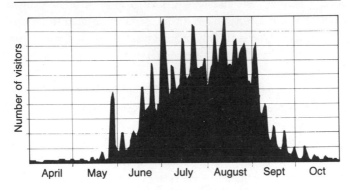

books of a sort are published in the form of CD-ROM disks (you need the appropriate disk drive). Much more can be learned via the Internet, the electronic network that allows information of all kinds to be moved from any computer to any other. Various outdoor publications, clubs, and management agencies have Internet "websites" (see Resources appendix for a few). Backpackers also swap information informally in "newsgroups." In some areas, updates on trail conditions are also available by fax.

Your sources will tend to lead you first to the well-known, well-used landscapes. That may be just what you want at the beginning—or perhaps much longer, if you don't mind a certain amount of company. It does appear, though, that many backpackers *are* disturbed by too much company. You can avoid it by going where other people do not, or by going *when* other people do not.

Weekends in the wild are always busier than weekdays; holiday and August weekends, in most regions, are busiest of all. Yet over much of the United States, autumn is a more welcoming hiking season than midsummer. In many regions, September is drier than August; a little later comes the wonderful bonus of fall color. Spring, too, is lovely and not very populous. But it should be noted that the soils in many areas are waterlogged in the spring, and easily damaged by human traffic.

In regions where winter brings snow, that clean, white surface covering the fragile meadows and the mountain roads creates a wilderness at once more spacious, starker, and less vulnerable to our abuse: see Chapter 24.

You can avoid the crowds in space as well as in time. Even in summer, and even in the best-known regions, use is anything but evenly spread. People flock to a few favorite lakes, a few peaks, a few trails. This is by no means a bad thing. You wouldn't want all parts of an area to be used equally. But the hiker who is slightly more adventurous, or simply better informed, can take advantage of the unequal distribution and go where others do not.

As a rule, you can be more alone on trails that do not lead straight to peaks or lakes or picture-postcard scenic climaxes. You can also be more alone on trails that are too rugged for stock.

In addition to less-visited parts of popular areas, there are whole wild regions where hardly anybody goes. Some are protected as wilderness; many, though thoroughly qualified, are not. In the western United States and in much of Canada, these unprotected de facto wilderness areas make fascinating destinations. You just don't know what you will find. And you have the added zest of knowing your visit can make a difference. If you visit an unlabeled wilderness area, take a few minutes, when you get back home, to write a letter in defense of what is there. You will be doing an important service to the country you enjoyed (see Chapter 31).

How do you learn where these places—by nature underpublicized—are found? The usual source is the grapevine, but a call to the nearest chapter of the Sierra Club may yield some information. Government land management agencies are of course aware of these areas, too—they have inventoried and studied them repeatedly. A visit to an agency office can net you a rich catch of information, once you get past the front desk (where only the most popular hiking areas will be mentioned).

A caution: unprotected areas are not, generally, the best destinations for your very first trips. Some of them, fascinating though they are, lack that instantly recognizable, photogenic charm that is always the first quality to be preserved. And you will need to check with the local offices of the land management agency about the condition of roads and trails. Maps are often out of date, and trail systems may have gone unmaintained for years. If you find uncertainty alluring, such an area is for you.

Then there is cross-country travel; it's more adventurous, more solitary, and more of an exploration. But this, like winter travel, takes preparation and skill (see Chapter 22).

Once you've settled on a general destination, check right away with the managing agency to find out whether a wilderness permit is required and how to get one (see below). For very popular areas, six months' lead time is not too much. If your party is larger than a handful, find out about size limits, too.

SECOND STEP: GET MAPS AND DETAILED INFORMATION

There is a pleasure in going off to the woods with no very firm idea of where you'll wind up. But this is not a pleasure for the beginner. As a rule, planning makes a better trip. Besides, it's fun.

Your basic planning tool is always the topographic map or "topo sheet" published by the U.S. Geological Survey or Geomatics Canada. These are webbed with thin brown lines that show elevation in feet or meters above sea level. For more about these maps and how to use them, see Chapter 16; for ordering information, see the Resources appendix.

U.S. topographical maps are now available in CD-ROM form from the U.S. Geological Survey and increasingly from private suppliers. The private versions come with programs that allow you to play with the maps on the screen, perhaps adding your own notes and information, and print the customized versions on your own printer.

In addition, management agencies publish maps for each national park, state or provincial park, national forest, national wildlife refuge, or Bureau of Land Management district. These maps are small-scale, representing a lot of country on a little bit of map, , and generally lack contour lines, but they are fairly up-to-date about roads and trails. Such agency maps are indispensable for exploring de facto wilderness, and in regions where there is a lot of private property intermixed with public lands. Of special value are the "recreation maps" published by the U.S. Forest Service for its extensive holdings.

Also very useful is the *Atlas and Gazetteer* series by Delorme. These volumes, extending rapidly across the United States, usually cover one state apiece. Based on topo maps, but on a far smaller scale, the Delorme maps fill the gap between the detailed sheets and ordinary road maps. They are great for general orientation and access roads.

Even if you already have the maps, even if permits are not a issue, you'll want to be in touch with the management agency office responsible for the region you're headed for. There are things they will want to tell you; there are things you will want to ask them. The more well known and populous the area you will visit, the more you need to learn about its rules; the less well known and populous it is, the more you need to learn about its physical realities.

Some questions you may want to ask: Has a certain trail been recently maintained? Which areas get the most recreational use and which the least? Which trails are heavily used by packstock? Are there routes on which you may meet off-road vehicles or mountain bikes? Are there areas currently being grazed by cattle or sheep? (You may want to avoid all these.) How reliable is a certain water source? Are there any extraordinary hazards you should know about? Are there current bear problems? Can bear canisters be rented near the roadhead? Where will hunters be active?

If you are doing something unusual and need more than standard information, you may have trouble finding someone knowledgeable. Explain your problem, get the name of the best person, find out when he or she will be in (most likely from 7:00 to 9:00 A.M.), and keep trying.

THIRD STEP: PLAN YOUR TRANSPORTATION

Most people can skip this step. They know already that they will be driving from their homes to the wilderness. But some hikers, bound for distant destinations, will be going by air and renting cars locally. It's a little difficult to get to wilderness trailheads without a car in the picture somewhere, but it is possible (see below).

Backpackers sometimes compare themselves smugly with people whose enjoyment of the landscape depends on internal combustion engines: motorcycles, jeeps, or snowmobiles. One implicit argument is that the mechanized recreationist burns up a lot more gasoline, and causes a lot more pollution, than the self-powered walker of the trails.

But that is only true if the backpacker has driven a merely moderate distance to the trailhead. If you live, say, in Cleveland, and drive (or fly) to British Columbia for your wilderness vacations, you may be using more fossil fuels than the busiest local off-road-vehicle enthusiast can burn.

Indeed, it can plausibly be argued that the worst thing any of us do environmentally in the course of a wilderness trip is to drive to its beginning.

Extreme? Possibly. Yet I like to avoid, at least, long drives before short hikes. I try to drive no more than 100 miles (one way) for each day on the trail. By this formula, day trips would lead to places less than 100 miles away; a weekend trip would lie within a range of 200 or 300 miles; the week-long trip within 700.

You will, naturally, take as few vehicles as possible. Sometimes, though, your party will want more than one. Maybe your hike will end miles from where it began; in the absence of public transportation, you need to spot a second car at the exit point (see Planning Shuttles, below). Then there's the case of travel in remote areas like the Canadian north or the Great Basin of Nevada and Utah. Here, where driving conditions are brutal and mechanics few, it is a bit foolhardy to depend absolutely on a single vehicle.

Yet one more point about cars. If you're traveling between regions, you don't want to be an unwitting botanical Typhoid Mary, introducing pestiferous plant species to distant wilderness roadheads. This is a more considerable problem than you might imagine, and authorities plead with roving backpackers to make sure their vehicles (and gear in general) are free of seeds and other plant materials from home (or landscapes they've traversed along the way).

What if you want to avoid the automobile entirely? This is a somewhat daunting proposition. But there are places where buses or even trains can take you directly to trailheads.

The carless backpacker in the eastern United States has relatively good pickings. Bus lines thread the Adirondacks and the Catskills, run through Cumberland Gap and across the Great Smoky Mountains, and intersect the Appalachian Trail at any number of points. There are even rail stops on the Appalachian. In the White Mountains of New Hampshire, too, wildland trails begin on the shoulders of main paved roads where buses run.

Out West, things get sparser. But there is regular transit service over Santiam Pass in the Oregon Cascades and Snoqualmie and Stevens Passes in Washington's part of that range; along Interstate 80, which runs close to interesting roadless areas in the California Sierra and elsewhere; and on other major western highways. There are also transit services to many national parks: Yosemite and Mount Rainier, Grand Canyon, Rocky Mountain, Yellowstone, and more. Glacier National Park has two Amtrak stations. Once you're in the right neighborhood, local recreational shuttles can be helpful. In Canada, many national parks are reasonably accessible by rail or bus. In general, approaching the wilderness by public transportation will put you in well-known and popular locales.

If you need to pick up a wilderness permit, perhaps at an office miles away from your trailhead, this can complicate matters. All the same, reliance on public transportation is not prohibitive—it just adds an extra layer of planning.

If you are going by air, be aware that you will not be able to take your stove fuel; you may not even be able to take your empty stove. Contact your airline about this. A duffel bag to encase your pack is a very good investment. For more about air travel, see Chapter 13.

FOURTH STEP: MAP THE TRIP

Now comes the pleasant job of laying out your trip in detail. You know how many days you have to spend: How many of those days would you like to spend resting, or on side trips out of a fixed camp? How many will you have left to use on moving forward, onward, deeper in? And how far can you walk in that time?

It all depends on the land. A crude but standard rule of thumb makes 10 miles an average day on easy terrain with pack. Some people routinely do much less, others much more. Another formula runs like this: allow 40 minutes for every mile of trail, plus an extra hour for every 1,000 feet you climb. Not as slow as it sounds, this rate is a good one to plan with. So you might allow 8 hours of actual hiking to cover 9 miles of easy trail with 2,000 feet of elevation gain—a longish day. Soon, of course, you'll know better than any book what you actually can do and want to do.

Now study the map for likely routes that take you to the places you want to see. One thing is obvious: you can enjoy a lot more country if you don't repeat yourself. Look for trails that loop back on your starting point or that bring you out to another roadhead. Sometimes a loop can be made by crossing a short gap between trails, but read the map carefully—are you going over a precipice?

How long is the line you have just traced? A guidebook may tell you and so may an agency's response to your request for information. You should, in any case, check the distance yourself using the map scale. A ruler won't help you much here, since rulers are straight and trails wander. One good traditional tool is a piece of fine wire (or a twist tie). Lay the wire out along your path, bending it to fit the curves; then straighten it out and compare the length you've used with the scale. This works best on the standard "7.5-minute" topo maps, less well on maps of less detail—it's easy to underestimate the bends. You can also buy little map wheels that you calibrate to the appropriate scale and roll along the route. They do no better than pipe cleaners, however, at estimating the very kinky bits. At the high-tech end, computerized topo maps can compute precisely the length of any line you indicate on the screen.

Try "walking" your entire route on the map. A skilled map-reader can get a clear mental picture of the place to be visited: here there is a sharp drop, there a gentle forested valley; here an easy stretch, there a sustained ascent; here a long view over the plain, here a closed-in canyon. If you like, you can use graph paper or a computer to prepare an "elevation profile"—a simple graph relating horizontal distance (the horizontal scale) with elevations taken from the map (the vertical scale). Again, the proper computer program can do this in a snap.

Give some thought to your camps. Estimate approximately where you will find yourself at the end of each day's move: is there reasonably level topography thereabouts? Be sure to consult the managing agency rules. There may be no-camping zones to be avoided, or (at the other extreme) specific sites you have to use. If you plan to build wood fires, you may find yourself limited to established spots, to particular, designated locales, or to lands below a certain elevation. Fires may also be permitted only at some times of year, or even forbidden entirely. If your trip is in the desert away from a perennial stream, or along a high ridge without lakes, springs, or snowbanks, you will have to take note of water points and plan your stops with these in mind. In desert travel it is common to plant water caches in advance (see Chapter 23).

In such eastern ranges as the Catskills, wilderness sometimes lies in narrow mountainous strips between lowland valleys. Often a long ridgetop trail will send short spurs down to roads on either side. This makes trip planning somewhat simpler, because you can make a quick exit to a road and perhaps a bus stop if the weather turns nasty, or if you get blisters, or if you simply run out of time. But in larger wildlands, you can seldom "bail out" except by going back.

If your trip will take you to high altitudes, try to allow time for adjustment to the thinner air. At a minimum, schedule a night's sleep at a high roadhead (see Chapter 28).

PLANNING SHUTTLES

Often you can see more country if you start and end your trip at two different roadheads. This requires some sort of a shuttle.

The classic method is to take an extra vehicle and park it in advance at the exit trailhead. Two cars must go to the exit point so that one can bring the shuttle driver back. If entry and exit points are well apart, this process can take many hours.

Given just one car and a slightly larger party, you can split into two groups that walk in opposite directions. Group A, say, can be dropped off at a northern trailhead to begin a southbound hike; Group B drives on to the southern trailhead and hikes northbound. Car keys can be duplicated, or switched when the groups meet in the middle.

A possibly viable alternative is to hitchhike. Even a grubby backpacker may find it easier to get a lift than would someone in street clothes. And you may bump into people on the trail or at the trailhead who will happily give you a ride in exchange for a tall tale.

Maybe the best solution, where available, is public transportation. As noted, some wilderness areas do adjoin roads where buses run, and long trails cross highways. In some popular areas, there are well-planned recreational shuttles. In California, a local taxi service transports parties, by arrangement, from roadhead to roadhead at the eastern base of the Sierra; a similar service connects the rims of the Grand Canyon (see the Resources appendix).

FIFTH STEP: DO ANY PAPERWORK

If you are going into a national park, into a designated wilderness zone in a national forest, or into certain state parks, you may need a wilderness permit. In the simplest case, you can do the paperwork at a self-service station at the trailhead, but ordinarily more human contact is required. This may mean a stop at a local ranger's office—no problem, if the office is fairly close to your trailhead and if you arrive at the proper time of day. In some cases you can secure your permit in advance, by mail; this is convenient and, if you plan to visit a popular area at a popular time, highly advisable. For some destinations, *all* available slots are now offered in advance. The confirmation you receive may or may not be the permit itself: you may still need to stop at an agency office near the trailhead to pick up the actual piece of paper. If your route goes through two jurisdictions—a national park and a national forest, for instance—a permit secured for the first area will do for both. In a few areas or parts of areas, permits (locally available) are required for day hiking as well as backpacking.

Wilderness permits are traditionally free, but this appears to be changing; any charge you encounter will be small. There may also be a fee for driving into a national park or other specially designated area.

Why permits? Their first purpose is simply to gather information. As wilderness use increases and impact problems grow, managers have a clear need to know more about hikers, their preferences, and their habits of travel. At certain trailheads, permits are further used to limit use: only a given number of people or parties are allowed to enter each day. You want to work the system to make sure you're among them.

When you get your permit in some national parks, you are required to list the general areas in which you plan to camp. A few parks insist that you reserve a specific camping *spot* for each night, but the trend seems to be to dispense with this extra, indeed chilling, bit of regulation.

Want to avoid the whole business? Go to less popular areas, or go off-season. The publicity about wilderness permits gives you the impression that restrictions are everywhere, but they're not. Permits are required in only a minority of wilderness areas, and they are used to ration use in even fewer.

One final note: even in areas that do not now require wilderness permits, you may be asked to produce a *fire permit*. These permits, available at agency offices, are commonly required not only for open fires but also for the use of stoves. And in some areas you may have to carry *both* a fire permit and a wilderness permit. A bit much, but those are the rules.

WHAT ABOUT YOUR DOG?

To begin with the formalities: some backcountry areas (in state and national parks, for starters) do not allow dogs at all. Some forbid them at certain places and times (as at deer fawning season or in bighorn sheep habitat). Some allow them on leash. Some merely require that they be under close control.

Behind the rules lies a big argument. Are dogs an undue impact on the wilderness? Certainly they can be. There are horror stories of dogs that bark incessantly, chase wild animals, get in trouble with bears, and even occasionally bite hikers. On the other hand, a dog's natural protectiveness can be reassuring, especially to a solo female backpacker or in a group with children; and the obvious joy the animals show on the trail can only add to our own.

What strikes me in this debate is that the pro- and antidog people are talking about different critters. A dog that is *very* well trained and supervised can be a blameless member of your party; a dog that is merely a pet on the loose can be a disaster.

If you want to take your dog, regulations permitting, do. But also take on the responsibility this entails. Make sure the animal is trained and also reasonably fit. Give it a load to use up some of its energy (there are many canine packs available). Keep it leashed when other people are near, otherwise under close voice control. Bury its feces as you do your own. Prevent more than minimal barking. On the trail, step aside for oncoming, dogless hikers. Don't let the animal beg food, especially from other parties. Prevent it absolutely from chasing animals. If you and the dog can't manage all these things—you'd better leave the animal home.

Two further cautions. Dogs should not be taken into wild areas where there are wolves or grizzly bears. In the first case, it's for the wolves' sake: dogs carry a parovirus that is deadly to their wild relatives. In the second case, it's for the sake of dog and owner. Though a specially trained dog can be an asset in dealing with a grizzly bear attack, the typical dog is more likely to provoke than to deter the bear.

PLANNING FOOD AND FUEL

Like many things in backpacking, the matter of food and cooking can appear more complicated than it is. Elaborate, time-consuming planning is not ordinarily required, and you can stock up for any trip of normal length at the local supermarket, with help, if you like, from a specialty store or two. Freeze-dried foods are convenient and, for long trips, essential, but they are pretty expensive. Most of the time you can do fine without them.

NUTRITION

The first thing you require of backpacking food is that there be enough of it. That means, simply, calories to keep your body running under fairly heavy work.

Even when you are getting very little exercise, your body burns about 15 calories a day per pound of body weight. On the trail, that can just about double—6 or 7 hours of hiking under a full load will do it. A 100-pound woman, authorities estimate, needs to budget 3,800 calories for a moderately strenuous hiking day; a 200-pound man, 5,600 calories. That's quite a bit of fodder.

Few people bother to compute these things precisely. It's useful to bear in mind, though, that pure sugars and starches provide about 100 calories to the ounce in dry form. Proteins are about the same, and pure fats run 250 calories to the ounce. Most foods are mixtures of these elements and fall somewhere in between. Surprisingly enough, most breads and crackers, and candies made mainly of sugar, provide relatively little energy—no more, per ounce, than dehydrated fruits and vegetables. Fattier foods like chocolate, nuts, bacon, and dried eggs cluster near 150 calories per ounce. Margarine and oils are over 200. (If you care to know more, the U.S. Department of Agriculture publishes *Composition of Foods,* a book giving calories and nutritional values for just about every imaginable substance: see the Resources appendix.)

What proportions of carbohydrates, proteins, and fats should you aim for? According to the (not universal) consensus, backpackers should get 60 to 70 percent of their calories from carbohydrates, 20 to 25 percent from fat, and the remaining 10 to 15 percent from protein. The carbohydrates are basic running fuel; they don't stick with you, but they keep the muscles working. Fats are energy in concentrated form and burn more slowly. In winter, and on sustained, difficult trips, backpackers carry more fatty foods. Proteins deliver about the same energy value as carbohydrates, only more gradually. They are somewhat harder to digest, which may sometimes be an advantage: the work of digestion can help you keep warm when you are *not* exercising.

The necessary calorie total, and the recommended proportion of carbohydrates, proteins, and fats, will take a little scheming to achieve. The typical backpacker is probably carrying rather too little food, and rather too large a fraction of it is in fat.

So how much food, in pounds, do you need to carry? You can probably reach your calorie target with 2 pounds a day of typical lightweight foods. Children and light eaters may be happy with less than that; in winter, everyone needs a little more. If you rely heavily on freeze-dried foods, 1½ pounds per person per day is an achievable daily ration.

Monitoring my own consumption, I find that I consume about 12 ounces of compact foods per day for breakfast and lunch combined, of which 3 ounces are breads or crackers, 6 ounces other carbohydrates like fruit, and 3 ounces protein and fat. That's less than I used to pack and less, it would seem, than the guidelines; but it works for me. It leaves about 12 ounces in the daily ration (pre-rehydration) for my share of dinner.

What about the finer points of nutrition: vitamins, minerals, balanced proteins, and such? By and large, on the trail, you can set such questions aside. Important though a finely tuned diet is over months and years, it matters little over the length of any ordinary wilderness excursion.

There are nonetheless a few special matters to consider.

First, many people find that they function better in the mountains if their wilderness diet is not too different from what they eat at home. Sudden changes can upset the system and lead to diarrhea or, more commonly, to constipation. Foods with roughage are valuable in the trail diet. Some people carry laxatives as well.

Second is the matter of food allergies and other negative reactions to specific foods. Some people must watch their sodium intake—if you are one of these, read labels carefully, and consult your physician about your wilderness diet. If you're one of the people who have unpleasant reactions to monosodium glutamate, you'll be relieved to know that it's rarely found in freeze-dried food today.

Third, women who take long wilderness trips during their reproductive years may benefit from taking iron.

PLANNING FOOD: THE PROCESS

Who plans the meals? Only on large trips, like those sponsored by organizations, are you likely to find a central commissary. In a party of more than three or four members, it's customary to split into smaller cooking groups, each of which works out its own menu and carries its own stove.

Dinner, if hot, almost has to be a group project. The other meals are often handled individually. Each packs his or her own breakfasts and lunches, plus a dinner for the entire group on one or several nights. For example, if four hikers are going out for four days, each can bring one dinner to feed four, plus four personal breakfasts and lunches. If you do it this way, you may want to make sure that you don't wind up eating noodles and chicken every night; aside from that, little consultation is required.

Whether you're planning for one or for ten, the first step is to work out a *menu*. Some people think they skip this step, but in truth they don't; they write the menu in their heads even as they push a cart down supermarket aisles. Most of us have to be a little more methodical, at least at the beginning. You may find it useful to check books on backpack cookery—there are many good ones—for recipes and sample menus. Soon your own preferences and your own experience will take over.

Given a menu, you can proceed to figure the quantities of groceries you need. When in doubt, it's perhaps better to make the main, cooked courses a little scant and fill out with finger food. A big glob of uneaten stew creates a real disposal problem in the wilderness: in fact, somebody is going to have to pack it out (see Chapter 18).

PLANNING FOOD: THE WILDERNESS MEALS

At *breakfast*, some people like to fire up a stove and enjoy a full-scale meal with cooked cereal and bacon and eggs or pancakes. Others limit themselves to just-add-water foods, such as instant cereals, drinks, and concoctions like Instant Breakfast. Still others prefer cold foods like granola, crackers, cheese, and sausage. There is absolutely nothing wrong with cold cuts, at breakfast or at any other meal, but to some people they just don't seem like food. Coffee or tea is pretty standard; pick your form.

Lunch, on the trail, is not an event but an occupation. Some parties never do declare a particular refueling stop to be the midday meal, but others like to schedule a longer break for some dedicated eating. Some even fire up stoves for hot drinks, soup, or whatever. On an exceedingly strenuous trip you may need such a lunch stop just to make sure you are taking in the necessary fuel. Common lunch foods are breads and crackers with or without spreads (not dairy butter—it doesn't keep); dried fruit; nuts; candy; modest amounts of sausages and cheeses; and, of course, cold drinks made from powdered mixes. Note that firm-textured cheese, despite what it says on the label, lasts perfectly well in a warm pack. Flour tortillas also travel well.

The classic trailmix—"good old raisin and peanuts"—usually has at least one additional ingredient, M&M candies. Many, many other mixes are around, some of which you can find in supermarket bins. All in all, lunch should contribute about 40 percent of the day's calories.

At higher elevations—say above 8,000 feet—many hikers find it best to avoid nuts, meats, and cheeses during the day. They find these fats and proteins hard to digest without a long rest after eating and don't want to risk exaggerating any queasiness brought on by unaccustomed altitude.

Dinner is almost always hot and is the largest meal. Commonly it begins with soup, goes on through a solid, one-pot main course, and ends with hot drinks, or dessert, or both. The main course usually follows the "macaroni and cheese" model: it consists of something starchy—pasta, rice, instant potatoes, bulgur wheat, couscous, quinoa—and something rich in protein—cheese, meat, beans. Other ingredients add flavor. You'll often see vegetable stew with beef, instant rice with meat or fish or cheese, and such prefabricated main courses as beef stroganoff and chicken tetrazzini. Side dishes add calories. Puddings are a convenient and popular dessert.

Ordinary dried beans will serve quite well on the trail; soaked a night and a day in an extra canteen, they'll cook up quickly when you want them. Dehydrated vegetables can be reconstituted the same way.

If you're going above 10,000 feet, don't rely on spaghetti and such; because the boiling point is lower up there, pastas, especially thick ones, don't cook well. Quick-cooking freeze-dried versions avoid the problem, and so do other carbohydrate bases, like instant couscous or mashed potatoes.

Food attracts bears. If you are going to grizzly bear territory, freeze-dried foods, which have less odor, are preferred. Don't take cheese, fish, bacon, and sausage—all backpacking favorites—or anything you have to fry. Even where the only bear is the less dangerous black, be aware that smelly foods can increase your problems. See Chapter 29.

BUYING FOOD

In general, you must buy food in forms that are *light in weight, small in volume,* and *nonperishable.* Cans, as a rule, are out (except for certain compact and popular foods like sardines). You also need dishes that are *easy to cook*—unless, of course, you pride yourself on camp stove miracles.

You have several types of stores to work from. Sporting goods stores stock mainly freeze-dried dishes and ingredients. Health and organic food stores carry some useful staples that you may not find elsewhere (powdered hummus, for example). Asian and other specialty markets can add some zestful components. But the supermarket, in truth, can give you most or all of what you need. There is no reason in the world to pay premium prices for such products as macaroni, cereals, dried milk, instant rice, or crackers.

If you use freeze-dried foods, be prepared to pay $6 to $8 for a main course for two, about half that per dish for side dishes, desserts, and breakfast foods. The most expensive procedure is to buy all dinners and breakfasts in this form. More selectively, you can choose freeze-dried main courses for your dinners, and round them out with cheaper foods. Another course is to buy concentrated bulk ingredients, like dried eggs, dried peas, and meat bars, to use in your own recipes. (Some gear stores carry these, but you may have to order by mail.)

One caution about freeze-dried foods. The instructions usually urge to prepare them in the package, simply by adding boiling water, stirring, and waiting a specified time. In my experience, though, these mixes do not get properly moist, soft, or even warm without a minute or two of simmering in a pot—even at low altitudes, never mind high.

Whether you are buying at the supermarket or in the gear store, be wary of the printed claim that such-and-such a packaged dish serves three, four, or six. With luck, a "serves four" carton from the local market will serve two on the trail. Gear store meals are more generous. The labels on freeze-dried dishes state what the reconstituted weight will be: "two 12-oz. servings," for example; and of course the weight and volume of the finished dish are essentially the weight and volume of the water you add. Twelve ounces is actually quite a lot of food, and two solid 8-ounce cupfuls, whether of one dish or several, will satisfy most appetites at dinner.

Despite the general need for economy of weight and volume, fresh foods do get taken on short trips, or for the first day or two on longer ones. Firm salad vegetables will travel well for a while; romaine is about the most durable of the lettuces. Apples will last if you can keep them from bruising, and you'll never taste anything so good as a great juicy orange, produced with a smirk on day five or six and shared around. Or not.

At the other extreme from the highly processed foods, many people concoct their own foods to eat on the trail. People bake journey-cakes and nutritional fudges; dry their own fruits and vegetables; jerk their own beef, chicken, turkey, and fish. A proper drier, which combines a small heater and a fan, costs about $70.

How much should food cost per person per day? This can vary hugely. For its outings, the Sierra Club plans $7 to $8 a day in most parts of the United States (more in Hawaii, where groceries run high). Buying for yourself or a small group, you may pay more, but $10 a day should cover it, even with considerable use of freeze-dried items.

TWO TO AVOID

There are a couple of forms of backpacking food that I regard more as expensive gimmicks than practical nutrition.

The first is the concentrated "energy bar," packed with all sorts of good stuff and costing between $1.00 and $1.50. There is nothing particularly bad about these—they deliver the nutrients they promise—but they are less than pleasant to eat, ranging from marginally edible to utterly out of the question. If they filled a genuine requirement, you might choke them down, but the point is that they don't. If you are eating properly in general, you simply don't need them. Have a handful of banana chips or some fig bars for a pickup instead.

The second gimmick, just as heavily hyped, is the electrolyte drink mix. Electrolytes are the trace elements lost in sweat. One of these is sodium chloride—ordinary table salt—but there are others, including, notably, potassium. Since these chemicals are vital to the body, you must restore what has been sweated away. Electrolyte drink mixes offer to do that.

Again, however, we are solving a largely nonexistent problem. Unless you're working very hard in hot conditions, electrolyte replacement need not be instantaneous; it can come from the general diet. And backpack foods are rich in these substances. Many foods are salty, and meats, dried bananas and apricots, raisins, nuts, and eggs are all good sources for the other electrolytes.

What *is* vital is that you take in enough water during the course of the day, and here the electrolyte drinks show their main disadvantage: they don't taste that good. A study comparing electrolyte drinks with ordinary water and flavored mixes (like lemonade) found that the sugary fruit drinks were the most helpful, simply because hikers drank them more readily.

While we're on the subject of gimmicks, you occasionally see wine and beer in dehydrated form. By all reports, they are awful.

PACKING FOOD

There are several schemes for packing food and the ingredients of meals. One traditional method is quite elaborate: each individual meal is pre-measured, prearranged, and packed in its individual, labeled plastic bag. Everything you need for that particular job of cooking will be there. Such packing can take a good deal of time at home, especially if meals are cooked from many bulk ingredients. It does save time on the trail, assures that you won't run out of food on the last day, and allows you to leave the menu at home.

A simpler method is to pack all the ingredients that will be used in dinners, throughout the trip, together in one large plastic bag (or several, to share the load). Needed directions, of course, go in the same bag, perhaps with a menu. Similarly, you can pack your lunch and breakfast foods in large bags of their own. Each morning before leaving camp, you extract the day's lunch and stow it where you can easily reach it.

Or again, you can sort foods simply by day: a bag for Monday, a bag for Tuesday.

However you arrange things, you will have to do considerable weighing and repackaging. (It's nice to have two scales on hand: a postage scale for small amounts, a diet scale for larger quantities.) Get rid of cardboard containers (but not the directions printed on them) and other excess wrapping. Crackers, however, travel better in the original packages. Purists may want to get rid of foil wrappers at this point, but I don't go that far: just make a resolution not to litter with these and not to toss them into fire (they won't burn).

Most foods can be stored in stout zipper-lock polyethylene bags, the kind found in any supermarket. Powders and greasy things should be double-bagged. Cheese, which sweats, can be wrapped in butcher paper or cheesecloth, or dipped in paraffin, and then double-bagged or wrapped in aluminum foil. Still larger, thicker plastic bags, sold in gear stores, are good for keeping related items together. Heavier bags will last many uses, so wash and reuse them as often as you can. Carry plenty of extra zip-lock bags in several sizes.

Fruits and vegetables, on the other hand, last much better in paper bags than in plastic. There are also now high-tech bags that are chemically treated to retard ripening and spoilage; using these, you can carry fresh items for up to a week. But you'll pay $3 to $6 per bag, depending on size, for the privilege.

You can also make some use of rigid plastic boxes and bottles; a few compact foods—meats and fish—are carried in their original cans. Butter and oils can't be bagged; they seem to dissolve their way through the seal. Cylindrical potato chip cans and well-cleaned milk cartons have their uses. Especially fragile items can be put in pots.

Figure out your plan for protecting food from bears and other animals. What will you use for a bearbag? If you haven't bearbagged recently, practice the skill at home (see Chapter 18). If you will be using a solid-walled bear canister, make sure your groceries will fit in it.

You don't want to cut your food supply too fine. Throw in an extra dinner, or at least some extra finger food, for a possible added day. Some people like to carry a packet of concentrated energy food for an emergency; it can be largely candy, pemmican, jerky—anything that will keep a long time. Wrap it tightly in a couple of plastic bags (you might seal them shut with a hot iron), stick it in the bottom of your pack, and forget it. Once a year go ahead and eat such items as pemmican and dried meats, and replace them; they don't last forever.

PLANNING FUEL

How much fuel do you need to cook the meals you have outlined?

That depends on your stove (some are thirstier than others) and on your cooking habits. A standard if economical allowance for liquid fuel is ¼ cup per person per day. That's with quick-cooking dinners and minimal use at breakfast—say 30 minutes of daily running time. More extensive cooking ups the quota considerably. On a first trip, I'd recommended taking ½ cup per person per day and seeing how much you come back with. You do want to come back with a little—the reserve idea again. One person alone uses more than 50 percent of what a pair would use. On snow, where water must be melted, fuel needs approximately double.

What about cartridge stoves? Again, consumption rates vary. With most models, 1 ounce of butane/propane mix runs the stove for 20 to 30 minutes. A typical large cartridge contains just under 7 ounces of gas. One such unit is adequate for two people for three days. If you use smaller cartridges or a lustier stove, adjust accordingly. Some older stoves use nondetachable cartridges: once the seal has been pierced, they stay put until empty. If you've mounted one of these and it isn't brand new, bring a spare. You may also want to bring a duplicate if you're taking a cartridge stove into cold conditions: assuming the units are detachable, you can help the stove function by occasionally swapping a warm cartridge for a chilled-off one.

As noted, you can keep fuel needs low by choosing foods that need minimal simmering. For some other fuel conservation tricks, see Chapter 18.

WATER

On most trips, water is taken for granted; there's no need to plan for it if it's plentiful along the way. But sometimes it is not so easily found. When a supply must be carried, it's important not to underestimate how much you need.

Even a person who isn't exercising needs 2 quarts of water a day, most of it in liquids, some of it in solid food. A hard-working hiker loses much larger amounts in sweat and breath. On a strenuous trip you require *a full gallon a day* or even more. That's more than you may find yourself prompted to drink by thirst alone. Though straight water is the very best thing to hydrate with, flavored mixes, hot chocolate, and such have the advantage of keeping you interested.

Most wilderness travelers today boil, filter, or chemically purify all water from natural sources. For the reasons and the options, see Chapter 20.

13 PACKING AND PREPARATIONS

You've got your gear. It's lying in great disorganized piles all over the living room.

You've got your trip. You're leaving tomorrow morning.

How do you get all that junk into your pack without utter confusion? How will you know where things are when you need them? How can you make sure of leaving nothing essential behind, and of taking not an ounce more than you need to take?

These are problems (if "problems" they can be called) that every backpacker must deal with. Every backpacker finds personal solutions, personal organizations, personal shortcuts and odd arrangements. What follows here is a set and rather fussy procedure to make use of, if you care to, the first few times you put a packload together.

FIRST STEP: MAKE A LIST

If you are more than usually efficient, you may in time be able to pack a good pack without a list, but don't skip this step at the start. When you make your first list of objects to be taken, divide it by category. List all items connected with food and cooking in one section, all items connected with shelter and bed in another, and so on. Think carefully about the places you are going. In such a month in such a spot, do you reasonably need to take a venom extractor? High-powered sunscreen? A spare pair of dark glasses? Clothing of cotton, or of synthetics and wool? Imagine the situations you may be facing. As a starting point, you may find it useful to consult the accompanying skeleton list.

Who hasn't heard the slogan "When in doubt, leave it out"? It's a good one, but it needs qualification. It applies properly to luxuries only. For other items—possible necessities and emergency items you may never need at all but could want desperately—the rule had better be "When in doubt, leave it in." If you aren't sure just when you'll finish the trip, take food for the longest possible period. If you aren't sure how cold it will be, put in the extra sweater.

When you're done packing, don't throw your new list away. File it. Later, as you walk the trails, you will be making notes—mental or written, conscious or unconscious—as you go along: "Flashlight should be in outer pocket . . ." "Didn't need down jacket this trip . . ." "Could have used a larger pot . . . ," and so forth. Remember which items you had but didn't need, and which you needed but didn't have. Then, when you get home, you can correct and rearrange your original list to make it a better guide next time you head into similar country at a similar time of year.

SECOND STEP: ASSEMBLE AND CHECK THE GEAR

Here's one way. Get a big cardboard box. Locate the items on your list one by one, place them loose in the box, and check them off the list. Examine each item as you go for needed maintenance. Fire up your stove. Run a quart through your water filter. Replace batteries as needed. (This is the point at which you find that none of your flashlights is working.) Actually, the better time to check your gear for major problems is immediately on your return from each trip, or at least while there's plenty of time to do whatever needs to be done. If you have any brand-new gear, be sure to get familiar with it now!

Especially if you are heading for grizzly country, old gear, including tent and pack, should be cleaned, and cooking gear rewashed.

THIRD STEP: COMBINE THE OBJECTS IN GROUPS

A typical pack may contain as many as 150 items, many of them small and losable. If you just dump them in, your confusion will be hopeless. Instead, handle them in groups. Keep all the kitchen items together, the medical kit together, the repair tools in their own small bag. Or forget superficial logic and work out convenient groupings of your own. Build a pattern that enables you to find what you need when you need it. In any case, avoid leaving tiny objects loose.

A typical frame pack, with its upper and lower compartments, suggests an organization. Almost everyone seems to use the lower level for clothing, for instance. In a pack with fewer built-in divisions, as in many internal-frame backpacks, hikers rely more heavily on cloth stuffbags to organize their gear. If you use these bags, you'll find yourself leaving much

Skeleton Pack List

This is meant as a starting point for a precise packing list of your own. Ask yourself: Do I need . . . ? and then: Do I have . . . ?

BED AND SHELTER

sleeping bag
foam pad or mattress
groundcloth
weather shelter (poncho; bivouac
   sack; tarp; rainfly; full tent)

KITCHEN

stove; cookware
method of handling pots
spare fuel as needed
any needed stove accessories
priming items (eyedropper?
   special fuel?)
matches, firestarters
personal eating tools
provision for dishwashing
bear protection

TOOLS

maps
compass
knife
cord
notebook/pencils
repair kit
flashlight or headlamp
spare batteries and bulb

CLOTHING

boots and socks
spare socks and underwear as
   desired
clothing for cold and wind; rain
   and snow
hat
glasses or goggles
bandannas

EMERGENCY

signals (whistle, mirror, bright
   cloth)
emergency shelter provision
matches/firestarters
medical kit; snakebite kit

PERSONAL

toothbrush, etc.
toilet paper
bug dope
sunscreen
other as needed

HAULAGE

stuffbags
plastic bags and closures
water containers
daypack (where appropriate)

of your gear parked in them between trips; this shortcut can make the final packing fairly quick and easy.

What about shared gear? In a group, items like tent and cookware must be allocated among the packs. If the hiking party is all from one household, this is easy. When people are converging, perhaps from far-flung places, the process is a shade more complex. The ideal is to meet beforehand, but it is more common to divvy up the community load at the last minute, on the road or at the trailhead. Each party member must be sure to bring the objects he or she is responsible for, and to leave space in the pack for a reasonable share of the combined community load.

FOURTH STEP: PACK IT IN

Now you start the pleasant task of loading the pack, the big cloth cupboard from which, in the next few days, everything you need for life must come. Especially if you haven't done it before, expect to load and unload several times before it seems just right. As you go, keep certain things in mind.

CONSIDER THE DISTRIBUTION OF WEIGHT

Stuffbags and other load components should be arranged to put as much weight as possible close to your back. Think of yourself as building a mortarless wall against the inner surface of the pack; if there's space outboard from that to be filled, use it for clothing or other light things. If there are load-compression straps, loosen them before you start and tighten them firmly when you are done.

The load must also be evenly divided between the *sides* of the pack. You don't, for instance, want 2 quarts of water and fuel in one side pocket and nothing but a sweater in the opposite one.

It used to be conventional wisdom that a trail hiker should carry a top-heavy pack, with weighty objects packed high and close to the back. With modern load-carrying systems, however, this advice has been challenged. Some treadmill tests with variously loaded packs have shown no significant difference in ease of carrying. Try different arrangements and see what you think. Many women, notably, seem to prefer a somewhat lower center of gravity in the load.

One thing remains clear: top-heaviness is definitely to be avoided when you are packing for cross-country hiking, for scrambling, or for travel over snow—especially if you are using an external-frame pack. Too high a load will move around disconcertingly on your back.

CONSIDER THE ORDER IN WHICH YOU WILL WANT TO GET AT THINGS

Try to cut down on the number of times each day you will have to burrow deep into your pack. Thus, there needs to be an accessible slot for the food you will eat for lunch each day. A water bottle should be ready to hand. Camera and accessories, if you carry such, should certainly not be buried, and neither should your medical kit. Likewise sunglasses, sunscreen, hat, bandanna, bug dope, sunscreen, map and compass, toilet paper and trowel, and whatever else you are likely to want as you go. This will never work out perfectly, and on a leisurely trip it doesn't matter, but it's nice not to be rummaging all the time. Accessibility varies, of course, with packbag design. In the least reachable regions (which vary by packbag design) you store the things you will not need till evening, like tent, dinner food, and possibly your stove (but see below).

CONSIDER SPECIAL PROBLEMS

Some objects shouldn't be packed together. Fuel and water should, when possible, be packed outside rather than in the main compartments of a pack (and of course right side up). Gasoline and food should never be together. Then there are a few fragile or aggressive items. Some stoves, for instance, won't take much mashing. Sharp objects like tent poles shouldn't be so packed that they could poke holes in a jacket, a food bag, or in the pack itself. A self-inflating sleeping pad needs to be in a good, tough stuffsack; if carried outside the pack, it shouldn't be on the bottom.

If you finish the trial packing job and find you have objects left over, or that the load is lopsided, or that things you want accessible are not, unload the stuff and try, try again. Often at this stage you change your mind about what is essential and what a luxury.

Make sure you know how you will manage objects that will only occasionally be carried on your back, like skis or snowshoes for winter travel. If there is likelihood of rain, consider how you will protect pack and contents. If you have a number of items strapped onto the outside of your pack, will your packcover or poncho fit over them? If not, how will you attach them outside the waterproof cover? It's easier to plan such things ahead of time than with water running down your neck.

In notoriously rainy areas, you will need more than one water-resistant layer to shield your pack. One veteran offers a fail-safe system for New England weather: he puts a plastic garbage bag inside his pack, places clothing in smaller plastic bags, and carries a coated packcover to go over the whole assembly. If the pack itself is of water-resistant cloth, it's a four-layer defense!

When your pack isn't quite large enough for the load, you can make more hauling room by adding a frame extension or additional tie-on patches, as discussed in Chapter 6. Shock cords and straps with buckles are always likely to be useful and can be tightened better than simple cord. Some people fasten things with carabiners, those heavy safety-pin-like links that climbers use; tiny versions, intended as packing aids only, can be had. Large, sturdy diaper pins will also serve. Additional carriers, like a beltbag, canteen, or camera pack, may prove their usefulness here.

Unless you live just miles from the trailhead, the last packing job you do at home is still in the nature of a draft. Even if perfect, it won't stay that way. You may have to dig things out of your pack while on the road; you may have to add in some community gear at the end of it. If the basic fit is right, don't worry about a little sloppiness: the time for last-minute adjustments is still to come. And, no, you won't be the only one who has to make some.

What about boots and clothing you will put on at the roadhead? If there's a lengthy road trip intervening, it is convenient to put these items in a duffel bag alongside your pack, together with any items you'll want in transit. A generous daypack may also serve as road duffel. It's especially nice to have your stuff compact and self-contained if you're going to be a passenger in someone else's car.

If you are traveling by air, you'll have to rearrange your gear for protection, not convenience. Anything rigid or breakable should go in the middle of the pack, with lots of softer things surrounding it. Shorten up the shoulder straps and sternum strap. Wrap the hipbelt around the base of the pack (the opposite of the wearing position) and secure it with added straps or by passing it through any handy exterior tie-on loops. Make sure that every tag end is cinched, buried, or fed back through a buckle. Bind zipper sliders in place with wire ties. For even more protection, you can wrap the pack in several thick garbage bags and secure it thoroughly with duct tape. (Carry more garbage bags and tape for the flight home.) Better yet, wrap your sleeping pad around the pack and put the whole thing in a hefty duffel bag.

Be aware that you cannot transport stove fuel by air: it will have to be purchased at the other end. Same goes for matches, butane lighters, and signal flares. Some airlines will not even accept camp stoves without fuel, and, if these are shipped, will destroy them.

OTHER LAST-MINUTE PREPARATIONS

In the hours and days before your trip, it's not a bad idea to drink more water than usual. Hydration is important, and you don't want to start out "down a quart." As a rule, fill your water bottles at home. A 2-to-5-gallon water can is a handy thing to have in a roadhead car.

If your toenails are not already trimmed short, trim them now. The last time you shower and wash your hair before you leave, forget conditioner and any skin lotions or antiperspirants. Such additives cause you to get grimier faster, and may even attract mosquitoes—or, more seriously, bears.

If you haven't already done so, this is the time to leave an informative note for a family member or friend, explaining your plans in some detail and indicating when you expect to be out of the woods or the hills. Include the license number and description of each automobile; names, addresses, and phone numbers of other people in your party; and the phone number of the local office of the land management agency whose jurisdiction you will be visiting.

What about that date of return? Most hikers, in telling their friends when they plan to return, ask that the alarm not be sounded unless they are *well* overdue, say 24 or 48 hours. They hate the feeling that people will begin worrying immediately if they switch to a longer route or take an extra day at an irresistible campsite. (Yes, a cell phone would be tempting.) However, if you give yourself this margin, be sure to pack food and fuel for the extra time.

TRAVEL ON THE TRAIL

Followers of trails and of seasons, breakers of camp in the little dawn wind, seekers of watercourses over the wrinkled rind of the world, o seekers, o finders of reasons to be up and be gone . . .

Saint-John Perse, *Anabasis*

14 TO THE TRAILHEAD

A sizable part of every backpacking trip is spent, not on the trail at all, but on the road. And while getting to the trailhead is by no means half the fun, the drive to the edge of wilderness is certainly a pleasure in itself. On the road you are in between, anticipating, imagining, watching the land unfold around you. The work is done, the decisions made. You're both excited and relaxed. You're on your way.

I have said already: "the *drive* to the wilderness." As noted in the previous chapter, you might be getting there by some other means. But when trailheads lie, as they often do, on remote and rugged roads, the end of your trip, at least, is going to involve a car.

Lost keys can produce major hassles. One ruefully experienced hiker suggests making extra copies and giving one to each member of your party; if you're driving a rental car, invest in at least one key copy. Have a credit card along, or enough cash to get home on if a car breakdown or change of plans requires you to do so (if, for example, your ride decides to leave the trip early).

TOUCHING BASE IN THE REGION

Unless you have completed the paperwork by mail (see Chapter 11), you will probably have to stop at a local land agency office for a fire permit, a wilderness permit, or both. (Requirements vary and cannot be readily summarized.) In a few well-trafficked areas you may find registration booths near the trailhead; more typically the responsible office is some miles away. Wilderness permits can sometimes be picked up after-hours at self-registration stations; fire permits, as a rule, cannot. Find these things out in advance!

Permits aside, it's an excellent idea to stop at a ranger station to ask some last-minute questions, or to double-check information received earlier. Are key roads in good condition? Have there been recent problems with trailhead crime (see below)? What is the latest local weather forecast? How high are the creeks running? What about snow on the passes? What's the risk of flash-flooding in a desert canyon you plan to travel? How are the bears behaving? (You may be advised to rent a bearproof canister, or even offered a free loaner). If there's been a problem bear in a certain area, you may have to make a last-minute change of plans. The less you learned beforehand by phone or correspondence, the greater the need to talk now to the local managers. There's a safety aspect, too: if a permit isn't required, it's a good idea to leave word of your projected route and schedule.

Most people have a last restaurant meal before they head in on a multiday wilderness trip. It's nice to do this in the town nearest the trailhead, and to let drop casually that you're in town because of the wilderness next door: a subtle message about its economic value. A decent tip never hurts. Repeat a few days later when you have the inevitable enormous "exit meal."

If you're in a very small town not geared up for tourism, be friendly to and respectful of local folk. Don't crowd them out at stores or eating places. If you need to park, hike, or camp on private property, ask permission and offer payment. Make a point of buying some supplies locally.

Many wilderness roadheads lie at the end of long, rough roads, far from the nearest service station. You may have some trouble tracing the maze of branching routes to your destination. And dirt roads eat up gasoline. Don't head into the hills without a full tank of gas.

TRAILHEAD STRATEGY

This trailhead business is sometimes more complicated than it seems. At many trailheads, three possible concerns arise: first, impact and congestion; second, theft and vandalism; third, animal raiders.

Some trailheads are major parking lots, designed for the traffic they get. Others are wide places in the road. People sometimes insist on parking where there is no room, damaging roadside vegetation—and sometimes getting stuck in ditches and mud. If there isn't room at the actual trailhead, park elsewhere along the road. Another half-mile on foot won't hurt.

More troubling is the problem of roadhead crime. It is no longer unusual for things left in cars to be stolen. Again, one solution is to leave the car elsewhere than at the obvious trailhead. For best security, park at a ranger station or in a patrolled camping ares (if a small fee is charged, regard it as insurance). If you drive an expensive car or plan to leave expensive items in it, this precaution is thoroughly sensible.

Wherever you park, stash any valuable items in the trunk or securest area. Leave nothing visible. Empty the glove compartment and leave it open, unscrewing the little bulb so your battery won't drain. Wallets and such go with you on the trail. (Better to leave all but essential cards and cash at home). Carry the keys, and don't leave spares hidden around the locked car. If you arrive in the evening and sleep beside the car, don't neglect to lock it for the night. To discourage theft, some people like to remove distributor rotors or otherwise disable their vehicles. In certain areas, it is unwise to leave a car with bumper stickers or decals that suggest conservation sympathies. It is also recommended that you not chat too casually about your plans with people met at the roadhead: thieves have been known to masquerade as hikers. It's all a damned shame.

If you are headed for bear country, which is most of our wilderness, you want to leave the car interior as clean as possible. Try not to leave attractants in it, like extra food or even cleanup supplies; any you're stuck with go in the trunk or most secure area. If possible, park in the shade so odors won't develop. Then there are the porcupines, which have the odd habit of chewing on brakelines. This is such a problem in parts of Canada that people shield the undersides of their cars with chicken wire.

If freezing temperatures are likely, be sure to leave the parking brake off (a frozen brake immobilizes the car). Nor should you set the brake if you have recently driven through water; the problem here is rust. If necessary for safety, place chocks behind several wheels.

THE BEGINNING

It always seems as if you could just start walking. Seldom does it work out that way. Unless you have done more planning, conferring, and prepacking than most hikers find time for, you will need to do some last-minute rearrangement. Most important, you will probably have to redivide community gear—shelter, stove and pots, food, fuel—to everyone's satisfaction. (A family group, of course, will have had more chance to sort out such details at home.)

Changing from car clothes to trail clothes, and putting on your boots, is about the final stage. Many hikers apply moleskin to their feet at this point, before the stresses of the trail begin. Chug some water now, too.

Should you stretch before you hoist your pack? Probably not—stretching cold muscles is not a good idea. Rather, plan to ease into the day with

15 minutes of not-too-strenuous hiking. If stretching is part of a regular fitness routine for you, by all means work it in later. Otherwise, this is not a good time for innovations.

One more thing as you set out: if a trailhead register is provided, take a moment to sign in. Even though you may have filled out a wilderness permit already, or left word with the office, the register is still the final record of who you are and where you are going. It also helps the agency gauge traffic on its trails. It may be objected that signing in provides more information for trailhead criminals; on balance, though, it's still the thing to do.

15 LIFE ON YOUR OWN TWO FEET

When the last stray object is stuffed into the last bulging pack pocket, when the car is locked and the map refolded, when the boots are securely laced, comes an end—and a beginning. You've been a planner, a list checker, a filler-out of forms, a chauffeur. Now that's over with. Congratulations: you're just a backpacker, now.

WALKING WITH PACK

As one kind of weight comes off, of course, another kind comes on. By now you'll have put your pack on many times, but let's review some ways of getting the thing up there.

The natural but strenuous method is to grab the pack by the shoulder straps (or, perhaps, by an upper crossbar), haul it up the front of your body, swing it around to the back with your stronger hand, and wriggle your arms, first one, then the other, under the straps.

To reduce the strain, you can start in a crouch and hoist the pack first to a bent thigh, parking it there for a moment before completing the maneuver and straightening your lower body. Even better, you can create the transitional thigh platform by placing one foot on a low rock or log. It's a little hard to visualize, but try it and see.

Or you can park the pack on a convenient rock, fence, or tree limb, or have a friend hold it in position for you, and back into it.

Then there's the dramatic flop or inversion method. It requires a light, tight pack with no dangling accessories. You hold the pack in front of you, straps toward you, *upside down.* Then you lift it up, over your head, and down onto your back, sliding your arms under the straps as it descends.

In the worst case, when the pack is heavy and there's nothing in sight to rest it on, you may simply have to set it on the ground, sit down with your back against it, slither into the straps, and surge to your feet—strong leg muscles, and maybe the help of a stick, required.

Whatever method you use, don't lean over to pick up the pack, and don't stoop over to shorten yourself to the level of a low rock or other pack-supporting platform: bend your knees instead.

As you walk, you will occasionally want to adjust the way the pack rides on your back. You may wish to tighten the hipbelt, since some rigs tend to loosen, if only slightly; or perhaps to slacken the belt deliberately to take more of the load on your shoulders for a few minutes (just for variety). If you come to a section where you have to scramble over stones or plow through bushes, more weight on your shoulders will reduce the lurching of the load.

Don't overdo shoulder carrying, however. It can damage the brachial nerves and give you what's called "pack palsy" or "trekker's shoulder," a numbness of fingers, forearms, or even the whole arm. Though temporary in most cases, it's best avoided.

The first time you carry a pack in a given season—and almost any time you carry an excessively heavy load—your hips will get red and sore. Aside from the slight discomfort, this does no harm, and will happen less as time goes on. Some people, early in the season, will put moleskin on their hipbones as well as on their heels.

ALL ABOUT WALKING

Does anyone seriously need instruction in how to walk a trail? Probably not. Complicated though the art of backpacking sometimes seems, the *act* of backpacking—the moving along with a load—is almost too automatic to describe. Walking is what we're built for. There are, nonetheless, some points worth mentioning.

The most comfortable trail pace for most people is not fast—at least the legs are not pumping rapidly—but it is very steady. Some experts recommend striding out, taking the longest steps you can manage; others see more efficiency in a deliberately shortened stride. But your own legs will tell you how far they want to swing. Let your arms swing, too, in the natural way.

A hiker in good condition can go up a fairly steep and sustained hill without either gasping for breath or slowing down to a crawl, though the stride will shorten. Avoid pointing your toes outward, which may seem easier but actually increases the strain on the knees. Tilting your pelvis slightly forward will bring the large muscles of the buttocks into play.

Breathe deeply. For some reason, expelling the breath, with a little effort, through rounded lips gives you the sensation of getting more oxygen.

If the rise is severe, you may switch to the *rest step*. In the rest step, you simply pause briefly every time you begin a new stride, at that moment when the forward foot is planted but has not received any weight. Each leg thus gets a series of tiny rests. On a steep slope, heavily loaded packers may break stride in this manner for a second or more with each step.

Going downhill can be hard on the knees. Although it's natural to plant the foot heel first, with quite a jolt, it's gentler to descend almost flat-footed in what might be described as a fast creep. Keep your knees slightly bent, unless you are plunge-stepping down a soft surface like snow or volcanic ash.

Some hikers adjust the lacing of their boots depending on the slope they are facing. At the start of a climb, they loosen the lower or toe-end laces and tighten the upper laces to stabilize the heel, which tends to shift and chafe in uphill travel. On the downslope they loosen the heel and tighten the toe, which prevents the toes from stubbing themselves against leather. Only your experience will tell you whether you need to bother.

In order to keep such customized lacing from evening out, you have to build in a high-friction "brake." Some boots have special clamplike retainers in the middle of the pattern for this purpose. You can get the same effect by wrapping opposite laces around each other two or three times in

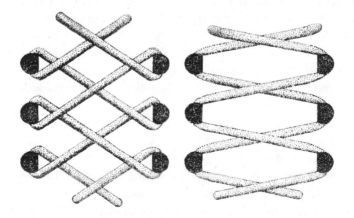

LOOP PATTERN (LEFT) VS. NORMAL LACING

a hitch. Where there are hooks, rather than eyelets, you can also reduce friction by running laces around the hooks in loops ("mountaineer's lace") rather than simple curves.

CARE AND FEEDING

You will need to adjust your clothing frequently. You may start out on a chilly morning with long pants, a heavy shirt, a stocking cap, even an insulated jacket, but be down to boots, socks, and hiking shorts by afternoon. You learn quickly that it makes sense to start cold; however chilly the air at breakfast, you'll warm up fast on the trail. If you start hiking in the clothes that are comfortable for puttering around camp, you will be hot and sweaty in a few hundred yards.

There are two competing principles here. One is: *keep comfortable.* The second is: *don't spend all your time fiddling with clothes.* With garments that you can adjust while you wear them, like shirts and sweaters with closures in front, you won't have to stop continually to add or subtract a layer.

But of course you can stop as often as you like. Unless you happen to want to make it one, this is not a marathon. There's always a picture to be taken, a snack to be eaten, or just something worth looking at. For hikers with a schedule, 10 minutes of rest an hour is a useful guideline.

Physiologically, several short breaks serve better than one long one. As your muscles work, they build up a waste called lactic acid. When you rest, you can get rid of about 30 percent of this waste in 5 to 7 minutes. But 15 more minutes of rest will eliminate only another 5 percent. Some people find long "flop-down" rests actually demoralizing: it can be hard to get started again, especially if tired legs have stiffened up. (But it's also true that a lunchtime nap can be marvelously refreshing.)

Whenever you do stop, don't block the trail; step well aside on an unvegetated surface. (A convenient natural pack table is nice, too.) In grizzly bear country, don't stop where there's bear sign or a food source (like ripe berries). In such regions, the resting group should arrange itself to look out in several directions. Don't spread food out too widely and don't shed crumbs. For more about bear safety, see Chapter 29.

Be sure to drink plenty of water as you go. Tank up in the morning, tank up in the evening, and sip incessantly during the day. Use plain water until that gets dull, then supplement with flavored drinks. You need, in fact, to drink more than thirst suggests. Many, many hikers become at least slightly dehydrated. A headache can be an indication of this problem, and in camp an insatiable "midnight thirst" proves that you've been shorting yourself on fluids. Muscle cramps may be one result, and dehydration can contribute to other, genuinely dangerous conditions (see Chapter 28). If you are getting enough water, your urine will be either clear or straw colored; darker urine means you must drink more.

Your intake of food is almost as continuous. Ninety minutes, the nutritionists say, is as long as a hiker should go without eating *something*. Some people subsist on snack food all day long. Some like to stop and eat, in addition, a distinct midday meal. It doesn't matter how you do it, but get the calories—mostly carbohydrates—in.

With nibbles of food in your mouth all day, you may wonder what's happening to your teeth. This is a sensible concern. It's not sugar and starch directly that do the damage, however, but rather bacteria in the mouth; the best defense is to brush and floss thoroughly in the morning, starting the day with teeth very clean. It also helps to slosh water around in your mouth after a snack. Tooth care in the evening is as necessary on the trail as at home.

HIKING WITH OTHERS

Almost inevitably, the members of a group will hike at different rates—some a little faster, some a little slower. A small difference in pace can produce quite a bit of separation. If this starts happening, talk about it. Spreading out may be quite all right, as long as the leaders wait at any trail junction, or it may not. It is miserable to be the one slower member of a group that is moving at racing speed: the only one who experiences as a struggle what should be pleasant exercise, who can't take the time to look around and enjoy. It's less of a trial for faster hikers to slow down or wait than for slower ones to puff and strain. Try to avoid the "Here you are, let's go" syndrome in which the stragglers, laboring up to the well-rested leaders, never get a proper rest themselves. It's important that fellow hikers be able to tell each other, calmly and at the appropriate moment, what they want and need.

If you do allow yourselves to spread out, make sure the people at the end of the line know what the plan is. For a person who simply follows, blind to the choices and landmarks of the route, getting separated can mean getting lost.

At the other extreme of things, don't follow the person in front of you too closely; unless you're in a long, slow line, leave 6 feet of elbowroom at least. If you want to pass, ask. If a companion wants to pass you, watch for a place where you can step off the trail onto a hard or barren surface, not onto vegetation.

If you meet another party coming the other direction on a slope, it seems natural for the downward-bound hikers to step aside: their momentum is less hard-won. A party with stock, however, always has the right of way. Pedestrians should step well off the trail on the uphill side and talk softly so the animals aren't startled to find someone there. Whenever a meeting is imminent, look for a spot where you can stand aside without compacting soft ground or crushing plants. Backpacking parties that meet on the trail or in camp tend to greet each other cordially, chat a moment, and then, as soon as politely possible, withdraw.

Be very careful about dislodging rocks along a steep trail. If you do, yell at the top of your lungs: *Rock!*

FIGHTING BLISTERS

The best way to deal with blisters is not to get them. Make sure your boots fit properly and that they are nicely broken in before you set out with them (Chapter 4). Do enough preliminary hiking to toughen your feet somewhat. If you aren't sure you're ready, or if you know you blister easily, you will want to cover the danger points with adhesive tape, moleskin, or the stretchable moleskin called Spyroflex before you leave the trailhead. Likely problem spots are the heel, the ball of the foot, the outside of the big toe, and the sides of the foot at the base of the toes. For best adhesion, wash and dry the spot first (a premoistened towelette is handy for this).

If you feel a zone of irritation forming as you walk—a "hot spot"—don't delay. Sit down, pull off the boot, and find out what's going on. Put on a protective layer; if you have one on already, make sure that it hasn't developed wrinkles (they can cause extra irritation) and reapply if needed. Check the boot lining, too: if there's a rough spot there, tape that. Make sure that your socks aren't wrinkled, holed, or more than slightly damp, and change them if needed. If boot fit seems loose, try adding another pair of socks. Relace your boots snugly. If the trouble spot is a heel, tighten the upper part of the lacing pattern, so that your heel is not rising too far inside the rear of the boot as you stride.

On a warm day, it's good to cool your feet in a stream at a rest stop—or at any rate to pull off boots and socks for a while. Don't soak your feet too long, though, as this can make them tender.

If you do get a blister, you aren't by any means crippled. Several treatments are popular. I prefer the simplest. First, wash the spot carefully with water and soap (or water and Betadine cleanser). Sterilize a needle by passing it through the blue part of a flame, and puncture the swollen area at one edge. Very gently press the fluid out. When the skin is dry, cover the blister with a thin sterile pad from your first-aid kit. (Some people apply antibiotic ointment.) Then put on a layer of moleskin or porous adhesive tape. If the blister fills again, repeat the draining after about 6 and about 12 hours, lifting just a corner of the tape to do so.

Another treatment commonly recommended is the "donut patch." In this procedure, you place a ring of moleskin or tape around the drained blister but not on it, leaving the blister itself exposed. (An unmedicated corn pad can also be used.) Then you add a second layer of tape or moleskin, this time covering the entire area. In theory, this arrangement takes pressure off the blister and prevents further irritation. On the other hand, it gives you something of a lump in your boot.

And some people swear by still a third procedure, "de-roofing": you trim the skin above the blister completely away, apply a dab of antibiotic ointment, and cover the raw patch with 2nd Skin, the burn dressing by Spenco. A layer of porous adhesive tape or stretch gauze goes on top.

A day's layover will help the healing process, but if this is difficult to arrange, it is not prohibitive to keep going. Walking a long distance with such a patch can be slightly uncomfortable, but it is by no means agonizing. Though blisters very seldom lead to any further trouble, it's important to watch the spot for signs of infection.

LOW IMPACT ON THE TRAIL

Everybody knows it but it bears repeating: if you're hiking a trail, *stay on it.* Cutting corners, taking shortcuts, walking outside the treadway—all these break down trail edges and cause erosion, gullying, and perhaps rockfall. If you're using a staff or trekking poles, plant tips inside, not outside, the trail tread, or on rocks.

Not all trails are well designed, and rather few are actually well maintained. Some are laid out so badly that it is hard to avoid doing damage. For example, a trail may push straight through boggy meadows or head directly up erosive slopes. In such places, people tend to move to one side or the other to avoid the mud or the rocky footing of an incipient gully. This is one of the main causes of *multiple trailing*, in which five or six parallel tracks scar open slopes and meadows. Such damage is not, strictly speaking, the hikers' fault—blame it rather on bad trail layout and poor maintenance—but you can best help by gritting your teeth and keeping to the original line. Always walk single file, not side by side, on a trail. (But in cross-country travel, where you wish to avoid establishing any visible track, the principle is precisely the opposite: you almost always walk abreast, each hiker on a separate course.)

Whether on a trail or on a cross-country route, you should restrain any impulse to build ducks (small rock cairns used as route markers) or otherwise to flag the path. Let the next travelers find their way as you did. Chances are they prefer it so. (However, there is one possible exception: the mapped, designated trail that is faint from lack of maintenance. Here you may be doing a service by building an occasional duck. It's wise to find out first whether such a trail is meant to be abandoned for some good reason—this is occasionally the case.) If a trail is intentionally blocked—if, for instance, a log has been carefully laid across it—respect the block.

Wildflowers, as a rule, shouldn't be picked or even touched. Although the amateur botanist can't be faulted for taking a sample, even this is technically forbidden in parks. If you don't know exactly what you're doing, don't transport plant materials from one area to another: you might be helping an exotic and damaging species to propagate.

PARTY SPLITTING AND SIDE TRIPS

There's no great harm in dividing your party—if you do it with some care, making sure that each splinter group has all the essential gear, and that everyone is clear about a place and time for coming back together. Note that in grizzly country there is safety in numbers—three or four are safer than two and much safer than one.

You may also want to vary a trip by taking side trips, even perhaps solo, with nothing but a daypack. If you take such an excursion, you must be certain to have some basic items with you. Always be prepared for an unexpected night away from your main camp (see below). As for your main pack, if nobody will be near it, protect it from animals by hanging it in a tree or over a rock face before you wander.

TWENTY ESSENTIALS

The classic list of "ten essentials," first formulated by the Mountaineers of Seattle, goes like this:

Map. At least the local topographic sheet.

Compass.

Flashlight or headlamp. Also spare bulb and probably spare batteries.

Extra food. Perhaps nothing more than a generous lunch; perhaps an emergency packet of high-energy food. It's true that a person can survive for days, even weeks, without food, and take no permanent harm, but in an emergency you need energy to work with and, still more important, to think with.

Extra clothing. This may be as little as a sweater or as much as a jacket, parka, and rainpants. Just as you do when you're packing the main pack at home, think of clothes to keep you *warm* and clothes to keep you *dry.*

Sunglasses. Advisable anywhere; doubly important above timberline, in the desert, and, most of all, on snow. Snow blindness is no joke.

First-aid kit.

Knife.

Matches. Waterproof/windproof matches are good for this purpose.

Firestarter.

Depending on local conditions, you will probably find yourself adding to the traditional ten. Here are some other items you may not want to be without:

Water. That the Mountaineers omitted this item says much for the dampness of the Pacific Northwest.

Water purifier. If you're treating your water (see Chapter 20), you won't want to stop now.

Sunscreen. Today this belongs in the core list of essentials.

Insect repellent. In some places, this seems like a survival item.

Provision for emergency shelter. If you don't carry a plastic sheet, bivouac sack, reflective blanket, or the like, be sure you know how to improvise a shelter of natural materials. (Such techniques are not for every-day or recreational use.)

Signal. Whistle? Mirror? Brightly colored item of clothing?

Toilet paper. Natural substitutes are possible.

Bandanna.

Notebook and pencil. You may need to leave a note somewhere.

STREAM CROSSING

On most well-traveled trails, at least in the regular hiking season, you will find simple bridges across large streams. More primitive routes, however, don't have bridges. Lacking stones that are dry and conveniently spaced, you wade.

Some people stride through such fords and keep walking, letting feet and socks and boots dry as they go. But wet feet in wet socks blister easily. It's a better plan to remove your socks and wade in boots alone, or in tennis shoes or river sandals if you have them. Don't try to cross a stony streambed barefoot (too easy to cut a foot or stub a toe). Don't try to throw boots across a broad stretch of water. A staff or trekking pole, or a pair, can add to stability.

Once across, drain and swab out wet boots as well as you can, replace your socks, and continue. When socks grow soggy, replace them with a dry pair; your boots should now be fairly dry. (Dry the wet socks on the outside of your pack if the weather's good.)

Most fords are very innocent. But there can be genuine danger in crossing a high-volume, swift-running stream such as you may encounter at the spring thaw or in cross-country travel. You may have to spend some time looking for a good fording point. Often it is better to wait for lower flow conditions or to turn back, even if it means abandoning a destination or going the long way around. Ask yourself what will happen if you are swept off your feet. An astonishing number of people have been carried over the terrible verges of Yosemite's thousand-foot cataracts after trying to cross the harmless-looking mountain streams above. Unless you know exactly what you are doing, it is not wise to tie onto a rope at a dubious crossing: the seeming protection can do more harm than good. For more about these tricky situations, rarely encountered, in ordinary backpacking, see Chapter 22.

LINGERING SNOW

In many mountain areas early in the hiking season—and in the North-west, the northern Rockies, and the mountains of Canada and Alaska at any time—you are likely to encounter snowbanks on the trail.

Old snow is slippery stuff when cold, and mushy stuff when warm. Either is difficult. Crossing a flat snowbank, you must adopt a rather tentative stride, lifting your feet cautiously and planting them very flatly. On hard snow, come down firmly to establish your footing. On hard-crusted snow that conceals a mushy interior, come down very gently and test the footing as you go: this should reduce the number of times you plunge in, swearing, to your knees. Be aware that snowbanks may have melted cavities underneath, especially at the edges.

Spring hikers who encounter a small melting snowbank on the trail often detour around the retreating margin of the snow, not wanting to wade in slush. By the following weekend the snowbank has shrunk; more parties come through and detour along a different arc, and then a third, until a whole fan of tracks is worn in the moist earth. The problem is so acute in some areas that managers close routes to public access during the thaw. If you encounter such a snowbank, don't detour (unless you can walk on rocks or logs): put on your gaiters and slosh through.

For something more about negotiating steep snowslopes in summer, see Chapter 22.

IN THUNDER, LIGHTNING, AND IN RAIN

The weather that hikers dread most is extended rain. Even rain, though, is troublesome only when it comes time to set up camp; walking in the rain, with the proper gear, can be a pleasure. If you have good water-resistant coverings for yourself and your pack, you will be relatively comfortable (though it is hard to keep water out of your boots).

That's if you're prepared. For the unprepared, there is real danger in wet, cool, windy weather. If you don't have the gear to stay dry and warm, you run the risk of losing so much body heat that you suffer the spectacular collapse called hypothermia. Common sense and proper clothing, however, are all that's required to prevent such situations. For more on hypothermia, see Chapter 28.

In brief, western-style thunderstorms, you may be able to wait out a swiftly passing shower under the shelter of a tree. But make very sure it's the right tree, and not a likely target for lightning. Lightning is a definite hazard in the American wilderness, much more to be feared than, for example, the rattlesnake. Yet, like most hazards, it's easy to avoid.

Lightning doesn't strike just anywhere. It is drawn to prominent objects: the highest outcrop on a stony peak; the sharp brink of a cliff; a tall, isolated tree. When the bolt strikes, the charge spreads out through the ground and can shock you badly many feet away from the original strike. The current tends to move along cracks in rock and down small, shallow watercourses, especially when water is running in them.

When you hear a thunderstorm working its way through the sky, stop for a moment and count the number of seconds that pass between a flash and the resulting thunderclap. Each 5 seconds that passes indicates 1 mile of distance between you and the flash. (Each 3 seconds indicates 1 kilometer.) If you are in a high or exposed place, don't wait till the last minute to start your retreat; thunderstorms typically move 1 mile every 2 or 3 minutes.

What are unsafe positions? A peak, of course, or a hilltop. A flat meadow or plain or rocky plateau where you yourself are a prominent object. The shore of a body of water. The foot of a prominent tree. The top of a cliff but also the *base* of a cliff. A shallow cave on a slope. You are much less vulnerable at the bottom of a valley; among low boulders or trees of fairly uniform height; or in a deep, dry cave.

If you have a choice of tree species to shelter under, avoid oaks. Favor spruces and beeches. Regard pines as intermediate. This bit of folklore has a sound basis: the trees most likely to be struck have deep roots that go down to groundwater.

If you're trapped on a mountain top or out in the open, with no time to retreat, at least get back from the highest points and from cliff edges. Among boulders, you can crouch between rocks of similar size and low profile. Members of a party should spread apart, keeping 30 feet or more of separation.

Take off your pack, your pocketknife, your belt, your camera, and anything else with metal in it, and move well away from the pile. If you can, try to get some insulation between you and the ground. A rope, if you are carrying one, is good; a foam sleeping pad will help some. Crouch or kneel on the insulation. You want stay low but also to minimize your contact with the ground. Keep your legs together (this posture tends to cause current to move along the skin rather than into the body core). If you hear a buzzing from metal objects, smell ozone, see objects rimmed in a blue glow, or feel your hair standing on end, make sure you're in position, and hope.

If a companion has been struck by lightning, your quick action may be lifesaving: see Chapter 26.

WILDFIRE

With the western fire season comes a disquieting thought. What if, in some summer-desiccated wilderness, you found yourself hiking in the path of a forest fire? I have never heard of a backpacker being injured in this fashion, but the situation bears thinking about. How do you react?

If you encounter a fire that is just getting started (don't let it be your own out-of-control campfire!), your best bet is to combat it on the spot. By kicking ground litter away, you may be able to create a miniature fireline good enough to confine a young, cool fire. If the fire escapes anyway, the already burned area may be the safest spot around.

If you become aware of a well-developed wildfire burning in your vicinity, you must try to stay out of its way. That may mean abandoning your trail. If you are near a ridgeline, go to it and move along it, away from the fire; if the blaze catches up with you, you can dive off the other side. If you're not near a ridgeline, it's best to move downslope: flames advance sixteen times faster uphill than down. If you can get down to a cool streambank, or even a dry, unvegetated streambed, that's ideal. (Watch for debris falling from above.) Stay away from draws, which provide natural chimneys for the flames. Wind direction matters, too: better to be moving against the breeze than with it.

If you realize that you can't avoid the fire, look for an area of relatively open ground. Remove nylon clothing, which can melt and burn you. Put a wet bandanna across your mouth and nose; wet yourself down all over if you have the water. Stay low to the ground. If the approaching fire front seems to be a thin curtain of flame, your best bet may be to dash through it to the charred ground behind. If the fire is more severe, survival may depend on finding or digging a hollow and hunkering down under a reflective blanket. When the fire front has moved past you, assess any burns or other injuries you or your party may have sustained, and seek help. By laying out three objects in a triangle, you can alert firefighters to your presence.

Needless to say, you don't want to be the source of a wildfire. For the all-important precautions in camp, see Chapter 18 . If you're a smoker and find you must light up on the trail, be exceedingly cautious about it: stop in a broad bare area, scatter ashes when cool, and pack out butts. When fire danger is high, don't smoke at all. In California and sometimes elsewhere, areas may be closed to access in the summer and fall, both for public safety and to reduce ignition. Respect such bans.

Let's face it. Few corners of the typical recreational wilderness are so remote, so trackless, or so primitive that they afford us much excuse for getting lost. Not truly lost, not lost without a clue, not North Woods lost. Nor do we need very complicated techniques to avoid losing ourselves. Navigation these days is most often a simple thing, a matter of keeping track of where you are, how fast you are progressing, what landmarks you are passing. It's a matter of awareness: common sense.

Yet people do get lost, and even in serious trouble, in the most populous of wild areas. And it is a rare hiker who has not had moments of disorientation along the way. Did I miss the junction? When did we cross into the watershed of Limbo Creek? What are those cliffs doing up there? Or just: What happened to the trail?

Even for the hiker who never moves on anything but the plainest of paths, navigation can be fun, not so much to tell you where you are as to identify what you see.

THE TOPOGRAPHIC MAP

The basic tool of navigation is the topographic, or contour, map. Add to it a compass and a little thought, and you can answer almost any question about your place in the land. These invaluable maps—many thousands of sheets in all—are published by the U.S. Geological Survey (USGS) and by Geomatics Canada.

In the continental United States, the basic map series uses a scale of 1:24,000. These sheets are also known as 7.5-minute quadrangles, "minute" being a unit of space, not of time. Each map covers an area of about 6 by 8 miles, though the field shrinks somewhat at northern latitudes.

In an older series of USGS maps called "15-minute" sheets, each map covered a region of about 14 by 17 miles. For backpacking, this style was far more convenient than the finer-scaled replacement: more compact (with fewer sheets to carry) and yet quite sufficiently detailed. Today, only Alaska is mapped at the 15-minute scale; 7.5-minute quads exist as well for a few regions in the southern part of the state.

Three other types of USGS maps are of occasional interest to the backpacker. Sheets of the 7.5-by-15-minute series have a scale similar to ordinary 7.5-minute quads (1:25,000) but are wider, covering twice the distance east to west. Moreover, they are metric, showing elevations and contours in meters. The 30-by-60-minute series is also metric, using a scale of 1:100,000 and portraying larger areas with less detail. Finally, the USGS still publishes the old 1:250,000 series, covering still vaster stretches; though not useful for close-up routefinding, these maps can be fun to consult in the car, giving you a sense of what's topographically what in an entire region.

In Canada, the base maps of the National Topographic Series have a scale of 1:50,000, making them rather comparable to U.S. "15-minute" sheets; 1:250,000 quadrangles are also published.

Government topo maps can be ordered from central offices or purchased at many private suppliers. Prices change from time to time. For ordering information, see Resources appendix.

On a regular topo map there are several kinds of information. Most important are the thin brown lines called "contour lines," or just "contours." Each traces a given elevation above sea level. If you imagine the map as a three-dimensional model that could be flooded with water, the rising surface would first touch the 1,200-foot contour wherever it appears, then the 1,400-foot, and so on. On U.S. 7.5-minute maps, the interval between contour lines is usually 40 feet. Every fifth line is heavier and darker, and marks a gain of 200 feet from the last such emphatic line; these heavy lines have elevation numbers attached. On the older 15-minute maps, the basic interval is generally 80 feet, and 400 feet separate the heavier lines. Don't take these intervals for granted, however. In very flat regions, smaller increments are used, and some older maps use other intervals for no special reason. (A notice at the bottom of every sheet tells you what contour interval applies—and the numbers printed on the heavier contour lines of course communicate the same information.)

Topo sheets ordinarily have a pale green shading to show forested areas. Green stippling indicates brush; uncolored areas are grassy or barren. Sheets are ruled with square-kilometer grids; in the United States, mile-square "sections" may or may not also be shown (see More About Maps, below).

Canadian topo maps are generally similar. Older sheets show elevations in feet; newer ones use meters. Canadian topos also differ from USGS quadrangles in having a legend printed on the back; in the United States, you need a separate brochure for maximum explanation. For the sparsely populated northern regions, Canadian 1:50,000 sheets are published in black-and-white only.

Topo maps today are both more and less accurate than they used to be. They are more accurate because satellite technology allows topography to be established more precisely than ever before. They are less accurate because remote sensing has all but replaced the laborious fieldwork called "ground truthing," especially with regard to little, evanescent things like trails. Don't be too quick to doubt your senses if your map seems to be wrong about some detail that can't be seen from the sky. Also notice the date in the legend. Many trails shown on older maps have been abandoned or rerouted, and the road systems in the rugged mountains of the western United States and Canada have expanded almost beyond comprehension since midcentury. Looking at topo maps from the 1950s, you get the impression that, even so late in history, the mountainous parts of the West were dominantly wilderness. That has changed indeed.

MAP MANAGEMENT

As maps get more expensive, people are looking for ways to make them last longer. Some people cut their maps into segments and mount them on backings, but this alone won't keep the pictured landscape from blurring away before your eyes in the rain. Several companies market liquid coatings you paint on map surfaces to keep moisture and mildew out; some hikers use mineral oil or acrylic varnish. And some cover the working side of the map with clear contact plastic. Maybe the simplest precaution is to store each map in a clear plastic envelope. You can spend up to $18 for such, but a plain zip-lock bag from the supermarket will do for most purposes.

USGS maps come rolled, not folded. Before you start creasing away at the pristine rectangle, plan a little. How big should each segment be when you finish? If your pack has a special map pocket, how large is it? Your folded map should be a bit smaller. A common procedure is to fold twice in each dimension, dividing the map into sixteen fields. An "accordion-style" fold allows you to see more fields without opening out the whole sheet.

It is useful to make your folds, and especially the folds that run the long way, very straight, so that these correspond to true north-south lines. The map gives you some help in this: both side margins and end margins are divided into thirds by little black tick marks with labels in the format 32′30″, indications of latitude (on left and right edges) or longitude (on top and bottom edges). If you were to draw lines connecting opposite ticks, you'd have a tic-tac-toe grid. At each crossing in that imaginary grid, the mapmakers place a tiny cross on the map surface. You can also go by the gray grid of kilometer lines or the red grid of section lines (see More About Maps, below).

Many hikers trim the margins from their maps, retaining only the actual representation of the land. But before you do this, consider how much of the marginal data is valuable. You may want to keep the scale (though you can move it onto an irrelevant part of the map surface). Do write down the name of the sheet (maybe on the back) and the declination number from the diagram at the bottom (more on this below). Finally, if you think you may use a Global Positioning System receiver, don't trim the margins at all (see Other Tools, below).

You can also, of course, carry a color photocopy of the map segment you need, and leave the original undisturbed. Or, having purchased the right maps on a CD-ROM disk, you can print out a segment with your computer (see below).

MAP READING

The basic skill is the ability to build, from the map, a picture of the land—to translate swiftly, automatically, from map to land and back again. You can practice this skill most easily by buying the topographic sheet for a familiar landscape near home and spending some time with it. Soon you'll know without thinking what a particular shape of land looks like in contour lines: that an outward eddy of lines along a slope indicates a spur ridge; that an indentation means a gully or a streamcourse; that one valley is broad and shallow, a second precipitous and deep. You will distinguish a short, steep hill from a long, gradual one, and a plateau from a knife-edge ridgeline. It is a fascinating study. The map begins as a dead graphic, a mere representation, but it comes alive as you learn it and instructs you endlessly. The map *becomes* the country.

The backpacker's navigation, in its essence, is not a set of techniques but a habit of thought; a custom of awareness; a matter of keeping tabs on where you are, and what the land is doing. In typical wilderness landscapes, unlike those of the city, there is seldom anything really inexplicable or arbitrary; there are broad, discernible patterns—drainages running one way and another; major and minor systems of ridges; plateaus and deep-carved canyons. If you keep alive this sense of pattern, it is rather hard to become entirely lost, whether you have a trail to follow or are striking out cross-country on a route of your own.

Some landscapes, certainly, are easier than others to lose your bearings in. Most confusing are areas that are level, rather patternless, or chaotically jumbled, and places where timber or topography cut off your long-distance views. Fog or low overcast can complicate matters, and every snow hiker knows (and somewhat fears) that brilliant-white, opaque, and snowy mist called whiteout. But these are special cases. For more information on advanced cross-country routefinding, see Chapter 22.

MORE ABOUT MAPS

Many popular recreation areas in the United States are now covered by what might be called privatized USGS maps. Some of these are essentially republications of the vanished 15-minute sheets, with some updated information. Others are based on the newer 7.5-minute quads and may not add much, beyond packaging, to the original source. Still others cover larger areas at varied, less informative scales. Commercial maps are likely to come prefolded, with tough plastic paper or water-resistant coatings. Prices run up to double those of government sheets.

For the computer-equipped, there's the option mentioned above: topo maps on CD-ROM disks. The maps for a substantial region (several hundred of the 7.5-minute sheets) can be housed on such a disk. If you buy from the U.S. Geological Survey, you'll get a set of individual sheets; you must also download a reading program from the Internet. Privately produced disks integrate the sheets into a mega-map, one huge regional expanse; the necessary reading program is part of the package. The private programs let you do some sophisticated analysis. For instance, you can highlight a length of trail with a cursor and get an instant readout of its length; or you can produce an elevation profile of a hike. Moreover, you can annotate the maps. Cost is from $30 to $100. See the Resources appendix for suppliers.

Although topo sheets are central, they are not necessarily the only maps you will need to consult. Usually you also want the maps published by the agency that controls the land you are hiking on—Park Service, Forest Service, Fish and Wildlife Service, Bureau of Land Management, or state agency. These agency maps, though mostly less detailed than topos, may reflect more recent changes in roads and trails, and they often have useful text on the back. For some designated wilderness areas, the agencies have prepared combination maps showing current roads and trails on a topographic base—ideal, if the base is sufficiently detailed.

Maps organize the world by grids. The oldest and fundamental grid system is latitude and longitude: every place on earth is a certain distance north or south of the equator and east or west of a Prime Meridian that runs through Greenwich, England. Latitude and longitude show up on map margins, expressed in units called degrees, minutes, and seconds (hence "15-minute" or "7.5-minute" maps). But there is a newer metric grid called the Universal Transverse Mercator system, which is actually printed in faint gray on U.S. and Canadian topographic maps, with identifications in the margin; this can usually be ignored but is very useful if you are carrying a Global Positioning System receiver (see below).

In the United States there is a third grid system that you sometimes need to know about. Most of the country is divided into squares, usually 6 miles on a side, called townships. Each contains thirty-six sections of 1 square mile, which are numbered within the township in an unvarying back-and-forth pattern:

6	5	4	3	2	1
7	8	9	10	11	12
18	17	16	15	14	13
19	20	21	22	23	24
30	29	28	27	26	25
31	32	33	34	35	36

The basic purpose of this system is to track land ownership, and land agency maps almost always reflect it, cutting the territory up into stacks and rows of section squares. Hikers and other people who work with the land soon become familiar with the pattern and use it to identify points on the map: "Looks like there might be a waterfall in section 17!" There's more than one "section 17," of course, but you usually know which one you are talking about, since the nearest neighboring section with the same name will be 6 miles away.

If you need to, how do you distinguish one township from another? Townships are stacked in vertical and horizontal rows. The vertical rows are called *ranges*. The horizontal rows are called *extended townships*, a term often shortened, as if for maximum confusion, to just *townships* again. Each extended township and each range has a designation marking its position in the broader land survey. Range 33E, to give just one example, is the thirty-third range east of a specified master meridian. Using these numbers, which often appear along map margins, it's possible to zero in on any point in the grid. But this is not especially a hiker's game.

One final point. On most maps, true north is at the top of the sheet, east on the right hand margin, west on the left, south on the bottom. However, sometimes the field is tilted for some reason. Look for an arrow labeled *north* somewhere on the sheet and adjust your thinking if it doesn't point straight up.

THE COMPASS AND HOW TO READ IT

With the map, the compass is the second fundamental aid in wilderness navigation. Its function is to help you place the map in the right position, so that the map's north and the world's north are exactly the same. This done, the compass helps you read the land, from the map, with precision.

Nothing is simpler, in practice, than using a compass. Nothing is more difficult than to describe this simple act without giving a largely spurious impression of complexity. I suggest that, after reading the next few pages, you locate a compass and reread them with compass in hand. Only thus will the seeming complexities dwindle.

THE CIRCLE OF DIRECTIONS

Before we talk about the compass itself, we have to deal with an essential concept: the idea of the *circle of directions.*

Imagine yourself standing on a peak from which you can see a hundred miles in every direction. Imagine yourself turning slowly in one spot—facing north, then east, then south, then west, then north again.

How do you name the directions you have been facing? The cardinal points—north, east, south, west—are easy. For the directions in between, you can combine and say: northeast, southwest; then north-northeast, south-southwest; then north-by-north-northeast; and so on. But obviously you can only go so far with this elaboration. For greater simplicity and precision, we switch from names to numbers. The circle of directions is divided into 360 units called *degrees*. Zero degrees is north; 45 degrees, northeast; 90 degrees, east; 180 degrees, south; 270 degrees, west; 350 degrees, just a smidgen west of due north; and 360 degrees, north again (zero and 360 degrees, in the circle, being names for the same point).

It may seem odd at first, this use of numbers for directions, but it is indispensable for any careful navigation. It allows you to define sharply a direction that, in words, might not be describable at all.

COMPASS ANATOMY

The essential part of the compass is the magnetized *needle*. The needle does not, except in a few localities, point to the geographic North Pole *(true north)*. Rather, it aligns itself to point *generally* north along a wandering web of magnetic lines that converge in northern Canada, at a point *(magnetic north)* a thousand miles short of the true pole. Thus the actual direction indicated by the "North" end of a compass needle varies from place to place; it can also vary over the years in a single location. The key to precise compass navigation is knowing where the compass needle is pointing, *this* year, in *your* wilderness—but more of this later.

There are many kinds of compasses. The type most used in backpacking is the *orienteering compass*. The needle rides on a pivot inside a round, fluid-filled plastic chamber. One end of the needle—the end that points (more or less) north—is specially marked, often with red paint. The surface of the chamber is a *dial* marked with 360 degrees running clockwise—the circle of directions. Though no small compass has room for a separate mark for each of the degrees, the better models mark every 5 degrees, or even every 2.

The needle-and-dial assembly sits on a rectangular *base plate* of clear plastic and can be rotated upon it. The bigger the base plate, the better for close navigation—5 inches is good. The plate is marked with a big lengthwise *directional arrow*; this extends partway under the dial and can be seen through it. There may also be two notched sights, one on each side of the dial, along the arrow's line. On many compasses the base plate is

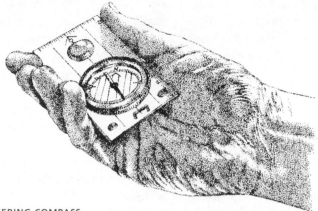

ORIENTEERING COMPASS

also marked with several *scales* to use in reading maps: inch, millimeter, and other intervals given because, on maps of different standard scales, they represent miles or kilometers.

One compass variation is often seen on the trail: the type that has a hinged lid and, mounted inside it, a mirror. This feature adds a little precision when you take a bearing (see below).

Good orienteering compasses without superfluous extras cost $10 to $20. The prominent brands are Silva, Nexus, Suunto, and Brunton. Very simple compasses, with small dials and no base plates, can be found more cheaply and may in fact be sufficient for your needs. If you plan to depart from the main traveled thoroughfares of the wilderness trail system, though, you need the more serious tool.

When you buy a compass, compare it with others in the store to make sure that the needle points in exactly the same direction. It is possible for a needle to be misaligned or to stick in a false position.

Compasses are confused by metal. You won't get an accurate reading from a compass held near a camera, a car, or other metallic object.

USES OF THE COMPASS

Although compass work can get finicky, most of the time it isn't. Most of the time you will be using the tool in a simple, casual way. Just a glance at the dial, now and again, can guide you when you are uncertain or keep you from drifting off an ill-marked route. If you know you are supposed to be heading essentially north, then something is plainly wrong if the compass shows you moving steadily east.

Now for the finicky parts:

COMPASS STEP ONE:
KNOWING WHERE YOUR NEEDLE POINTS

In most of the United States and Canada, compass needles point either just east or just west of true north. To make good use of your compass, you have to know how much east or west. The name for this difference, measured in degrees, is *declination.*

Every topographic map has, in one or another margin, a diagram that purports to give this information. The vertical line with the star represents true north; the slanted line labeled "MN" indicates magnetic north, or the direction in which the needle is actually supposed to point (once the compass has been transported to the region depicted). The angle between these lines, expressed as a number of degrees, tells you how far you have to go left or right from zero on your compass dial to find the number that represents the point toward which your needle will actually aim when you are in the mapped area. If the declination is "west," you'll be going around the dial toward west—counterclockwise; if the declination is "east," you'll be curving toward east—clockwise.

Got that?

It has always struck me that the standard way of expressing "declination," as a deviation from an imaginary norm, is needlessly confusing. All that matters is that the needle, in a given region, points to a given spot on the circle of directions. Know that spot, swivel the compass dial until the needle points to that spot, and you're in business.

There is a potential catch. Unless your map is very new, its stated declination is out of date, perhaps so much so as to be useless for careful work! But let's set this fact aside for now.

COMPASS STEP TWO: ORIENTING THE DIAL

Suppose the declination in your map area is 19 degrees east. This means, simply, that your compass needle will point in the direction represented by 19 degrees—about north-northeast. To orient your compass for that region, then, you rotate the dial until the number 19 comes into position at the tip of the needle. With your compass dial thus oriented, it has become

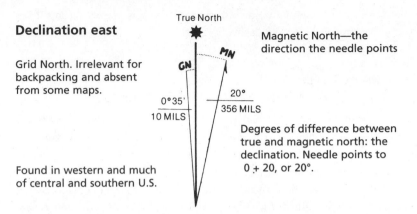

Declination east

True North

Magnetic North—the direction the needle points

Grid North. Irrelevant for backpacking and absent from some maps.

GN

MN

0°35'
10 MILS

20°
356 MILS

Degrees of difference between true and magnetic north: the declination. Needle points to 0 + 20, or 20°.

Found in western and much of central and southern U.S.

an accurate guide to all directions. True north on the compass matches true north on the land; southeast on the compass is southeast in the outside world; and so on.

In the eastern United States, compass needles lean west from true north. Say the declination is 10 degrees west. Rotate the dial so that the needle rests at a point 10 degrees to the west of north. This point bears the number 350: 360 degrees (north) minus 10 degrees (declination west) = 350 degrees. (To go west from north, counterclockwise around the dial, you have to subtract degrees.)

On some compasses, you can turn a tiny screw to rotate the lower surface of the needle capsule in such a way that parallel lines imprinted on it align with local magentic north. This makes orientation just a shade faster. Cost is a couple of dollars. Worth it? Up to you.

COMPASS STEP THREE: ORIENTING THE MAP

Once you know how to orient the compass, the next big step is to get the map lined up as well. (Remember, you are doing this in the field, standing on the territory represented by that map.) The trick, essentially, is to go back one stage and orient the compass again—this time *with* the map, as though they were one thing.

First, take the unoriented compass and rotate the dial until the directional arrow on the base plate is seen to pass through the mark on the dial that represents true north. Second, place the compass on the map, with the directional arrow in line with north on the map. (To line it up

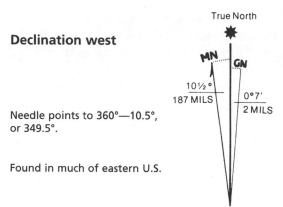

Declination west

Needle points to 360°—10.5°,
or 349.5°.

Found in much of eastern U.S.

exactly, use a margin or an accurate north-south fold.) Third, hold this map-and-compass combination firmly in your hands and turn it as a unit until the compass needle points to the number on the dial that matches magnetic north. You have now oriented the compass and, with it, the map. The map now parallels the land.

COMPASS STEP FOUR: TAKING A BEARING

Now that both map and compass are oriented, you can use them together to give you many kinds of information. Often a simple procedure will do. If you already know within a mile or so where you are on the map, it is easy to read the identities of prominent points. The big massif just east can only be General Steele's Backbone; the forested valley can only be the drainage of Horsethief Creek; what is glinting in the socket below can only be Hungry Packer Lake.

But sometimes you will need to read the land more precisely. Perhaps you don't know at all where you are; perhaps the topography is downright confusing; perhaps you must make a difficult choice of route. All these problems are reasons for taking *bearings*.

How is it done?

The idea is to find the precise direction from you to a particular object, say, a prominent peak. Raise the compass to just below eye level. Make sure it is correctly oriented. Now, keeping the dial in that same correct position, turn the base plate underneath it so that the arrow on the plate is pointing exactly toward the object you want the bearing on. Now look down through the transparent dial (or through sights if your compass is so equipped). You will see that the directional arrow is visible and cuts the circle of degrees at a particular point. Read the number at that point. This is your bearing.

If your compass is the kind with a mirrored lid, you'll notice a vertical line etched down the middle of the glass. There will be also be two sights, one taking the form of a hole in the lid, near the hinge. Adjust the lid so that the compass dial appears in the mirror, with the etched line crossing it at the needle's pivot point. Check dial orientation. Look through the sights at the object whose bearing you want. Note where the line cuts the mirrored dial. This is your bearing.

This information has many uses.

You know where you are and want to know what you're looking at. Take a bearing on the feature you want to identify. (For convenience, say it's a peak.) Note your own position on the map. Place the (properly oriented) compass on the (properly oriented) map with the center of its dial at your position. Say the bearing on your landmark was 120 degrees, or about southeast. Simply draw (or imagine) a line running from your position to the number 120 on the dial and on across the map. (The line printed on your compass's baseplate will do for a start. Swing the baseplate around to the proper position without disturbing the actual compass dial.) The first height along that line that seems of proper height and distance is the one.

You know what you're looking at and want to know where you are. Take bearings on two known peaks (or any other prominent features). The farther apart they are, the more accurate your fix will be. Placing the compass on the map as before, draw (or imagine) lines running from those landmarks toward you at the proper angles. Where these lines intersect, you have your exact position. To double-check, you can sight on additional points.

Or perhaps you already know that you are on a certain *line* in the landscape: a major stream, a trail, a ridgeline, a road. This simplifies matters. Just one bearing, just one additional line on the map, may be enough to show you the single place where you can reasonably be standing.

You have the whole picture but want to find this place again. Say you've discovered something interesting, some distance off the trail: an old cabin not shown on the map, a hidden shortcut through a band of cliffs, a good fishing spot. You want to come back next year. But there's no obvious landmark along the trail to tell you where to leave it next time you come along. A bearing on a more distant landmark will do just as well. Write yourself a note: "Next time walk east along the Kangaroo Trail until Sawtooth Mountain is on a bearing of 315 degrees; then cut down the ravine to the left." You can further describe your cross-country route as a compass direction: "Then head downslope on a line of 125 degrees."

DETERMINING DECLINATION

As noted above, the declination figures given on topographical maps are not always accurate because declination varies over time. For casual compass work, the difference between a map's declination figure and the actual declination in the territory it represents may not matter much. But if you want to know true declination, you can get it from a printed source, or figure it out yourself.

The printed source is *Magnetic Field/Declination U.S.*, updated every few years by the U.S. Geological Survey (see Resources appendix). In Canada, get the equivalent *Magnetic Declination Chart.*

To use the commonsense method, make your way to a place that is unmistakably mapped on the topo sheet in question: a road junction, a hilltop, a USGS benchmark or whatever. Take a bearing on another unmistakable landmark. Vary the normal procedure, however, by ignoring declination: pretend for a moment that your compass needle points to true north.

Next, look at the map. Place your compass on it so that the center of the dial is at your position and "North" on the dial matches north on the map. (Forget the compass *needle* for now.) Read off the mapped bearing to your landmark.

Finally, compare the bearing you got from the landscape with the bearing you got from the map. The difference is the actual current declination. If your compass said that Landmark Peak was at 60 degrees in your personal circle of directions and the map says that the peak lies at 80 degrees from your position, the real declination is 20 degrees clockwise, or east. To put it another way, when your compass needle points to 20 degrees on your dial (the point 20 degrees east of north), all the directions shown on the dial are correct in the outside world. To check yourself, repeat this procedure several times, using different landmarks.

OTHER TOOLS

For very fine navigation, especially on big mountains, an altimeter/baro-meter can be helpful and fun. This is a device, mechanical or electronic, that measures air pressure. Because air pressure decreases rather steadily with height above sea level, this measurement can indicate your altitude. Air pressure also increases or decreases with the weather—falling pressure usually signals an advancing weather front. An air pressure sensor that simply tells you the local pressure, in a unit called millibars, is a barome-ter; if it expresses its data as elevation above sea level, it is an altimeter; many units do both.

Of course, the double meaning of air pressure readings can lead to some confusion. If you find your campsite has risen a hundred feet dur-ing the night, you may be in for a storm! The pressure changes due to weather, however, are usually both slower and much smaller than changes due to your own climbing and descending.

Some wristwatches now contain built-in navigation aids and weather-sensing tools: altimeters, barometers, thermometers, and compasses. One watch has a compasslike directional arrow on the face. Point it where you like, push the "Bearing" button, and a reading pops up. On other models, a not-very-useful little compass is mounted on the wristband. None of these added tools, however, can replace the traditional compass, a truly versatile object.

Neither can the backpacker's newest and most glamorous naviga-tional plaything, the Global Positioning System (GPS).

The Global Positioning System is an array of twenty-five satellites launched and maintained by the U.S. military. By picking up signals from three or more such satellites, a little handheld receiver can calculate your position exactly, expressing it as a pair of coordinates. It can also tell you the direction and distance to any other point on the map whose coordi-nates you enter.

Coordinates? What coordinates? You can use either of two grids indi-cated around the margins of your topo map: latitude and longitude, measured in degrees, minutes, and seconds; or Universal Transverse Mer-cator (UTM), measured in kilometers and meters from specified master lines. The UTM grid is the one actually shown, in faint gray, across the map field. Of course, your target is unlikely to be exactly at a marked intersection of the grid, so you have to interpolate, something done far more readily with the metric UTM. The language of these coordinates is slightly complex but quickly learned.

Each point you have described and entered stays in the receiver's memory as a "waymark." Once you've got the hang of it, you can map out a whole trail, or cross-country route, as a progression from waymark to waymark. To chart a curvy course using GPS, you have to break it up, establishing many waymarks linked by short, straight segments. (As far as the GPS unit is concerned, the only way between two points is a straight line.) In cross-country travel, you might get a bearing on your target from the GPS, head off in that general direction, and check again as you close on the destination.

There are circumstances in which this aid could be very helpful. In a snowstorm, or in heavy fog. On flat or undulating forested terrain. When you're closing in on a target that is not visible or distinctive, or adjacent to something that is. Be aware, however, that a GPS unit needs to "see" as much of the sky as possible; clouds and tree cover interfere with reception, and canyon walls can block it absolutely.

For ordinary wilderness travel, do you need to buy and master this technology? Not remotely, in my view. As a rule, it is only doing for you what you can do far more cheaply and simply—and, it seems to me, pleasurably—with map and compass alone.

If you do buy a GPS, make sure it's one that can work with the UTM grid, and be prepared to pay $250 to $400. Weights are well under a pound.

Another technological innovation now seems inevitable. We have GPS receivers; we have regional mosaics of topo maps on disk. How long before we're offered the two elements in one portable device: an all-purpose navigator that would project a map of the landscape you're in and mark it up with symbols showing where you have been, where you are, and how you should proceed to get where you say you want to go? I can't say I'm looking forward to it.

LOW-TECH NAVIGATION

Let's go to the other extreme. Far from having high-tech gadgetry, suppose you've even lost your compass? There are some rough-and-ready methods of determining direction. Except for the first, none of these

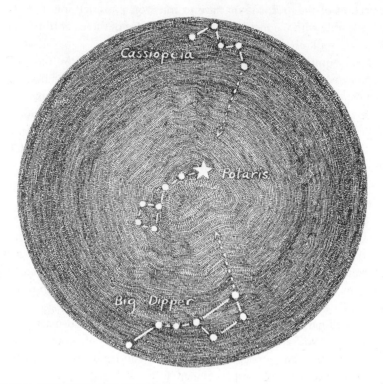

USING ADJACENT STARS TO FIND POLARIS

tricks will do much more than straighten you out if you are grossly turned around.

STARS

Our polestar isn't always at true north, but it's close enough for emergency purposes. To locate it in a clear night sky in summer, first find the Big Dipper. The two stars that form the end of the Dipper's "bucket," opposite the "handle," point almost straight toward Polaris, a star of medium brightness.

If the Big Dipper is beneath the horizon, you can go by another constellation, Cassiopeia, which lies on the opposite side of Polaris and about the same distance away. Its five stars form a distinctive, flattened W.

Whether the W appears right side up or upside down, its open, three-starred side points toward the North Star.

All stars, in fact, give directional clues. Here's a trick you can use without special knowledge. Pick any star (or planet) near the horizon and note its position relative to something distinctive, maybe a tree branch. Wait a quarter of an hour and watch how the celestial body moves. If the star rises, you are facing generally east. If it sets, you are facing west. If it moves to the right, you're looking south. If it moves to the left, you're looking north.

THE SUN

It's well to be aware of the arc the sun follows in the sky at a given time of year. North of the Tropic of Cancer, it is always in the south half of our sky at noon, but its rising and setting points vary. At the equinoxes, mid-March and mid-September, the sun rises and sets very close to due east and due west. In mid-June it rises somewhat northeast and sets somewhat northwest; in mid-December, it rises somewhat southeast and sets somewhat southwest. (Exact tables, organized by date and latitude, are available to pin this down.) Above the Arctic Circle, of course, there is a period at midsummer when the sun never sets at all.

You can use a watch or a stick to extract some of the directional information that's implicitly contained in the daily path of the sun. Though none too accurate, these methods are kind of fun and might provide some reassurance in a pinch.

If you carry a watch with hands, first set it to standard time (subtract one hour if it's on daylight saving time). Second, hold the dial level and point the hour hand toward the sun (or the ground point that appears to be beneath the sun; you can align the hand with a straight shadow). South will be a point on the watchface halfway between the hour hand and 12:00, going in whichever direction the arc is shorter. (Before 6:00 A.M. and after 6:00 P.M., you have to go the longer way toward 12:00 and split that arc.) If it's 8:00 A.M. standard time, south will be at about 10:00 on the dial; if it's 4:00 P.M., at about 2:00 on the dial. If your watch is digital, you can translate, drawing the watchface on a piece of paper or scratching it on the ground.

Lacking a watch, you can read direction, roughly, from the shadow thrown by a straight stick. There are different versions of the technique. In the quickest procedure, you plant your stick in the ground, not straight up, but slanted toward the sun, so that no shadow is thrown. Then wait until a shadow appears. This shadow will mark an approximate east-west line. The reading can be taken at any time of day.

SIGNS IN THE LAND

In the Northern Hemisphere, the north and northeast sides of objects are heated less by sunlight each day than the south and southwest sides. Other things being equal, then, moss *does* tend to be thicker on the northern side of trees; different plant communities tend to grow on north- and east-facing slopes; snow and ice linger longest on the northern sides of ridges. In rare cases, you may also be able to guess directions from the effects of a strong prevailing wind: lopsided trees, sand patterns, and so on. But all of these signs should be used with extreme caution. Local conditions complicate them, and, at best, they are crude.

"SENSE OF DIRECTION"

Do human beings have a built-in "sense of direction"? Just possibly. It turns out that there is a bone between the eyes that is rich in iron; it may be a vestigial navigation device. But "vestigial" would seem to be the word. Study after study finds that people who try to walk straight lines without constant correction go around in circles instead.

FOLLOWING A TRAIL

Ordinarily, there's no skill to following a trail. It's there, unmistakable, and you just plod. But even obvious trails grow faint at times. And in the United States there is a huge network of what might be called "ghost trails"; built in the 1930s under the New Deal, they have never been maintained since. (As fast as the American hiking public is growing, our trail system seems to be shrinking still faster.)

Faint trails, especially above timberline, may be marked with small stacks of stones called "ducks" or "cairns" or "birds." Occasionally these piles are high, but most are just large enough to be clearly artificial. Often a single stone, placed at one side of the main stack, indicates the direction of the continuing trail.

In wooded country, the guiding marks are *blazes:* deep, clean ax cuts that have chipped out whole sections of bark and underlying wood. They are usually shaped like a capital T or a dotted lowercase i, with a smaller separate cut above. Usually, blazes are placed at about chest height. Often they are stacked in groups of two or three; this stacking may or may not signal an impending turn. Blazes ordinarily face along the line of the trail, so if you see one facing sharply off to the left or right, it probably marks a bend in the route. However blazes cut by different workers at different times aren't necessarily standard.

Recently, plastic tags, metal disks, and paint spots have been much used instead of classic blazes. Throughout the East, marks of different colors routinely distinguish trails.

When the trail is clear, of course, you don't have to be too much concerned with these guides. But if the path starts going hazy on you—if it disappears under patches of snow, if it threatens to dissolve in a maze of deer trails, if the brush starts closing it over—begin watching the blazes meticulously. Don't go on for long without locating one. Stop and hunt if you must. A surprisingly official-looking trail can be made by deer and bear. Be aware, too, that natural marks can counterfeit ax-cut blazes—occasionally a rock bounding down from a cliff gouges a good imitation. Yet another caution: lines of blazes are sometimes used to mark the boundaries of land survey squares, or sections, away from any trail.

When the ducks and blazes fail you, there are other signs you can look for. Have the branches of trees or shrubs been cut or clipped? Is there a terrace effect where the path was cut into a hillside? In a place where brush has obscured a route, the treadway itself may be free of new stems; plants are slow to root again on compacted ground.

If such detective work is required for long, though, you are probably no longer just bridging a difficult section of an otherwise plain path. Rather, you have to count the trail as defunct and regard the trip as a problem in cross-country routefinding. Bear in mind that the original trailbuilders may have taken the most logical line through the landscape; it may be worthwhile continuing on that line as indicated on the map, even if the trail refuses to reappear.

WHAT IF YOU DO GET LOST?

What *is* getting lost, anyway?

If you lose the trail in the undergrowth; if you hesitate at a junction; if you see a landmark you don't recognize; then you aren't lost. You're disoriented merely, and though disorientation can be the beginning of "lost," it is not the thing itself.

You are lost when you do not know how to retrace your steps to a place where you feel sure of your bearings. But perhaps even more than a situation, being lost is a state of mind: panic.

If you find yourself disoriented, whether you are "lost" yet or not, sit down. Get out map and compass. Think back on where you have been in the last hour. Think back to the last point at which you were sure of your position. Scan the landscape for features you can reason from. Consider the lay of the land—are you, for instance, in a valley that drains in a certain direction? If you find yourself initially too worried to think, start by making this a rest stop. Eat something, take a picture, have some lemonade.

If you have a Global Positioning System unit and a map, you can get unlost in a hurry. Just figure the Universal Transverse Mercator coordinates of some spot where you've recently been, or where you'd like to be. The unit will consult the satellites and tell you what direction to walk in. But of course if you have this gizmo and the skill to use it, you probably aren't lost in the first place.

Even just using your head, you should most of the time be able to reconstruct where you are, or at least how to get back to known ground. After all, a pedestrian moves only so fast. You won't be two counties away.

And if you can't reconstruct? Sometimes, especially on flat terrain, it is appropriate to walk a *search pattern,* a sort of rectilinear spiral widening out from your starting point. This can be useful if you are looking for something—say a trail—that is probably nearby. One caution, though: never lay down your pack or daypack while you search. You might not find it again, and this could turn a minor problem into a major one.

If you get lost on a side trip, away from your party, try to make contact with the rest of your group. Shout, blow your whistle, flash your mirror. Three signals of any kind are a distress signal; two signals of any kind indicate response—"We read you." Most stray people are collected, sooner or later, by their companions.

If none of this works, about all you can do is make yourself comfortable, keep signaling from time to time, and stay put until searchers turn up. Eventually your friends will report you missing, or an alarm will be sounded when you fail to return at an appointed time.

Your first priority now is *warmth and shelter*. If you are hiking alone with a full pack, you will have everything you need to make yourself cozy. Otherwise you may have to improvise.

If there is wind, getting out of it will be important. If you're on the windward side of a ridge, cross over to the leeward. Look for a natural barrier like a boulder or massive tree. A dense thicket of vegetation also cuts wind. If there's no easier escape, you can build a windbreak of stones or, if available, snow. For warmth, you can rake together a pile of forest debris and burrow into it.

If rain is in prospect, however, you need a roof as well as a wall. A cave or overhang is ideal; sometimes there are sheltered spaces among room-sized talus blocks. Lacking a previous tenant, a hollow log or tree will also serve. There may be a persistent dry zone near the trunk of a large coniferous tree.

If you have to build a roof, don't get fancy. The basic plan calls for a *ridgeline*, which may be a stout stick, a taut cord, or a fallen log; transverse *ribbing* of sticks or cord; and *thatching* of grasses, reeds, chunks of bark, fallen leaves, green foliage, or whatever else you can find. If there's a convenient fallen log or stone, the ribs can lean against that. Thatching 6 to 12 inches thick will keep out most of the rain. Build the shelter just big enough to fit into. Pile material under you, as well, so that you don't wind up lying in a puddle. If you need to cut boughs for your shelter, this is of course justifiable in a genuine emergency.

Though insulation is more important than the positive warmth of a fire, by all means build one if conditions permit. If you've found a semi-sheltered pocket at the base of a cliff, for example, a fire in front of you can make it downright cozy.

If you have to search far to find shelter, leave a marker at your first position, like a bright cloth or a circle of stones. Leave also a note saying who you are, what condition you're in, what kind of gear you have, what date it is, and what you're doing next. And don't just blunder away from the starting point. You can't afford to get still further lost. Rather, follow a definite landscape feature or a compass line.

The second survival priority (under some circumstances the first) is *water.* If you have to move around to find it, follow the precautions noted above. As for food, that can wait.

After basic comforts are assured, your job is to wait. But it is also to keep trying to draw attention to yourself; and it is also, very importantly, to think.

Nothing attracts the interest of the authorities so quickly as a smoky fire. Distress or not, be careful how and where you light it. Don't try to send up puffs in threes: just make sure the smoke is plentiful. This is one situation in which there is an excuse for putting green wood or foliage on a fire.

As time passes, keep pondering the land and your position in it. You may well sort it out yet. But don't strike out across country until you are quite sure of what you are doing (and then leave a note). Be cautious in following such traditional a advice as "Follow water downhill." It all depends on what water and what hill. Sometimes a downhill grade leads not out of wilderness but deeper into it. On the other hand, heading uphill may frustrate searchers if they can't tell which forks you choose when a watercourse branches.

So much for the lost person. What should the unlost members of a party do when they realize someone is missing? The first rule is not to throw away your greatest asset, your known and inherently reasonable position in the neighborhood. Don't split up and scatter. Wait for a while at a distinctive point like a trail junction, stream crossing, or pass. Shout or otherwise signal, continually. Wait some more. If you think your partner may be behind you, send someone down the trail to a specified point or for a specified time. If you think the wanderer may be ahead of you, do the same. Pursue possible branching trails in the same way. (If you have the numbers, each search party should have two members.) If you are the only companion, don't move from your original position without leaving a prominent marker and an explicit note. If you think your friend may have left the trail, it may be appropriate to walk a search pattern, or a series of compass courses, across the area of concern. But return to your base by dark and stay there, signaling frequently with a flashlight. A campfire makes a good beacon, too. If the absent person doesn't show up by midmorning, you have to consider the possibility of injury and send for help. For related subjects, see Chapter 26.

To repeat, however: in summer backpacking, and in our modern wilderness areas, so small and so well mapped, nothing should be easier than staying out of this kind of trouble. And in fact it is fairly rare for well-equipped backpackers, traversing the deep backcountry, to lose their way. Casual hikers, wandering away from their cars without maps, are much more at risk. If you know what you are doing, and walk with a mind aware, the land should have no unpleasant surprises for you—or for your friends.

MAKING AND MANAGING THE CAMP

It is legitimate to hope that there may be left . . . the special kind of human mark, the special record of human passage, that distinguishes man from all other species. It is rare enough among men, impossible to any other form of life. It is simply the deliberate and chosen refusal to make any marks at all.

Wallace Stegner, *This Is Dinosaur: Echo Park Country and Its Magic Rivers*

17

Low-impact travel means many things. But among them, one is paramount: the proper making, managing, and breaking of the wilderness camp.

It is hardly surprising that the agencies responsible for our wilderness are particularly concerned with camping habits. In fact, of the guidelines they set, most have to do with campsites and camping practices. That's something of a pity. You'd prefer not to have the feeling of someone looking over your shoulder, in thought at least, when you stop for the night. But until all wilderness travelers are using sensitive common sense, the rules can hardly be spared. When you're confronted with them, examine them; ask questions and learn from them.

Regulations are not uniform across the country. Different regions have different problems; different experts have different ideas to propose. Sometimes the managers seek to concentrate use in a few areas, leaving the rest untouched; sometimes the plan is rather to disperse campers widely. In many areas there is a double standard: campers who build fires must stay at designated sites; those with stoves may camp at large. Sometimes particular areas may be closed, not only to fires, but to any camping—all the time or at given times of year, for various good reasons (wildfire danger is one; the welfare of vulnerable species is another). Local codes of conduct are generally printed on the back of wilderness permits of brochures. Don't be put off by the way the rules change from place to place. The agency people, like conscientious hikers, are feeling their way in a complex and many-sided matter.

In what follows, I may speak as if these regulations did not exist, as if nothing affected your choice of site but your own good judgment. This does not mean, of course, that official advice is to be ignored; on the contrary, I hope and assume that you will follow it.

CHOOSING THE LOW-IMPACT CAMP

Where then *should* you camp? What standards do you go by—not only for low impact on the land, but for comfort and convenience as well?

We need to begin with a vital distinction. There are two very different sorts of camping spots in the wilderness. First is the pristine site: the piece of unmarked ground that, for a certain time, you make your own. If you camp in such a place, you take onto yourself a considerable responsibility. It is your job to leave that land exactly as you found it: still unscarred, still unfrayed, recognizable to no one as a place that has been used. Some sites are much more vulnerable to scarring than others, and these the low-impact camper must be at pains to avoid.

Campsites of the second type, in contrast, are unmistakably marked by use. They have worn paths, fire rings, bare ground, perhaps even terraced tent platforms cut from a hill. Logs and stones may have been shifted to make tables and seats. Such camps, if you find them vacant, can be both convenient and charming. And from the point of view of low impact, they have a telling advantage: they are already barren. It is relatively hard to injure them further. The price has already been paid.

What about the ambiguous case: a site that is just beginning to show wear and tear? Squint, and it looks pristine; look closer, and you see a little zone of trampled ground around a fire ring. This type of site, which can still melt back into its unaltered surroundings, should *never* be used; fire rings in spots like this should be dismantled.

Even among established sites, all is not equal; some should be avoided. In many open mountain landscapes, you find many more firespots and devegetated tent locations than anyone needs; the same may be true along popular forest trails. Many of these excess sites, built at random by the uninformed, could not have been worse chosen if the makers had drawn up a plan for maximum disturbance to land, wildlife, and the human experience. Then there are sites so punished by use that soils are badly eroded and tree roots exposed. Choose instead a spot that is still pleasant. You are not obligated to camp in the ugliest place!

Now the criteria:

DISTANCE FROM STREAM, LAKE, AND TRAIL

This is the rule that the land managers tend to put first, perhaps because it is easy to grasp. We are instructed to camp a given distance away from streamsides, lakeshores, and trails, or (in some areas) from private property. Specified setbacks vary, but 100, 200, and 300 feet are common. Two hundred feet is 70 to 80 normal walking steps.

The reasoning here is no mystery. Campers do tend to cluster needlessly close to water and to trails (and especially to points where trails reach water). Loss of privacy is one result. Increased pollution is a second. The formation of large trampled zones is a third. Perhaps most importantly, water-dependent birds and wildlife may be displaced. Loons, for example, nest on lakeshores and may abandon their nests if disturbed. In arid areas, where isolated springs are vital to wild animals, you can disrupt a whole web of natural patterns by settling down near the local waterhole.

Yet I do think setback rules are sometimes applied too mechanically. The camper who favors unmarked, pristine sites may have little trouble complying; but how about the more typical backpacker who prefers to use established sites? In some wilderness areas, the majority of the existing campsites violate the letter of the law, and many of these are unobjectionable in every other respect. I would call it less damaging to use one of these technically illegal sites than to establish a new spot on previously unmarked ground. If *everyone* obediently dispersed into the woods, the result would be far more impact, not less.

Nonetheless, do your best to stay legal. If you want an established site, choose whatever available spot best fits the model. If an effort is obviously being made to "roughen" and renaturalize an old site, avoid the spot. If, on the other hand, you are camping in the dispersed style (which requires fanatical attention to low-impact matters), go much *more* than 100 or 200 feet from the trail or lake or stream. In the lake basins of western ranges, search for sites behind low trees on the hillsides, several hundred yards back from the water. Often you will find little terraces of twiggy soil, just the right size for a small party, or at least for a bed or two.

There are good selfish reasons for getting away from, and if possible above, the water. Since cool air sinks, it's going to be warmer up there. You will also have less dew, mist, and mosquitoes.

GROUND SURFACE

This is *indisputably* important. The best kind of ground to camp on is forest duff—the springy cushion of needles, leaves, and twigs, free of green vegetation, that covers many woodland floors. The second best is bare ground: sand, gravel, rock, rocky soil, or an area already worn bare by human traffic. Deep snow is fine, too. Avoid damp places and don't camp on vegetated areas when it can possibly be avoided.

Not all vegetation, however, is equally sensitive. Low-growing leafy and woody plants, such as may be found on a shady forest floor or above treeline, are extremely fragile. Grasses vary in their vulnerability; although moist meadows can get scarred rather quickly, expanses of dry grasses and sedges are actually quite slow to degrade. In certain wilderness areas, campers who are not using established sites are positively urged to camp on such "shorthair" meadows.

Students of the matter make a distinction between resistance and resiliency. Resistant plants are those that can take a fair amount of pounding before damage begins to show; resilient plants are those that grow back quickly once the disturbance ends. Species may be resistant but not resilient; resilient but not resistant; both; or neither. Dry mountain meadows are of the first type: once they do wear thin, it takes a long time for them to recover. (So if you camp on such grass, do it for one night only.) The species that make up tundra, the low-growing vegetation found at heights where it's too cold for trees, may or may not be resistant, but, given the short growing season in this alpine zone, they are almost never resilient. (Thus, in some areas, camping above timberline is simply forbidden.) The cryptobiotic crusts that form on desert soils (see Chapter 23) are neither resistant nor resilient. (Stay off them completely.)

You might wish to find out from a local agency office which species and plant communities in its territory it is most concerned about. Failing that, you can fall back on the one-sentence rule: don't camp on growing things at all.

SIZE, FLATNESS, AND DRAINAGE

The site you pick must have not only the right kind of surface but also a sufficient expanse of it. A large party stuffed into a small site will naturally tend to trample adjoining, perhaps less suitable, ground. It is obviously also important that the site be fairly level; besides the comfort factor, steep ground, if it is anything but solid rock, is easily disturbed and easily eroded. On the other hand, if a site is too flat, or actually concave, it may be a place where water pools or flows. Stay out of pockets that might become ponds; stay out of dips, or swales, that might carry runoff during a rain. In the desert, during the thunderstorm season, be careful not to camp in dry streambeds (called washes); arid though they seem, a flash flood can turn them into rivers deeper than a tent is high.

SAFETY

Be aware of other possible hazards: snags or branches that might break in the wind, cliffs from which stones might fall, and, in the winter, avalanche paths. If lightning is a possibility, don't camp near an isolated tree or rock outcrop.

Various animal hazards may need consideration. If there are "bedding sites" where something large has slept and crushed the vegetation, move on. Abundant bear scat and obvious game trails suggest the same. You may also want to avoid a site that other campers have left dirty and thus attractive to bears; if you must camp there, clean it up. Avoid also an area where numerous burrows suggest a rodent colony: fleas or droppings may carry disease. For the same reason, don't use an abandoned cabin. Steer clear of a hornet's nest. In bear country, your site must include a proper outlying tree to hang your food from at night.

WATER SUPPLY

Water near camp is pleasant but not essential. Given enough container capacity, you can fill up at a convenient stream in the afternoon, and then make your evening stop with no need for a local supply. Where good sites are few or crowded, this extra degree of freedom can help you find the best.

PRIVACY

Consider your own and others.' Researchers find that many backpackers prefer an uncomfortable but solitary camp to an ideal spot with neighbors. Even if you don't feel that way yourself, it's courteous to assume that others will. Try to be out of view and out of earshot of the next camp. Remember, sound carries readily across lakes and meadows, less so through trees.

LOCAL CLIMATE

Cool air settles at night in basins; night breezes move downslope along ravines. A hillside flat or the top of a knoll may be as much as fifteen degrees warmer than lower ground. Whether you want more warmth or less, you can take advantage of these variations. Consider also the wind; you may want to escape it behind a natural windbreak or use it to blow away mosquitoes. If you are hoping for an early start, a site with an eastern exposure, bringing early sun, will help.

SUITABILITY FOR LONGER STAYS

If you are planning to stay in one place for several nights, you'll be somewhat choosier about the site. Now you consider the overwhelming view, the nearby swimming hole, the peaks to climb, the canyons to explore. But it is also important that you find a specially impact-free site for such an extended stay; vulnerable areas, if they must be used, should not be used long at a stretch.

SETTING UP THE LOW-IMPACT CAMP

Alhough experienced backpackers can settle in quite quickly, it is far better to allow yourself several daylight hours. Blundering around with a headlamp is no fun. And an early stop gives you time for good cooking, for relaxation, perhaps for a side trip, a splash in the lake, a boulder problem, or a few minutes with a camera or a natural history guide.

If your target campsite is very specific—as when a particular spot has been assigned—you're there when you're there. But if you have a choice of sites—and anytime you are camping on unmarked ground—you will want to reconnoiter a bit, comparing alternative locations before you start unloading.

What happens first when you've made your choice? In the rain, or late in the day, raising the shelter has to be the first job. Otherwise, water treatment and cooking may take first place; or the priority may be finding the bearbag tree. The weather, the time of day, the number of people, the site, and personal preference decide. A large group may have to organize itself to get things done; in a smaller party, there's nothing so formal about it.

A campsite has to contain these elements: a water source; a kitchen; a place to protect food at night; a place to sleep; and an area for sanitary needs. Depending on circumstances, all these components except the last may be within a small radius, or they may spread out quite widely.

Your water source may simply be a waterbag hanging from a tree. If you will be going frequently to lakeshore or streambank, choose an access spot where there is a clear trail, or rock and sand; avoid vegetated and undercut banks.

Should your hanging waterbag contain water that has already been filtered or otherwise treated? Or should it contain "raw" water, a substitute creek? I've seen it done both ways. If your water treatment method of choice is filtration (see Chapter 20), you can spend a long time crouching on the bank before you have a bagful—but on the other hand, the job is done for a while.

If you build a fire, your kitchen will cluster around a fire ring. Even if you don't, the rocks of a ring may make convenient shelves and tables. In any case, the kitchen area must be on bare ground where trampling does no harm (this spot will get more traffic than any other part of camp). Then there's fire safety to consider (even a stove must not sit on twiggy duff!). If there is a constructed cooking shelter, use it.

Food storage may be a tree or a rock face from which bags can be slung; in some places, there are lockers.

Sleeping areas may be one or several.

A small group, especially at a little-used camp, needn't specify a toilet area, so long as everyone resolves to go well away from camp, trail, and water and uses normal care (see Chapter 20). But in a large group, it is well to select a general area in advance, choosing a zone where no one else is likely to be camping. If a latrine is to be dug (done only by large groups and not always by them: see Chapter 20), it should be set up first thing, not as an afterthought.

It's natural to have most of these camp elements in a tight cluster; but campers in western Canada, Alaska, and the Rockies of Montana, Idaho, and Wyoming have formed other habits. To minimize the nuisance, or worse, that raiding grizzly bears may cause, things get spread. Beds are well separated from kitchens and night larders, and dishwashing is done at some remove from all the other elements. Wind direction is taken into account as well, with beds upwind and dishwater disposal down. Thus a bear pursuing food odors is less likely to stumble on a sleeping human being.

Engineering has no place in the design of your camp. The perfect site is found, not made. Spend your time locating the right piece of ground, not reshaping the wrong one. Don't clear brush, drive nails, build cupboards, or move any more logs and stones than is absolutely necessary. However hard you try, it is never possible to restore such objects so perfectly that the natural effect is completely recovered.

Living in a well-marked site, you limit your traffic almost completely to ground that is already bare, already stamped by human presence; a little more traffic won't alter it further. When paths and pads are there, use them. But avoid doing anything to extend that barren area. If you are at a pristine site, most especially if there is vegetation underfoot, the strategy changes. You try to avoid repeated traffic over any one piece of ground. In moving between kitchen and spring, or tent and toilet area, take a slightly different route each time, and try to walk on duff, rocks, and mineral soils. Try not to mill around too much in one place, as at the entrance of a tent or near the stove. If you go in soft camp shoes or sandals, you will automatically be more careful how you step. If you're wearing regular boots in camp, walk softly.

One final point. If you see a tiny tree trying to get started—even in what looks like a wasteland—improvise a fence around it and take care not to crush it. In the not-so-long term, many of our forest campsites are going be sunbeaten clearings, simply because no young trees are surviving to replace the old ones that will die.

THE PLEASURE OF WILDERNESS CAMPING

Of necessity, this chapter has contained a lot of "don'ts." Because good wilderness practices so often go against obvious convenience and the tradition of "woodcraft," it may take a little conscious effort to adopt them.

But soon enough, new methods, like the old, are automatic. And you are free to enjoy each campsite you find for yourself—the smells and sounds of it, the views (short or long), the quality of its light, its trees and plants and birds. Every campsite, when you come onto it, seems strange and even a little unwelcoming (why just here and not a mile farther on?). Every campsite, once you have eaten and slept there, becomes a known place and a comfortable one. Your camps, after all, are the spots in the wilderness of which you have most knowledge; it is your campsites that you particularly remember.

The low-impact game has added to the pleasure of wilderness camping a new, keen edge. To wander through a landscape, never guessing that you could damage it, or that you have done so, is one thing. It is quite something else to know that you might have harmed a place and that you did not; to know that your skill and knowledge were great enough to let you use the wilderness without consuming it.

It's enough to make you grin with pride.

18

FIRE AND FOOD

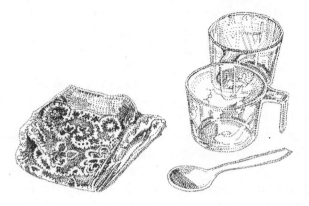

Let's start with a piece of advice from the nutritionists: During the first half hour after you stop hiking for the day, take a moment to eat some carbohydrates—especially if you have big plans for tomorrow. In this immediate postexercise period, the body recharges its stores of glycogen, the muscles' running fuel.

Somewhat later comes the proper evening meal, and what is possibly the trickiest moment of your day: lighting the stove or fire.

OPERATING A STOVE

Cooking on a portable stove is, at its easiest, almost like cooking on a range at home. Yet the use of stoves, like that of open fires, has its headaches, even its hazards. Fuel tank overheating and ignition of spilled fuel are notable dangers. Although normal and careful use is enough to prevent most problems, it's important not to let familiarity breed carelessness. The suggestions that follow are cautious in the extreme.

Stoves vary; no single procedure applies to them all. (For the kinds and their basic anatomies, see Chapter 9.) Consult your manufacturer's directions! But the following steps seem to cover most cases.

STOVE STAGE ONE: PREPARATION

First, pick your site: a level, wind-sheltered spot out of the line of traffic (so that nothing gets knocked over). Just set the stove on the spot. Don't dig a hole for it, or bury it, or build up a hearth of stones around it (though a flat-topped rock can make a handy counter). The stove should be some distance from any other flame, from the rest of your gear, and from burnable underbrush.

Consider wind shelter: though a really good windscreen will protect the flame in quite a breeze, the less moving air to contend with, the better.

If you are camping on snow, you'll need to place the stove on a scrap of wood or perhaps foam padding: to prevent a fuel tank from getting chilled, or a warm burner from melting itself a pit, or both. Finally, if there is a natural bench to sit on where you work, that's ideal.

Second, check the fuel supply. With a bottled-gas stove, this may mean replacing one cartridge with another; it may also mean prewarming a cold cartridge for better operation. Before use, you could carry the fuel next to your body; wrap it in insulation; take it into your sleeping bag; let it sit in the sun. Don't shake a cartridge, however. While the stove is running, you can warm the fuel with your hands. You can also carry two cartridges and switch them each time the active one cools.

Follow directions carefully in removing and attaching cartridges. Some must be held carefully upright. Some can be removed between uses; others, once attached, must be left until empty. Some stoves use cartridges that screw on; others plug in. With screw-on cartridges, be careful not to strip threads. Especially with the screw types, a little fuel may spray out at the moment of connection: not a problem unless it persists (see below).

White-gas stoves with small built-in tanks should be filled each time you use them. Don't overdo it; an air space should remain under the cap (see your model's instructions). In moving the gas from storage bottle to tank, use a pouring cap or, better, a funnel with filter. If you spill fuel, wipe it up and let the residue evaporate (it will do so quickly). If a spill has soaked into the ground beneath the stove, better shift the operation.

If your stove is the type with a pump that plugs into a larger fuel bottle, "refueling" may not arise; but on a long jaunt you will have to switch bottles or top off the current one from a reserve. Again, don't overdo it:

with the bottle upright, an inch or so of air space should show at the top. Many bottles are marked with a fill line.

With two-piece stoves like MSR's, you must next put the stove together by screwing the pump assembly into the fuel bottle and plugging the fuel supply tube from the burner into the pump assembly. Lubricate the end of the inserting tube with saliva or lip salve. Do not overtighten any connection.

After refueling and assembly, close every cap and valve (firmly, not excessively) and check for leaks. A butane/propane cartridge that is losing gas will feel cold; there may be an audible hiss. Check that the burner is connected properly; then try another cartridge. Manufacturing defects are not unknown. If the stove is a liquid-fuel type with a pump, use that item to raise pressure in the tank (instructions will specify how many strokes). Then hold the whole stove upside down; check carefully for drips or wet spots. If there's a leak you can't troubleshoot, don't light the stove.

On a few traditional pumpless stoves, the cap of the tank has a safety release valve; make sure this is pointed away from flammable objects. If you are using one of the several Optimus stoves that have separate tanks mounted behind heat shields, confirm that the shield is clean and shiny and that it has not been knocked out of alignment.

Make sure that the burner plate (if there is one) is firmly attached (you'll see metal tabs that can be crimped to hold the plate more tightly to the burner head) and that pot support wires are firm.

With liquid-fuel stoves, this is a good point in the routine to clean the orifice where the jet of fuel issues. Older stoves may have separate cleaning needles that you insert by hand; on others you operate a built-in needle by turning the fuel-flow valve control; on still others, you activate a built-in needle by gently shaking the burner unit. If a separate needle is used, be careful to come at the jet directly from above: a simple poke, not a reaming action. You don't want to widen the opening, which can lead to malfunction. If you're burning white gas, clean the jet every several days; if your fuel is kerosene or auto gas, do so daily.

STOVE STAGE TWO: PRIMING

Cartridge-stove users can skip this part, and so can owners of Peak 1 stoves. When a liquid-fuel stove is running, its own heat vaporizes the liquid fuel as it rises from the tank—a self-sustaining process. But in order to get the stove started, you have to apply heat to the vaporizing tube beneath the burner. You simply burn something—anything—in a little priming cup that is built in around the base of the vaporizing tube.

What fuel do you use? How do you get it into the priming cup?

It's traditional to make the stove cough up some of its own fuel for priming. On pump models, nothing could be simpler: just crack the fuel-flow valve after pressurizing the tank, and the liquid will flow. With pumpless stoves you have a choice of methods. After opening the fuel-flow valve, you can warm the tank with your hands and your breath until the expanding fuel rises into the priming cup. Or you can leave the stove in the hot sun till the fuel expands; then open the valve and let it flow. There are other variations. Before pumps came along, priming was a whole conversation.

It's not so traditional, but often convenient, to put the priming fuel into the cup yourself. In that case, you use any burnable substance you like: white gas, drawn from the stove tank (or a fuel bottle) with an eyedropper; alcohol from a squeeze bottle; bits of woody or fibrous firestarter; or even toilet paper. The nongasoline alternatives have the advantage of producing less soot. If your cooking fuel is something other than white gas, you should definitely use a separate primer; kersosene is hard to light, and auto gas produces nasty fumes.

How much priming fire do you need? Under good conditions, a single eyedropperful of white gas, or the equivalent, may do it. But any amount is okay as long as the liquid fuel doesn't overflow the cup. Some bizarre accidents have occurred when people drenched their stoves with several cups of fuel. They were surprised at the resulting bonfires!

Before you put a match to the priming fuel, make sure that the fuel-flow valve is shut off, that the tank cap is screwed on firmly, and that all containers of liquid fuel are capped and set well away from the stove.

Then light. If you have primed generously with white gas, the flame may rise quite high before it fades; this is normal. By the time your priming dose has been consumed, the vaporizing tube should be hot enough to do its job, and (in pumpless stoves) the fuel tank should be warm enough so that vapor pressure within will keep fuel flowing upward toward the flame.

STOVE STAGE THREE: LIGHTING

To light a butane/propane stove, hold a match to the burner; then and only then open the valve to let the gas stream out. Under good conditions, you'll have a strong blue flame from the start. If not, you may have a temperature problem. You may need to increase wind protection, or perhaps to warm the cartridge further.

Lighting a standard liquid-fuel stove isn't quite so simple. Just as the priming flame fades, open the valve to admit fuel from the tank; it should catch. If you miss the moment, reduce the flow briefly while you apply a match. With luck you'll get a blue, clear crown of fire. If instead the flame flickers and wavers yellowly, you'll have to prime again. This is common, especially in the cold.

Under good conditions, stoves by Peak 1 will start up without any discernible priming phase. Pump air into the tank, touch a match to the burner, turn the fuel-control valve to "Light/High," pump some more to strengthen the flame, and you're there. Under not-so-good conditions, however, you may get a weak flame or none at all. If this happens, do not pump the stove up further but prime manually with a dab of paper or other solid fuel placed in the burner under the vaporizing tube. Then re-light.

STOVE STAGE FOUR: COOKING

Once a stove is burning with a fine blue flame, arrange its windscreen for maximum protection and put on your first pot of water. If your white-gas stove is the older style that has a metal valve key for flame adjustment, remove this between adjustments; otherwise, it gets too hot.

With pump stoves you'll need to maintain tank pressure by pushing the plunger a few times every 4 minutes or so. Also keep an eye on the temperature of a built-in fuel tank. If you find it getting too hot to touch, better shut down and see what you can do to increase ventilation. Be alert to this problem if you have an improvised windscreen that encloses the tank or a broad pot or frying pan that overhangs it. With bottled-gas stoves, a cartridge should always remain cool enough to hold in your hand. Some stoves link burner and cartridge with a flexible hose; watch that neither hose nor cartridge rests too close to the flame.

Simmering on a two-part white-gas stove can be a challenge. Some

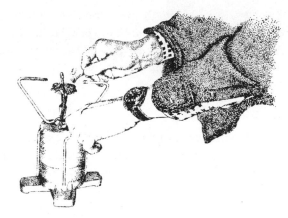

find it helps to start with a half-empty fuel tank, which evens out the fuel flow, or simply to pump fewer pressurizing strokes than the instructions call for. Mountain Safety Research suggests turning down the flame on its stoves after 5 minutes of full-bore operation. Maybe the best solution is to place a metal plate between the flame and the pot, diffusing the heat, or to use a double boiler.

To conserve fuel, make sure you have something heating at all times; make sure the windscreen is effective; and keep lids on as much as possible. Often it's practical to stack your cooking, with a second pot of something warming on top of the first.

Even the smallest cartridge or tank of fuel will last through one meal, maybe two, except in a winter camp where quantities of snow must be melted. If you run out of gas midmeal, don't refuel without first letting the burner grow cool enough to touch. Do not, of course, remove a tank cap while the stove is running, to check the fuel level.

STOVE STAGE FIVE: SHUTTING DOWN

When you shut down a standard liquid-fuel stove, a small flame will linger for a moment at the jet. Instead of letting this die, blow it out. The tiny puff of unburned fuel still in the pipeline will tend to clean the aperture.

If the stove is to be used again at the same site, you can leave it set up. If not, let it cool, wipe off any food spills, and pack it away. Loosen caps to let pressure out of tanks, then tighten them again. Close fuel-flow valves. Some cartridge-stove users report that partially used cartridges of the detachable sort can leak in the pack; they suggest putting tape across orifices. Don't discard a cartridge until you have burned it dry; even then, never toss it into a fire (enough gas may be left to cause a sharp explosion). Of course you'll pack your empties out of the wilderness with you, for eventual recycling.

COOKING IN A TENT?

Cooking inside a tent is one of those things you're sternly advised against but may someday find yourself sorely tempted to do. If you think you may be tempted often, get a stove that can burn kerosene—or consider an alcohol unit.

Much safer than cooking deep within the tent is cooking just outside it, through the open door, under the sheltering roof of a vestibule. You can still work from a lying-down position, with most of you snug in your sleeping bag. Make certain the burner isn't too close to a roof or wall. Especially if you prime with liquid fuel, beware of a high-flaring priming flame; have a pan lid ready to interpose between the flame and the nearest nylon.

Stoves put out carbon monoxide. This gas is absorbed into the bloodstream far more readily than oxygen; if you breathe enough of it, you can die of lack of oxygen. Symptoms of monoxide poisoning may be headache, dizziness, and nausea, or just a deadly sleepiness. At high elevations, where there is less oxygen to begin with, carbon monoxide is doubly dangerous. Make sure your tent has lots of ventilation.

If fuel spills on nylon, wipe it up, let it evaporate, and air the tent before you strike your next match. All fuels are bad for the waterproofing compounds on tent floors, as well as for clothing.

FIRE

Campfires these days are not popular with wilderness managers. The impact of fires on the land—so many people have come to feel—is simply unacceptable: not because any single fire does much harm, but because so many campers are lighting so many. One fire ring may be welcoming, but twenty are obtrusive, and two hundred in a single camping area constitute a plague. The trampling caused by wood foraging in popular areas is itself significant, and if the wrong sorts of fuels are selected, real ecosystem damage is done.

But in this, as in so many impact questions, there's no substitute for common sense. A fire in an old ring of stones in a middle-elevation forest littered with down wood can't possibly be called an attack on the land. A similar fire built (illegally) of green wood on a peak in the crowded Catskills, or built (illegally) against a granite boulder in an unscarred alpine meadow, is an atrocity.

What makes a fire acceptable?

An abundance of appropriate wood.

An existing firesite in a good location.

And very great care.

If the cooking fire is in disfavor, still more, in some circles, is the pleasure fire: the comfortable blaze you sit around after the meal is done. Yet, if fire has a legitimate use in the wilderness, it is not, in truth, for fixing food (stove cooking is simpler) but for fun. For fun and for something a little more than fun: for relaxation . . . for sociability . . . for the odd beauty of flames . . . as a special focus (*focus:* Latin *hearth*) of a place and time you enjoy. It may well be argued that the occasional small pleasure fire, lit as a deliberate luxury, makes more sense than a succession of cooking fires lit for a dubious utility.

SITING A FIRE

The fact that you find a fire ring does not necessarily mean that you should use it. Lake basins in western ranges may contain several hundred rings, many of them badly sited.

Why so many firesites? Partly, no doubt, because many people still put value on the *creation* of a camp, the carving out of a home in the wild world. But there's another reason. Established rings are often left dirty, unpleasant, full of cans, aluminum foil, and organic garbage half rotted and half charred. You'll be doing a service if you choose one of these ruined rings, clean it up, use it, and leave it clean. This, in fact, is an argument for building a fire that you might otherwise forgo.

The ring you choose should be on bare ground well back from water. Make sure that there is nothing flammable within an 8-foot radius: no low branches overhead, no dry grass or brush close by, no duff through which worms of fire could burrow. Keep your other gear well away. Sparks burn holes in nylon.

If you have a choice of rings in otherwise acceptable places, you can afford to consider such things as sun (nice for cooking in the morning, sometimes too hot for cooking in the afternoon) and the direction of the wind (typically upslope during the day, downslope after dark).

If the ring you've chosen is choked with old ashes, remove them and scatter them widely, well away from camp, at several different locations. If it is huge, move its stones together until you have a hat-sized central chamber.

Now, fuel. If you have settled on a well-used site, the chances are good that the woods within, say, 300 feet will be pretty well picked over. Yet it is astonishing how much suitable wood you will find just outside that narrow circle. Scavengers have been lazy. In your own gathering, take a few pieces at a time from a considerable area; don't pick any acre clean. (If you know you'll have a fire in the evening, it's smart to pick up a few pieces of wood along the trail late in the day.)

Every stick of wood that you gather must pass three tests. Each piece must be *dead*; it must be *down* (not attached to a tree); and it must be relatively *small*. Avoid chunks that are green or rotten. Larger logs on the ground have special value in the ecosystem, and rooted snags are not firewood: they are habitat and hunting territory for owls, woodpeckers, and a whole community of animals small and large. Don't use wood you can't break by hand. Ax, hatchet, and saw are no part of the wilderness tool kit today.

OPERATING A FIRE

Get together a reasonable supply of wood, in various sizes, before you begin. Then take a final look at the weather and the site. (Has the day turned windy? Could sparks get into dry underbrush?) The risk of starting a brush or forest fire is not one you want to take. Always have water and a trowel at hand.

If yours will be a cooking fire, you may want rearrange stones and place a grate or perhaps a "dingle stick" (a sort of jib, braced at one end by stones, resting on a fireside rock or log, and protruding over the fire). From this you can hang your largest pot. If you do much campfire cooking you may find it convenient to rig pots with bails of thin wire attached at *three* points around the rim, so that they do not tip when hung. Don't cut a green branch for a dingle stick, or a marshmallow stick, or for any other use.

Starting a fire is both straightforward and slightly tricky; skills that were automatic to generations of firemakers may be less familiar in the age of stoves. Your starting point can be paper or knife-whittled, paper-thin shavings; *fuzz sticks,* sometimes useful, are shaved sticks with the shavings still attached. Some firemakers always lay the whole fire, small to large, before they touch a match to it; others start with the tiniest sticks, get them burning, and then add larger bits and pieces gradually and carefully. If you lay the fire in advance, don't pack the wood in overtightly; fire needs air. Don't put on fragments of wood larger than you can reasonably expect to burn completely to ash or to very small coals.

What if it's raining? Here's where your firestarters come in. Fetch out your dry tinder, magnesium block, or candle. Wax dripped on anything flammable makes a good starter. So does a fragment of porous wood, soaked for a few minutes in a pool of white gas. What does not work, though many people try it, is to pour white gas over a stack of wet kindling: the fuel just flares off, leaving the stubborn wood untouched. In a real emergency, you might sacrifice a nylon stuff sack—they do fine.

Traditionalists look for help in pitchy wood, which you can find as unrotted streaks in the decayed trunks of fallen conifers. This stuff burns delightfully. So, in a pinch, do the waxy needles of many trees. If it hasn't been raining long, you may be able to whittle away the damp exterior of a wood fragment and find dry wood at the center.

Once a fire is burning brightly, of course, it will dry and burn even the most sodden logs. But when all wood is truly waterlogged, as in rain-forest country, only the experts seem to get that far.

Whenever conditions are drier, fire is a beast that has to be watched with the greatest care. Never leave untended one that is burning or even smoldering (though a low fire may be left to consume its embers on a windless night with sleepers close by). Whenever you leave camp, of course, the fire must be absolutely and unmistakably cold.

FIRE AT AN UNMARKED SITE

There is rarely either reason or excuse these days for building a fire where none has been before. This is true without exception throughout the crowded wilderness lands of the East and in well-used areas of the Far West. In remote and little-visited sections, though, even this principle may be slightly bent.

The ideal vanishing firesite is a sandy or gravelly spot where any mark that is made can simply be erased. Sea beaches and river shingles, washed periodically by tide or flood, are best of all. Given any kind of loose mineral surface, you can dig a small trench for the fire; when done, you can scatter ashes and smooth over the site with clean material.

Lacking such a favored spot, you can build what is called a mound fire. This technique, developed by the National Outdoor Leadership School (NOLS), is designed to keep the fire's heat away from unscarred ground. Picking a safe spot on unvegetated soil, you lay out a piece of groundcloth or fireproof blanket a yard square. You locate a deposit of mineral soil—perhaps sand from a streambank or humus-free dirt from the pit where a fallen tree has ripped from the ground. On the base cloth, you create a mound 6 inches thick and several feet across. On this you build your fire, using only such fuel as will be completely consumed. Finally, when you break camp, you scatter the ashes and put the mound material back where you found it.

Is this rather laborious procedure worth the trouble? Not in my book. It would seem to make sense only if you were going to stay at one spot for several days—and that in itself is bad practice at an unmarked site. I think the mound fire is a gimmick, and I wish NOLS would just drop it.

Distinctly out of a favor now is an earlier NOLS technique, the pit fire. It seemed like a good idea: you'd carefully dig a hole, removing a block of ground surface intact; you'd build, use, and douse your fire; and you'd replace the surface plug. It turned out, however, that depressed areas remained, and animals would often dig up the sites.

Another option, for people who *must* have fires, is to carry a metal fire pan. River rafting supply stores have them; you can also use a garbage can lid or an oil pan. Perch the pan on stones so that heat doesn't sterilize the ground. The result is pretty blameless, though the weight of the barrier is daunting.

Whatever the technique, pioneer fires are acceptable only where few parties travel. Little of this sort of thing can be done, even with extreme care, before an area begins to seem subtly scuffed and scarred. Signs of use attract more use.

For my part, I will simply not build a fire except in a well-sited existing ring. Period.

FOOD HANDLING AND CLEANUP

Food handling and dishwashing in camp must balance several concerns. The first is to prevent any transmission of disease from person to person. The second is to minimize food odors that may attract animals. The third concern, which may seem contradictory, is to put as little soap as possible into the environment.

There's one situation in which you don't want to spare the soap. Hands that cook, or even pass food to other hands, should be as clean as possible. Wash them well before dinner. Wash them especially well after taking care of sanitary needs (see Chapter 20).

While you are cooking, try to avoid wiping your hands on your clothing (use a bandanna instead). In areas where grizzly bear problems are acute, it may actually make sense to bring a light apron or coverall for the cook; or light waterproofs may be worn. At night, such items will be bearbagged.

Do your dishwashing well away from any spring, creek, or lake. In a small party, each person can clean cup and cutlery separately, using little or no soap (you decide). Whenever a number of people's dishes are washed together, however, soap has to be used. It must of course be non-detergent, biodegradable, and phosphate-free. Some people like to carry sponges treated with antimicrobial agents. In a family-sized party, the largest pot can serve as dishpan, and will get cleaned up in the process. Fallen cones, fallen tufts of conifer foliage, sand, and snow can supplement your scouring pad. So can fire ash. You can finish off with a boiling-water rinse. Let everything air-dry.

What about the dirty washwater? Before disposal, it should be poured through a small strainer or a bandanna, and the solids added to your garbage. Then water should be scattered widely, away from potential campsites, on porous ground among brush or stones, without dosing the same spot repeatedly. But in grizzly bear territory, it's advised instead to pour washwater into a small pit dug in organic soil and filled in after the last use.

You would never think of dumping wastewater into a stream, but the authorities note a couple of situations in which it makes sense. If you find yourself on the bank of a large southwestern river, rolling cloudily along through a desert environment, go ahead and dump your (strained) waste-water right into the waves. It turns out that the river is better able to absorb it than is the adjacent, parched terrain. Again, if you're on the banks of a sizable stream in grizzly country, safety argues for in-the-water disposal; pots and utensils should be rinsed in the current as well.

As for solid garbage, all the old rules have given way to a simple, single principle: *pack it out.* The only exception, and then only if you build a fire, is material that can be readily, totally burned: paper and also plastic bags, which combust cleanly if they are fed, a little at a time, into a very hot flame. (Allow them to smolder, though, and you get smoke, dark, rancid, and probably poisonous.) Aluminum foil won't burn: it only breaks up in fire. Watch out for packages that have a foil lining inside paper. Cans, if you have any, should be flattened, then washed or seared, and carried out.

What if you find yourself with half a pot of uneaten stew? See first if you can't finish it off; an excess of dinner may make a very good breakfast if you can keep it well-chilled overnight. Failing that, you simply have to take it with you as garbage. Neither burial nor burning is practical, and scattering, depending on the local wildlife, is somewhere between dubious and dangerous. You're training raccoons, bears, and other animals to scavenge and make camp nuisances of themselves.

What about fish viscera? In remote areas, away from trails, campsites, and the water's edge, they may be scattered on the ground. In high-use areas, or within day-trip range of the roadhead, they should be packed out. But if you are lake-fishing in grizzly bear country, the authorities recommend that guts be tossed into the water.

PROTECTING YOUR FOOD

Depending on where you are, you will have to take more or less elaborate precautions to protect your food from animal raiders. Procedures differ somewhat in regions without bears; with black bears only; and with both black bears and the more dangerous grizzly or brown bears.

Shelters and developed campsites especially attract animals. If you camp at a spot that has food lockers, metal hanging posts, overhead cables, or other built-in protective devices, by all means take the hint—and take advantage of what's there.

Many animals are inclined to piracy. In bearless country, you can protect open packages by putting them under pots or in pots with the lids wired on. Don't store food in packs overnight, and leave all zips and flaps open; otherwise, critters may gnaw right through packcloth to get at interesting smells.

In regions where bears are common, sterner measures must be taken. In more and more areas, that means stowing your groceries in one or several bearproof canisters. In black bear terrain, these can be left on the ground; the bears are quickly learning that the containers cannot be cracked. In grizzly country, the authorities recommend that even canisters be suspended if there are suitable trees. A plastic liner bag will minimize bear-attracting odors.

The more traditional technique, bearbagging, still works in some places, however. If you do bearbag, it is vital to do it exactly right. Otherwise, you are contributing to the education of the "garbage bear."

To hang your food, you need two large stout stuffsacks, not less than 50 feet of cord, and the right kind of tree. Finding the last item may take a while. You need a tree with a living, spindly branch about 20 feet up—thick enough to support the weight of your food, but too thin to support the weight of a scrambling bear. Once you locate your branch, take a good length of stout cord, tie a rock to one end, and lob it over the limb at a point at least 10 feet out from the trunk. Place your food in one of the stuffsacks, and tie it to the end of the line where the stone was. Now haul the load into position, fully 15 feet above the ground and 5 feet below the supporting branch.

In the old days you finished the job by simply tying the free end of the line around a tree. But in many regions the bears have learned that food comes down when an accessible cord is gnawed. For more protection, use the counterbalance method. Instead of tying off, haul on the free end to raise the load up close to the branch. Now place in a second stuffsack a weight equal to the food bag and tie it to the available line, as high up as you can reach. Wrap the remaining free line around this "counterbalance" so that nothing dangles. Finally, use a long stick to nudge the counterbalance as high as you can. Counterbalance and food bag should finally be hanging side by side.

To get your food back, you must push the food bag still higher, thus lowering the counterbalance to within reach. A loop tied near the counterbalance is helpful at this point—you can snag this with your stick to

BEARBAGGING

pull the load down. It is also possible to wrap the extra cord in such a way that you can dislodge it with a poke and make it fall within reach.

No stick? Tie a loop in the line near the food bag and run through it a second, separate piece of cord, with both ends dangling toward the ground. Hauling on the double line will pull food bag down and counterbalance up. When the bags are hanging side by side, you can get the loose cord down by hauling on just one end, like recovering a rappel rope. That doesn't solve the problem of retrieving the cache down in the morning, of course. Another solution is to leave a dangling recovery cord of fishing line, too thin and slick for a bear to get a grip on.

Although I have spoken of "food bag" and "counterbalance," the typical procedure is to divide your food and put equal weights of that on both ends of the line.

In regions where the bears aren't quite so educated, a less exacting method may be used. It requires two trees, 20 or so feet apart, and 100 feet of cord. Tying a weight to an end of the line, you toss it over a limb on tree

#1, about 20 feet up, and tie it off by wrapping around the trunk. Repeat the tossing maneuver with tree #2. Attach the food midway between, haul up, and tie off. The food should wind up 17 feet above the ground and at least 10 feet from each tree.

Along with food, a number of other items in your kit should go in the bearbag. Include scrubber pads, any wooden utensils, and canteens that contain, or have contained, flavored drinks. Include also shampoos, soaps, insect repellents, sunscreens, toothpaste, and other scented personal products.

If you are camping in an area where grizzly bears have been making problems, a still more comprehensive, indeed daunting, list of items will have to be bagged. Include all pots and utensils, even clean; all water bottles, even if they have contained only unflavored water; and the clothes you have cooked in. Ideally, packs should be hung as well. See Chapter 29.

Rainproofing your bearbag can be a problem; when a stuffbag is hung from its drawcord, water will get in at the top. The simplest solution is to wrap the contents in a large plastic bag and insert this, opening down, in the cloth sack that is actually suspended. Waterproof bearbags can also be purchased in stores.

Lacking a suitable tree, you can hang food bags over a vertical rock face, or under a pile of stones, with pots and pans on top to provide an alarm. A canister, of course, is better.

What do you do if you actually see a bear investigating your suspended cache, or, worse, heading down the trail with your food bag in his jaws? If you're in Canada, Alaska, or the northern Rockies, and think the animal may be a grizzly, swear at yourself for carelessness and don't argue. But if it's a black bear—now the only possibility in most of the United States and eastern Canada—you can safely fight back by shouting, flashing lights, banging pans, blowing whistles, and such. It's okay to advance on the bear (but not too close and not in such a way that the animal is cornered). It's even okay to throw small rocks toward but not directly at the bear. Black bears are seldom combative and are likely to retreat or even drop what they have taken. Don't start picking up scattered food, however, until the bear is out of the picture. For more on bear concerns, see Chapter 29.

Keeping your food out of the jaws of wildlife is more than a selfish concern. Careless food handling causes animals to regard camps, packs, and even automobiles as sources of food; a bear that has gotten this message will probably end up being destroyed ("A fed bear is a dead bear," the slogan goes). The penalty for smaller mammals isn't so drastic, but our involuntary gifts of food can lead to local population increases that natural forage can't support.

Do you really need to pitch a tent or other shelter? Weather and mosquitoes permitting, there's nothing like sleeping outside—really outside, with no cloth canopy between you and the big, brilliant dark. It's also far easier to choose a bedsite if you have no tent to consider. If the weather is uncertain, you have the further option of setting up shelter but starting the night in a bed outside.

There is, unfortunately, one excellent safety reason for preferring a tent: bears. Grizzly bears and even occasionally black bears have been known to investigate open-air sleepers; since the animals' investigating tools are teeth and claws, this can hurt. Bear experts recommend flatly that we sleep in tents, always. I refuse to take their advice in black bear country, the risk seeming too slight to matter; but in grizzly territory the case for tenting is awfully strong.

SITE SELECTION

Sleeping sites get picked early in the process of making camp. The choice may be casual and obvious, or it may require some thought. The requirements are the same commonsensical ones that apply to the camp as a whole.

You obviously need a piece of flat or nearly flat ground: a narrow piece for one person sleeping out, a broader one for a tent and its occupants. You can settle for less than perfection: a gentle slope from head to toe won't hurt, but you don't want a roll-inducing sideways tilt. Lie down on the spot to test it for comfort.

A soft or malleable surface is nice. The most comfortable upholstery is fine forest duff; sand and gravel are also good, if smoothed and shaped in advance. Grassy ground is hard. All vegetation, indeed, should be avoided.

Good drainage is vital. Watch out for hollows and subtle drainage paths that might gather water in a sudden rain.

Take account of wind direction. Sleeping out, or in a flimsy shelter, you may want to look for natural windbreaks. With a good tent, this becomes less important. But if there is a chance of a considerable breeze, make sure you have room to pitch the tent parallel to the direction of the wind, rather than crosswise.

Consider what you'll use for anchors. For a regular tent you want ground firm enough to hold any stakes you use but soft enough to drive them into. Look also for rocks, trunks, and sturdy snags to which you might tie guylines. A cord stretched between trees can provide a roofbeam for a tarp; a boulder or big log may serve as one shelter wall.

If cold is an issue, remember that high ground is warmer. Cold air flows downhill and gathers in moist and chilly pools. A site under trees will be warmer than one open to the sky, and will have less dew.

If your tent will be standing for several days in the same spot, look for a shady place, or plan to pitch an extra tarp or groundsheet above it, for comfort and to prevent premature deterioration of sunbeaten nylon.

Only after the basic requirements are met, consider such luxuries as morning sun (a great help in prodding you out of bed) and the view.

PITCHING SHELTER

Once you've chosen a site, smooth and police the ground, removing sticks and stones. Unless you are working with something loose like leaf mold, snow, or sand, don't level or engineer. Don't dig ditches in solid ground to carry off water; you don't need them, and they make all-but-permanent scars.

If you aren't pitching a shelter, you can proceed to make your bed. Spread your groundsheet—dirty side down—and mattress or pad. If the air is not too humid, unpack your sleeping bag and bivouac sack (if you use one) and lay them out. You may want to let the bag fluff up for a while before inserting it in the outer cover. If you've found a spot with a natural hollow for your hip, or if you can scoop one in sand or duff, that's fine. The digging of hipholes in hard ground is no longer recommended.

Pitching a tarp is both simpler and more tricky than setting up a real tent: there are so many possible variations. You can arrange the tarp in an A-shape, with a long ridgeline and sloping sides; like a lean-to, with one side high and one close to the ground; or even like a pagoda, with the center raised. Your choice depends most of all on the natural anchor points you find. Most tarps come with stout grommets built in at several points along the sides. Some have tie-on cords as well. If you need an attachment

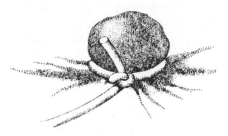

LINE ATTACHMENT USING
PEBBLE AND NOOSE

where none is provided—like the middle of the sheet—you can make one by wrapping a small, smooth pebble in the fabric and tying it off with a noose of cord. There are commercial devices that mimic this arrangement. A walking stick can be a useful prop. If your tarp is a light one, you'd do well not to put too much stress on any one part. For instance, run a line under the entire ridgeline rather than attaching a short line at each end and letting the sheet pull taut between them.

Nine people out of ten, probably, will be pitching genuine tents. Before you start unpacking, make sure that the site is large enough and otherwise suitable. Decide where the main door is going to be; if there is any slope, you usually want the entrance uphill. Decide where the higher end of the tent is to be; as a rule, you want it downwind.

Now spread a groundcloth or a fitted tent protection groundsheet. Make sure that the sheet does not protrude beyond the edge of the tent when you're done, possibly funneling rain beneath the floor.

Most tents these days are freestanding. Once you have slid various poles into various sleeves, or clipped various clips around the poles, or both, you have a stable structure you can lift and move around. (It can also blow away, so watch out if the wind is high.) A few light and popular tents, however, won't stand up until the corners have been staked and at least one guyline secured, providing tension.

In assembling shock-corded poles, unfold and join the segments gently. Resist the urge to "shake them out," whiplike: it works, but weakens the elastic and can damage metal. When you slide poles into or out of sleeves, be careful not to pinch fabric between segments. Always push from the base, rather than pulling from the forward end. At each end of its arc, a pole will seat in a brass grommet, usually marking a tent corner.

Grommets are typically set in rows of three, permitting different degrees of tension; if your tent is new, don't choose the tautest placement now but save it for later years, when fabrics may have stretched a bit.

Next, position the tent as you want it. Before committing yourself with stakes, lie down inside to see if a further shift is needed to keep you off roots, rocks, and such. Then stake the corners firmly. Given an assortment of stakes, choose the thinnest style that will hold in the local soil. Where the ground is very hard, you may be able to improvise alternative anchors, like short lengths of cord tied to sizable stones.

What about the rainfly? In most current designs, it's a cinch to install. Classically, it has grommets in the corners that get impaled by the tent-pole tips, or "ferrules." Some designs make the linkage easier still with clips, straps, or elastic cords.

The final action is to extend stabilizing guylines. As noted, some tents won't stand up until at least one of these is set. Even where they are not structurally necessary, guylines draw walls out tautly, help the tent shed wind, and may give it a little more room inside.

In low-impact terms, you might think it better to attach guylines to natural anchors rather than to stakes, reducing ground disturbance. That depends, however. In Rocky Mountain National Park at one point, so many cords were being tied around trunks that timberline trees were dying because of girdling! If you do run lines around young trees, provide padding against the bark.

Guylines tend to grow slack after they have been set. It's useful to set them up to be adjusted without moving the anchors. To do this, pass the line through the loop or grommet where it joins the tent; then double it back and tie it to itself, using any of several knots that will grip under tension but slide when you loosen the strands. The most common is the *taut-line hitch*. Some tents are pre-rigged in this manner; commercial gripping devices are sold to do this same job.

HOUSEKEEPING AND BEDTIME PRECAUTIONS

Should you unpack your sleeping bag immediately, or leave it in the stuffbag? If the air is not humid, it's good to let the bag expand as long as possible. Down, particularly, takes quite a while to regain its maximum loft. But on a cool, damp evening, the bag may start getting clammy as soon as you expose it to the air; in this case, you're better off leaving it

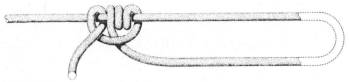

TAUTLINE HITCH

stuffed until you can get inside it. When you unpack a down bag, shake it out gently to fluff the fill.

Avoid bringing dirt, debris, and wet clothing into your tent or tube tent. (This is less a concern beneath a tarp.) Muddy boots come off just outside. Dirt that does get tracked in can be left to dry and shaken out the next time the tent is struck. Snow, though, must be removed before it melts.

Whether you're sleeping outdoors or in, you don't want to be too fascinating to the local wildlife. This means, above all, *not* taking food to bed with you: your evening snack has to happen before the bearbag ascends, not after.

Before you turn in, police the campsite. Loose objects, especially bright ones, are likely to be carried off by pack rats (in many regions). Various animals are also drawn to salty things. If there are porcupines around, packs, with their sweat-salty straps, should be indoors or hung out of easy reach; drying socks should hang well off the ground.

Your clothing and paraphernalia come into the tent with you, stashed in the handy netting pockets; boots can be left in the vestibule. If you're sleeping outdoors in the dew, stick small belongings in a "possibles bag." Turn boots sideways or put them in a bag as well. On a cold night, you can take removable insoles into bed with you for a warm start in the morning.

Warm nights with mosquitoes can be troublesome for the tentless sleeper. For this situation you need a headnet, with a brimmed hat worn under to lift it away from your face, or a separate piece of netting to hide under. Repellent can prevent most of the bites, but it won't spare you the sense of being under siege. In desperation, lacking a net, you can breathe through a sweater.

In the morning, shake out boots and clothes before dragging them blindly on; just occasionally you'll find some small crawling thing has found its way inside.

A GOOD NIGHT'S SLEEP

Nothing should be more automatic than a restful night in the wilderness. The harder you have worked during the day, the more luxurious the warmth and softness of the sleeping bag become; the colder it is in the world outside, the lovelier the contrast feels.

If you've been accustomed to softer beds, however, you may find it odd and even uncomfortable at first to sleep on a thin foam pad. This is one excellent reason for beginning with the relatively luxurious self-inflating air mattress, despite the extra weight. For a pillow, rolled up clothing in a bag will generally do.

If you don't use a sleeping bag liner with a down bag, it's a good idea to wear a layer of clothing to bed. Body oils gum up fluffy down; the cure, washing the bag, destroys some of the all-important resiliency of the plumules. Wear a stocking cap, or put a shirt under your head, to protect the bag from oils in your hair. Bags filled with polyester insulations, by contrast, aren't damaged either by dirt or by washing.

If you've planned well, you shouldn't find yourself in a sleeping bag too cool for the region you're visiting. But maybe you're testing the limits of a summer bag in winter, spring, or fall. If you do find yourself getting chilly at night, there are a number of things, some mentioned already, that you can do about it.

- Speed up your metabolism. Take a brisk walk or get some other exercise before you crawl in (some people do isometrics in the bag). If you feel warm when you lie down, your body will heat the bag quickly and give you a good start. Don't linger outside getting chilled. When you're cold or likely to be, it's good to eat something last thing before bearbagging your food, preferably protein (the best fuel for warmth when you aren't exercising).
- If tentless, move under cover. Lying in the open, you radiate extra heat to the sky. Even the branches of a tree will cut that loss somewhat. And protect yourself from any chilling breeze; for instance, you can put your head downwind so that the cold draught won't enter the open end of your bag.
- Put on more clothes. The single most useful item is a knit cap;

the head loses more heat than any other part of the body. Dry socks are also important. Then come pants, shirt, sweater, mittens, possibly a jacket—even, if required, your waterproof breathable raingear—until your whole wardrobe is on. Or, instead of wearing it all, you can stuff some items into your sleeping bag, especially at your feet, to stop air motion and hold warmth in.

- ➡ Build up the insulation beneath you. A wind parka, a rope, the emptied pack itself—almost anything will help. Make sure there's something under your feet as well.

- ➡ If you get seriously cold, you can try sticking your hands and feet in waterproof bags: moisture won't escape, but neither will the considerable warmth that is carried off with it.

If none of these ideas works, you are probably badly underequipped for the trip you're taking. If it's any comfort, you can lay plans for next time: perhaps a longer, thicker foam pad, or a second pad . . . warmer clothing . . . a bag cover or an inner bag . . . even a pair of down- or polyester-filled booties for your feet.

Whenever the wilderness world is both cold and wet—in winter camping especially—keeping dry is an important part of keeping warm. Sleeping gear always gets damp at night. Although synthetic bags will keep on warming you to some degree even when wet, down bags will not, so you have to fight any buildup of moisture. If the weather allows, you can dry a bag by hanging it on a branch, a ski, or over your pack as you walk. It will also dry well in a sunny tent on a layover day. Don't attempt to dry damp clothing by taking it into the sleeping bag with you.

If you should ever feel that you are dangerously chilled, don't keep quiet about it. If you act early, there is an easy corrective: strip and get into a warm sleeping bag with a companion. Hot drinks also help; alcohol, when you're cold, only does harm. If you recognize in yourself or in a companion the symptoms of what is called *hypothermia*, it's a true emergency (see Chapter 28).

SANITATION AND CLEAN WATER

Time was when nobody dreamed of a wilderness being anything other than *clean*, clean beyond the measure of any city or town. One writer observed happily that wilderness dirt was "perfectly sanitary, being rendered so by oxygen and remoteness from human habitation." Then there was the notion that running water purified itself every 200 feet.

But gradually we began to hear a different, disquieting story. Lakes and streams along the John Muir Trail in California began to be called polluted. In backpacking areas all over the country—in Idaho, in Colorado, in the White Mountains of New Hampshire—researchers began to find unexpectedly high counts of the bacteria known as coliform, which indicate contamination by the feces of warm-blooded animals.

And then came worse reports—a few, then more, then seemingly an epidemic. Backpackers were reaching home only to suffer punishing bouts of diarrhea, caused by any of several unpleasant organisms found in human and animal feces: notably the protozoan *Giardia lamblia*, the bacterium *Campylobacter jejeuni*, and the recently notorious protozoan *Cryptosporidium parvum*. These organisms can be transmitted in water, and it was the water that was blamed. From the 1970s onward, we were advised to boil, filter, or chemically treat every drop of wilderness water we drank.

Several things are unclear about this situation, however. It isn't clear whether we have seen a true explosion in infections, or rather a surge in reporting and publicity. If the risk really has gone up, it's not clear why. Are we catching these ailments from increasingly polluted water, as conventional wisdom holds? Or are we rather catching them from each other, in camp, because of poor sanitation, as some dissenters suggest? Some people carry giardia without showing symptoms—estimates go as high as one-fifth of the population. A person who is a carrier, and who fails to clean up scrupulously after defecating, could infect a companion just by sharing a piece of cheese.

Backpackers, fortunately, don't have to resolve the debate about what is going on. What we do have to do is to defend ourselves, in two ways. First, and absolutely vital: each of us must be scrupulous in disposing of body waste, keeping all traces of it both far away from natural water and out of our food supply. Second, and somewhat more debatable: each of us had better make a practice of purifying all water taken from the land, or carefully gauge the risks of not doing so.

SANITATION

You need only spend a few days in a popular hiking area to know that many people still are careless in their toilet habits. Feces left on the surface of the ground, especially anywhere near water, can contaminate a large area. And though humans are not the only carriers of *Giardia*, we *are* the only carriers of other, more dangerous diseases that afflict our species: the several types of hepatitis, for example.

If you are traveling in a group of unusual size, say, ten people or more, and if you plan to use one spot for several days, a common latrine is probably the best solution. You'll need a shovel. Choose the spot and do the digging soon after arriving in camp, not as an afterthought. Find a spot several hundred feet away from trails and water. The drier the location, the better. Avoid low-lying spots that are, or could be, moisture traps, and areas that look like natural runoff channels. And look for *soil*, not cavities among rocks. Organisms that are filtered out effectively by soil can travel long distances along cracks in rock. Finally, try not to dig in a place that has obvious appeal as a future party's bedsite or kitchen.

A latrine should be 12 to 18 inches deep. If you need more capacity, make it longer or wider, not deeper. In digging, do not cut roots. Only excrement and toilet paper go into a latrine; garbage must be dealt with otherwise, and tampons, sanitary napkins, and disposable diapers must be packed out with you. Throw in fresh soil after every use, and tamp down the clean surface to compress the waste below. Don't overfill the latrine; leave enough space so that, when breaking camp, you can top it off with at least 4 inches of soil.

Most hikers, however, will never build or use a latrine. Instead, we turn to what is rather comically labeled the "individual cat method," digging a succession of small, single-use holes.

Members of a party should scatter widely to find their spots and get as far as they can away from trail, camp, and waterside. Around some camps, late in the season, you may find so many catholes that it's hard to locate fresh ground. This is a sign of too much use, but also indicates a certain laziness: go far enough from camp and you won't have this trouble. (Maybe you can collect some wood at the same time.) If your bodily schedule permits, it's good to take care of these needs during the day, when the party is between campsites; this prevents the buildup of waste in popular areas.

With catholes as with latrines, surface is important. Again, you want a deep-soiled spot that is neither too dry nor prone to waterlogging; the shady side of a log is good. With trowel, boot, or stick, excavate your pit, not deeper than 8 inches, but deep enough so that you can cover your deposit with a couple of inches of soil. If the soil surface is sodlike, held together with rootlets, cut out a slab and set it aside. When you finish, use a stick to mingle feces with soil and drop the soiled stick into the hole. Then replace the surface plug, or rake in clean, scooped-out earth, and restore surface litter.

Although catholes and latrines serve well to isolate waste, they don't do anything to hasten its decomposition: quite the contrary. In cold alpine environments, studies have found, buried feces remain both recognizable and infectious after several years—as wildlife feces, left on the ground in reach of sun and air, do not. This disquieting fact gives rise to one more disposal option: surface smearing. If you are traveling off the trail in a truly remote area that is either high in elevation or very dry, you might consider this variant. Look for a sunbeaten spot well away from water and from any likely travel route; spread excrement thinly with a stick or a stone; and pack out any toilet paper. However, this method need hardly be considered for ordinary travel, or in warm, well-watered regions.

Yet another situation needs a brief mention: if you find yourself on an extensive glacier, dispose of feces into a crevasse. They will emerge years later at the downstream end of the ice, unrecognizable and, so the experts tell us, harmless.

Last of all, there's the pack-out option. In a very few situations, you may actually be asked to carry feces out of the wilderness. The way to do it: put the waste in a paper bag containing a scoop of cat litter, with a plastic bag outermost. Then deposit the whole package, after removing the plastic, in a vault toilet at trailhead or campground.

What about toilet paper? The old advice was to bury it or, with extreme caution, to burn it. The new doctrine is simpler: pack it out in essentially all cases. Carried in a doubled plastic pouch, the soiled paper won't be objectionable. Once out of the wilderness, dispose of it in the normal way; but never put plastic down a toilet. If you're packing TP out, you have an incentive to use as little as possible. Sometimes you can clean up adequately with such found objects as bits of wood, smooth pebbles, and (carefully chosen) vegetation. Snow works, soo. Even if you adopt such methods, however, you'd better have some TP in your pack, if only in case of diarrhea.

It isn't necessary to be so fastidious about urination. In the way that matters most, the urine of a healthy person is quite clean: that is, it contains few or none of the organisms that can cause disease. However, the acid in urine does burn vegetation, and some animals like to nibble urinous leaves—yes, these matters have been studied! The ideal is to besprinkle barren rocks.

WASHING AND SWIMMING

Having taken due care to keep the pathogens in human waste out of the larger environment, now take extreme care to keep them out of your immediate environment: by washing your hands scrupulously with soap. Just a palm-to-palm scrub won't do it: work up and down and around each finger, and scour around the nails. Conclude with a copious rinse, starting with clear untreated water and finishing with a splash of the disinfected kind (see below).

In principle, all washing—of yourself, of your clothes, of your teeth, of your dishes—should be done well away from the water's edge. Aside from the after-cathole, precooking, and dishwashing cases, skip the soap. For general personal cleanliness, rinsing off soapless should make you feel fresh enough. To get warm water, you can heat it on the stove, or leave it in a dark container in the sun; a shower attachment can be fitted to a waterbag. Some find that a sponge with a scrubber pad, applied gently, cleans the skin better than a cloth. Alcohol wipes from your kit can be refreshing every once in a while.

Swimming is delightful and usually harmless. Don't swim if you are ill, however, and make sure you aren't introducing any fecal traces into the lake or stream. It also does no harm to sponge off a few layers of sunscreen, bug dope, and general grime before you plunge. At the shoreline, avoid stepping on plants and undercut or crumbling banks.

Two special cases alter these practices.

On the bank of a large, rushing stream, it may be just as well to wash clothes, soapless, in live water; in a remote area, you can even suspend them in the flow and let the current do the job for you. In grizzly bear country, streamside washing is positively recommended.

At the other extreme are water bodies so sensitive to contamination that you should make minimum contact with them. An example would be a desert pothole filled with rainwater. Generally speaking, wherever there is a little water in a harsh environment, better just keep your distance, or at most tap the source for drinking water only.

WATER TREATMENT

The pollution problem in the wilderness has led to a striking change in habits. We are now routinely advised that every drop of water taken from the land must be boiled, microfiltered, or treated with iodine. I don't go that far (see The Old Way, below); but plainly every hiker now must know how to treat water and be equipped to do so.

BOILING

Boiling is the classic water treatment. Most experts feel that a momentary full boil is the maximum necessary for practical purposes, even at high elevations. A brief boil unquestionably kills *Giardia*. Suggested boiling times of more than a minute reflect bureaucratic caution and can safely be ignored. Boiling, of course, consumes fuel, and it can only conveniently done when you are in camp. So other alternatives are more widely used.

IODINE TREATMENT

For many purposes, chemical treatment is most convenient. Treatments involving chlorine—in the form of Halazone tablets or bleach—are out of favor. (The substance is not the most effective, and tablets lose potency quickly.) The recommended chemical today is iodine.

Alas, it is not quite as recommended today as it was a few years ago. Iodine was long thought effective against all pathogens. It now appears that one organism of great concern, *Cyptosporidium*, may resist iodine treatment. In the absence of more and better-focused research, I'd be slow to jettison my iodine kit; but people are wondering.

Iodine for water treatment comes in several forms.

Tincture of iodine. *Tincture* means a solution in alcohol; the bottle you buy must say "2 percent" or "USP standard." (It will also say "Poison," but don't let that scare you.) The standard dose is five drops of 2 percent tincture per quart of water. Let stand for half an hour. If the water is very cloudy, double the dosage; if very cold, double either the dosage or, better, the time. A much more concentrated tincture, designed specifically for water treatment, may be on the market soon.

Iodine tablets (tetraglycine hydroperiodide). Potable Aqua is the familiar brand. The normal dose is one tablet per quart. Give tablets 3 minutes to dissolve, then let stand for at least 20. Since tablets lose potency on exposure to moisture and air, keep them in a tightly sealed container; avoid opening the bottle with wet fingers. Potable Aqua kits are now available with companion pills of ascorbic acid—vitamin C—which can be added (after treatment is complete) to neutralize the iodine flavor. Discard unused tablets at the end of each season. Cost: about $5 without C tablets, $8 with.

Iodine/water solution. The kit consists of 4 to 8 grams of iodine crystals in a small, tightly capped glass bottle, capacity 1 to 3 fluid ounces (exact numbers don't matter, but a larger container is easier to handle). You can find the ingredients yourself or, easier, pick up the ready-made setup by PolarPure ($9). When the bottle is filled with water and shaken vigorously, some crystals dissolve to form a solution. This solution—*not the solid iodine in the bottom*—is the treating agent. The recommended dose depends on the temperature and clarity of the water you are treating: check instructions. Each time you use some solution, replace the drawn-off water, twist on the cap, and shake again; more iodine dissolves, and the concentration stays the same. One caution: the solution is weaker when cold; in chilly weather, carry it in a shirt pocket or warm it before using. And store the unit in several layers of plastic. It tends to leak a little and turn things around it a violent purple.

Some tricks and precautions apply to all these iodine treatments:

- If uncertain of the normal dose, remember that the treated water should look slightly brown and taste a little funny.

- Consider the treatment times recommended in kit directions to be the absolute minimum: there is evidence that *Giardia* cysts can hold out for several hours. Letting the water sit overnight before drinking is ideal.
- There are tradeoffs between time, temperature, and dosage. You can cut back on chemical if the water is warm; you can also use less if you're able to wait for several hours.
- Thorough mixing helps the treatment. After adding the iodine, rattle the bottle with lid slightly loose so that the threads are moistened.
- Cloudy water should be cleared by straining it through cloth or letting it stand for several hours before treatment.
- It's fine to add vitamin C or flavorings to kill the slight iodine taste, but only *after* treatment is complete.
- Iodine is slightly toxic in large doses; avoid ingesting solid iodine, and don't let kids play with the kit. Pregnant women, people with thyroid problems, and people allergic to iodine shouldn't use this method at all. And iodine shouldn't be relied on heavily during multiweek hikes.

FILTRATION

The most used water treatment today is filtration. Half a dozen makers now offer filters suitable for backpacking. Weights range from under 8 ounces to a couple of pounds; costs range from under $10 to $300; selling points vary widely. What's to choose?

The first question is just what you want to filter out or kill. All reputable filters stop *Giardia* and *Cryptosporidium*. Many claim to stop bacteria, but only some of these models actually have a pore size tiny enough (0.2 microns "absolute") to do this job impeccably by mechanical means. In some designs the filter is impregnated with iodine, which attacks smaller organisms as they float by. Only this type can deal with viruses, which are minuscule. Finally, some filters use carbon to remove organic chemicals like pesticides or herbicides (but may or may not counter bacteria and viruses—these functions are separate). Carbon can also remove the after-treatment residue of iodine.

In the North American wilderness, where the water is pretty clean by planetary standards, any filter that blocks the protozoans will probably serve you well enough. Indeed, there is some disadvantage to buying a more capable unit: it is likely to weigh more, cost more, and clog more frequently.

Ease of use is a second and key criterion. Pumps require varying amounts of force and produce varying amounts of clean water per minute.

Easiest of all are filters that you don't pump at all: they work by gravity. This process is too slow for on-trail use but fine in camp. Lacking moving parts, gravity-feed filters are somewhat less prone to fail. On the minus side, they are notably heavy. Some regular pump models come with gravity-feed adapters.

Filters work by catching things. Therefore, and inevitably, they get plugged up in time. Some clog faster than others. Some can be readily cleaned in the field, some not so readily. On certain models, a clogged filter element must simply be replaced.

Several options may come with your filter, either as part of the package or separately sold. Often handy is a *prefilter* that attaches to the intake hose and screens out coarse material. Another useful item is a bottle fitting that allows you to pump without spillage straight into a wide-mouthed bottle or waterbag.

You may see very small filters designed to be used like straws, slurping directly out of a water source. They don't yield enough water to be practical and can be ignored.

Filter technology is changing rapidly. If you're in the market, seek the current advice of stores, magazines, catalogs, web pages, and friends.

USING AND MAINTAINING A FILTER

With the advent of filters, a new chore has been added to the backpacking day: crouching by the waterside, pumping away. It's a slow business at best, and when your filter acts up (as is not unlikely), it gets slower. Indeed, water filters seem to be among the most troublesome and hated items of gear. To keep problems to the minimum, get to know your filter and follow its instructions carefully.

As with any treatment method, you'll start with the cleanest, clearest water you can find. Moving water stirs up sediments and contaminants, so draw from quiet pools if you can. Keep the intake hose off the muddy bottom (some models are usefully equipped with floats). Cloudy water should be dipped into a container and left to settle, an hour or two or

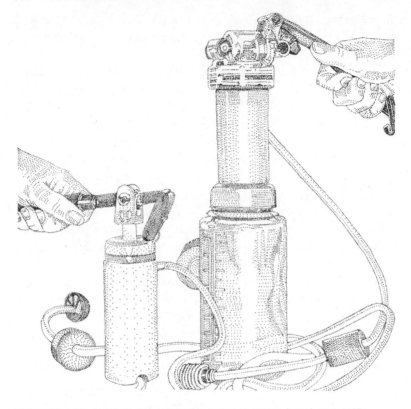

WATER FILTERS: SWEETWATER GUARDIAN MICROFILTER (LEFT) AND MSR
MINIWORKS

even overnight, before filtering. (Glacial flour—the fine suspended rock
dust found in some high-mountain streams—is almost instant death on
filter elements.) If you have a prefilter, use it. Particularly ugly water can
be filtered twice, or treated with iodine as well.

When water starts coming through the device, let the first few spurts
go by before you start collecting. Keep the outlet tube—the spigot where
treated water emerges—scrupulously clean. Touch it as little as possible
and don't let it flop into the source. After each use, pump air until the last
drops are gone, shake out the hoses, and wipe surfaces dry. In the pack,
keep the outlet tube in its own bag or wrap a plastic bag around it. To permit further drying, carry the filter as a whole in the mesh bag it came in.

When it's cold enough, ice forms in filters and slows the action. Prevent this by taking the gizmo into your tent, or even into your sleeping

bag, in a plastic bag. If a filter gets dropped onto the rocks, suspect the worst; any sudden change in its action probably means you need a new filter element.

If the filter seems to be gradually flagging, it's time to clean the works. Usually, this task takes one of two forms. You uncover a ceramic filter element and scrub it with a pad or brush to remove surface contamination. Or you "backwash" a nonceramic filter element by rearranging hoses and pumping clean water through it in the reverse of the usual direction. In some cases, a clogged filter element must simply be replaced with a new one.

If you are scrubbing a ceramic element, you'll be handling a contaminated surface. Do this job away from food and try to avoid splattering yourself. Some elements then need to be sanitized, as by boiling. Wash your brush or pad in clean water, and wash your hands with soap when you are done.

Backwashing, which doesn't require exposing the filter element, might seem a simpler process. Some instructions, though, call for sanitizing at the end with a chlorine bleach solution you're unlikely to have available on the trail.

At home after a trip, instructions usually call for sterilizing the unit by pumping a weak bleach solution through it. If so, repeat the operation at the beginning of the hiking season. In between, store the filter in a dry place in its netting bag.

After a certain number of cleanings, filter elements must be replaced. (On longer trips, take a spare.) Generally, ceramic filters have longer cleaning intervals and longer life overall. Replacement cartridges will cost somewhere near half the price of the complete original unit.

COMBINATION METHODS

Since each type of water treatment method has its drawbacks, many people switch off among methods. At dinner, for instance, they boil water; overnight, they iodinize at low concentration; on the trail, they filter. You can also combine methods in treating a given batch. For instance, water may be filtered first through a unit that stops protozoans only, and afterwards treated with iodine at half the standard concentration to dispose of bacteria and viruses. Or it may be treated with iodine first and then filtered through carbon to remove the chemical residue.

One final caution: some water is dangerous because of naturally oc-

curring chemicals like arsenic and won't be made drinkable by any sterilizing treatment; even carbon filters may or may not help. Suspect a spring
without insects or signs of use by animals; avoid water draining from old
mines or areas with hot springs, geysers, or fumaroles.

THE OLD WAY

What if (like the author) you're unwilling to forgo the very special pleasure of drinking water straight from the country, flat on your belly, suck-
ing it from a stream, or getting its tang across the cool rolled lip of a metal
cup? Are you crazy? No: but be very careful about where you pursue your
habit.

Giardia and *Cryptosporidium* can be found in just about any water; so
the branchwater drinker is taking a certain risk. That risk, though, is less
than current publicity might have you think. In the California Sierra, the
"worst" water has yielded one *Giardia* cyst per 10 gallons! This no doubt
understates the problem—the critters are notoriously hard to isolate—but
the actual numbers are certainly far smaller than the populations used to
test filters and treatments in the lab. Many people have drunk natural waters for years, and continue to, without ill effect. And if you do come
down with giardiasis, it's less than a disaster for a basically healthy person.
Some other water-borne diseases, hepatitis E for instance, are far more serious, but these are derived from human contamination only, and typically via waters far more polluted than you'll encounter in the North
American wilderness.

When you look for water, *think watershed.* Where does a stream come
from? What pollution sources might there be in its drainage area? Don't
drink downstream from a known camp or trail crossing; rather, go upstream, or find a smaller stream draining from a basin containing no trail
or major cross-country hiking route. In regions with beavers, be aware
that their dams are sources of major contamination. (In beaver country,
filters clog in a hurry.) Don't patronize streams that have their sources
outside wilderness, in civilized territory; this is a not-uncommon situation, especially in the Southwest and in the Ozark region. Water fresh out
of a remote snowbank is likely to be safe (as well as exquisite). Watch out,
though, for colored "watermelon snow," tinted by algae that can give you
indigestion or worse. Merely scraping away the pink layer isn't enough—
the clean-appearing snow below it may also contain the organism.

Lake water does not quite follow the watershed rule. Large bodies of water act as settling basins, and water from a lake outflow is likely to be safer than that from inflow streams. Where streams wander across meadows, something similar happens: they are likely to be cleaner where they leave than where they enter. Other things being equal, it's better to drink from still water than from a current (which can stir things up).

Some otherwise wild landscapes are grazed or overgrazed by livestock. If you see many cows or much dung, better treat the water, period.

In the region bordering Lake Superior, including Isle Royale National Park on the lake itself, all waters without exception must be treated to kill a regionally ubiquitous parasite, *Echinococcus granulosis*.

WHAT IF YOU DO GET SICK?

Giardiasis develops 5 to 7 days after exposure. Since most wilderness trips are shorter than that, you're unlikely to come down with this particular affliction on the trail. The similar disease caused by *Cryptosporidium*, however, can develop in as little as 2 days, and so can diarrheas caused by bacteria. If you do get sick on the trail, make sure you keep up your fluid intake and get to civilization as fast as you can (see Chapter 26).

In all these diseases, diarrhea is the main affliction; accompanying miseries vary. Untreated, you can expect to be laid up for a week or more (up to three weeks for giardiasis). There are drugs for giardiasis; bacterial infections can be treated with antibiotics. There is at present no treatment for cryptosporidosis. Only a stool analysis can tell exactly what you've got. By all means, seek your doctor's advice.

Some campers, very careful when they choose their campsite and organize their brief life there, are rather casual and careless when they depart. Yet breaking camp is a moment of special responsibility for the conscientious traveler.

Suppose you have camped at an established site. It is, inevitably, a beaten-down, impacted place. That is its great advantage. Even here you can look around before you leave and ask yourself: How much have we added to the problems of this place? How much can we undo?

There is little point in getting rid of a properly located fire ring that the next party may want to use. But if you see a ring where no ring should be—at the lake's edge on grass, for example—it can be a good service to remove the stones and disguise, as much as you can, the scar. Make sure that the ring you used yourself is completely clean, ready, and inviting. Otherwise you may be encouraging the next comers to construct a fresh one.

Your fire must, of course, be unmistakably dead. Stop adding wood to the flames well before you are ready to leave so that coals will burn into ashes. Never bury the fire with dirt; this may fail to kill it properly and also spoils the ring. Instead, douse a still-warm fire with quantities of water. Comb through the ashes with your fingers to make sure they are cold clear through. Be certain to pull out any unburnable fragments like aluminum foil (which should not be there in the first place) and pack them away with you. If, in spite of all care, you do have sizable chunks of wood left over, it's okay to leave them in the ring.

If a ring is choked with ashes, should these be scattered, buried, or left alone? There has been quite a debate about this, but the consensus now is for scattering to restore nutrients to the soil. Take cold, gray ashes away from camp and fling them widely in several places. Black, extinguished coals, however, should be left in place for further combustion.

Gather up all litter—your own and as much as you can carry of what may have been there before.

So much for the typical, relatively civilized site. If, by contrast, your camp has been in a place not obviously used before, there is more to do. Your tracks must be made to vanish. Some instructors in wilderness programs like Outward Bound have made a game of it. They ask their students to imagine themselves fugitives, with hostile trackers behind them examining every yard of ground for signs of their presence.

If you have used only a stove at the pristine site, your job will be simple; with a fire, it is more complex (see Fire at an Unmarked Site in Chapter 18). It is truly important in this situation that *all* charred wood be consumed to ash. Ashes pass quickly back into the soil, but charcoal lasts so long that archaeologists count on it for dating ruins. Make sure you don't wind up with a big half-burned log, there being no good way of disposing of such an object.

Ashes, again, should be scattered, with even more determination to make them inconspicuous. If you've managed well, you won't have coals; if you do, these had better be buried. Exception: where wildfire has left obvious traces in the scene, a few more embers won't bother anyone.

If you cannot make all traces of your fire disappear from the pristine site, you should never have built a fire there in the first place.

Sleeping spots need policing too. Restore any rocks you've removed. Ruffle the smooth surfaces you've made. Scatter twigs, leaves, or gravel to replace the natural litter you've swept away. You won't succeed in eliminating *every* trace, but you should be able to restore the natural scene well enough to fool any casual eye. Weather, in a little time, will do the rest.

F VARIATIONS

At the same time that we are earnest to explore and learn all things, we require that all things be mysterious and unexplorable, that land and sea be infinitely wild, unsurveyed and unfathomed by us because unfathomable.

Henry David Thoreau, *Walden*

22 CROSS-COUNTRY TRAVEL AND OTHER VARIANTS

Of all the miles that backpackers travel each year, 90 percent are probably hiked in summer. And of that 90 percent, 90 percent are hiked by trail. Sometimes we speak of wilderness as "crowded," but for those who are ready to take a further step into wildness—to leave behind the busy channels of the summer trails—the wild country still has room and to spare.

Not that you could call these remoter lands underused. Wilderness serves purposes beyond recreation; the lands where the hiker seldom comes may be the best preserved of all for wildlife, for watershed, for scientific study. None of the backcountry is wasted. Wilderness itself should have within it a deeper wilderness—wilderness, so to speak, to the second power.

The hikers who take advantage of that deeper wilderness are not numerous. And here's a paradox: wherever they do become numerous, the experience they seek vanishes before them. Whenever a cross-country route begins to carry more than a handful of people a week, informal paths start to appear, and then to erode and deepen. When this point is reached, the land-managing agency has several choices: to restrict use ... to build a formal trail ... or (as happens too often) simply to let the land take scar upon scar. A well-built trail is not a convenience merely, but also a way of accommodating use without excessive damage to the land.

Take the High Peaks of the Adirondacks, 4,000 and 5,000 feet in elevation. In that region, 4,000 feet is already subalpine. Yet these summits are not barren, but green with a thick fur (unlikely though it seems) of sphagnum moss—"inverted bogs," one writer has called them. Many of these peaks are trailless, and most people seem to want them that way. But so often are they ascended by cross-country hikers that their sides are striped with steep, eroding gullies. These are trails in all but name, and the mossy tundras on the narrow crests are being trampled away.

What can be done in cases like this? Except where access roads can be shortened, adding a filter of distance, the answers seem to come down to two: either the authorities must limit the number of people allowed to make these climbs, or they must build formal trails and overlooks, protecting the fragile summit vegetation with railings and with signs: "Keep off the moss." Neither answer is appealing. But where there is little wilderness and many who would use it, we come to such uncomfortable choices again and again.

Meanwhile, the trailless outback is still there. And for a certain number of hikers, it is the only wilderness that really counts, the one experience that has the full reward.

TRAVEL OFF THE TRAIL

It's hard to offer rules for hiking cross-country, because "country" itself is endlessly diverse. A trail along a talus slope may not be so very different from a trail in a rainforest or a trail through a thicket of chaparral. But leave the path and you deal with the land in every shape and texture it has. Here you may struggle at ½ mile an hour through an enormous, fragrant field of azalea; here you slip and slide on scree or the abominable sliding stuff called rock mulch; here you jump from stone to stone in the bed of a rushing stream; here you scramble up a steep rock scarp; here you clamber over and around the trunks of fallen trees.

Cross-country travel is typically slow. If 2 miles an hour is a lively pace with a pack on a level trail, 1 mile an hour is good progress through woods and brush. And yet not even this slowness of pace is predictable. There are open, parklike forests as well as thick and tangled ones. And on the smooth granite expanses of certain western ranges, it may be scarcely harder to move off-trail than on. In the desert, too, marked trails are rare and scarcely required.

To hike off-trail you need a serious backpacking boot, weighing 3 pounds or more the pair in an average size, and with a good high top; lighter boots, so comfortable on easy ground, offer too little protection for rugged travel. Make sure you have plenty of adhesive tape in your kit. A sprained ankle can often be stabilized with tape, allowing you to retreat under your own power (see Chapter 27).

For travel in rough country, you will be happiest with an internal-frame pack that rides close to the back. If you have an external-frame already, though, it will serve. Just try to lower the center of gravity of the load. Put your heaviest objects at the bottom and mount the sleeping bag on top rather than underneath. On some models, you can shift the entire packbag lower on the frame. Before you wade into vegetation, make sure that zippers are shut tight, and get rid of any trailing loops or protrusions where bushes and branches could catch hold. Stow away any objects that are hanging on the outside of your pack, or at your belt.

When crossing scree and loose ground, as well as snow patches, you may be grateful for a pair of gaiters. These zip-on cuffs fit tightly over the gap at the top of the boot, preventing loose rocks and the like from bouncing in.

Two animal problems, common in many regions, become slightly more troublesome when you leave the trail. In brush country, ticks are hard to avoid. Gaiters help here, and so do dabs of insect repellent at neck, wrists, and ankles, but about the only sure defense is to strip and inspect each evening and get rid of the creatures before they get attached.

Second, snakes—rattlesnakes and, in the east, copperheads and cottonmouths—are somewhat more of a hazard off the trail. Snakes can't function either in heat or in cold and are most active on warm nights and in the morning and the evening of hot days. Thus you are often warned to watch for them at those times. But in the heat of midday there is another danger: a snake, lying low, may be too torpid to move out of the way of a descending boot. Watch where you put your feet and hands. Don't step down on the far side of a rock or log without first getting a look at the ground there.

You are no more likely to see wildlife off-trail than on—perhaps less so. But there may be more risk of sudden bear encounters. In grizzly country, be cautious in bushwhacking in dense vegetation; you don't want to stumble on a resting bear. Brushy avalanche paths are favorite bear retreats; before crossing such an area, pause and look for moving bushes or other sign. For more about animal problems, see Chapter 29.

LOW IMPACT OFF THE TRAIL

On established paths you deliberately confined your impact to places impacted already. On the trail you walked single file. In camp you built fires (if at all) at old sites. You concentrated your traffic in the smallest possible area.

But in off-trail travel, exactly the opposite applies. To avoid leaving traces, you disperse. A party walking through the woods, or on any surface where a mark could be left, should always walk abreast, each hiker in a separate line, so far as the land allows. A little impact, spread over a lot of land, will simply vanish. To make sure this is the case, off-trail parties should be small—two or three is best.

Don't build cairns or ducks; don't blaze trees or break branches. Don't spoil the experience of others by reminding them, oppressively, that Kilroy has already been here. Although they may know better, walkers on the trackless ridge or in the empty forest would like to imagine that no one else has been in that place, at least this year. Don't kill the illusion for those who come after.

What kinds of land are most easily damaged by cross-country hiking and camping? The types are familiar: leafy plants of the shady forest floor . . . timberline vegetation of all kinds . . . wet meadows and bogs . . . erosive slopes. Although subalpine meadows are proverbial for their fragility, woody shrubs and heathers at the same high elevations are in fact more vulnerable still. Dry mountain grasslands, though slow to repair themselves, are also rather slow to scar.

ROUTEFINDING AND NAVIGATION

Routefinding—picking your detailed line through the landscape—is perhaps the central cross-country skill. What is the least impossible way through this prickly brushfield? Which of several gullies will get us through this band of steep rock? Can we get around the head of this valley without losing too much elevation? Where is the safest spot to ford the stream? Will the going be easier up the creekbed or on the ridge to the side? Shall we pass to the left or the right of that sharp horn? Decisions are made every minute. The cross-country hiker is constantly looking both near and far; the route that looks easiest in the short run may lead you into problems later on.

It is always good to travel the wilderness with a mind aware, conscious of the shapes of the land, their correspondence to the map, and your own progress among them. Off the trail, this attentiveness becomes essential. Nobody in a cross-country group should be a passive follower. Every member must understand what's going on. Don't neglect to look behind you now and then, noticing landmarks as they appear in reverse, in case you must retrace your course.

In trail travel, it is rather hard to get seriously lost, even if you should lose track of your exact position on the map. You know, after all, that you are on a certain *line*, or at worst (if you think you have overlooked a junction) that you're on one of several lines. Either way, you have only half a problem to solve.

Even off-trail, you may at times be following a prominent linear feature—a major stream, a ridgeline without confusing branches, an ocean beach. In orienteering, they call such features handrails. But much of the time you'll have no handrail to hold to.

In rugged, mountainous country, topography—the lay of the land—typically tells you a lot. Shapes are bold and distinctive. Your problems start when you can't see to read the land—because of fog, or clouds, or darkness, or winter whiteout—or when what you *can* see is uninstructive. Some landscapes are like that, flattish and jumbled, or flattish and forested, with no particular pattern to go by. In featureless country, as in blind weather, navigation has to go beyond the obvious.

There is one situation in which even quite experienced backpackers can get lost: coming down from a height, particularly from a large, conical mountain. On the way up to such a summit, ridges converge; the terrain gathers itself together toward the peak; you can hardly go wrong. On the descent, however, the land fans out in front of you. A mistake of a few yards, one way or the other, will put you on the wrong ridge, in the wrong drainage, or even on the wrong side of the mountain. Again, the vital thing is to have noted, *on the way up*, how things will appear on the way down. Where visibility is likely to be a problem, mountaineers may carry *wands*, light bamboo stakes to which flags of brightly colored plastic tape are tied; these can be placed at decision points to mark the proper way. They must, of course, be collected as you descend.

Here are a few more navigation tricks that veterans rely on.

TRICK #1: WALKING A STRAIGHT LINE

Sometimes, with nothing else to go by, you need to walk with compass in hand, following a selected direction or bearing. Even with a compass, it's hard enough to keep straight. At one point you circle left around a thicket or a massive log; at another you turn right along a stream, looking for stones to cross on; you zig and zag simply in moving among closely spaced trees. In general you try to zig about as often as you zag. If there is even a little visibility, you can also check your line with *backbearings*. If you are supposed to be moving due north from a prominent tree, for ex-

Plotting a course around an obstacle

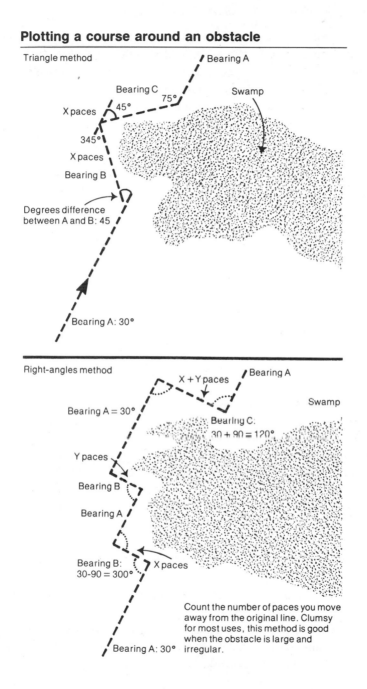

Triangle method

Bearing A

Bearing C

75°

45°

X paces

Swamp

345°

X paces

Bearing B

Degrees difference
between A and B: 45

Bearing A: 30°

Right-angles method

X + Y paces

Bearing A

Bearing A = 30°

Swamp

Bearing C:
30 + 90 = 120°

Y paces

Bearing B

Bearing A

Bearing B:
30-90 = 300°

X paces

Count the number of paces you move
away from the original line. Clumsy
for most uses, this method is good
when the obstacle is large and
Bearing A: 30°   irregular.

ample, you can turn around now and then to confirm that the tree is due south of you.

Sometimes you have to veer well off course to get around an obstacle. Don't do it blind. Instead, plot yourself a whole new track around the barrier. Suppose, for example, you have to turn left around a large marshy area. Simply note the compass bearing of your new line. As you go, count your strides. When you clear the obstacle, turn back toward the original line of travel at the same angle you used in leaving it, and walk an equal number of paces. Then return to the old bearing. When you've done all this, you should be more or less back on track.

TRICK #2: AIMING FOR A DESTINATION LINE

Nobody, no matter how careful, can walk a perfectly straight course by compass. If you try to follow a bearing to a particular point—a campsite, a car, a water cache on a remote desert road—you are almost certain to miss it. You may drift left, you may drift right; you won't be precisely on target.

What's the answer? This: you give yourself an easier assignment. You don't try to reach one particular point; instead, you aim for a recognizable *line* on which the point is to be found. This line may be a stream, a lakeshore, a ridge, a road, a trail—even (if you can see large distant features) a compass direction to a landmark (when Big Marvine Peak is at 210 degrees, you're on the intended line).

Once you're on the destination line, the problem is only halfway solved. Assuming you have no further landmarks to work from, how do you know which way to turn along the line to find whatever it is you're heading for: the car on the road, the camp on the stream, the cache on the compass line? There are two main ways of making sure you know: *aiming off* and *bracketing*.

TRICK #3: AIMING OFF, OR DELIBERATE ERROR

It's a bold, simple way of protecting yourself from confusion: instead of heading straight toward your destination point, you consciously veer to one side or the other, making *an error you know about*. Let's say you're hoping to reach a car parked on a road. Angle deliberately left or right from the course that would take you straight to it. Don't err blindly, but use a compass bearing, and make your error large enough so that your smaller, uncontrolled deviations won't matter. Say you've angled, con-

Using deliberate error

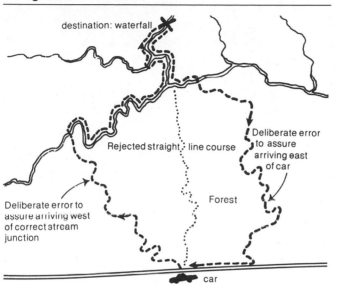

destination: waterfall

Deliberate error
to assure
arriving east
of car

Rejected straight line course

Forest

Deliberate error to
assure arriving west
of correct stream
junction

car

ciously, to the right. You'll know, then, when you reach the road, that the
car can *only* be somewhere to your left.

Here's another application. Say you are following a faint trail down a
ridge toward a stream. The trace disappears in the underbrush, but you
want to locate the exact point at which the old route crosses the water, in
hopes of picking up a plainer trail on the other side. If you try to follow
the mapped line of the trail, you won't know, when you reach the water,
whether you should search upstream or downstream. Unless, by unusual
good luck, you're right on target, your error may have led you either way.
All you can do, lacking landmarks, is pick one direction and try it, continuing until you have either found your spot or traveled so far that you
know you've made the wrong choice.

But if, coming down the hill, you had *deliberately* angled upstream,
then you'd have known to search downstream, possibly saving an hour or
more of time.

TRICK #4: BRACKETING

Remember the problem: how do you find your destination *point* once
you've reached the destination *line*? Bracketing is an additional solution.

Bracketing

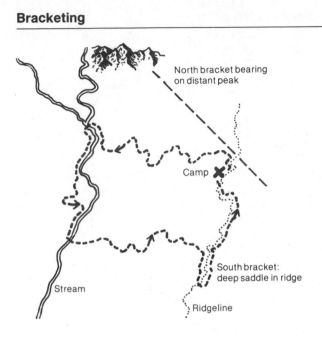

North bracket bearing on distant peak

Camp

South bracket: deep saddle in ridge

Stream

Ridgeline

You establish two landmarks—two things to look for—on the destination line, one on each side of the point you are planning to reach and far enough apart so that you're sure to come out somewhere between them.

There are several kinds of brackets and several ways of "establishing" them. Sometimes you can set up your own artificial landmarks in advance. Say you've parked your car on a road through featureless woods and have to make sure of getting back to it. Then you can simply tie rags, or leave some other markers, a mile or so away from the car in either direction. More often, though, brackets must be natural features, predicted from study of the topo map. Maybe you are trying to reach a given point on a stream; the map tells you that your destination lies between a waterfall upstream and the junction of a major tributary downstream. Or, to take a third case, brackets can be compass bearings to a landmark visible in the distance (but not visible from the destination point; if it were, there would hardly be a problem).

It doesn't matter what your brackets are, or how you establish them. When you encounter your destination line, somewhere between the brackets, little harm is done if you guess wrong at first and head in the wrong direction. You'll soon run into a bracket and be turned back to the center.

TRICK #5: USING THE GLOBAL POSITIONING SYSTEM

If you own a Global Positioning System receiver, of course, you can skip these mental exercises. The unit will read satellite signals and tell you where you are; it will also give you a bearing to any point whose coordinates you enter. In closing on an invisible target, you can head in that general direction without concern for minor deviations, getting a new bearing as often as you like. A complex cross-country route may be laid out as a series of short straight lines leading to a succession of targets, or "waymarks."

STREAM CROSSING

One of the most difficult wilderness obstacles is the major, rushing stream. There is a whole craft of stream crossing and less than perfect agreement about some of its details.

If you expect to be encountering significant creeks, branches, brooks, or runs on your cross-country trip, by all means seek the advice of the management agency and other local sources. As always, try to get through to rangers who know the conditions and won't just advise you to follow the crowd. If you expect many crossings, bring river sandals or soft shoes as well as boots. Where streams are very cold, consider wetsuit booties.

A fast, shallow stream is not a particular problem, though it can be tricky if the current is fierce enough, or cold enough, or both. A slow, deep river may be easier than it looks. You can usually swim across, floating your pack in front of you on an air mattress, or buoyed up by contents stored in airtight bags. As for powerful, foaming whitewater, you needn't worry about that either: you *know* you can't get across.

What makes you think twice is the swollen mountain stream, knee-deep to thigh-deep, fast moving and possibly murky. You can probably cross it, yet you may or may not want to try: there are real dangers to weigh.

When you reach such a stream, stop and study it. Assess its temperature, speed, and depth. Can you see the bottom, and what it is made of? Gravel is the best footing to wade on; sand is often okay but may erode underfoot in a fast current; rocks are more or less slippery and can trap a foot, perhaps disastrously. Will the opposite bank permit an easy exit from the water? Consider what would happen if you were swept off your feet. Downstream are there rapids, falls, or prolonged steep banks? Are there fallen trees—"strainers"—that might fatally trap a person caught in the current?

Unless the spot you've hit is obviously benign, reconnoiter upstream and down. If you are below a junction of tributaries, your stream will be smaller above. Unless you find a natural bridge like a log or a beaver dam, the best spot will be a stretch that is wide, straight, and relatively shallow. The broken water of a submerged gravel bar, or shingle, is preferable to a deeper, apparently calmer area. In picking out a detailed path, take advantage of eddies, swirls where the current is weaker. Avoid pockets of deep water, often indicated by darker color.

Consider the time of crossing as well as the place. Streams fed by snowmelt will be lowest in the cool of the morning. Releases from upstream reservoirs may be a factor, too.

When you're ready to cross, change to your sandals or lighter shoes. (If you use your boots, retie the laces for quick release if needed.) Remove any bulky outer clothing that might impede your ability to swim. Repack your most vulnerable gear in several layers of plastic bags. When you put on your pack, loosen the shoulder straps and leave the hipbelt unbuckled (so that, if you must, you can easily shed your load).

Now for the actual crossing. If alone, you're best off facing upstream so that the current won't tend to buckle your knees. Set your feet wide apart and take short steps, moving one foot at a time and always keeping the same foot forward. Test each new footing before you shift your weight. A long-handled ice ax, a staff, or a trekking pole will give you a third foot and help you keep your balance against the tugging flow.

Several hikers, crossing together, can give each other extra support in a circle of three, with linked arms; in a line, each gripping the belt of another, facing upstream but moving sideways; in a V formation, point facing upstream; or abreast, with arms linked and wrapped around a long pole, facing across the water. In this "line-abreast" method, all move forward at once; otherwise, only one person moves at a time.

What if you are swept off your feet? The proper reaction varies from case to case. If the current is not too deep and fast, you may be able to recover your footing. In the more potent stream, you're advised to shed your pack and go with the flow, floating on your back with feet pointing downstream, working all the while to paddle your way to the shore.

Should a river crosser, like a climber, tie onto a rope and get a belay? No. A rope can actually add to your danger. If you're swept off your feet, the force of the current, dragging your weight against the rope's resistance, can press you down into the streambed until you drown. If the water's that fast, the person on the bank may not be able to retrieve you.

There are various ways, all more or less involved, of using a rope to better effect. In a large group it makes unquestionable sense to string a rope across the water for the middle members to use as a rail or "handline"; only the first crosser and the last will then be unprotected. The line should run diagonally downstream, so that it can't form a V-shaped trap in the middle; hikers should hold onto the downstream side.

Hazardous crossings are sometimes made in very cold water, or weather, or both. If someone takes a spill or otherwise gets dangerously chilled, he or she may have to be stripped, dried, and put into a sleeping bag, following the drill for hypothermia (see Chapter 28). Lacking a hypothermia crisis, though, the best post-immersion treatment is to put on whatever dry clothes you have available, eat starch and sugar, and start hiking, fast and hard, to produce a lot of body heat.

STEEP SUMMER SNOW

In the northwestern United States and alpine Canada, snow may linger on mountain slopes for most of the summer. A snowbank is only an interruption, but what if your route simply vanishes under a steep, white snowfield? Even if you were on a trail before, you are now facing a moderate cross-country challenge.

In climbing a gently sloping snowfield, walk flat-footed, taking full advantage of the friction provided by your bootsoles. As the angle increases slightly, you can point your toes outward and waddle up duck-fashion (a maneuver that skiers will recognize as the herringbone). Steeper slopes are best ascended by traversing at an angle, making switchbacks as required. If the snow is at all firm, you will have to kick steps as you climb. Use a scraping, arcing motion of the boot, and make the step no deeper than you need to feel secure. On short, steep sections, head straight up the slope, kicking steps into it with your toes. If you are the first in a party, remember that other people will be using the footholds you create; restrain your stride if long-legged, and don't space steps too widely.

On any but very gradual slopes, you will find an *ice ax* helpful; on steeper ascents, it is essential. An ice ax consists of a stout metal shaft fitted to a head with two blades, one narrow (the pick) and one wide (the adz). For occasional use, a rather long ax is best; with the tip of the shaft on the ground, you should just be able to rest your hand on the blade. A suitable tool will weigh under 2 pounds and cost at least $60—and you will see some models at twice that price.

The ice ax is used, on an ascent, as a movable anchor. You grip its head with the hand on your uphill side and thrust the shaft deep into the snow. After a couple of steps, you pause momentarily in a stable position, remove the ax, and thrust it in again ahead of you. When you change directions at a switchback, you plant the ax, place both hands on it, and shift the grip to the hand that is now going to be uphill.

Descending snow slopes looks scarier than going up and is, in fact, a little trickier. On steep sections, or if nervous, you can face the slope and kick steps inward with your toes, maintaining your ax as anchor all the while. A better technique on moderate slopes is the *plunge step*. You stride downhill, facing out, legs stiff, punching into the snow with your heels. Each time your weight comes down, you compress a wad of snow and make a solid platform. It is important in this maneuver to keep erect, with your weight over your feet. Though plunge stepping takes a little getting used to, it is both easier and safer than creeping downslope in a gingerly fashion. For added security, hold your ice ax ready to thrust into the snow, shaft first, to arrest any incipient slip.

What if you *do* slip, and find yourself careening downhill? If your slope has bare rocks, trees, or a cliff at the bottom, you must be able to stop yourself quickly. The best technique is known as *self-arrest*. You throw yourself face down in the snow across your ax, with its shaft pinned beneath your chest and its pick cutting into the snow beside your head. In a good arrest, the pick creates so much friction that you stop very quickly indeed. The art, however, can't be learned from a book. Seek instruction.

If you do much of this sort of thing, you don't want to lose your ax: have it tethered to you somehow. For casual use, a wrist strap is okay; mountaineers prefer the more positive attachment of a leash tied in to a climbing harness.

If you find yourself up the snow without an ax, you can improvise a substitute. For instance, an old-fashioned metal cup, dug into soft snow with the bowl downhill, can generate a surprising amount of braking power. Tent pegs can be used the same way. Your hands and feet are better than nothing. Don't give up and just slide!

Unless, of course, you're *glissading:* zooming quite deliberately down the slope. This should only be done when you can see the course ahead and know it to be free of obstacles and sudden drops. Make sure there is a snowy run-out at the bottom, not a bruising exit onto stony ground or into trees. In a *sitting glissade,* you sit down on the snow and simply coast. An ice ax, held diagonally across your torso with the tip of the shaft scraping the snow beside one hip, can serve as speed control. A safer though less easily learned technique is the *standing glissade.* Here you stand erect, facing downslope, and slide on your bootsoles, using them somewhat like skis, with your ax serving again as control (or held ready for a possible self-arrest). If you feel yourself picking up too much speed, you can dig in your heels and convert the glissade to a plunge-stepping descent. Glissading, once mastered, is a fast, exhilarating way down. It is also a trifle dangerous: use with care.

To travel across hard snow or icy areas, you need an additional item: *crampons.* These are sets of spikes that strap or clamp onto the soles of your boots. Though you won't need them for backpacking in most regions, crampons become almost standard equipment in parts of the North Cascades, the Canadian Rockies, and Alaska. Even an iced-up grassy slope can be a slippery hazard. Partial or instep crampons, with just four spikes, will do for many situations. If you use full crampons, which have ten or twelve spikes, make sure that you get the two-piece type that comes with a hinge under the sole. Rigid one-piece crampons can't be worn with flexible-soled hiking boots. The cheapest and lightest full crampons cost about $75 the pair and weigh something under 1½ pounds; instep crampons run about half that in both weight and price.

Lacking crampons, try to time your crossing of icy slopes for midafternoon, or whenever a particular slope has had sun on it for the longest possible time. Most summer snowfields will get soft as the day goes on.

For much more on the skills of travel on steep snow and ice, see the Mountaineers' *Freedom of the Hills* (listed in the Resources appendix). Some of these techniques come naturally, or can be self-taught; but the best preparation is to travel with more experienced hikers and learn from them. Self-arrest, as noted, takes instruction and a lot of practice. If you are going into country where steep snow problems are likely, take the time to master the tricks of this trade and to review them every season. If you plan to do a lot of sitting glissades or to practice self-arrest—a wet business— take raingear with slick outer surfaces (snow clings to rougher fabrics).

ON THE EDGE OF CLIMBING

This is not a book about mountain climbing. But if you begin taking trips away from the trail, you may sooner or later want to learn at least the simplest of the climber's methods. With a little gear and the skill to use it, you can deal with unexpected obstacles; more important, perhaps, you can plan trips in country where obstacles *are* to be expected. A rope-carrying party isn't balked if, hiking down some desert canyon, it comes to the brink of a steep, dry waterfall. It isn't precluded from crossing a stretch of crevassed glacier. Peaks that are out of reach to most hikers, because of a little steep rock at the top, are open to the party with a rope and some slings and hardware to use in setting up anchors.

BELAYING

The great point of the rope between climbers is this: it allows one partner, braced (and usually anchored) in a strong position, to protect a second, who is moving on hazardous ground. As the moving climber advances, the stationary partner—the *belayer*—feeds out rope. If the climber slips, the belayer can stop the climber's fall.

For the system to work, obviously, both partners must be tied in to the rope. Most climbers these days wear harnesses, securely encasing the pelvis, to which the rope is in turn attached. For occasional purposes, though, you can fall back on an older, direct method of tying in, wrapping the rope around your waist several times and securing it with the knot called the bowline-on-a-coil.

There's another technique that can be of use in cross-country travel, and that is the *rappel*, a way of sliding, slowly and safely, down a doubled rope. This is sometimes the only way to get down a cliff without leaving the rope behind you. Running the line around a tree, knob of stone, or artificial anchor, with both ends dangling, you slide down it, and then recover the rope by pulling on one of the strands.

This isn't the place to describe these methods further. Climbing basics are much too important to be learned from a thumbnail sketch. Consult instead *Freedom of the Hills* (see the Resources appendix) or some other specialized climbing text, look for instruction, and practice again and again.

THE VERY LONG TRIP

Yet another variation on the brief "normal" backpack is the trip measured not in days but in weeks. Such a journey may be within a single very large wilderness area; more commonly, it follows a lengthy trail that traverses both wildlands and regions that are relatively tame. Either way, the extended trek requires very detailed planning and preparation, and it is likely to require resupply. The ultimate that can be managed without reprovisioning or living off the land would seem to be about two weeks.

Especially if the area traversed is isolated, food planning for the longer trip is complicated. Your appetite will grow as time goes on; experienced long-distance trekkers add about ½ pound per person per day to the normal ration of 1½ to 2 pounds per person-day. Just about everything must be dried or freeze dried. High-calorie, high-priced "energy bars" make sense as lunch foods in this kind of travel. Balance in the diet—scarcely a consideration on the shorter jaunt—becomes important on a long trip.

The ingredients for each meal need to be packaged together in a sealed, informatively labeled bag.

At some point it becomes necessary to replenish food, fuel, and miscellaneous supplies. This may mean connecting with a cache you have placed in advance; hiking out to a roadhead to meet a friend; making your way to a town with a post office; having supplies packed into you by friends or commercial outfitters; or in very remote areas receiving an air drop.

Supply caches take various forms. You can leave food on the ground in tightly sealed metal boxes (available at some gear stores) or hang it from trees in boxes or in waterproof bags (as for bearbagging).

If your route passes close enough to towns, you can mail your supplies ahead (Special Handling, Insured). You can also buy groceries at such places or, for that matter, pause for a restaurant meal. The Appalachian Trail, the prototype of all the long trails, passes quite close to many settlements, and the Pacific Crest Trail approaches a few. Along with food, you may need to replace first-aid supplies and some of your minor gear as the weeks go on.

On a long trail like the Appalachian, climate will change as you hike, because of the passage of time and also perhaps because of progress north or south. You may want to ship a heavy jacket home, for example, and replace it with something lighter.

Most long-trail hikers favor all-leather boots of middling weight. A good pair of leather boots should make it at least 1,500 miles. Find out when you buy what the store, or the manufacturer, will do for you if the end comes sooner. Veteran long-distance hiker Karen Berger recommends picking up two identical pairs before you start and breaking them both in, so that a substitute is ready. Just as your feet swell a little in the course of an active day, they seem to grow during a very long hiking trip. Some people report gaining a full size. So start with a marginally generous fit rather than a marginally snug one.

If feet are prone to grow, the rest of you is likely to shrink on a very long journey. This can affect the fit of your pack. Unless you're already pretty skinny, it's best to start with a belt that feels a bit tight when cinched in to the maximum. You may in any case wind up changing belts along the way.

Water treatment can be a challenge on the very long trip. Appalachian Trail hikers report almost universal headaches with filters used week after week (clogging is the major complaint). The easy alternative, iodine, isn't recommended for long-term use, either. Boiling consumes fuel. Drinking water off the land is risky. Most people seem to settle on a mixture of these methods.

ULTRALIGHT HIKING

Throughout this book we've envisioned packs of 30 to 40 pounds, of which 16 pounds or more is the irreducible "dry weight." It is possible, however, to get pack weights much lower than that. This is accomplished partly by doing without things; partly by buying (or making) lightweight versions of things; partly by carrying rather small reserves of consumables like food, fuel, and water; and partly by sticking to fairly benign hiking climates and conditions.

Weight savings start with the pack, which need not have high capacity or the elaborate suspension systems found in packs meant for heavy loads. You can find very good and rugged packs (not inexpensive!) that weigh 3 pounds or so. If you're willing to forego some ruggedness, you can get packs lighter than that. Ray Jardine, whose *Pacific Crest Trail Hiker's Handbook* (see the Resources appendix) is something of a bible for ultralighters, carries a homemade pack weighing under a pound. An off-the-shelf pack can also be altered to remove items that are extraneous with light loads, like tie-on patches, sternum straps, and compression straps.

The next major point of attack is shelter. If a tent is carried, it will be a simple tunnel design, much lighter though slightly harder to pitch than the standard self-supporting dome. More probably, the ultralighter will rely on a lightweight nylon tarp weighing less than 2 pounds.

The sleeping bag in the ultralight kit is likely to be down, perhaps with a waterproof breathable shell. The pad will be thin closed-cell foam.

One of the lightest stoves will be carried; to reduce the amount of fuel carried, campfires will be used as much as possible.

Once these heavy items are accounted for, possible savings come in tiny increments, item by item. Ultralight hikers prepare master lists including the weight of every component to a tenth of an ounce, and scan each item ferociously: do I have to have this, and can I buy or create a lighter version? Here's where the handles really do come off the toothbrushes. Jardine and his hiking companion have basic dry weight down to about 8 pounds apiece.

A very light pack has multiple advantages. It permits the hiker to move along in comfort, almost oblivious of the load. It enables older or slightly handicapped hikers to continue the sport longer. And for those so inclined, it allows much faster movement. There is currently a vogue for what is called fastpacking or speed hiking, in which the energy saved by toting a tiny pack is spent in multiplying miles traveled.

HIKING ALONE

"Nobody should ever hike alone."

If the land agencies had their way, if the rescue workers had their way, that's the sentence that would stand at this spot. The authorities don't welcome anything that might encourage people to undertake adventures. You can't blame officialdom for that. It's too accustomed to retrieving—at great effort and expense—the overambitious, the overconfident, and the underprepared.

You may even hear that no party is safe with less than four people. If someone is injured, after all, there should be one companion to stay with the patient and two (since no one should hike alone) to go together for help. When a single hiker gets in trouble, it may be quite a while before anyone knows about it, and the problems and dangers increase.

Okay, there is risk in hiking alone.

There is double risk whenever the solo hiker leaves the beaten paths—when he or she ventures into cross-country travel, or into the desert, or into the world of snow and winter storms.

And yet there are people who do all these things, matter-of-factly and without mishap, year after year. And they have their reasons. Some of the sharpest and most memorable statements of the wilderness idea—the formulations of a John Muir, an Edward Abbey, an Aldo Leopold—have been made by the solo travelers. Whatever it is that wilderness gives you, you come back with a double dose of it when you go out by yourself. And then there are the practical advantages. "The man who travels alone," Thoreau observes, "can start today; but he who travels with another must wait till that other is ready, and it may be a long time before they get off."

So if you feel like taking up solo hiking, by all means do it. Do it, though, with preparation, with understanding, and even (the word is not too strong) with healthy *fear*. Things *can* happen out there. You may want to start your solo travel on frequented trails where you will meet many parties a day; later, you might find yourself drawn to remoter country, perhaps even to off-trail and off-season adventures. But take it slow. Don't overrate yourself. Don't underrate the wilderness. The wilderness is bigger.

Be aware that grizzly bears, and to some extent other animals, are distinctly more dangerous to one person hiking alone.

If you do head out alone, take special care to leave a precise itinerary, both at home and with the local office of the managing agency. For best clarity, include a map with your roadhead, routes, and projected camps marked on it. In the information left with family or friends, be sure to include phone numbers of the land managers and perhaps the local police; in the version left with the rangers, give your home data. Provide in both places the description and license number of your car. Indicate when you plan to be out, and discuss with your backup person how late you can be before the alarm is to be sounded.

Take extra food and fuel (also water, if that's a limiting factor). For other gear, the beginning solo traveler's rule can only be: *when in doubt, leave it in.* You'll have nobody else along this time to loan you the item you forgot, the thing you unwisely decided to do without.

Give more than the usual thought to how you might attract attention in case of difficulties. That will depend largely on where and when you are going: is the country open or wooded, the weather cloudy or likely to be clear? Things in threes and the color orange are universal signals of distress. Fire is an old standby, attracting attention by smoke during the day and by flame at night. Pencil flares and smoke bombs are not too useful: they burn only briefly, and somebody has to be looking. You may be able to attract the attention of a distant airplane with a mirror, though you don't read too many reports of this being successfully done.

For shorter distances, as when searchers are closing in on you, a mirror can certainly be effective, and so can a whistle: good ones can be heard a mile away. Some orange surveyor's tape might come in handy, especially if you must leave a prominent point in search of shelter. At night, a flashlight or headlamp will work. Aim it directly at an approaching aircraft or ground party, and blink it on and off in sets of three.

In solo travel, indeed, you might be sorely tempted to carry a radio or a mobile telephone, even at the risk of sabotaging the whole idea.

23 BACKPACKING IN THE DESERT AND OTHER ODD PLACES

There are many kinds and degrees of desert in the United States and many types of desert travel. For the backpacker, there is a practical definition: you are hiking in the desert when you have to think, and more than just occasionally, about *water*—when H_2O is not just a gift of the land, to be counted on, but the center of all your plans.

Much hiking done in regions loosely called desert is not, by this measure, desert hiking at all. Much of the arid West is basin-and-range country, marked by a pattern of alternating valleys and mountain masses. Some of the highlands reach 10,000, 12,000, even 14,000 feet, high enough to yield abundant water. Hiking in the Toiyabe Range of central Nevada, for instance, or in the forested Deep Creek Mountains of Utah, you are *in* the desert only as an island is in the sea.

The desert is also interrupted, here and there, by perennial streams that flow in deep-cut canyons. Many famous "desert" treks follow these arteries: you wade the shallows and push through the green streambank thickets of an Aravaipa, an Owyhee, an Escalante River.

Take away the wet mountains and wet canyons, and what you have left is the desert itself, the real thing. It's true desert hiking when you park on the shoulder of a rugged road from nowhere to nowhere and head up a long alluvial slope toward the hard, stark summits of a mountain range that appears in no guidebook. It's true desert hiking when you clamber up the branches of a bone-dry, precipitous gorge. It's the real thing when you strike out across the featureless expanse of a playa, one of those dead-flat, lifeless, cream-colored sedimentary plains that fill the low points of many desert valleys. And if it is solitude you are after—perfect, silent, almost scary solitude—these are the places to find it.

PLANNING AND CACHING WATER

Your objective in planning desert travel must be to avoid being short of water—*ever*. Dehydration is a nasty, insidious disease. It is not something you want to take chances with.

How much water does a desert hiker need? Not quarts, but gallons—at least 1.5 gallons a day, in liquid form and in food, and sometimes double that. Figure a 6-quart daily minimum and add a quart to that for every 5 miles to be traveled—in reasonably cool weather. In the heat of summer, figure more. If you insisted, for some reason, on camping in Death Valley in midsummer, you would need 9 quarts a day simply to survive, sitting quietly in the shade. ˙

Water is heavy, 2 pounds to the quart. Two days' supply at 2 gallons a day would already weigh some 32 pounds (plus a few ounces for the containers). Of course, if you're hauling water anyhow, you hardly need to carry dried or freeze-dried edibles: you might as well get some of your moisture in real food, fresh or canned.

If you have to carry *all* your water, your hiking range is necessarily limited. Many desert hikers wind up taking successions of short trips rather than one longer outing—going out just for a day or two and looping back to the car between excursions. This type of travel—call it the cluster trip—is a desert specialty.

There are several ways of increasing your range. One is to find water on the land. Often it is there to be found. What you must not do, however, is to put yourself in the position of depending on a supply that may not exist. Don't count on local sources just because a map shows the blue squiggle of a spring. You may or may not find it; it may or may not actually be flowing. Plan your trip so that the presence of on-the-ground water will be good news, its absence not dangerously bad.

Converging animal tracks may help you zero in on a spring, and so may birds, which circle water at dawn and dusk. Look for wet spots below cliff bands and up shady side canyons.

In addition to permanent springs, you sometimes find natural catchments or "tanks" that hold water for several days after a rain. There may also be livestock watering tanks somewhere around. As an emergency measure, you may be able to reach water by digging into the gravelly floor of a streambed. Dig at the outside edge of a bend, at a spot where vegetation indicates that roots are reaching the water table. (Cottonwood trees are the surest sign of all.) A hole that is dry in daylight may show some water after dark, when trees release some moisture into the ground. In winter in higher desert mountains, a ready source of water is snow.

Even prickly desert vegetation, and even desiccated desert soil, contain a trace of water. You can extract it, in a pinch. For instance, you can gather plant matter (the more succulent the better) and place it in a plastic bag that you inflate with your breath, tie off, and leave in the sun; moisture will evaporate from the green stuff, condense on the plastic, and pool. More elaborate is the solar still. You dig a hole in the ground and roof it with plastic, anchored at the margins and sagging in the middle, where it is weighted with a stone. Below the low point you place a container. Moisture will evaporate from the soil, condense on the ceiling, run down to the low point, and drip into the container. If you have vegetation to place in the hole, all the better. Think twice before embarking on this project, however: at best you'll get under a quart in 24 hours, and there might be better uses for your energy and time.

Most desert waters must be purified. Many are polluted by domestic stock or by feral burros. (You can count on one drowned scorpion per spring.) A few sources are so alkaline as to be obviously undrinkable; a very few contain poisonous minerals. These are usually identified on maps, but be wary of pools that have no sign of life whatever around them. Also don't drink water running out of mines or mine-disturbed areas.

Caching water is another way of extending your range. The process can be simple. For instance, if you will be hiking out and back on the same line, you can start out under a heavy load of water and plant a generous supply a few miles up the route. For a greater extension of range, you will have to do advance work by car, planting caches near (but not right next to) roads. Figure to place one cache for every day and a half of hiking. Plan locations and quantities so that, if you failed to find a particular cache, you would have enough water left to reach the next.

For containers, you can use solid plastic bottles (not gallon water bottles from the supermarket—too flimsy), or tough, collapsible waterbags. Smaller containers allow the load to be split among party members, and also reduce the consequences of any one leak. Food and other supplies can also be cached; any food that is not canned or freeze dried must be contained in several layers of plastic to block odor.

The ideal cache site is a place you can easily recognize, but that other people aren't likely to stumble on. It is good to choose a site near some prominent *line* in the landscape: a road or track or fenceline, the toe of a mountain slope, or the bank of a dry streambed, or wash (but not down

SCORPION

in the wash in summer thunderstorm season). Avoid areas trafficked by off-road vehicles. Desert veterans take care to place caches unobserved. It is not quite unknown for vandals to steal or destroy supplies.

The tradition was once to bury cache containers or place them under massive cairns, but the resulting disturbance is now frowned upon. It is still fine to nest bottles in sand and perhaps to wedge them upright with stones. A site at the north side of an adjoining shrub or bush will get a little cooling shade. Attach to the cache a note stating when the stockpile was placed and when it is to be removed. If your cache includes food, cayenne pepper scattered around it will discourage rodents, coyotes, and foxes from taking too much interest. The desert has no bears.

Before you leave the site, make absolutely certain that you can find the place again. Mark the spot on your map. Take at least three compass bearings and write them down. Make a sketch of local topography. Mark the spot on your map. If you're using a Global Positioning System receiver, note precise coordinates. Some people document cache sites with photographs from several angles.

Cache placing is a good occasion to practice precise navigation skills. For instance, flag several locations a mile or so apart, approach the area from a new direction, and try to locate each of your flags in succession.

If, on the actual hike, you have trouble finding a cache, don't search at random. Sit down and reconstruct. If you're sure you're close and still can't spot the target, you can walk a search pattern. Choose a starting point and start moving outward in a series of straight lines: say 20 paces west, 20 paces north, 30 paces east, 30 paces south, 40 paces west, 40 paces north, and so on. You will pass within ten feet of every point. Scrutinize the landscape all the while.

When you retrieve a cache, remove all trace of it, filling any hole, smoothing sand, and rescattering any rocks you have gathered. If you skip or miss a cache, go back later by road to retrieve it.

With due care it just won't happen. But what if the worst possible situation does somehow develop: you find yourself short of water and miles away from the next source? Research shows that a healthy person, not dehydrated to begin with, can walk about 10 miles in the desert in daytime without additional water. If it's hot, hole up in the middle of the day. Move at a steady, moderate pace. If help or water is more distant than 10 miles, walk at night. If you have any water at all, don't hoard it; it is better to drink it as you become thirsty and keep your body functioning well as you move toward help. To reduce water loss, keep your skin covered with clothing, even in hot weather. Do not smoke or drink alcohol. Eat only a little (carbohydrates), and avoid salt. A pebble in the mouth may make it feel less dry. Talk as little as possible and breathe through your nose. If you find water that is undrinkable, you can cool yourself with it by moistening the skin; urine, in a pinch, can be used in the same way. You needn't force yourself to drink urine, however: it does the body no good.

OTHER ASPECTS OF DESERT HIKING

We think of the deserts as hot, but that isn't quite right. The North American deserts stretch 1,000 miles north and south (even omitting the Mexican portion) and range 5,000 feet or more in elevation. Nowhere is it hot *all* the time. Death Valley, where the summer temperature in the shade can climb above 120 degrees Fahrenheit, is chilly in the winter; in the high desert of Oregon, winter nights may be deeply subzero. By picking your hiking season, you can keep to a comfortable range.

If you steer clear of the extremes, you will need nothing extraordinary in the line of gear. For shelter, a light tent will do and often just a tarp or poncho—or nothing at all. Cotton garments will do fine, are even preferred. A sunhat with a neck-protecting "havelock" is essential, as are sunglasses and sunblock cream. Nights may require warm clothes. A light, three-season sleeping bag is fine. Do be prepared for rain (sometimes even for hail or snow).

If you want to hike hot desert country in the summer—and a few people do—special precautions are required. It is vital that you understand the process of overheating or *hyperthermia* (see Chapter 28) and know how to prevent and counter it. The body can acclimatize to hot conditions, and a summer desert hiker should allow time for this adjustment before beginning a serious trek. Water consumption, of course, must be very high; electrolyte replacement drinks can be helpful in this special case. Summer desert hikers often move at morning and evening—even at night—and take a long siesta in the heat of the day. They wear loose, light-colored clothing, not heavy but densely woven enough to block ultraviolet rays. For maximum eye protection, some choose wraparound goggles instead of mere sunglasses. They may also carry canopies to pitch for the midday stop, tentpoles to pitch them with (since vegetation may be sparse and low), and thick foam pads to keep their bodies off scalding ground. (Avoid air mattresses in southern deserts full of prickly things like cholla cactus.)

Watch how you park your pack in desert heat. Left harness side up, it will be unpleasantly hot to put back on; harness side down, it may pick up spines. Better stand it up, being careful not to lean it against some thorny thing. To keep water (relatively) cool, carry bottles inside.

Perhaps the most vital piece of "gear" for the desert hiker is the auto mobile. Out here that vehicle is more than transportation; it is a vital home base. Make certain it has *lots* of water in it, together with food, stove fuel, and first-aid supplies. Desert driving is hard on cars. A little mechanical knowledge and a basic toolkit may serve you better than the fanciest backpack ever made. In remote areas, it is a good idea for even a small group to travel in two vehicles. If you are expecting to drive rough roads, your equipment should include a stout shovel, tire chains, a piece of plywood, and a pump—all aids to getting through sandy spots and other rough areas. Partly deflated tires traverse sand more readily, and of course need reinflation afterwards.

Once you're on foot, desert travel is overwhelmingly cross-country, without explicit trails or reassuring signs. Formal trailheads are rare. Navigation, though, tends to be straightforward. Views are long; topography tends to be on a grand and simple scale. Often you are following an unmistakable ridgeline or canyon. Vegetation is seldom so thick that you cannot work your way through it.

But obstacles and confusions do occur: unexpectedly continuous bands of cliffs, thickets of fiercely spined cacti, labyrinthine canyon networks, jungles of streamside growth. Elsewhere you may encounter webs of abandoned, rugged roads, confusing rather than helpful. Sophisticated compass work becomes important if you strike out across a featureless playa, of if you are aiming for a water cache.

Flash floods are a major desert hazard. Thunderstorms, common in the Southwest throughout the summer and fall, reach a climax in July and August. Keep an eye out for distant thunderheads. Even if the air is dry where you are, floods may be sent down by downpours elsewhere in the watershed. Avoid camping in streamcourses, especially in the narrows of a gorge. Never try to cross, either on foot or in a vehicle, a wash that is filling with water.

Another hazard to steer clear of is the abandoned mine (Nevada alone has 50,000 of these). Most are horizontal tunnels into slopes; some are vertical pits. Some have been plugged or capped and some have not. Resist the temptation to explore. You don't want to trigger a collapse or run into a pocket of poisonous gas.

The desert has its rattlesnakes, but no more than the woods. Carry a venom extractor. Arizona and California desert travelers should inform themselves about one highly venomous scorpion, *Centuroides exilicanda*. See Chapter 29.

LOW IMPACT IN THE DESERT

Easily scarred, slow to repair themselves, America's desert lands are taking a beating. Desert hikers are not contributing much of the damage. It stems much more from overgrazing, from uncontrolled mining and prospecting, from off-road vehicle use and proliferating roads. The conscientious hiker, though, will want to use care here as elsewhere. All the familiar low-impact principles apply, and a few extra ones besides.

You might think the desert soil invulnerable to any disturbance as tiny as a hiker's footfall; actually, it may be uniquely sensitive. In many areas, the ground is covered with a blackish coating of algae, fibrous cyanobacteria, mosses, and other tiny plants, together making up what is called cryptobiotic or cryptogamic crust. Undisturbed, this crust absorbs rainfall, limits erosion, enriches the soil, and encourages the growth of taller plants. Once broken, it is terribly slow to heal. In the old days, virtually all treeless terrain in the deserts had this crust; now only a few relatively undisturbed areas are so protected. Go to great lengths to avoid trampling cryptogamic surfaces. Walk as much as possible in washes or over areas naturally paved with embedded stones. If you must cross cryptobiotic crust, go single file: in this case a single footfall is as destructive as ten. At roadheads, avoid crushing the crust, or indeed any surface not already damaged, with a tire track.

Another key point: don't compete with wildlife for limited water. If you draw from an isolated waterhole or a short section of perennial stream, don't then camp beside the source, but move a good distance away, say, ½ mile or more. This is crucial in desert mountains where bighorn sheep are struggling to maintain themselves. Leave watering spots before dusk, when the desert animal world comes most alive.

In desert wilderness, as at timberline, fires have no place. You won't find much burnable material anyway; what you do find belongs on the land. Some people burn their toilet paper to speed decomposition, but fires have been set that way and desert land management agencies now commonly discourage the practice. Instead, pack out TP. Depending on the popularity of the area, feces may be buried or left on the surface for rapid degradation by ultraviolet light.

Historical or prehistoric artifacts you find in the desert must be left alone. Yes, this applies to arrowheads and chips! If simple respect is not an adequate reason, consider that all such objects, simply by being where they are and arranged as they are, communicate information. Rather few sites have been properly studied. Stay out of ruins; if a trail leads through them, don't wander off it. Don't dig. Don't comb through shards. If you find something attractive, like a pot, that seems likely to be scavenged by someone else, leave it alone but report its location to the authorities. And don't be too reflexive about knocking over cairns: in some areas, these too may be ancient artifacts. Such cautions apply to all wilderness, but it's in the southwestern deserts that one's conscience is most likely to be tested.

If you encounter range fences across your route, don't climb the strands (which may break), but part them and slide between. If you go through a gate, leave it as you found it—open if it was open, shut if shut. Such courtesies lessen friction between hikers and the ranchers who utilize vast tracts of publicly owned arid land.

WET-CANYON HIKING

Overlapping true desert backpacking is the sport of canyon travel. This can be a very dry business or a very wet business, depending on the canyon.

In a dry canyon system, the major obstacles are likely to be dry waterfalls. Topographical maps may not reveal all steep drops. If you hike a canyon not known to be easily passable, take a rope and appurtenances for setting anchors, and know how to use these tools. In traveling multibranched canyons, keep track of the choices you make at each junction.

Many larger canyons of the Southwest have perennial streams in them. You walk beside water and ford it so frequently that your feet are always wet. Leather boots are no good for such travel: you want sneakers or cloth boots with drainholes that let water as readily out as in. Sport sandals work well if you're not rock scrambling or carrying too much of a load. It may be necessary to swim across pools, floating your pack on an air mattress. If you do a lot of this, you may turn to an inner tube, an inflatable miniature boat, or a drybag (a waterproof pouch with a rolled-over closure at the top).

In some wet desert canyons you may encounter quicksand, created where springs well up through fine sediments. Contrary to its reputation, quicksand does not suck you down; think of it as a kind of heavy water. You can swim the morass if there's no other way to cross.

Flash floods are a more serious danger. Just as in hiking a normally streamless canyon, consider what may be happening in the watershed and keep an eye out for escape routes. The stream may warn you by turning muddy and rising slightly in advance of the main surge.

Most challenging is travel in very narrow, very rugged "slot canyons" containing vigorous streams, high waterfalls, plunge pools, log jams, and boulders wedged between walls. Traversing such a slot may involve ropes, rappels, wetsuits, and all manner of special equipment. There is an emerging sport of "canyoneering," combining elements of climbing and spelunking and requiring similar knowledge and preparation.

COASTLINE HIKING

Another unusual environment for backpacking—one that can be desert-like, at times—is the beach. On the Atlantic and Gulf coasts of the United States, hikers can walk for days along low barrier islands with the ocean on one side and protected bays or sounds on the other; in more rugged regions, beaches alternate with stony promontories.

Beach walking has its peculiarities. Typically, you'll choose to walk next to the waves, where the sand is wet and firm. Sneakers or running shoes are normal footwear. Water may be a problem; on an Atlantic barrier island, for instance, you may have to carry or cache your supply like a desert traveler. (In some areas you can find fresh water by digging in a pocket between dunes, well back from the beachfront.) For cooking, washing, and brushing your teeth, brine can be used. Salt on your skin and sand in all your gear will simply have to be put up with. Lack of shade makes summer an unpleasant hiking season on southern coasts; autumn may be ideal. In many regions, fall is also the best time of year to catch the spectacle of migratory birds.

In coastal walking, especially on rugged shores, tide table and watch are essential tools. If a coastwise route is punctuated by rocky points, the tides may control when you travel: although some headlands can be clambered over, some can only be rounded at low water.

Ordinarily, the beach walker camps above high-tide line, as indicated by sandmarks and debris. But any fires should be built lower down, where the next tidal cycle will remove the traces. Managing agencies rarely object to fires so sited (inquire, of course), and you can count on driftwood for fuel. On coasts where grizzly bears roam, the whole camp should be in the intertidal zone so that odors are washed away. (This is for the sake of future parties; you don't want the bears drawn to the waterline by residual good smells.)

A tent on a beach needs to be very well pitched, and that can be tricky. Skinny stakes won't hold. Snow stakes, broader in section, may work; or you can anchor with "deadmen," stakes or other objects buried crosswise in the sand. Stuffbags, filled with sand and buried, also serve. Driftwood, too, may offer solid anchors. Salt air, by the way, is hard on the metal of tentpoles, which must be rinsed and wiped down when you return home.

On a really wild shore, the disposal of human waste takes an unusual form. It is actually better to throw excrement into the sea, tossing it perhaps on a flake of rock, than to bury it in the sand. Look for a spot where waves or currents won't bring it right back in, and lob your missile out as far out as possible.

Hiking on a little-visited coastline, you can live off the land, if you choose, to an unusual degree. Besides fish, there are all those shellfish, like mussels, crabs, and clams. Tidepools, of course, are for admiration only: don't collect or even touch the living things within them.

On some beaches at some times of year, birds that nest on the sand may be vulnerable to disturbance. One such is the snowy plover, found on the Gulf of Mexico coast and on Pacific Ocean shores; it nests from April through September. Avoid disturbing the line of debris that marks the highest recent tide: it may contain plover nests. If you notice a small shorebird circling nervously, calling obsessively, or feigning injury, it probably has eggs nearby. Move on.

24 THE WINTER WILDERNESS

In snow the wilderness grows and is wilder.

Except in the South, in the deserts, and in the coastal West, most of our wild country is snowed in during winter. The new white surface covers scars, smooths old mistakes, shelters fragile ground. It covers the trampled campgrounds, the beaten trails of summer. Most of all, it closes roads. In winter the California Sierra becomes once more the huge mystery that John Muir explored. Yellowstone, clean of cars and noise, is once again an amazement. In forested mountains, the labyrinth of logging roads becomes a land of flat, white corridors—still artificial but no longer ugly and (except by snow machines) no longer drivable. Peaks that were an hour away by summer trails become the reward of a three days' march.

Once the snowy hills were pretty much unpopulated. Even now, winter is, by comparison, the empty, spacious season. But the winter wilderness today is tracked by two species of travelers, specially equipped, and moving with the extra vigor that seems natural in cold places.

There are, first of all, the cross-country skiers. Moving swiftly on narrow, lightweight skis, carrying only daypacks, they don't often push very far into the wild.

But besides the daytrippers there are those more committed travelers, the winter backpackers. Some shuffle along on snowshoes; some slide along on skis of heavier make than those of the daytime skiers they meet on the first miles of trail. Some are climbers heading for remote winter summits. Some are downhill skiers weary of busy commercial slopes, come to labor up steep peaks for the long swoop down. Some are simply backpackers, moving, camping, enjoying, dealing with the white, crisp world. But these travelers have in common a shared problem and a fairly similar set of solutions to it.

The problem: how do you stay comfortable—and more important, safe—in the beautiful, strange, and unforgiving country of the cold?

GETTING INTO WINTER

Winter is another planet. So different are its rules, so special its demands, that it would take a separate book to deal with them thoroughly—as several good books do.

The great reality, in snow, is *cold*. Never underestimate it. On a typical winter trip you will be cozily warm while you travel, and cozily warm once you're lying in your sleeping bag, drinking soup. But the times in between are rarely perfectly comfortable. Fingers get cold and disobedient. Bare metal can be so frigid that it stings and sticks to flesh. Flashlights balk, cameras jam, water freezes solid in canteens. Everything you do takes longer—and there is more to do: more gear to deal with, more fixing, more finding, more figuring, more rigging to be gotten through. To add to it all, there may be less daylight to work with.

Then why camp in the snow? Because the world of the snow is endlessly, cleanly beautiful. Because experiences in it—the good and not so good alike—seem to happen with double intensity. Because the land is emptier, ornerier, wilder. Because you have, more than you have in any summer travel, the sense of being on a frontier.

Some backpackers value these things so much that they turn the year upside down, like downhill skiers or Australians; it is November that sets them to scanning the maps and checking out their gear, not May. Even if you don't go that far, the taste for winter camping gives you a twelve-month hiking season.

It's a real jump, the move into winter camping—almost like learning to backpack all over again. Most people will want to break into it gradually, starting with day trips, and then short overnight jaunts not far from the road. Don't take on too many problems at once. Test all your gear where retreat is easy. If you need a heavier sleeping bag, if your summer stove is going to balk in the cold, you want to know about it before you're committed. It helps to travel, the first few times, with more experienced companions. Outings clubs offer very valuable courses.

For much more about the medical problems that can overtake hikers in cold conditions, see Chapter 28.

WINTER GEAR

For winter travel you have to make some changes in your gear—some substitutions, even more additions. The most obvious new requirement is a pair of skis or snowshoes: for more on the possibilities, see below.

What about footwear? If you will be traveling on skis, you'll need specialized boots that mate to compatible bindings. For snowshoe travel, you have more choices.

The traditional snowshoe boot is simply a heavy hiking or light mountaineering boot, built of top-grain leather (or possibly plastic), weighing 4 pounds or more the pair. There are other solutions, however. Somewhat lighter winter boots are now being made that incorporate high-tech insulating and waterproof breathable layers. *Much* lighter boots—even running shoes—can be worn inside an insulated *overboot* or *mukluk.* Then there are the high rubber boots known loosely as *shoepacs.* These cover most of the foot with a single piece of vulcanized rubber; the rest of the upper—ankle and calf—is leather; the interior is lined with foam or felt. L.L. Bean and Sorel make familiar versions. Cost of either overboots or shoepacs is under $100.

There are several ways of increasing the warmth of any boot that you fear may be chilly. If it doesn't spoil the fit, you can add inner soles or extra socks—but don't overdo it (you don't want to risk frostbite by cutting off the flow of blood to your feet). Dry socks are important; take spares.

Then there's the vapor barrier trick, which can be done with a plastic bag or a special nylon liner. The impermeable layer, pulled on over a thin inner sock, blocks the evaporation of sweat and keeps the foot noticeably warmer. A second plastic bag, placed outside the main sock layer, can be further protection if you're working with an imperfectly waterproof boot.

SHOEPAC

A more expensive solution for the chronically cold-footed is the *Gore-Tex sock* ($40–$50 a pair).

Some cold-footed people have recourse to chemical warmers, little packets that deliver heat when you break an outer package and allow air to penetrate; placed in a boot (or glove), they can produce a lasting glow. These gimmicks can certainly be helpful to someone who has to sit quietly in the cold, and they might have a place in an emergency kit. They're no substitute, however, for the real winter furnace, your body's own metabolism.

To keep snow out of your boots, you wear tall, spatlike *gaiters*, usually of waterproof breathable fabric. Greater protection comes from *super-gaiters*, which cover the entire boot and cling to the edge of the sole with elastic rims called rands. Don't leave these on the boot for more than a few days between trips, as they can cause the soles to curl. Depending on fabric, height, and features, these coverings cost can cost as little as $15 and as much as $100.

Of course you need more clothes in winter, and to some extent different clothes. Cotton is absolutely out; synthetic fabrics and wool are in. Synthetic underwear, designed to wick sweat away from the skin, is almost universally worn; many people use long johns as their basic trousers, with a pair of shorts on top for modesty, and supplemented as needed with insulating layers and waterproof breathable shells.

Pants or knickers for unladen cross-country skiing may have elastic waistbands and no provision for a belt. If you're carrying a full pack, however, you need a belt or, more commonly now, suspenders. If such support is lacking, the process of getting the pack on and off tends to drag the trousers up and down unpleasantly.

For extreme conditions there are "bibs," shell pants that rise well up the torso and hang from the shoulders with suspender-like straps; worn with a parka, these give a degree of protection you can only exceed by going to a one-piece coverall.

Even more than in summer, you'll be glad of clothes that allow easy adjustment. You don't want to let yourself get either cold or hot—excessive sweating will chill you by evaporation later on. Front zippers or buttons or hook-and-loop closures, and adjustable openings at the wrists, are good. The more accessible pockets, the better.

Some combination of gloves, mittens, and shells goes on your hands. I like three independent layers, permitting a choice of coverages, but many people prefer a one-piece shelled mitten worn over the light inner glove.

You must have a balaclava, a knit cap that pulls down over the neck, leaving a gap for the face. For colder and windier places, you may need a cap with a built-in facemask to prevent facial frostbite. For warmer days in bright sun, an ordinary broad-brimmed hat is of course essential.

You must have dark glasses or goggles—two pairs, in fact, in case the first goes missing. For the fierce, bright lands above timberline, you need glasses with opaque barriers at the sides of the eyes. Though glass lenses block ultraviolet light most completely, plastic lenses will do for altitudes to 14,000 feet. Sunglasses suitable for winter start at about $36.

Internal-frame backpacks are almost universally used in winter. A snowshoe traveler, however, can get by with an external frame. Whichever kind you have, make sure you can fit all your needed gear into it, or onto it, tied to the outside. If zipper tabs don't already have pull-loops of cord attached, add some: these make it easier to work stubborn zippers with cold hands or mittens.

True winter sleeping bags are inevitably heavier than summer types. A bag with 7 or 8 inches of loft, in a mummy style, takes most sleepers down to about 0 degrees Fahrenheit in comfort. "Three-season" bags, a little lighter, can be made to serve, especially within the protection of a tent. If the insulation is waterfowl down, a waterproof breathable shell will keep it dry; a separate bivouac sack is a second choice. You also need more ground insulation: two long closed-cell pads, or, more typically, a thick self-inflating air mattress.

For shelter you'll need a tent that can carry heavy snow weights and stand up in strong winds. Where snow is deep, you can build your own shelter—igloo, snow trench, or cave. You'll need a folding snow shovel ($40 or more) for this work; some igloo builders also carry light snow saws ($30–$50). You also don't want to be without a shovel in avalanche terrain (see below).

Doesn't all this add up to a heavier load in your pack? You bet it does. It is difficult, in winter, to trim your pack weight much below 40 pounds on an overnight trip. Winter mountaineers, adding ropes and other paraphernalia, seldom carry less than 60 pounds. This is a price you pay.

SNOWSHOES

For the person just getting into winter backpacking, the snowshoe is the simplest tool of travel. Wearing snowshoes, you walk much as you would on bare ground without them. At first you will step on yourself a few times and take some comical falls, but the skill teaches itself. Snowshoes, though cheaper than skis and their appurtenances, are no longer an economy item: you can expect to pay $200 to $400 for a pair suitable for backpacking.

As you gain experience, you may want to switch to skis, or at least to substitute skis part of the time. It depends partly on personal taste (how much does speed matter to you?) and partly on the kind of country you visit. In lands that are largely flat and rolling, or steep but not densely forested, nothing moves like a pair of skis. Yet in rugged, timbered mountains such as the northern Appalachians or the Siskiyous, snowshoes, being more maneuverable, may actually serve you better. In deep, fresh powder, too, skis, as basic transportation, lose some of their advantage. Don't be overawed by skiers who dismiss the snowshoe as a beginner's tool.

The classic snowshoe was a piece of basketwork: rawhide stretched across a framework of blond ashwood. It was possibly the most exquisite object used in wilderness camping. Though several companies still make traditional models, they are most often seen decorating mantelpieces.

The typical modern snowshoe has instead a metal *frame* and a mostly solid *deck* of neoprene, copolymer resin, or other tough synthetic material. A vast range of traditional shapes has resolved itself into the style known as the Western. Shoes of this type are rather long and narrow, 8 to 10 inches wide and from 2 feet long to a shade over 3 feet. Both front and back are rounded, and the leading edge has a moderate upward bend. A *binding* encases your booted foot. Your foot rests on a stout *hinge rod;* your toe dips into the snow through an opening in the deck. Bindings usually incorporate *snowshoe crampons,* toothed or knifelike projections mounted below the foot, to help in climbing steep or icy hills.

The backpacker's snowshoes need to be at least 30 inches long and a shade wider than most. Toting a load and sometimes traversing untracked snow, you want big platforms to spread your weight and keep you from sinking in. If you are heavy to begin with, buy the most generous shoes you can find.

Toe styles vary somewhat. For flattish terrain and fairly firm snow, a fairly flat prow—one that curves up just slightly—will suffice; it is also good for kicking steps in crusty snow. On powder snow, such a toe will bury itself and trip you; you need instead a moderate upturn—say, 3 or 4 inches. Sharply upturned tips, hardly found any more, are good in just one circumstance: very deep, light snow on gentle terrain.

Beyond these basics, many special features are now built into snow-shoes and their bindings. At least one maker builds asymmetrical shoes, with a differing right and left. Some shoes are built to drag their tails on the snow; others get lifted off the surface with each step. The former is better in powder, where you're likely to acquire a load of snow on the deck behind your foot; the latter is better on packed trails. "Dual rotation" systems have it both ways: ordinarily the shoe lifts as a unit, but if snow has piled up behind, the weight overrides an internal spring and the tail drags, saving you pointless labor. You can also get bindings that release at a touch and bindings with insulation that double as foot warmers. Some shoes even let you change their shape by trading one modular part for another, for instance replacing the normal stubby rear end with a point (which can act as a sort of rudder in deep snow). Bindings ordinarily come with the shoe but may also be purchased separately with or without crampons ($70–$170); check compatibility with your shoes.

On snowshoes you need at least a third leg for balance. One or two ski poles, or trekking poles with large baskets, will do in most terrain. If you expect to cross steep, icy snow on snowshoes, you may want to carry a long-shafted ice ax as well, and switch from pole to ax when an exposed traverse begins. There used to be clip-on ski baskets that converted axes to dual-purpose tools, but this handy item seems to have disappeared.

SKIS

Unlike the beginning snowshoer, the novice backpack skier definitely has some learning to do. The learning process starts with the subtle task of picking the right gear, and goes on to mastery of various strides, turns, and ancillary techniques. It's an excellent idea to rent several ski packages (skis, bindings, boots, and poles) before plunking down the $500 or more your kit may end up costing you.

You won't find a rack of skis in the gear store identified as for the ski backpacker. Most people buying skis will be going out on day trips only, and product descriptions are geared to this majority. Generally, you'll see *track* or *skating* skis, intended for fast work on groomed surfaces; *touring* skis, designed for movement across country in moderate terrain; and *telemark* skis, which are built for ski mountaineering, including steep, alpine-style descents. The skis the backpacker wants straddle the border of these last two categories and are sometimes distinguished as backcountry or *mountain-touring* models.

Even within that group there is a spectrum of possibilities. Some people favor skis that are relatively short and wide; others prefer models that are somewhat narrower but also longer. Generally speaking, the wide-and-short kind is easier to get started with; the more traditional "skinny skis" may be more fun as you gain skill. A familiar ski of the first type is the Karhu Catamount; the Fischer E-99 is a classic representative of the second.

Besides basic style, you'll need to come to a few decisions on these characteristics:

Length. Once you've chosen a ski, let the salespeople advise you on the proper length for you. Recommended lengths keep coming down, but you need enough surface area to support you and your load in soft snow.

Sidecut. Skis are somewhat hourglass shaped. The narrowest point, the "waist," is beneath your foot; it will be something between 50 and 70 millimeters wide. The tip or "shovel" is traditionally about 10 millimeters wider. The difference in width between waist and tip is called sidecut. Makers have lately been building skis with sidecuts of 15 or even 20 mm. A ski with pronounced sidecut will turn more readily than its straighter cousin, but is less adept at blazing down a slope, gliding on the flat, or breaking a straight trail in deep snow. It's really a matter of taste. Drastically curvaceous "parabolic" skis, however, are not for the backcountry.

Stiffness and camber. Skis are not just flat boards. Rather, they bow upwards from the snow, resisting the skier's weight. Put a pair together, base to base, and you'll see daylight—the camber—between. Some curve decidedly and can be flattened only with difficulty: it may take a two-handed effort to close the gap. Others are fairly limp and can be pressed together easily. Stiff, high-cambered skis glide better, perform better on icy or windblown surfaces, and generally reward skill. Softer skis are more controllable, especially in fluffy snow. As a backpacker, you'd like to have it both ways, but you have to settle for a compromise, which may vary by region. Ski backpackers out West are likely to favor the soft end of the scale; easterners, accustomed to fighting heavier snow, may go for stiffer skis. Heavy-bodied skiers may also need a little more stiffness to resist their weight.

Edges. Many heavier skis have metal strips running down each margin of the ski, and you probably want this feature. Edges assist greatly in crossing icy slopes, in making turns on downhill runs, and in keeping control while laden with a pack. Some skis have edges just partway, but the backpacker in hilly terrain had better go for the maximum version.

Weight. Weights per pair for backpack-worthy skis, before bindings are added, will run from 5 pounds to almost 7 pounds.

WAXES, PATTERNS, AND SKINS

There's one more big choice to make in the ski department: the one between waxable and "waxless" skis.

In skiing cross-country on the flat, you fall into a steady, gliding gait called the diagonal stride, which looks (and sometimes feels) practically effortless. For this technique to work, your skis must grip the snow at certain moments and glide freely forward at others. This magic can be worked in different ways.

Traditional cross-country skis have a smooth undersurface (or "base") made of a plastic called P-Tex. (Porous or "sintered" P-Tex is best.) On the trail, you coat this surface with one or more layers of cunningly formulated waxes. When the ski is stationary, snow crystals press into this coating and grip the ski. When you push forward, the projecting granules melt and let the ski glide. When the stride is finished, the surface refreezes and the bond is restored, giving you a firm base for the next forward push.

One wax won't serve for all temperatures and types of snow. In fact, there are a dozen or more grades suiting the most varied conditions. To some people the skill of choosing and applying the right waxes is at the center of the skiing experience. For those less fascinated by the challenge, adaptable broad-spectrum waxes can simplify the craft. Many skiers get by with just two hard waxes for fresh snow (one grade for snow below freezing, one for soggy snow), together with one tube of sticky wax, *klister*, for snow that sun, wind, and time have stripped of its crystal-bristling surface.

Along with the waxes themselves, some accessories must be carried. You need a cork to get wax on and a scraper to get wax off; to remove klister, you'll need a rag soaked in solvent (white gas will do the trick) and rags.

Some regions are more hospitable to waxers than others. In the deep, dry snow of the Rockies, where conditions tend to remain the same all day, a good wax job in the morning may keep you in trim all day; but in the wet snows of the Pacific ranges or the icy, crusty packs of New England, continual, fussy adjustments are likely to be necessary. For people not caught up in the challenge of the technique itself, it can seem an awful lot of trouble.

That's where "waxless" skis come in. Their bases have been impressed with tiny steps or other one-way patterns that permit the forward slide but catch in the snow whenever motion is backward. These skis don't move as fast or climb quite as well as perfectly waxed conventional models, but they certainly do move. The textured bases make them rather noisy, a drawback in some ears. Despite the name, waxless skis do benefit from a little waxing: a slick wax, applied to tips and tails, helps them to glide; and if you're pushing their limits up a hill, a grip wax, applied to the zone beneath the foot, helps them to stick. Waxes for "no-wax" skis are differently formulated than those for conventional models.

Waxed or waxless, there are limits to the slope a ski can attack directly. After that, you have to zig and zag. Even on the flat, you may have trouble getting enough grip for the forward stride when you are first in line, slogging into deep snow, with a pack on your back. At that point, you pull out your skins.

Climbing skins are strips of fabric covered with stiff artificial hairs. To use them, you hook one end (equipped with a loop or ring) over the toe of each ski; the rest of the skin is held to the ski with a layer of strong, temporary adhesive. The bristles of the skin point backward and resist any downhill slide. With skins, you can shuffle right up a pretty severe slope, or keep going on icy surfaces, at the edge of exhaustion, against a headwind.

SKI BOOTS, BINDINGS, AND POLES

When you buy your first pair of skis, you'll buy compatible boots and bindings at the same time. The classic boot-binding combination is called the Nordic Norm. The binding, mounted by the shop, consists of three short pegs, a toe clamp, and a ridged heelplate. The corresponding boot has three small pits in the sole beneath the square, projecting toe. To get into the binding, you press the toe of the boot into position, fit pegs to holes, and close down the securing clamp (called a bail). It takes just a moment to step into such a binding (unless ice has built up in the holes). The heel of the boot rises freely, as it must for effective skiing on level or rising ground; the boot flexes behind the toe. Nordic Norm bindings are made to accommodate boots 75 millimeters across at the toe and either 12 or 15 millimeters thick. (Older bindings, however, may not accept 15-millimeter soles.)

For greater control, you can get a three-pin binding supplemented by a cable running around the heel. This is an increasingly popular combination. An alternative refinement is the *Voilé plate*, a flexible plastic strip that runs back under the boot from the binding and clamps to the heel; it also aids in control, especially if your boots are somewhat soft.

Another, totally different boot-and-binding system is the New Nordic Norm Backcountry (NNN-BC) by Rottefella. The bootsole contains a metal bar that mates to the binding more positively than pins and holes;

CROSS-COUNTRY SKI BOOTS, THREE-PIN (LEFT) AND NEW NORDIC NORM
BACK-COUNTRY

the binding, not the boot, does the flexing. Salomon has a similar binding called the SNS-BC. Some like these "system" bindings, some don't. Yet another option for moderate backcountry skiing is the pure cable binding (no pins), which comes in many variations and will accept various boots.

A backcountry ski boot must be reasonably heavy and thick, with a fairly high top (avoid slipperlike models). Though plastic is gaining, top-grain leather still predominates, as does the classic Norwegian welt construction, in which the upper turns outward at the sole and is stitched firmly to it. Extra insulation built into the boot can be nice. Some boots have buckles as well as laces. Ski boots must bend readily from front to back, but should resist twisting. Hold the toe in one hand, the heel in the other, and rotate in opposite directions, as though you were wringing out a towel. A proper boot will not twist very far.

More ambitious skiers—telemarkers, "randonnee" skiers, ski mountaineers—will wear more rigid and massive boots, probably made of plas-

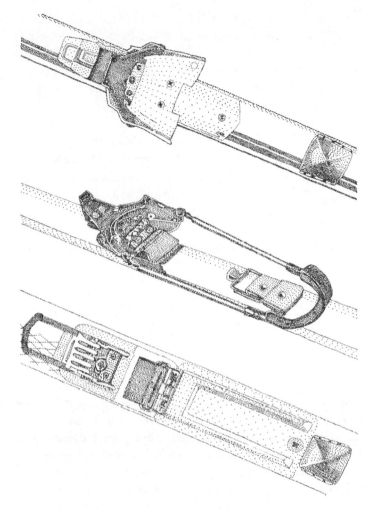

THREE-PIN BINDING, TOP; THREE-PIN WITH CABLE, CENTER; NEW NORDIC
NORM BACK-COUNTRY BINDING, BOTTOM

tic, and fit them to more elaborate bindings set on heavier skis. If you're
that good a skier, you need no advice from this book. Snowboards, too,
are sometimes now seen in the backcountry; their owners carry very light
skis and ski boots to use in getting up the hills their boards will carry
them down.

Of course you need *ski poles*. The best are aluminum, though fiberglass is also seen. The old rule for pole length—up to the armpit—still applies. (The ski poles you'd use at a downhill resort are too short to serve.) Back-country poles may adjust to different lengths—a feature some people like and some don't—and they may also allow you to remove the baskets and screw the shafts together to create a long avalanche probe. As a back-packer, you need pretty large baskets for soft snow.

Taken together, skis and the required accessories add up to a pretty pricey list. The naked skis run $200 to over $300 in the types backpackers are most likely to use. Boots cost $130 to $300; if you're on a budget, spend on the boots and compromise elsewhere. Bindings cost $30 to $60, poles a similar amount. Add $20 for a waxkit and $50 to $100 for skins. All in all, you'll be lucky to hit the snowy trail for less than $500, and it wouldn't be hard to double that. Special package deals, frequently offered in stores, may save you a few dollars; end-of-season sales in the spring will save you a bundle.

REPAIR KIT

The winter repair bag includes all the summer items and a few more be-sides. Have plenty of duct tape, wire, and cord for emergency ski or snowshoe fixes. A pair of pliers or vise grips is likely to be useful. Skiers carry overlength screws for remounting pulled bindings, and screwdrivers to match; however, this trick doesn't work with all ski constructions, so inquire when you buy. Some skiers like to have a spare ski tip: an emer-gency substitute, metal or plastic, that you can slide over the stump of your ski if you should break the point. If you use cable bindings, carry a spare cable. A spare ski basket will come in handy someday, too. If you use skins, you'll want to have a spray can of glue.

Skis take some home maintenance. Edges need sharpening, which you can do; bases need resurfacing from time to time, which most people del-egate to the shop. Modern snowshoes are pretty close to maintenance-free.

Boots for winter, of course, need fanatical waterproofing and seam sealing, especially around the welt and at the toe, where bindings may rub. Three-pin ski bootsoles sometimes crack beside the pin hole, making the binding useless; if this happens in the field, your best bet is to impro-vise a cable binding with wire, cord, or an elastic band, and head for home (and a cobbler).

TRAVEL IN THE SNOW

Especially on your first trips, don't commit yourself to covering too much ground too fast. One mile an hour is a good pace on snowshoes in open country; 3 miles an hour is excellent progress on skis. Often you will do much less. A 10-mile day on snowshoes, when you carry a pack, is an extremely long one, as is a 20-mile day skiing day. In some situations, skis may be no faster than snowshoes.

Take into account how much, or little, daylight you have to work with. At the winter solstice near the United States–Canada border, the day lasts less than 9 hours. If you allow 2 hours after dawn for breaking camp and 1, at dusk, for getting settled in, that leaves only 5 or 6 hours for travel. Still farther north, the days are still shorter; at the Arctic Circle in midwinter, the sun does not rise at all: not camping weather. On the other hand, much snow travel is done in spring, when daylight hours make up more than half the day; again, the effect grows stronger to the north, to the point of perpetual midsummer sun.

Whether you're on skis or snowshoes, the first problem of snow travel is keeping warm (but not hot) and, so far as possible, dry. Don't delay any changes in your armor of clothing that will keep the balance of heat production and heat loss. Allow all the ventilation you can. If there's snow in the air, you need to be wearing smooth-surfaced fabrics from which the flakes will slide; brush them off when they accumulate. Knock snow from low branches *before* you pass under them.

The thermometer doesn't tell you everything about cold. What chills you is the loss of heat from the skin (as well as from the lungs), and warmer air that is moving will remove heat as quickly as colder air that is still. If you are wet, evaporation in the wind will still further accelerate chilling. Humid air, too, is effectively colder than dry air. If your body keeps on losing more heat than it can make, you will enter the dangerous and even deadly condition called hypothermia, described at length in Chapter 28.

Nibble starchy or sugary foods as you walk, and drink plenty of water, more than you feel you want. If it's cold enough that water freezes during the day, insulate the containers. For instance, you can pull a thick wool sock over a bottle. Fitted foam sleeves are also available. Pack canteens up-

Wind-chill chart: effective temperature

Thermometer reading, degrees fahrenheit

Wind speed	50	40	30	20	10	0	−10	−20	−30
calm	50	40	30	20	10	0	−10	−20	−30
5	48	37	27	16	6	−5	−15	−26	−36
10	40	28	16	4	−9	−21	−33	−46	−58
15	36	22	9	−5	−18	−36	−45	−58	−72
20	32	18	4	−10	−25	−39	−53	−67	−82
25	30	16	0	−15	−24	−44	−59	−74	−88
30	28	13	−2	−18	−33	−48	−63	−79	−94
35	27	11	−4	−20	−35	−49	−67	−82	−98
40	26	10	−6	−21	−37	−53	−69	−85	−100

Read down from the thermometer reading, right from wind speed, to find effective temperature in wind. Jagged line marks the degree of chill at which travel becomes dangerous; unprotected flesh can freeze.

side down, so that plugs of ice won't form in the necks. Mixtures like lemonade stay liquid longer than straight water.

A constant minor frustration in winter is the way your glasses keep fogging up. Antifog solutions are available, and they help a bit (by causing moisture to form drops and migrate downward). Ventilation helps, but will be limited in glasses with side barriers. Double glasses are effective (but expensive). Wearers of prescription lenses may carry contacts instead, but this choice leads to other miseries. (Ever try to find a dropped contact lens in a world of sparkling snow?) This is one of those problems for which there is currently just no good solution.

In some areas, trails are as useful in winter as they are in summer. Abandoned roads or even railroad beds, healed over into simple paths, make especially good and obvious routes for snow travel in rugged country. Even if nothing is visible but a line of blazes or markers on tree trunks, these may mark the best path through the terrain. And trail blazes encountered while you follow a course of your own can help you pinpoint your location.

Most of the time, though, trails simply cease to matter in the winter. Navigation is cross-country, with the snow the whole new country that you cross. Be sure you understand the navigation tricks described in Chapters 16 and 22. In winter travel, as in other cross-country hiking, no one can afford to be a passive follower; each person in a group must be aware.

Winter weather can make it hard to keep track of your position. Your views of distant landmarks will almost certainly disappear in any overcast. Under some conditions the outlook shrinks to yards. Sooner or later you'll encounter one of those opaque snowy ground-mists called whiteouts. Shapes will be strange, unrecognizable. You can lose all sense of place and direction. Here as nowhere else the compass becomes your lifeline. You need to know, not only how to walk a compass course, but also how to plan a whole trek as a succession of compass lines, or bearings as they are called—so many paces on bearing A, so many paces on bearing B. A Global Positioning System receiver can also be used.

Your detailed route over snow depends largely on the skis or snowshoes you are wearing. Skis and snowshoes, and different models of each, handle differently; some are more able, some less able, to cross icy slopes, to float in deep, soft powder, or to climb steep hills. Often the snowshoers in a mixed party will head directly up a soft slope while skiers will circle around, or climb in a series of switchbacks.

There are certain hazards in traveling on snow. Tree trunks, warmer than the surrounding snow, melt "tree wells" around themselves, embarrassing to fall into. More serious is the risk in crossing snowbridges over flowing streams: a collapse can dump a backpacker into bitterly cold, rushing water. Look for the thickest bridge you can find, and cross one at a time; the leader should probe ahead with a ski pole or ice ax. Rope-carrying parties may give crossers a belay. Very fresh, very light, very deep snow can also be dangerous: people have actually suffocated in it.

AVALANCHE

Nothing else in the winter wilderness is quite so terrifying as the avalanche. About twenty people a year die in avalanches in the United States alone. There is a whole science of avalanche safety, and every winter traveler should know at least the rudiments.

Avalanches, or snowslides, are of several kinds. The most dangerous is

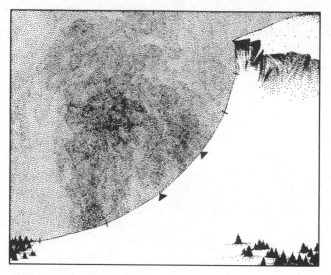

AVALANCHES ARE MOST LIKELY ON SLOPES OF MODERATE
STEEPNESS: BETWEEN 30 AND 45 DEGREES.

the *slab avalanche,* the great mass of snow that breaks, all at once, from a mountainside and plunges into the valley. Slab avalanches are likeliest during, and just after, heavy winter storms. The more new snow that comes down in a storm—and the faster it comes down—the greater the risk. It's cause for concern if more than a foot is added, especially if it piles up at the moderate rate of an inch an hour, or more. High wind adds to the danger. Remember that it may be snowing and blowing much harder up the ridge you must cross tomorrow than it is at tonight's campsite in the valley. Rising temperatures during a storm should also make you worry, for they mean that heavier, wetter snow is being dumped on top of lighter.

Once snow has fallen, it immediately begins to change and consolidate, generally growing much more stable. If it's not too cold, this will happen quite rapidly, and the risk of massive slides may vanish within hours. In very frigid weather, however, the snow changes slowly, and danger can last for many days or even weeks; north of the U.S.–Canadian border, it can last all winter. Watch for tiny "sloughs," harmless slides of loose, powdery snow; they indicate that the snow is settling nicely.

Slab avalanches can also form without fresh snow if it's cold and windy enough. Winds over 25 miles an hour can build up dangerous hard

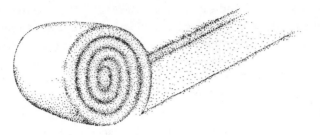

SUNBALL

drifts on the lee sides of ridges. These "hard-slab" avalanches of wind-packed snow are especially important as a danger in clear but windy periods following storms.

Not all snow is equal. How prone a given slope is to sliding depends largely on the history of that year's snowpack. Thaws followed by freezes, to take a simple example, will create icy layers within the pack, on which later-deposited snow is prone to slide. The matter gets complex and subtle. In avalanche safety classes, you're taught to dig pits, analyze the strata, and test snow stability. For an inveterate winter traveler, such training is a very good investment.

Up to a certain point, warm temperatures mean lesser risk. There is, however, such a thing as a *wet-snow avalanche*. Such snowslides occur in warm conditions or late in the season, when snow becomes waterlogged and loses its grip on the surface below. Watch for "sunballs," curious wheels of snow that run down the slope, rolling up the surface layer of the snowpack in a sort of scroll. Small sunballs don't indicate much danger, but very large ones, several feet thick, suggest danger of wet avalanche. Wet-snow avalanches don't kill as many people as the slab type, but they are dangerous enough. They are especially prevalent in the mountains of the Pacific Coast and as far inland as the Tetons of Wyoming.

AVALANCHE DEFENSE

Before you head into the wilderness, inquire about current avalanche conditions. In some U.S. states there are Forest Service avalanche numbers to call; the National Ski Patrol will certainly have information. The land agency office nearest your destination should know about local conditions.

Whatever the type of avalanche, the danger is greatest on treeless slopes of middle steepness, between about 30 and 45 degrees. Gullies and open swaths in forested landscapes are especially risky. Dense timber provides some reassurance, but a few trees on an open slope don't prove a lack of avalanches there. Avoid the lee sides of steep high ridges. Keep out from under cornices, the solid waves of snow and ice that hang over the crests of windy ridges like paralyzed ocean breakers.

If an indicated avalanche path lies across your course, it's best simply to go around it. The safest course is to circle it on safe ground at the top; the second best, often more practical, is to bypass the swath on gentler terrain at the bottom.

If you find no way around an ominous path, try to judge the risk. Is it "avalanche weather"—has it been snowing or blowing a lot? Consider also what might happen if you were caught in a slide. A short avalanche path that widens at the bottom is not quite so perilous as a long chute that funnels in. Are there rocks and trees at the base of the slope against which you would be crushed, or a cliff over which you would be carried? In some cases, by far the best choice is to turn back.

In crossing, move one at a time. Every member of the party should watch the crosser carefully; the last to go is in no less danger than the first. If you have a rope, by all means provide a belay. If the risk zone is wide, take advantage of any natural safety islands like clumps of trees and patches of bare rock.

If you do trigger an avalanche, things will happen terribly fast. On skis, you may just possibly be able to glide out to safety. If you're sucked in, survivors report, it's a little like being caught in a flash flood, but a flood at the same time fluid and solid. Don't just go along for the ride, but fight it. Immediately shed your skis and poles (there's not much you can do about snowshoes). Make the motions of a swimmer; try to keep on the surface of the tumbling snow, and to work over to one "bank" of the flow; grab onto vegetation. If you see the unmoving snow surface that underlies the avalanche, claw at that. If in spite of all this you feel yourself going under, cover your face with your arms to preserve a cavity of air. When you stop moving, make an attempt to widen that space in the moment before the snow hardens around you. Don't bother to shout; sound carries very poorly out of snow. If you can't dig, there's really nothing to be done but discipline yourself to calmness, and wait.

If you, the person spared, see a companion carried off in an avalanche, watch the process carefully. Your friend may appear and disappear several times. Note the last-seen point with reference to local landmarks. Then follow these steps:

1. Mark the point where you last saw the victim. Make a quick search down the apparent main line of the avalanche. Mark the location of any pieces of gear you find. Look carefully behind trees, on ledges and benches, and wherever any obstacle might have slowed or diverted the rushing snow.
2. Next comes the careful search. Probe systematically with skis, ski poles, ice axes, or avalanche probes assembled from ski poles. Reexamine the likely "traps" where the victim might have been stopped; then spread out to cover the whole surface of the avalanche.
3. When you find the victim, you may have to give artificial respiration. Get snow out of clothing and place the victim in a sleeping bag, head downhill. Treat, as needed, for trauma, shock and hypothermia (see Chapters 26 and 28).

What about summoning help? If you have a radio or portable telephone, by all means use it now. But sending someone out to civilization is almost never worth the loss of time and person-power. Half of all buried avalanche victims die within 30 minutes. Unless you're right next to a ski resort, every member of your party should stay and search. Keep it up for 6 to 8 hours: although very few victims last beyond the second hour, there have been astonishing exceptions.

In an attempt to improve the odds, many people now carry special short-range radios called *avalanche rescue transceivers*. Every member of a party carries one, leaving it switched off most of the time. In a hazard zone, however, all units are turned on, set to "transmit." If there is an avalanche and someone is buried, the remaining members of the party switch their radio units to "receive" and zero in on the signal from the buried companion unit.

Transceivers aren't cheap—over $200 apiece—and they are somewhat controversial. Some question whether they actually save lives. The reassurance, though, may be worth it. In putting together a party, just make sure that the various units people carry are compatible. The old standard frequency in the United States was 2.275 kilohertz; Canada (and Europe) use 457 kilohertz, which is becoming a worldwide norm. Dual-frequency models are available, but produce a weaker signal. If you buy transceivers, don't neglect to study the instructions and practice in the snow before you use them in earnest.

CAMPING IN THE SNOW

Might as well admit it: no winter camp is without discomfort. The snow camp can be, on balance, very pleasant or pretty miserable. It depends partly on things you can't control (like the weather), but mostly it depends on your gear, your skills and your common sense.

In some areas you can simplify camping by hiking in to established shelters. It's unwise, though, to count on finding the less elaborate shelters free of snow, and those that are open will sometimes be crowded. It is dangerous to head out so underequipped that you would be in trouble if you didn't make it all the way in to a distant refuge.

You generally have a wide choice of campsites in winter. The distinction between established and pristine sites disappears: you don't have to worry about trampling when the vulnerable earth is yards beneath your feet. It is polite, though, not to set up your tent right beside a route down which other travelers are likely to come.

If you don't find a level place, you can make one. The winter camp, of course, *can* be engineered without harm. Build a whole city, if you like—it will last, at latest, to the thaw. Make sure that you are out from under dead limbs and standing snags and, of course, away from avalanche paths.

One consideration is the availability of liquid water: not a necessity, if you have adequate fuel, but a luxury. You can lower water bottles to a stream rushing in a trench of snow, or maybe carve steps down to waterline. If you dig a deep enough well, you can also get water from under the ice of any sizable lake. Stream and lake water, of course, need the usual treatment; water melted from snow ordinarily does not. Filters tend to freeze up, so boiling and iodination are preferred water treatments for winter.

The first camp job is to pitch your tent. Without taking off skis or snowshoes, stamp out a level site. (If time permits, let the snow set for half an hour before proceeding; the platform will be less likely to get "post-holed" by boots and knees.) To anchor guylines in snow, you need special, broad, aluminum *snow stakes*; or you can use "deadmen," bits of wood or other small objects stamped into the snow and buried. Stakes and deadmen will quickly freeze into place, and you may have to dig or chop to free them when the tent comes down.

The moment your tent is up, you begin to face the challenge of keeping it dry inside. Avoid bringing snow in with you. Keep a whisk broom and a sponge just inside the tent door. Brush yourself off as you crawl in; take your boots off at the entrance and make sure the snow is out of the laces and the spaces between lugs.

Depending on the weather and the capacity of your shelter, packs may stay outside. Certain objects, however, need to be spend the night inside the tent and even inside your sleeping bag: your boots (in a plastic bag, or in your sleeping bag's stuffbag, turned inside out); your flashlight or headlamp; and batteries from any electronic gear like a camera. (To prevent damaging condensation, though, the camera body had better stay cold.) If the temperature is much below freezing, water bottles will have to taken to bed or, at the least, tucked alongside your bag, on the side away from the tent wall. (Make sure the caps are on tight!) Alternatively, you can bury some of your bottles outside under several inches of snow— which, believe it or not, acts as insulation. (Make sure you know exactly where to dig in the morning. Fresh snowfall can obliterate all surface signs.) Fuel should be brought inside as well.

If you have good weather and daylight, you can dig out a luxurious kitchen in the snow. Start with a natural depression, like a tree well. Straighten the vertical wall, and then dig out a waist-high "counter" for your stove and cooking gear. But when conditions are less pleasant, hikers cook and eat lying down, setting up the stove in the vestibule just outside the tent door. In truly awful weather, you may be forced to cook entirely inside, an intrinsically hazardous business. Watch out for any flare-up when you prime a white-gas stove, and keep ventilation generous. A pot with a bail can be suspended from the ceiling to minimize spills. Be aware that a tent that has been cooked in will absorb food odors and should not later be used in places where bears, especially grizzly bears, are a concern.

Winter cooking can be something of a struggle. Stoves that worked beautifully last August may require multiple primings now. Propane/butane cartridges may have to be warmed to function. Even liquid fuels may give trouble in deep cold: frozen impurities can gum up stove passageways. Put insulation under fuel tanks. Be terribly careful in handling fuel: besides being flammable, it can freeze the skin when spilled.

Tent cooking produces a lot of steam and adds to the moisture problem. Keep air flowing through the tent. Give the humidity inside every possible chance to escape. Be quick to mop up spills.

Winter dinners tend to be simple. Except in the leisurely, fair-weather camp, the standard is the meaty one-pot meal, with hot drinks, possibly soup, and cold snacks on the side. If water must be melted, cooking only starts your evening in the kitchen: you may be at it for hours. Don't drink up the last of your old supply before you begin to the melting process: you need a half cup or so to moisten the bottom of the pot. As you melt, keep drinking; have more tea, more fruit juice, more chocolate. If you wake up with a violent thirst toward morning, it's a good sign that you've been shorting yourself. Make sure that each person is getting at least a full gallon of water, in food and drink, each day.

Clothes hung from a line run along the peak of the tent, inside, may dry out at least partway. Don't take wet clothing to bed in an attempt to dry it. Unpleasant though it is to put on wet and frozen clothes in the morning, it's not as unpleasant as a wet sleeping bag. Even if it's very cold, leave your nose and mouth uncovered in the hood opening; your breath shouldn't be trapped inside. (You can breathe through something like a stocking cap instead.)

The ultimate luxury in winter is a warm, comfortable bed. Nights can be long; you spend a lot of time there. If your sleeping bag isn't really intended for winter, you may wind up wearing most of your clothing to bed. Wet clothes, though, will only chill you. It's particularly important to put on dry socks at bedtime and, if you have them, insulated booties. If you're brooding on boots and such, you can arrange them not too uncomfortably at your feet, behind your knees, or under your head as a pillow. Some people carry wide-mouthed bottles to use for indoor urination on nasty nights. On any clear night, though, the predawn stars when you go out are worth a few shivers.

Speaking of sanitation, the winter hiker obviously has a problem. Unless you happen to find a patch of clear, unfrozen soil, digging a "cathole" is pointless. All you can do is go even farther away from lakes or streams than you would in summer. As for toilet paper, pack it out always.

SHELTERS MADE OF SNOW

Although many never bother, every winter camper really ought to get some experience in building a shelter in the snow. These skills can be invaluable in an emergency, and quite a few travelers use snow shelters all the time, saving considerable weight. (Typical two-person winter tent: 8 pounds; shovel and snow saw for building a snow shelter: under 2 pounds.)

The simplest and quickest snow shelter is the *trench*. It's just what it sounds like, a moat, 3 or 4 feet deep, 6 or 7 feet long, and wide enough for a couple of sleepers (the wider the trench, the harder to cover). In the old days you would make a roof of interwoven conifer boughs. That won't do now, of course, unless a life is at stake; instead you use a tent fly, a tarp, or some such, laid on beams made of ski poles, axes, or whatever you have (downed branches, should you find them, make good supports). For insulation, cover the roof with snow. Be sure to leave an opening for ventilation.

More elaborate is the *snow cave*. To build one, you need soft to medium snow and a good thick snowbank. Suitable drifts often form near creekbanks (watch out for any concealed flowing water).

There are at least two ways of digging a snow cave. The traditional method is simple to describe but difficult to carry out. You burrow into the snowbank, making an entry tunnel. About 4 feet in, you angle the tunnel upward; you then excavate a flat-floored, round-roofed chamber. The job takes 3 or 4 hours even with a snow shovel, and the excavators get soaking wet.

It is possible to shortcut the process a bit. The trick, essentially, is to dig the snow cave with an oversize entryway, so that you have room to work without burrowing like a mole, and then to close off the extra gap. Proceed this way:

First, cut away at your snowbank to make it as close as possible to a vertical wall.

Second, dig into that wall a horizontal shelf or alcove about 4 feet wide. Make the floor of this opening level with your belt; make its ceiling about 18 inches above. This alcove is the beginning of the inner room of the cave.

Now start expanding the opening backward into the snow. Don't make the initial gap bigger; just hollow out behind it, inward, sideways, and upward, but not downward. The floor should run back on a level.

When you've dug out all the snow you can get at from your first position, excavate a trench for your legs, cutting into the incomplete cave, so that you can stand up in there.

Snow cave construction, shortcut method

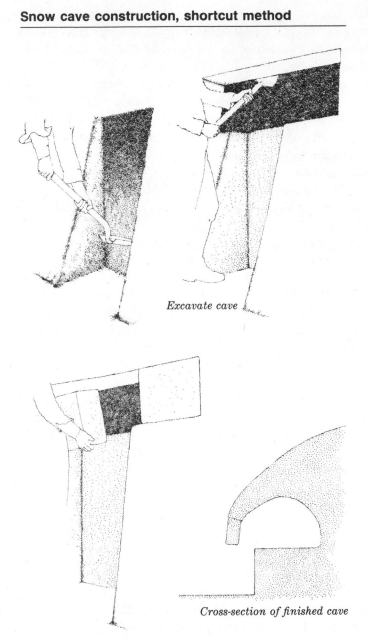

Excavate cave

Close off the excess opening

Cross-section of finished cave

Now finish the cave. Make it as large as you like: a typical plan is more or less a rectangle, 7 feet wide, 5 feet deep (into the snowbank), and 3 to 4 feet high. It may be split-level, with a lower floor and a higher "sleeping shelf." Make the ceiling a smoothly rounded dome.

What you have now is a snow cave with one side gaping open to the air, a sort of cutaway model. It remains to close off the open side. You do this by cutting several big snow blocks and placing them in the unwanted window. One of these blocks will bridge the trench you cut for your legs, turning it into a short tunnel—your permanent entry. Fill in the cracks and gaps between the blocks with loose snow.

Complex as it sounds, this method eliminates much of the misery of building a snow cave, and you don't get terribly wet (though it still is wise to work in waterproofs). Practiced cave-makers can do the job this way in an hour or so.

After the shelter is essentially complete—by whatever method—you "furnish" it. Cover the sleeping area with a groundsheet, and cut niches and shelves for a candle, your stove, and odds and ends. Punch a ventilating shaft up through the high point of the dome and a second above the stove. Narrow to start with, these shafts will widen as heat rises through them.

An *igloo* is something like a snow cave above ground. To build one, you need snow firm enough to hold its shape in blocks cut with your shovel (or shovel and saw). If loose snow is all you have, you can trample it down with skis or snowshoes, then let it set for 20 minutes or so. The bigger the blocks you work with, the faster the job gets done: 18 inches by

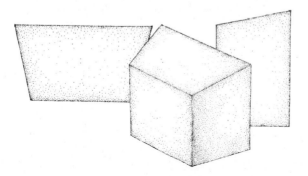

10 inches by 15 inches is typical. Because you're building a dome, the blocks must be beveled, with top and end surfaces sloping inward.

To guide yourself, outline the base of the igloo (round or oval—an 8-to-10-foot diameter). Then choose the location of your entry. The best position is downhill and crosswise to the prevailing wind. Dig a trench from the center of your circle to the entry and several feet beyond. Remove the snow from this trench in usable blocks.

Trench dug, you begin laying blocks around the circle. (One of them will bridge the trench.) When you finish the first circuit, trim the first couple of blocks you placed to make a gradual ramp, and take the second course right on up over them, starting a spiral. Then just keep going.

Typically, one of the snow masons works outside cutting blocks while the second stands inside to take them, place them, and finish the shaping. Five or six courses will be required. Because of the shape of the blocks, the walls will lean increasingly inward. If the blocks are regular enough and carefully beveled, they'll support themselves clear to the final large key-

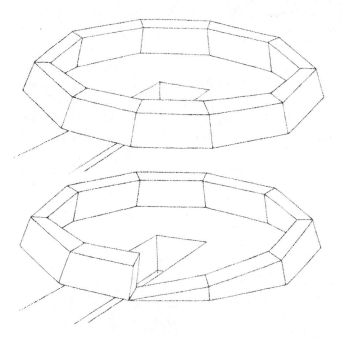

stone block that closes the top. When it becomes convenient, cut an arched lintel into the block that spans the trench, making a better door.

At this point you have your basic igloo. For extra protection you can add a raised roof of blocks over the trench outside the wall, creating a longer covered entryway. Then coat the outside of the igloo with loose snow. You should be able to move inside, and out of the wind, in an hour. The structure will knit together quickly as it warms up inside. As with a snow cave, you finish the interior for convenience, punching or cutting a generous air vent at the peak.

Igloos and snow caves are quite astonishing places: dead silent, comfortable, sheltered, almost warm. A blizzard outside can't touch you—it can scarcely make itself heard. The snow admits a curious daylight, col-

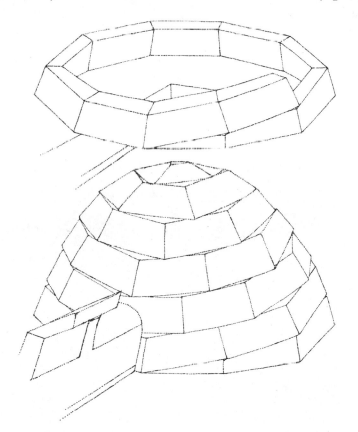

orless, dim, yet very clear. If their roofs are properly thick, both caves and igloos are very strong.

There are things to be aware of in any snow house. Just as in a tent, you have to make sure your ventilation is good. Don't block the air shafts or your entryway. See that the entry doesn't get sealed by drifted snow; a low, outlying shield wall of two or three blocks may trap a drift where it does no harm. Then there's the moisture problem. When stoves are running, the snowy roof will drip. Since drops collect on projections, the smoother you've made the roof, the less drizzle there will be.

It is an excellent idea to practice shelter building near the road, when nothing at all depends on quick, successful execution.

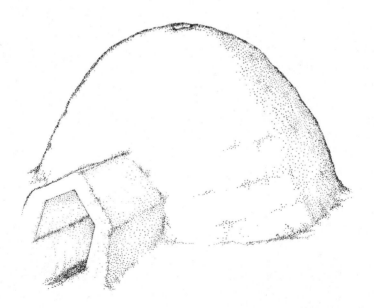

25

HIKING AND CAMPING WITH KIDS

A majority of wilderness travelers—so say the studies—are married, and most of them have children. (Interestingly enough, married couples who do *not* have children are relatively scarce in the wild places.) For more and more people, backpacking has become what, in earlier years, it was for few: a family sport. And more and more often the kids, even the very young ones, are coming along.

It's perfectly feasible to backpack, not only with middle-sized children, but also with babies. In fact, people who have done it—who have raised their children half in the wilderness, half at home—seem to find the process delightful.

True, you won't be able to go very far or very fast; true, you will have to carry a certain amount of extra gear and do some extra chores on the trail and in camp. But a slower pace can be a pleasant change in itself. And the child who has among earliest memories the woods, the streams, the far-off mountains, may well have gained an advantage that will last a life-time. Even very young children, too, seem to value the sense of being part of the enterprise their parents are carrying out. Something important, pleasant, and adult is going on, and they are part of it, not excluded. To older children, the actual responsibilities of the trail—even scaled down to their size—are a firm link with the parents, and a kind of preview of growing up.

Parents who backpack with their children, and enjoy it greatly, warn that you mustn't expect the wrong things. A trip with kids is quite another experience than a trip with adults; it's another style of travel. It is—it has to be—more leisurely. You have to give yourself more leeway, more margin, than you would on an ordinary trip. It isn't just that children have shorter legs than their parents; they also have different attitudes. Up to a certain (and quite variable) age, kids just don't look at the wilderness the way their parents do. They enjoy it for different reasons, value different things.

Most kids are tougher, physically, than we give them credit for. They'll make out just as well in the wilderness as out of it—maybe better. They won't be as clean as they might be at home, but you quickly learn not to bother much about *that*. A couple of matters merit more concern. First, children, and even adolescents, are more sensitive than adults to certain environmental hazards, including altitude sickness and ultraviolet radiation. Second, there's no denying that you're far away from the doctor. If you've put off learning first aid on your own behalf, you'll definitely want to take it up when you begin traveling with children.

When you're starting backpackers small, you want to start them slow—partly for their sake, even more for yours. All those special items, all those modified routines need shaking down. It's best to begin with day hikes, very short at first, then longer. Here's where you test (and inevitably add to) your list of necessary items; here's where you get the hang of familiar chores performed in unfamiliar places. It's also at this stage that you find out about temperaments and problems. How happy is the two-year-old in the baby carrier? How much walking does the five-year-old feel up to? Before you move on to overnight camping, you may want to test your methods on safe ground. Try cooking meals on day trips; try a risk-free "camp" on the back lawn or at an auto campground.

As you move on to backpacking, begin with trips in known territory. Make plans that don't put your group under pressure, and plan excursions you'll enjoy whether or not you make it all the way in to such-and-such a pond or such-and-such a waterfall. Most people who hike with young children don't fight bad weather when it catches up with them; they just go home. Don't let a youngster get the feeling that misery and wilderness belong together. Take it easy. Make it easy.

For backpacking purposes, you can say that children come in three sizes. There are the very small ones, the *portable* ones, who aren't able to walk much yet. There are the older ones, five years and above, who (if not exactly hikers at first) are more or less *hikable*. And in between are the youngsters of two and three and four—kids who want to do things for themselves but can't very well. Backpacking parents find it most challenging to travel with children of this age. But many people do it, and the young and the old seem both to enjoy it.

PORTABLE KIDS

How soon do you start taking an infant into the wild country? As soon as you like. Some families backpack with babies only a month old; most wait till about six months. In some ways these youngest children are very easy to manage. You will, of course, be slowed down somewhat by feeding and diaper changing, and most of the family's gear will have to ride in a single pack. On the other hand, the baby will go happily as fast and far as you feel able to manage.

Not all destinations are suitable, though. Young human beings are not at all coldproof, heatproof, or sunproof. Sunburn can be very serious in a small child, and infants have practically no ability to adjust to thin, high-mountain air. Because babies won't stand for wearing protective glasses, they can't very well be taken onto snow or to elevations above timberline.

What do you carry your passenger in? The choice is wide. (The old leather papoose-carrier, lined with sphagnum moss as an absorbent diaper, was elegant, but the materials are hard to find these days.) For very young children, you can use soft slings. These hold the baby against your chest, or on your back, or at either side, depending on the model. Expect to pay $60 to $75 for such a carrier.

As soon as the child can sit with head upright, you can begin using a backpack-style transport: a soft, padded seat, slung inside a metal frame, with the rider facing forward. The best models have high backs and sides, almost encasing the passenger. Different designs fit kids from 20 to 60 pounds; seats may adjust to provide differing amounts of support as youngsters mature. A carrier is first of all a pack, and must have comfortable, adjustable hipbelts and harnesses. There is typically a kickstand so that the unit can be parked upright on the ground. A child seatbelt is essential; a sunshield/rain hood is a useful accessory. Incidental storage room is nice. Good backpack-style carriers cost $100 to $200.

Most babies, delighted by the motion, ride well on parental shoulders. Not until a youngster has begun to walk does a prolonged ride seem confining and dull. A familiar toy, tied to the frame, makes a good diversion.

When you have a passenger perched behind your ears, you obviously have to watch out for low branches and be careful about leaning over. The rider, who isn't doing any work, must be dressed much more warmly than you are. If it's the least bit chilly, pay extra attention to keeping the baby dry. Make sure also that eyes and skin are protected from bright sun.

The same baby clothes used at home will usually do on the trail. Elastic one-piece garments, lighter or heavier or doubled-up according to the season, are good. Whatever clothing you bring, carry a *lot* of changes: you can hardly bring too many. Make sure at least one set is noncotton. Raingear? Standard waterproof "slickers" coated with vinyl, available in department stores, work well for most young children. Get rainpants as well as coats. Since youngsters perspire less than adults, and don't tend to drown inside their waterproofs, you won't need to scour the stores for miniature garments in Gore-Tex.

In camp, very young children aren't likely to crawl or toddle clear away into the forest. But they are quite likely to head for the attractive flames of a fire (stove cooking is a little safer; cooking with kerosene or alcohol is safest of all). A tent can serve as a playpen. You can also make a pen out of a tarp, hung low at the middle, raised around the edges. Some parents even use a leash and a harness.

As for feeding, make it as simple as possible. Breastfeeding is of course the easiest all around. Whatever the child has been eating at home should be continued; this is no time to introduce big changes. Kids who are just learning to feed themselves need a deep, generous cup with a big graspable handle. Also bring the usual plastic cereal bowl, bib, and washcloth. You may be able to minimize your use of pureed baby foods: quite a few freeze-dried foods are fine textured anyway, and you can always mash solid food to make a usable paste. You will of course avoid glass containers.

In diapering, most people continue whatever routine they use at home. This is not the place to revisit the debate about the environmental effects of using cloth versus disposable paper-and-plastic diapers. Whichever you choose, take plenty—more than you expect to need—along with all the incidentals. Stools, of course, should be carefully buried, but not even the liners of disposable diapers go into the ground—much too slow to decompose. You'll need a strong, leakproof plastic bag (or several, one inside the other) for carrying soiled diapers. Be scrupulous, of course, about washing your hands.

What about warmth at night? A baby can be tucked in (cautiously) with a parent, or between two sleepers in a double bag. You can also use the upper part of a bag built for an adult or larger child, doubling over the excess material and filling in with insulating things. Again, an infant, warmly dressed and wrapped in a fleece blanket, can be tucked into a stuffsack. With a little home effort, you can create a tiny tailored sleeping bag—for example, by cutting off the arms and stitching up armholes and waist of an old insulated jacket. Since down is damaged by repeated wetting and washing, synthetic insulations are naturally preferred in the infant bedroll; Polarguard is known for its durability. You'll also need a bit of plastic sheeting and a small pad of closed-cell foam.

IN-BETWEEN KIDS

It's not the infant—the object to be carried—that parents find most difficult to take to the wilderness with them. Rather, it's the two-, three-, and four-year-old who is neither a mere passenger nor quite a self-operating human being. Too heavy and restless to carry for long, the child can't walk fast or far. A 4-mile day, with such a companion, is about the most you can plan on. At this stage quite a few people sign up with organized groups for aid and comfort and take mostly easy trips to accessible base camps.

In the earlier part of this period, youngsters are of course still mastering the basic skills of being alive: learning to walk with confidence, to talk, to feed themselves, to use the toilet. Wilderness toilet methods, in particular, can be upsetting. When you've just learned that virtue is the porcelain bowl, it may seem not just odd but even downright sinful to squat over a hole in the ground. Some families stay close to campground outhouses at this juncture; others ease the transition by bringing along light plastic toilet seats. When operations commence, a parent should stay with the youngster and be patiently reassuring. Make sure that hands get washed thoroughly afterwards—in a basin, not in a lake or stream.

This is the time when kids are exploring, handling things around them, getting into trouble. There are plenty of dangerous objects around a camp to be concerned about. But there's also a lot of gear, soft, harmless, and fascinating, for a child to play with.

Clothing gets more ordinary at this stage. You still need generous spares but not quite so many. For the bed, pint-sized synthetic-filled sleeping bags with hoods are available in various lengths; most cost under $100. Though kids need some insulation under them, they're generally happy without the generous padding that many adults require.

HIKABLE KIDS

Once youngsters are able to walk at a fair clip, the problems change; some of them disappear. Older kids will wear what anybody wears on the trail. Footwear, though, can be a problem. Tennis shoes don't really do the job, once serious hiking begins; sturdy boots, even if you can find them in the proper sizes, are expensive overkill for rapidly lengthening feet. Choose trail shoes or boots at the very lightweight end of the scale.

Few families are large enough these days for much "handing down" of boots or other wilderness gear, but sometimes several families can get together in a sort of pool. Then there are the invaluable thrift shops.

Most kids seem to enjoy carrying packs from an early age. The first "load" may be no load at all, or a favorite toy. Use a daypack with shortened straps. Kids of about nine and older have no trouble with a full load—that is, a load of about one-fifth of their weight; a rucksack with a hipbelt is a sensible pack in this stage, or perhaps a small, cheap frame.

Even after children can walk pretty well, they may think of it as a chore. It takes some encouragement to keep a young hiker going. Although your range will be longer now, you still don't want to be in the position of *having* to get to a particular, distant place. You'll need to take frequent breaks to rest, to eat, to play a game, to look at something entertaining like a stream. It can be fun to look things up in guides to flowers, trees, rocks, birds—if you aren't too high-handedly "educational" about it. (Do it for your own sake and let your enthusiasm spill over.) Some favorite playthings should be there to fall back on.

In matters of safety, your judgment will have to substitute for the youngster's, and that can take a good deal of your time. Give each kid a whistle, pinned to the shirt. (You'll have to convince them not to blow it for the fun of it.) Keep younger children in sight and middling ones within earshot. Older kids may want to run ahead, but have them wait at a given, not very distant point (a trail junction, the foot of a slope, whatever). If you're in an area where grizzly bears or mountain lions are of concern, don't let kids run ahead at all.

Tell them what to do if they lose you. The rule: sit down, blow the whistle a lot, and stay put. Talk to them also about the possible hazards of the land: snakes, bears, falling rocks, rapid currents, poison oak or ivy or whatever. It can be hard to do this without making the country sound forbidding, but it's not a step to be skipped.

Discourage kids from eating while they walk (some of them can't hike and chew gum at the same time, and there's a risk of getting a food fragment stuck in a windpipe. Having taken a first-aid course, you'll know exactly how to deal with "foreign body obstruction of airway.") You'll have warned them, of course, against munching the unidentified leaf or berry; still, a handbook on local poisonous plants is one good item to have along. The usual first aid for plant poisoning is to induce vomiting. For more on these matters, see Chapter 26.

In general, watch out for problems children may be having. Some, as you might expect, complain very readily; others, surprisingly, do not. Check now and again for developing blisters. You need to make sure that kids stay comfortably warm or cool; watch for signs of hypothermia and hyperthermia (see Chapter 28). Above 6,000 feet or so, be very alert for altitude sickness, and head downhill decisively if you suspect it. Fortunately, even relatively stoic kids don't push themselves as dangerously far as prideful adults may sometimes do.

When you get to camp, check the site for any particular dangers—a steep drop, a rotten snag—and point them out. Experienced parents set limits: kids don't go beyond that creek, that rock, that stand of firs. With especially adventurous youngsters, one adult may have to spend most of the time keeping watch.

Any animals you encounter will be fascinating to the young. Teach the kids to understand them, to like them, and to respect them. Teach equally firmly that animals must not be fed, or petted, or even approached too closely. Critters that seem oddly unafraid may have something wrong with them. *Hands off the cute and furry.*

Kids, being small, are more likely than adults to look like potential prey in the eyes of a mountain lion or (rare case) the genuinely predatory bear. In regions where these animals live, you have yet one more reason to keep youngsters with you and, especially, to prevent any kid from wandering off alone. The wild animal hazard can be exaggerated, and almost always is; yet it is not zero. See Chapter 29.

Many or most kids like to do small chores at camp. This is fine, of course, and should be encouraged. (With the younger ones, it won't speed the chores up any: contrariwise.) Wood gathering is a pleasant assignment, and so is help with tent pitching. If weather and wildlife permit, kids may want to lay out their own open-air bedsites. Older children get a lot of pleasure out of a tent of their own. Then there's help with the cooking—safest are those jobs, like mixing a cold-water pudding, that don't get the small-fry too close to fire or stove. Be sure to tie back long hair when there's fire around.

There's nothing special about backpacking food for these relatively grown-up children. If anything, the food you take on a trip with youngsters should be even simpler, even easier to prepare, than you would otherwise favor. Some foods—desserts, of course, individually packaged hot-cereal breakfasts, and such—have entertainment value. Happily, the problem of the fussy eater is likely to solve itself on the trail.

LOW IMPACT: ENTERTAINMENT VERSUS WILDERNESS?

Alt kids may enjoy a trip immensely, they aren't at first likely to enjoy it for "adult" reasons. They are more likely than adults to want to return to familiar ground. And when they're in a wild place, they look for the same sorts of entertainments they would find at home: things to *do*. Toys, cards, and games are valuable, especially for rainy days.

Since nothing can fail to be new to them, babies just coming alive to their surroundings are as fascinated by one place as by another. Older kids want places they can play in. Above all they like *water:* a stream (especially with a swimming hole), a pond, an ocean shore, mud, or—best of all—summer snow. They tend to be unimpressed by the subtle detail of the forest. The appreciation of wilderness as wilderness seems to come later in life, though you're establishing the basis for it now.

Kids' energetic playfulness can lead to certain problems, for some of the things that seem most entertaining are also hard on the landscape.

Children (and boys especially—by nature? by social example?) are engineers. The first thing they want to do when they find a stream is build a dam across it; the first thing they want to do with dirt is turn it into miniature roads, walls, and earthworks. Even when no special project is underway, children, moving around as much as they do, can accomplish much more than their share of vegetation trampling and path beating. Some might say there is legitimate argument for not taking youngsters into the wild places at all.

And yet there is every advantage to doing so. The taste for wilderness is best learned early, and so are the habits that protect the land. Though it may not come easily, it's never too soon to start teaching kids those wilderness manners that consist partly of courtesy, partly of safety, and partly of concern for the fabric of the country. During the day's hike, make sure kids don't trample down trail edges, cut across switchbacks, knock rocks down the slope. Discourage the random collection of plants. Making camp, select a suitable well-used site and explain why you choose the spot you do. Point out sensitive areas, like plants that shouldn't be trampled. Try to steer games in harmless directions. Low-impact methods, indeed, can be presented as a kind of game or entertaining drama. Even adults find it sometimes useful to think of it that way, and kids have the ability to throw themselves into a fantasy without irony. (*The bad guys are after me. Did I leave any marks they can track me down by?*) At any rate it's worth a try. Think of it as an investment. You're training tomorrow's wilderness user to go gently in the fragile wild places.

By about age twelve, youngsters graduate from daypacks and rucksacks to external-frame packs essentially like those worn by adults, though a little smaller and usually simpler. (There are very few internal-frame packs to consider.) Adjustable frames and interchangeable harnesses will prolong usefulness as bodies lengthen. Cost is usually under $100. You'll need to monitor loads—kids, like some adults, may feel compelled to fill up every cubic inch they've got, not always with very light or very practical things.

When full-scale packs begin to be worn, serious boots with good ankle support become necessary as well. Kids tend to buy for looks and brand name; they may not be very attentive to fit, and it's your job (with help from a fitter at the store) to make sure they don't wind up in blister machines.

THE CHANGE

In the middle of all this there comes a time—a different time, for different youngsters—when the young person begins to regard the wilderness somewhat as the adult regards it. Reports vary, but clearly some children begin to show this change of attitude as early as eight or nine. Wilderness travel is, after all, more play than work, for anyone; the gap between child and adult is not so great here as it would be, for instance, on a visit to the office where a parent earns a living.

Somewhere along the line, youngsters start to see the land as a place to adventure in, to admire and value for its own shape, its own interest. At this point they have already begun to be "real" backpackers, and this is the time that backpacking parents especially look forward to. At this stage some parents (fathers especially) can't resist forcing the kids to walk farther, carry more, and achieve more than they may really enjoy. This is a mistake that can just possibly spoil things. But most kids who discover for themselves the pleasure of the wilderness seem to be addicts for life.

A few years further on, the situation changes again, and the kids, long-legged and energetic, will be waiting constantly for *you*.

TROUBLE AND HOW TO DEAL WITH IT

It must be poor life that achieves freedom from fear.

> Aldo Leopold,
> *A Sand County Almanc*

But it is a characteristic of wisdom not to do desperate things.

> Henry David Thoreau,
> *Walden*

26

We may not admit it, but there's a certain peculiar glamour to the thought of facing danger, of defending life and limb, especially in remote and photogenic places. People *like* to read about wilderness hazards and narrow escapes, to listen to other people's "war stories." But the charm quickly vanishes when threats become personal and real. And there's a thing you can just about count on: spend enough time in the wild places, and you're going to have some part, sometime, in dealing with an all too genuine emergency—another person's, or your own.

The wilderness, make no mistake, is full of danger. Granted, the risks, when you compare them with the hazards of driving a car or running a power lawnmower, don't look unreasonable. A couple of hikers may be killed each year by snakebite; a couple, in a bad year, by bears or mountain lions or lightning; perhaps a dozen by accidents or by weather they're not prepared to handle. Small numbers, as such sad numbers go. But wilderness dangers, because less familiar, can be more daunting.

The way to stay out of trouble is to think in terms of trouble. This doesn't mean a hypochondria, a fretfulness, or even a conservative unwillingness to take *considered* risks (that's up to you). What it does mean is awareness. Don't go out underequipped. Don't go out underinformed. On the trail keep a slightly wary eye on the world around you and on yourself.

Be alert to objective outside hazards: the approaching thunderstorm, the loose rock ready to fall on companions below, the hazardous ford, the red-hot stove. Some of these you will avoid; others you'll have to deal with. Either way, the great virtue is simply to know what you're about. Most accidents seem to happen to people who take risks *without knowing it*, casually, carelessly, unprepared.

Watch also for physical problems in yourself, or in your companions, that could become serious if not attended to. Deal with nuisances promptly, before they become more than nuisances. A cold, drenching rain, for instance, is only an annoyance—but if you don't handle the situation properly, it can lead to a life-endangering chill.

FIRST AID

First-aid training is simply vital. Every adult or teenager in a party should have some. The shortest medical course in the world, 6½ hours of Standard First Aid, is available through local Red Cross chapters for $50. It's ideal if at least one member has had additional instruction. Most useful of all (but not available everywhere) are courses in mountaineering medicine or wilderness first aid. However, there is a fair amount that the relatively unpracticed first-aider can safely do, and in a pinch you have to work with what you know.

One sometimes useful item in the pack is a booklet setting out, precisely and in order, the steps to be worked through when you have a seriously ill or injured person on your hands. Several such guides exist; your prefabricated first-aid kit may contain one. Among more-than-minimal handbooks, Steve Bezruchka's *Pocket Doctor* is a standard (see the Resources appendix).

If the emergency is fairly minor—and most are—you will have time to consider, to consult the manual, to talk things over with the cooperative victim. It is the major injury, or the physical collapse, that is most frightening. Such cases are rare in the extreme but too serious not to consider in advance.

Details vary, but in general there are three steps in dealing with a major wilderness injury or illness.

First, you *save life.* A few problems are so dangerous that action must be almost instantaneous.

Second, you *stabilize things.* Chances are you won't be able to treat a major injury in any fundamental way; all you can do is make the patient as safe and comfortable as possible and follow, with caution, the instructions in your manual and the dictates of common sense.

Third, you *get the victim home.* Sometimes a person in distress can get out under his or her own power, slowly, and with help. If not, you'll have to arrange for outside aid, or, in some cases, carry your companion out yourself.

The notes that follow here are not meant to substitute for a first-aid manual, still less for actual training. I've tried to select, from the long list of things the hiker needs to know, a few that seem absolutely basic. Please do learn more.

THE FIRST STAGE: SAVING LIFE

Let's say you find a person, a member of your party or not, seriously hurt, or unconscious, or both. Go to him, if you can do so without danger to yourself. Speak loudly to him, asking him how he is; if there's no answer, touch him, not roughly, in a further search for response. Unless he's plainly "all right," consider him your patient and proceed.

As a rule, you examine victims where you find them. You don't try to move them. (There are exceptions. A drowning victim won't be left in the water; someone struck by lightning had better be moved from the vulnerable spot; any immediate danger, as from falling rock or avalanche, can't be ignored.)

First things first: establish that the victim is *breathing.* Look for chest movement; listen for exhalation; try to feel his breath on your hand. If you can't quickly confirm respiration, make sure that there is no physical blockage of the breathing passages or *airway.* Place one hand under the back of his neck to tilt the head back sharply—this keeps the tongue from plugging the throat. Note this, however: neck injury is likely in any accident involving force or impact. If you even suspect such a problem, don't press up under the back of the neck. Rather, place your hands along the side of the lower jaw and draw it forward, closing the nose with your two thumbs. (This jutting of the jaw may also help whenever the airway remains stubbornly blocked by the tongue.)

If some foreign object is blocking the airway, you should be able to dislodge it by fishing it out of the throat, by slapping the victim on the back, or by applying the thrust to the abdomen known as the Heimlich maneuver. In a first-aid course, you'll be taught how to do these things correctly, and in rotation, until the blockage is removed.

If opening the airway does not restore breathing, you move on to *cardiopulmonary resuscitation,* or CPR. In the pulmonary part of this procedure, the rescuer breathes for the victim, mouth to mouth. Place your free hand on the victim's forehead and close his nostrils with finger and thumb. Seal his mouth with your own, and breathe deeply into him. Remove your mouth to let him exhale. For an adult, provide breaths at the rate of one every five seconds; for a child, every three seconds.

The CPR procedure can also provide—but only if needed—an artificial heartbeat, produced by rhythmic pressure on the breastbone. Full CPR is exacting and energetic, especially if performed by one person alone, and must be learned by practice under supervision. The Red Cross incorporates CPR in its standard first-aid course, and in more intensive courses as well; the American Heart Association has similar programs. If you are traveling with young children, be sure to master the somewhat different version of CPR that applies to them.

If a patient isn't breathing but has a pulse, you must provide artificial respiration indefinitely. But what of the victim whose heart has stopped? In the city, the rule is to start the full version of CPR, including chest compressions, regardless of how hopeless the victim's condition may appear— and to continue it until professionals arrive. In the wilderness, the choice isn't always so clear. A badly injured person with no heart action is most unlikely to be saved by CPR this far from hospital care. The same is true for a heart attack victim. On the other hand, the technique can make all the difference to someone who has suffered a lightning strike or a near-drowning. If a life is to be saved, it will be saved quickly: a person whose heart is not restarted within 1 hour, at the very most, has lost the battle.

Should you wear a surgical mask when doing CPR? Due to our newly strong concern about diseases that may be transmitted in body fluids, some people think so. Prefabricated aid kits may include such masks. However, the risk of contagion in mouth-to-mouth contact is really very

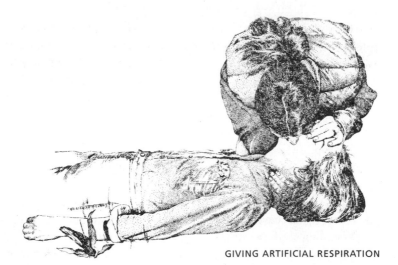

GIVING ARTIFICIAL RESPIRATION

slight. As Dr. Gordon Benner, Sierra Club medical officer, puts it: "I personally would do it without a mask and I hope that you would do it, too."

Three other problems can be listed with the instant emergencies. One is massive *bleeding.* In almost every case, you can stop the flow simply by pressing on the wound. (In this situation, do protect yourself from infection with a surgical glove or by placing a thickly folded cloth over the site.) Ten minutes of firm pressure should allow clotting and prevent further hemorrhage. If the wound is on an arm or a leg, it also helps to lift the limb above the level of the heart. Rather than removing the blood-soaked cloth, make it the basis of the dressing you later apply.

A second problem that won't wait is *heat stroke,* the late stage of bodily overheating, or *hyperthermia.* The treatment is obvious: cool the stricken person down. For more on this problem, see Chapter 28.

The third hurry case is *poisoning.* No matter what was swallowed, the initial step is to have the victim swallow water to dilute the substance. The next step is usually to induce vomiting. Neither of these can be done, however, if the victim is unconscious, or having convulsions. For certain poisons—petroleum products (stove fuel!), strong acids, and strong alkalis—you do *not* induce vomiting. These substances may do further damage to the esophagus if they are vomited up; there is risk, too, of getting them into the lungs.

THE SECOND STAGE: STABILIZING THINGS

When the instant emergency is over, the next danger is *shock.* Shock is essentially very low blood pressure, and can be caused by trauma, blood loss, dehydration, pain, and emotional reaction. It can occur with any accident or illness, and is sometimes a sole cause of death. Thirst, nausea, and increasing anxiety are symptoms. The skin will grow pale, damp, and cool. Heartbeat will be rapid and weak, breathing quick and shallow. The victim may get dizzy or black out. In the last stage of severe shock, blood pressure drops toward zero.

Treat for shock whether or not it has yet appeared. Lay the victim flat on her back. Raise her legs 8 to 10 inches if practical (but not if there is severe injury to head or torso). Loosen constricting clothes, especially at the neck. Her body will have lost much of its power to maintain its temperature; depending on the weather, you must keep her either warm or cool. If she's aware, be certain to reassure her, to listen to her, to satisfy her requests where you can. If she's awake, give sips of cold water. If she can't keep it down, try again in a couple of hours. Don't give fluids to someone who's spontaneously vomiting or suffering convulsions.

Along with treatment for shock, do a second, more thorough examination. Look, touch, and listen. Check for all sorts of injuries: wounds, fractures, burns, dislocations, frostbite. (Sometimes the most dramatic problem is not the most serious.) Count heartbeats per minute and breaths per minute. Get all the information you can from and about the victim. Take notes. Even an amateurish medical history may be of value later.

Special precautions apply whenever someone has taken a hard blow on the upper body, especially if the victim loses consciousness. First, until you know otherwise, assume the person has a broken neck; make sure the back of the head is supported and pad the sides to prevent movement. Shift the victim, if at all, with extreme care. Always move the body as a unit, avoiding any twisting that might damage the spinal cord.

Watch the victim's state of consciousness. Does she become alert and then hazy again? As time goes on, does she become more aware and responsive, or less? If there is any pattern other than steady improvement, it's vital to summon a rescue.

Now decide, with deliberation, what happens next. That may be nothing more than signaling or sending companions for aid. Or you may need to apply whatever treatments you are fairly sure of, guided by common sense, a manual, the patient's own reactions, and whatever training you've had. (The idea is not to "fix the victim up," but merely to prevent further injury. Don't do a thing unless you can tell yourself why you are doing it.)

Don't stop paying attention to your patient after the first crisis passes. Keep on noting vital signs. Talk to her. Let her know what you're doing. First-aid experts remark that, if you don't talk to the person in your care, you're practicing veterinary medicine!

In the excitement, don't forget the welfare of the rest of your party. Among other things, it's often important to set up a safe and comfortable camp.

THE THIRD STAGE: GETTING OUT

In few of our wilderness areas is there much difficulty about swift rescue, at least in summer, and at least for hikers on busy trails. If the victim can't move under his own power, the problem is simply to attract the attention of rescuers, or of other hikers who can send for them. If there are several healthy people in your party, send one (or better, two) for help. Be sure the party you send out knows how to describe your whereabouts. If you have a radio or cellular phone, you will of course use that.

If you can't send people to the outside world, or want to send an additional message, nothing attracts the attention of the authorities like a smoky fire. A triangle of fires, 50 feet apart, will certainly be read as "Trouble Here." There are also recognized ground-to-air signals that you can form by arranging gear or objects on open ground. The most important one to remember is the simple vertical bar (I), which means "serious injury." Then there is the double L (LL), which means "all is well"—worth remembering in case there has been some sort of false alarm.

How do you decide if an injured person can walk out? This decision can be hard. On the one hand, you don't want to risk further injury. On the other hand, many accident victims *can* make it out, slowly and with assistance. Helicopter rescues are damnably expensive. (Who pays? Policies vary. In some cases the victim and companions must pick up the tab themselves. If not, the public pays. Such an operation should not be unleashed casually.)

If you travel away from the trails, or if you visit remote areas in winter, it is a good idea to learn some rescue techniques yourself: how to make a litter, how to splint major body injuries, and so forth. These are set out in books and courses on first aid, rescue, and mountaineering medicine.

27

SOME COMMON
MEDICAL PROBLEMS

Most of the time, medical problems on the trail take a form much milder than the accident or collapse that demands your fast, clear-headed action. The typical complaint is a nuisance, not a danger; even rather serious injuries usually allow you time to think. Here is a list, short and by no means complete, of problems you may face sometime—the common cases, and a few uncommon ones in which a little information may be reassuring—together with the treatments that mountain medicine experts recommend for them.

SURFACE WEAR AND TEAR

Cuts, punctures, and scrapes. You step on a porcupine quill; you skin your elbow; you gash a thumb with your pocketknife. If bleeding is copious, stop it by pressing directly on the wound. If the bleeding wound is someone else's, especially a stranger's, you may want to put on latex gloves from your first-aid kit, or at least interpose a cloth: it isn't paranoid to think of AIDS. Especially if there's almost no blood (as with a puncture), try to produce a little bleeding by kneading the surrounding flesh (object: to flush out germs). If bleeding alone has not completely washed out the wound, finish the job with plenty of clean water. A plastic bag with a pinhole in it makes a good "hose." You do not need to apply a dressing unless the wound would get dirty without one. A gaping cut can be kept closed with one or more "butterfly bandages," strips of adhesive cut in an hourglass shape, with the thin part over the cut. A minor wound is certainly not a cause to head for home; a larger one might be. (All hikers should be sure their tetanus immunization is up to date; one booster shot is needed every ten years.)

Burns and scalds. These account for a large percentage of backcountry injuries. Whether the affected area is large or small, your first priority is to *cool it as fast as possible*. Remove clothing first (if it isn't stuck on). Immersion in cold water is ideal. Cooling will quickly lessen the pain, inhibit further damage, and promote healing. Prolong the cold treatment for up to 2 hours if it continues to soothe. Then clean the site with soap and water and apply a water-based gel dressing, such as Spenco 2nd Skin. Some sources recommend an antibiotic ointment as well.

Minor burns—burns that raise few if any blisters—will probably require no further attention; but do watch for infection. Burns that raise numerous blisters, or that penetrate the skin, are more serious. Be especially concerned about any blistering burn on the face, hands, feet, or genitals; any *large* blistering burn elsewhere; and any blistering burn at all on an infant. If a person has burns about the face, be aware that the breathing passages may be scorched, and watch for any breathing difficulty. People with serious burns should be evacuated.

If first aid continues more than a day, dressings will need changing every 24 hours. If you're using ointment, flush off the old coat with a stream of water and apply new.

For *sunburn* and *snow blindness,* see Chapter 28.

Eye problems. Getting a fragment of the wilderness in your eye is annoying and can be hazardous. The first thing to remember is not to rub the eye, which will only add irritation. Instead, get a wooden match or a thin twig; place it horizontally halfway up the outside of the upper eyelid; then fold the lower margin of the lid upward around it, watching the maneuver in a pocket mirror. Foreign objects tend to stick to the inside of the lid and can be safely removed with the corner of a bandanna or a cotton swab. Sometimes the problem is no more than an inturned lash. Sometimes the irritating object has already floated away, but leaves a scratch that causes the something-in-my-eye feeling. If this persists, soothing eyedrops may be helpful; seek a doctor's attention for a persistently inflamed eye.

If someone's eye is actually penetrated by an object, your immediate job is to calm the person and instruct him *not to move his eyes.* Do not try to remove the invading object. Cover both eyes (so that the injured eye won't move in tandem with the healthy one) and summon help.

BROKEN BONES

Broken bones are scary and usually painful. Broken arms and legs, fortunately, are rarely very dangerous in themselves. If you even suspect a fracture, assume there is one. Fractures are not always marked by obvious deformation; check also for discoloration, swelling, pain, and tenderness. Unless a life is in danger, never move a person until all fractures, known or suspected, have been splinted.

Splinting—binding the broken part to something solid—prevents motion, keeps broken bone ends from damaging adjacent tissue, and generally makes the victim far more comfortable. The details of this craft make up a large part of advanced first-aid courses. For starters, remember that a fracture of a bone in the arm or shoulder can usually be splinted by placing the forearm in a sling across the lower chest and binding arm and sling to the body; most fractures of leg bones can be dealt with by splinting the broken leg to the healthy one.

In some first-aid courses you may be taught to leave a broken limb exactly as it is and merely to immobilize it with splinting—"splint 'em as they lie." In the wilderness, where help is more than minutes away, you will probably have to modify this principle. The injured person will be more comfortable, and the broken bone more stable, if you restore the limb to something like its natural or functional shape. This means straightening to some extent. While one person cradles the limb, another can take hold of the hand or foot and pull, gently and persistently, parallel to the normal alignment of the bone. When the injured limb looks more or less like the healthy one, proceed with splinting.

A particularly worrisome case is the *open fracture*, in which a wound reaches the fractured bone, or a broken end of the bone pokes out through the skin. Should you try to clean such a wound, or scrub the bone end, before splinting? The consensus is that you should simply remove visible particles of dirt and then proceed with straightening by gentle traction, causing the broken end to retreat back under the skin. All such fractures must be examined and cleaned thoroughly in the hospital, anyhow.

Anytime you apply a splint, you must make sure that blood is reaching the region of the limb beyond the break. Locate a pulse in the healthy limb; then make sure you can find the same pulse in the broken one, both before and after you apply the splint.

Head, neck, and back. As noted in Chapter 26, injuries that may affect the brain or spinal cord need a special degree of care. A patient who has been unconscious more than momentarily should probably head for home; any delayed effects are better dealt with there than on the trail.

SPRAINS AND DISLOCATIONS

A sprain is damage to the ligaments that bind bones together in a joint: depending on the severity of the sprain, tissues may be stretched, torn, or actually severed. A dislocation occurs when the bones shift out of their normal positions in the joint.

Ankle problems. The badly twisted ankle is something every hiker, especially the solo hiker, dreads. Fortunately, most ankle injuries are not immobilizing. Often the sharp pain that seemed to indicate a major problem will go away by itself. Even a moderately damaged ankle can be walked on—with adequate reinforcement. On the other hand, if you mistreat a minor injury, you can just possibly make a long-lasting problem for yourself.

You've "done something" to your ankle. Consider it. Where does it hurt? Most of the time the painful spot will be on the outside of the ankle, below the bony bulge that marks the end of the smaller leg bone (fibula). This suggests a sprain, or, at worst, a fracture of the fibula. These injuries will allow you to walk out, with proper support. By contrast, pain at the inner side of the foot indicates a more troublesome problem; you probably shouldn't plan to do any walking.

If the ankle joint is actually torn, the foot will flop at an odd angle to the leg. This is a far more serious injury. The foot should be restored to its natural position and splinted. Wrap a jacket or other soft object around the foot in a U shape and bind it around the ankle, not too tightly but firmly enough to keep the foot steady. In this case there is no question of trying to walk.

In the case of a typical sprain, the immediate treatment is to *cool* the painful area with a cold pack (snow or a canteen of cold water, wrapped in cloth). At the same time *compress* the area by wrapping it with an elastic bandage. Begin at the toes and wind it around and around the foot and clear up the ankle. Place some padding under the bandage right at the painful spot to increase the pressure there. The third element of the initial treatment: *elevate* the leg to keep blood from pooling in the foot. The objective at this stage is to limit swelling.

Keep this treatment going for at least an hour—up to a full day. Then you can wrap the ankle for walking. Start by cutting three strips of adhesive tape 1 inch wide and about 3 feet long. Next, make sure that the foot is correctly positioned, at right angles to the leg. Now run a tape strip down the inside of the calf, around the heel, and up the outside of the calf, pulling a little in the last stage to rotate the foot gently outwards. Apply the remaining strips in the same fashion, each overlapping the last and a little farther forward on the foot. Over the tape layer goes the elastic ban-

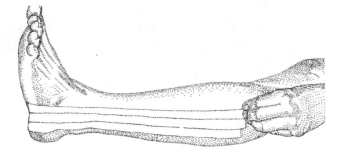

TAPING A SPRAINED ANKLE

dage, and over the bandage go sock and boot. Lace the boot firmly but not ferociously. If you don't have a staff or a trekking pole, find a stick to be used as a cane.

At this point, most people with twisted ankles find it quite possible to walk without excessive pain. A small amount of pain does not mean that it is dangerous to proceed. Move along slowly. Check from time to time that the ankle is not swelling; if it is, loosen the elastic bandage slightly.

Dislocated shoulder. This is a rather common wilderness injury. It is relatively easy to treat a dislocated shoulder in the field, and there is good reason to do so, because it becomes much harder to deal with as time passes.

There are several rival methods of restoring, or reducing, a dislocated shoulder. This is about the simplest. Have the injured person bend over, resting her chest on an object or on someone's hands. The injured arm hangs limp. Now take that wrist and pull the arm first downward, then downward and forward, turning it slightly in such a way that the thumb moves toward the outside. The tug should be strong and decisive, yet not so abrupt as a jerk.

A slower method uses a weight instead of muscle power to provide the traction. Give the victim your best painkiller and have her lie face-down on a tablelike surface with the bad arm hanging. With tape, attach a 15-to-20-pound weight to wrist or forearm. In 15 minutes or so, the pull should exhaust the arm and shoulder muscles, permitting the bone to pop back into place. Give it 2 hours; if it hasn't worked by then, abandon the effort and seek help. Not many hikers with stubbornly dislocated shoulders can be expected to walk out—the jolting is too painful.

Dislocated kneecap. Another dislocation that can be dealt with in the wilderness is that of a kneecap (as opposed to a dislocated *knee,* which involves major damage to the whole joint). It is not uncommon for a kneecap to slide out of position, usually to the outside of the knee; you can probably make it slide back by straightening the leg and pressing the bone gently from the side.

Dislocated finger. This ailment is also pretty manageable. Have the person flex the finger slightly; pull on the fingertip while you press on the dislocated segment from the end nearest the wrist and from the backside of the hand.

Other dislocations. By comparison with these cases, most other dislocations are serious business—much more dangerous, in fact, than typical fractures. The rule is to splint them and leave them alone. But always make sure there is a pulse beyond an injured joint. (First locate the pulse in the healthy limb; then try to find it at the same spot in the injured one.) If you can't feel a heartbeat out there—say in the wrist beyond an injured elbow—it may be necessary to shift the joint carefully in the hope of unkinking an artery.

Strains are injuries to muscle tissue. Minor ones are common and not serious; occasionally, though, a muscle in the calf or back will tear so badly that it cannot bear weight. This may be a considerable injury requiring medical attention. First aid is much like care for a sprain: cool, elevate, and gently compress the injured area. Some people with seriously strained muscles can walk out; some can't. A crisscross layer of tape and an elastic bandage, as with a twisted ankle, may help.

With sprains and strains, as with most other problems, the injured person himself is your best source of information. Only he can tell you how bad it feels, and whether or not he can travel on foot after your best efforts at first aid.

BODILY ACHES AND ALARMS

So far we've talked of problems that arise because you are where you are, doing what you are doing: hiking in the wilderness, or anyway on a trail. But other, homelier complaints can arise out here as well as anywhere else, and sometimes do.

Headaches can ordinarily be treated with your light analgesic; usually insignificant, they may be connected with another problem like altitude sickness (see Chapter 28). A headache that comes on during the hiking day may well be due to dehydration. A quiet hour with a canteen should clear it up.

Earaches tend to be due to infection; antibiotics can be taken if they persist. *Nosebleeds* are best stopped by pressing a cold compress on the bridge of the nose for as long as it takes. *Sore throats* may be a sign of another illness or may occur at high altitudes for no discernible reason; pus on the tonsils suggests that an antibiotic be taken.

Garden-variety upper respiratory infections—*colds and flu*—are certainly not emergencies. They're no fun, either, and if you're really under the weather, you may want to creep for home. Considering the number of people moving around in wild areas, it is truly astonishing how rare it is to encounter these common complaints out there.

Chest pain is alarming—everyone thinks heart attack—but can have other causes. There is little first aid for genuine heart problems in a wilderness situation, beyond comfort and reassurance and, if required, basic life support. People with known chronic heart problems will have medication along.

Abdominal pain. A growing pain in the belly, and anybody who still has an appendix thinks *appendicitis*. If the pain does not settle in the lower right quadrant (below the navel and to the right of the midline of the body), it probably isn't an appendix that's complaining. Abdominal pain that does not increase when you press on the bothersome spot is probably superficial, not involving an organ, and not worrisome. Simple constipation can produce a suggestive pain but not the other symptoms of appendicitis: nausea, loss of appetite, and mild fever. If you do suspect the disease, start taking the antibiotic in your first-aid kit and head for civilization with all deliberate speed.

Indigestion happens out here, too; if you know you're susceptible, or are responsible for a group, carry an over-the-counter remedy. Pink bismuth in tablet form is favored by many. *Constipation* is not uncommon; drinking lots of water helps prevent it. Some hikers carry laxatives. *Diarrhea*, if serious, is more of a problem. You are not very likely to come down with a serious case in wild country in the United States or Canada. (Giardiasis, the infamous "backpacker's diarrhea," will not develop for at least a week after exposure. If you do come down with it, you will need a doctor's care. See also Chapter 20.) The essential thing to remember about any severe diarrhea is that you must replace fluids. Some first-aid kits contain oral rehydration salts, designed to replace not only water but other chemicals lost.

28

THREATS FROM
THE ENVIRONMENT

New backpackers are often too much afraid of wild animals. They may be too little afraid of other, less obvious, yet sometimes menacing dangers: the heat, the cold, the wet, the wind, the alpine sun, the lack of oxygen at altitude. All these things affect the hiker. Some of them can make you very sick, and some can kill you. One of the "environmental" disorders—the disease called hypothermia—probably endangers more backpackers in a single year than animals do in decades.

THE BODY'S THERMOSTAT

To keep working properly, the human body has to stay near the normal 98 degrees Fahrenheit. A very precise balance has to be maintained between heat gained and heat lost. If the balance shifts too far in either direction, the hiker becomes a victim, a person in trouble.

You generate heat just living. The harder you work, the more you generate. At the same time, the body loses heat, constantly, in the breath and from the skin. Survival depends on conserving this body heat when your surroundings are cold and getting rid of it when the neighborhood is hot. There are natural mechanisms for doing each.

What happens when the problem is *cold?* First, the muscles tense just slightly in what is called preshivering tone; this burns calories and generates a surprising amount of heat. (So you may be exercising in the cold without knowing it.) Then comes shivering, an even more effective heat producer. Meanwhile, the small arteries near the skin, where heat is radiated to the outside air, close down. Less blood approaches the skin, and less heat is lost. In dangerous cold, the body may cut off a large part of the circulation to the arms and legs, risking the limbs to keep the head and torso warm. After that, the natural defenses are exhausted. To operate in cold climates, we depend on artificial ones. Clothing, our added insulation, has made us a species that can live in the Arctic as well as in the tropics, where we evolved.

If the problem is *too much* warmth, there are different mechanisms.

Vessels in the skin and in the arms and legs expand, bringing blood to the surface, where its heat is lost. Perspiration begins, and sweat, evaporating, takes large quantities of heat away. Clothes only get in the way of the cooling, except when you need to block the direct heat and burning ultraviolet rays of the sun.

This, oversimplified, is the system. The diseases of heat and cold—hyperthermia, hypothermia, and frostbite—attack when it is pressed too far.

HYPERTHERMIA

Hyperthermia is what happens to you when your body is unable to dispose of heat as fast as it manufactures it and absorbs it from outside. As the temperature of the vital organs rises, you begin to feel sick.

The overheated person may feel faint and nauseated. The heartbeat may be fast and irregular. Sweating is profuse, yet the skin may feel oddly cool. The face is likely to be pale. The symptoms are generally those of shock (see Chapter 26). However, they don't always appear in neat packages. The most important thing to watch for is a growing indifference to surroundings. ("Whenever a person says he wants to sit down and catch up with the party later," one M.D. remarks, "it's a worrisome sign.") In this early period, the disorder is often labeled *heat exhaustion.*

As the body's core temperature rises to high-fever levels, the system goes haywire. The body may lose its ability to regulate blood flow to the skin. There may be a pounding pulse, labored breathing, and seizures. In the textbook case, the victim stops sweating: skin will be hot and dry. But experts warn that this is not always the case. Because the symptoms vary, it is most important again to focus on the person's attitude: a severely overheated hiker will lapse from indifference into major confusion. At this stage, the disease is commonly called *heat stroke.*

If the condition is far advanced, you have an instant emergency on your hands: heat stroke will kill. The treatment, early or late, is the same: rapid cooling. This is best accomplished by removing clothing, sprinkling water on the skin, and fanning to produce evaporation. The water does not have to be cool or clean; in a pinch, even urine can be used. Once the person is clearly aware and able to swallow, give plenty of water by mouth.

Once the crisis has passed, you face the decision of whether to continue the trip or head for home. Except in very mild cases, the latter is probably the better choice—especially if the weather continues hot. In any event, an attack of hyperthermia is a signal to take it easy: the body has tried to handle a taxing combination of effort and heat, and failed.

How did it fail? Probably by being unable to sweat profusely enough. That ability is partly a matter of hydration—you have to drink a lot to sweat a lot—and partly a matter of training. In hot-weather hiking, one may have to perspire 2 quarts an hour to stay healthily cool. Hardly anybody can do this on the first hot hike of the season. But as time goes on, the body adapts to heat stress, "learning" to sweat more copiously and with less loss of the salts called electrolytes. An otherwise fit hiker needs about a week of intermittent exercise in a hot climate to make this adjustment. If you plan to hike the desert in the warmer part of the year, bear this in mind. Really intense hot-weather work requires conscious effort to replace sodium, by salting food or by consuming electrolyte-replacement drinks.

When the air is both hot and very humid, however, no amount of training will help: sweat just won't evaporate. Under these conditions, don't hike.

Heat cramps—painful involuntary muscle contractions, usually in the legs—are another misery that may affect unacclimatized hot-weather hikers. Rest, rubbing, and stretching help. So does salt intake, but don't take salt in tablet form (likely to cause indigestion). Rather, drink slightly salty water, made by adding no more than ½ teaspoon of table salt to 1 liter.

HYPOTHERMIA, THE KILLER

Of all the diseases of heat and cold, hypothermia has the ugliest record. As in heat stroke, the body's defenses break down, struggling vainly not against an excess of heat but against a lack. The temperature of those organs that are vital to life—the organs of the head and torso—begins to drop. All the conserving mechanisms are tried. All fail.

How do you know when hypothermia is coming on? It can be hard to tell. Cold feet and hands are not hypothermia; neither is a generally "chilly" feeling. Take these rather as warnings: signs that you're in a hostile environment and that your guard should be up. Cold-clumsy hands may make it harder, for instance, to adjust your clothing properly.

Real hypothermia begins when the body's core temperature drops below 95 degrees. Violent shivering, though not always present, is a classic early sign. The sufferer grows somewhat clumsy and may have trouble talking. And yet the hypothermia victim may push on—toughing it out—

when she should not, wrongly convinced that she is only a little chilly and tired. Deteriorating judgment is itself a symptom.

If the cooling process is not arrested, this borderline condition will tip over into *profound* hypothermia. Body temperature, now, has dropped to 90 degrees. Shivering has tapered off or ceased. Muscles are very stiff indeed. Most notably, the person will start acting very oddly: she will stumble, mumble, say and do peculiar things. No longer is she competent. Finally she will simply fall to the ground. If nothing is done for her, coma will follow, and then death.

If you notice the early signs of hypothermia in yourself or a companion, you take the obvious action: stop the loss of heat and make it possible for the person to warm up again. At the very beginning, it may be enough to get out of the wind for a few minutes and eat some candy. If the problem has reached the serious shivering stage, stop and set up shelter. Get your friend out of wet clothes, under cover, and into a sleeping bag. It may be helpful, and it cannot hurt, for a second hiker to take off outer clothing and get into the bag with the victim, sharing body warmth. If the victim can swallow, give her sweet liquids—hot, if possible, though the sugar is the main thing.

Profound hypothermia is not so easily dealt with. What if you come across a solo hiker semiconscious, or even seemingly dead, on a snowbank? In this instance, the right kind of first aid can save a life, but the wrong kind can kill.

In deep hypothermia, the heart muscle is chilled. One result is that the heart is prone to go into ventricular fibrillation, a random fluttering that pumps no blood and leads quickly to death. Any shock to the system can trigger this condition.

In such a case, the sufferer must be handled *gently*, with extreme care. Do not allow him to stand up or walk. (Sudden effort will shock the heart by bringing cold blood back from the limbs to the body core.) Even rewarming, if done too rapidly, can deliver a fatal blow. Don't, for instance, place a hypothermia victim in a warm spring.

Having avoided these errors, your first task is to prevent the person from getting any colder, typically by placing him in a sleeping bag. Your second, much less urgent job is to help rewarm his vital organs *but not, initially, his arms and legs.* Hot water bottles can be applied to points where heat can go quickly to the core—at the scalp, the neck, the armpit, the groin. (Hot mush in a plastic bag makes a good head-warmer.) In a tent, light a stove and boil water; the warm, steamy air will get heat to his head and lungs while the rest of him stays cool inside the zipped-up bag. Once the victim can swallow, sugary hot liquids are helpful. (Never try to get food or liquid into an unconscious person, though—it may be inhaled.)

A deeply hypothermic person may not be breathing and may lack a detectable heartbeat. In such a case, you certainly want to give artificial respiration, the pulmonary part of cardiopulmonary resuscitation. (Along with its primary purpose, it will help with rewarming.) Professionals debate, however, whether the chest compression part of CPR should be attempted. A cold heart may in fact still be beating, terribly slowly; intervention could produce a fatal fibrillation. As an amateur, you'd better not chance it. Meanwhile, don't assume the worst. "They're only dead," the saying goes, "when they're *warm* and dead."

If someone in your party has a brush with mild hypothermia, that need not necessarily alter your plans. A hiker who has been definitely hypothermic should probably be taken home. In a case of *profound* hypothermia, move the victim as little as possible; send someone out to summon a rescue.

We tend to think of hypothermia as a winter problem, and that's of course not wrong. But a surprising number of cases also occur "out-of-season"—in the warmer half of the year. On New Hampshire's Mount Washington, four hypothermia cases once had to be rescued within 48 hours—in August! Washington, one of the most weather-beaten summits in the United States, is hardly typical, but there is some risk in any cool region. Spring and autumn hikers in cool places are especially vulnerable, because, so often, they take gear and clothing suited only for midsummer.

Remember: it doesn't take bitterly cold air to make "hypothermia weather." The problem can arise even on a mild day that is both *windy* and *wet*. A hiker in wet cotton clothing on a breezy ridge can die of hypothermia when the air temperature is in the forties or fifties Fahrenheit.

FROSTBITE

Frostbite is, essentially, freezing: the freezing of a part of the body. Feet and toes are the likeliest parts, by far, to be bitten; most of the other cases are fingers and hands.

Unlike hypothermia, frostbite can only happen when the air temperature is freezing. That makes it almost exclusively a winter problem (though on some peaks and at some latitudes it can happen anytime). Winter campers, the first few times out, may worry about frostbite every time their hands or feet get unpleasantly cold. With more experience, you learn that mere chilliness isn't frostbite. Still, it's better to be oversuspicious than to be complacent.

The fact is that frostbite can sneak up on you. The *typical* pattern—a cold sensation, followed by pain, followed by no sensation at all—doesn't always hold. The best defense is to ask yourself frequently whether you have full feeling in fingers and toes, and to do something about it if you don't. It's especially important not to have your boots too tightly laced, and to loosen them further from time to time.

If you think a finger is beginning to be frostbitten, you can quickly warm it in your armpit. If you are worried about your toes, there's the belly treatment. You stop, strip off your shoes and socks, and plant your feet on somebody's warm belly—not nearly as uncomfortable for the companion as it sounds! Groins and armpits work, too.

A part that is frostbitten will look waxy, feel cool to the touch, and be numb. If it is still soft and movable, however, the damage hasn't gone too deep. It will hurt while you rewarm it, but there should be no permanent harm. Seriously frostbitten flesh is inflexible and hard. If your fingers or toes have gotten like that, what do you do about it?

Your instinct might be to warm things up, fast. But this is sometimes the worst action you could take. In deep frostbite, the real tissue damage is done during the initial freezing and again when the flesh is thawed. While the part is actually frozen, nothing much is going on. Moreover, it doesn't hurt. Thawed, it will hurt like hell. People can walk many miles, without discomfort or further damage, on frozen toes and even frozen feet; but once thawing has taken place, a seriously frostbitten person must be carried.

There's another good reason for not rewarming deep frostbite too soon, and this is the risk of another bout of frostbite on the outward trek. Thawing and refreezing can turn a minor case into a major and crippling one.

So if you discover, in the middle of a bitter winter day, that someone in your party has a frozen toe, don't stop. Head as quickly as you can for the roadhead, or to a place from which rescue will be easy.

If you must make camp, you can hardly avoid rewarming a frozen part. Authorities now agree that this should be accomplished quickly rather than gradually. Soak the injured limb in a bath of warm water. Mountaineering doctors debate the recommended temperature, but the consensus puts it between 100 and 105 degrees Fahrenheit. If the water feels hot to the first-aider, it s too hot for the patient. Keeping the water at that temperature as nearly as you can, soak the part for 20 to 30 minutes. Never pummel the damaged flesh, rub it with snow, break any blisters that appear, or try to exercise the limb. Never apply direct heat. After re-warming, bandage loosely.

Overtight boots can lead to frostbite when you might not otherwise expect it. Overstuffing your boots with socks, in the attempt to keep your feet warmer, may actually impede circulation and make them colder. Tight crampon straps, cinched over pliable boots, can do the same. If your feet feel chronically cold, try easing up on straps and laces.

Deep frostbite is another of those subjects that *have* to be talked about, because the problem is so frightening and serious when it occurs. But frostbite simply won't overtake a well-equipped and knowledgeable backpacker.

PREVENTING THE DISEASES OF HEAT AND COLD

We've touched many times in this book on some of the basic practices that should keep you safe from the diseases of heat and cold. Reviewing them quickly:

Keep comfortable. On cold days keep warm—on hot days keep cool. Adjust your clothing whenever you need to. Don't be so strong minded that you let yourself suffer for hours—if nothing else, you'll be wearing yourself out, and that can lead to trouble.

Drink plenty of water. Thirst isn't a reliable guide to your need for water—when it makes itself felt, you are already somewhat dehydrated. Drink *more* than thirst would suggest, something between 1 and 2 gallons of liquid water a day. Notice the color of your urine: if it is dark, you know you need to be guzzling harder.

Get plenty of food. This is doubly important in the cold. Nibble all day long. The body can and will run on its own fat, but this is an inefficient source of energy unless new sugar and starch are coming in.

Don't push on to exhaustion. Some readers will smile ruefully at this advice—climbers, and others with fixed ambitions, are perhaps unlikely to follow it. But whenever heat or cold is a problem, exhaustion can help precipitate heat stroke, hypothermia, or frostbite. It can complicate other health problems as well.

Be in good condition when you set out. This means reasonable exercise at home as a matter of routine, and a good diet. Some Americans, though technically healthy, don't have the reserves they need to deal with stressful wilderness environments.

Avoid most drugs. Winter campers, snug and warm at nightfall, often take a swallow or two of liquor. No harm in that. But whenever cold is becoming a major problem, it's best to stay away from that and any other "stuff." Different stimulants and depressants have different effects, but they commonly interfere with the normal working of the body's heat machine. (Coffee and tea are okay, however.)

Deal early with incipient trouble. Learn to watch for the signs, and resolve to act on them.

ALTITUDE SICKNESS

"Altitude sickness" is a name for several related physical problems. Naturally enough, it is mostly encountered in high western ranges. More people than we realize get sick at altitude, sometimes running considerable risk without ever knowing it. In one study, 84 percent of the people who climbed to the 14,410-foot summit of Washington's Mount Rainier were found to have at least some symptoms.

Altitude sickness is brought on by rapid rise in elevation. Though symptoms rarely start below 9,000 or 10,000 feet, they can begin as low as 5,000. How fit you are doesn't seem to matter a great deal. Neither, surprisingly enough, does smoking.

Ordinary altitude sickness, the kind experienced by thousands, is known medically as "acute mountain sickness." Coming down with it, you will probably notice first a headache, mild or intense. If you're hiking, you'll feel exhausted and short of breath. You'll lose your appetite and may feel nauseated. In more severe cases there is vomiting. Many people get a few symptoms toward the end of a long first day that ends above 9,000 feet, feel better when they stop hiking, and wake up perfectly fit in the morning. Others are uncomfortable for several days. Aspirin and acetaminophen will help against the headache; the prescription drug Diamox (see below) will alleviate all the symptoms. Avoid alcohol and salt.

All of this is a nuisance at worst—for most of us, most of the time. But acute mountain sickness can develop, on the second or third day, into one of two other conditions, both highly dangerous. For either there is only one cure: *pack up and get down the hill*—if possible, while you can still move under your own power.

Cerebral edema, a rare but deadly condition, is an accumulation of fluid in the brain. The current belief is that ordinary mountain sickness is actually a very slight cerebral edema, but the more intense form is unmistakably different. The headache turns violent. The victim will be alarmingly weak. She may stagger, babble, hallucinate. If she isn't taken to lower elevations, she falls into a stupor, followed by a coma and then by death.

Almost as serious, and considerably more common, *is high-altitude pulmonary edema,* an accumulation of fluid in the lungs. Over a hundred people die of this disease every year, some at elevations no higher than 9,000 feet. The symptoms are somewhat like those of pneumonia. There is coughing, shortness of breath, quickened breathing, and fast heartbeat. The lungs feel tight, stiff, constricted. There will be creaking or bubbling noises in the chest, slight at first, and then increasing. As the victim gets worse, coughing will bring up a pinkish foam. The last stage is a stupor brought about by lack of oxygen.

Again, the one real answer is to go down. Sometimes a drop of a couple of thousand feet will bring a dramatic recovery. If you can't evacuate immediately, have the victim sit up, and try to keep him alert. Bed rest only makes the condition worse.

Pulmonary edema is by no means unknown in older adults, but the danger is much greater for people under twenty-one. Hikers who have had it once must be on the watch for it afterwards. And here's a curious fact: people who spend a long time at high altitudes, return to sea level for several weeks, and then go up again, run the greatest risk of all.

AVOIDING ALTITUDE SICKNESS

The body has the ability to adapt, within limits, to the lack of oxygen at unaccustomed altitudes. On the typical short backpacking trip, however, this adaptation has barely begun when the party heads for home.

The more slowly you ascend, the fewer problems you will have. It's good to start with several days at 9,000 or 10,000 feet, and to increase the altitude of your camp no more than 2,000 feet per night. If you must start at a high roadhead, try at least to get a full night's sleep there on the eve of the trip, and schedule a fairly leisurely first day.

People with heart and lung problems should certainly ask a doctor's advice before setting out on trips in the high country.

There is a prescription drug, Diamox (acetazolamide, a diuretic), that is often effective both in preventing and in treating mild altitude sickness. People who are allergic to sulfa drugs can't use Diamox, however: it makes them hypersensitive to ultraviolet rays and gives them severe sunburn.

SUN EXPOSURE AND SNOW BLINDNESS

It's painful to admit it, but the case is clear: sun exposure—*any* sun exposure—must now be recognized as unhealthy for human skin. Ultraviolet (UV) light, an invisible component of sunlight, is a serious health hazard. Darker-skinned people may burn less, yet are also susceptible to long-term hazards. Nobody who spends a lot of time outdoors can afford to be complacent about the effect of ultraviolet radiation on the skin. Skin cancer is on the rise, and sun exposure contributes greatly to general epidermal wear-and-tear. Damage is done even if you acquire a lovely tan, or do not noticeably burn. The eyes are similarly punished; several conditions, including cataract, are promoted by ultraviolet exposure. People up to about age eighteen are especially at risk for skin damage, and young eyes remain extremely vulnerable up to about age twenty-five.

The higher you climb, the worse it gets: the more ultraviolet rays come through the filtering atmosphere. At 10,000 feet, ultraviolet dosage is half again as strong as at sea level. Moderate overcast does little to stop this radiation. Be aware that burning rays bounce up from glittering granite, sand, water, or snow.

Protection takes the form of clothing, hat, and sunglasses, and of sun-blocking lotions for exposed skin.

Sunscreen lotions are graded according to "sun protection factor" (SPF), prominently noted on containers. A lotion with an SPF of 8 would theoretically permit you to remain in the sun eight times as long, before burning, as you could with no lotion on at all; an SPF of 15 would give you a fifteenfold safe period. You can now buy goops with SPFs as high as 50, for a price. These are worth the investment if exposure will be intense, as on alpine snow, or if you've been badly burned before. Backpackers also favor lotions billed as waterproof—they do float off with sweat, but not too quickly. Apply screen an hour before the sun hits you, and renew it from time to time. Don't neglect to apply lotion under your chin and around your nostrils, where rays bouncing up from below can burn you badly. Beyond sunscreens are opaque sunblockers, intended to shut out all ultraviolet radiation. Two types are zinc oxide lotion and clown-white makeup. Some people like to smear zinc oxide on their noses. For lips, use SPF-rated waxy sticks containing sunscreen.

A single layer of thin cloth is surprisingly transparent to the sun; a T-shirt, for instance, gives you no more protection than a coating of lotion with an SPF of 7 or 8. Thicker cloth, or multiple layers, can block UV radiation totally, but may be too warm for the conditions you are hiking in. Several firms now make light, well-ventilated garments designed specifically to block ultraviolet. Sun Precautions is one (see the Resources appendix); its Solumbra shirts and trousers are rated with sun protection factors, like lotions. The most important article of protective clothing is a broad-brimmed hat. For very bright conditions, special sunhats with neck cowls, or havelocks, are valuable.

Sunglasses are also necessary, and not only in the high country (where of course they are vital). Suitable glasses are of the "special-purpose type." These will block 60 percent or more of the ultraviolet radiation wavelength called UVA and 99 percent or more of the more damaging UVB type. The apparent darkness and color of the lenses is unrelated to sun protection. Gray is a popular, nondistorting tint. Polarized lenses are useful if you are trying to spot fish in water. Glass lenses cost more than polycarbonate and break more readily, but they are clearer and less likely to get scratched: take your pick. Sunglasses for outdoor use need virtually unbreakable frames.

For extra-bright conditions—altitude, snow and ice—you will want "glacier glasses" with lenses that block out most of ordinary, visible light and all ultraviolet, and with opaque or translucent shields of some sort at the sides. In an emergency, in such conditions, you can peer through a tiny hole in a bandanna, or make slit glasses by putting tape across an empty frame.

If you wear prescription lenses, eye protection gets more complex. Clip-ons, though available, are awkward. A spare pair of regular prescription lenses can be given appropriate coatings. Specialty sunglasses made to prescription cost $150 to $400. Talk to an optician or optometrist.

Should you neglect your eye protection on the heights, you risk coming down with the frightening condition called *snow blindness*, sunburn of the eye. The first symptom will be a scratchy, sandy feeling. That's the time to hurry off the mountain. In another 6 or 7 hours the eyes may swell almost shut, and the touch of light will become a physical, painful thing. At that point, to get down the hill, you may have to be led. The first-aid treatments are cold packs, total darkness, and perhaps aspirin or codeine for pain. The condition should abate in 1 to 2 days.

What about ordinary, epidermal sunburn? In mild cases, your sunscreen lotion will also do for a salve. Creams with aloe vera seem unusually helpful. Really severe sunburn can be incapacitating, with blistering, severe pain, swelling, headache, even nausea, fever and chills. Moist, cool dressings will help somewhat. So will lotions with cortisone.

29

PROBLEM ANIMALS
AND PLANTS

The animals of the mountains, woods, and deserts are among the things that draw us there. The word *wilderness,* in fact, comes from roots meaning "the place of the wild beasts." Still, animals (and some plants as well) can make problems for the hiker, or worse. Although these dangers account for far less injury or death than do the environmental hazards discussed in Chapter 28, they loom larger in our imagination. (How dare these other organisms harm or prey on *us!*)

MOSQUITOES AND OTHER INSECT PESTS

The bugs have probably caused many times as much misery as the snakes and the bears combined.

Mosquitoes lay eggs in shallow water or damp soil and hatch when days are warm and moist. In the mountains of the Southwest, where the soil is dry by August, they vanish early. Elsewhere, and especially in wet lowlands, mosquitoes may swarm much longer. Though mosquitoes in the United States and Canada don't transmit diseases to anything like the degree they do in the tropical world, there have been cases of mosquito-borne encephalitis and dengue fever in several states.

Then there are the various stinging or biting flies, a whole tribe of species going by variable common names. *No-see-ums* ("biting midges," "punkies"), found in low-lying areas over most of the country, are so tiny that they vanish in most lighting and can pass through all but the finest netting. The *black fly,* a famous torment in the north woods, is also known as the buffalo fly. There are horse flies and deer flies and sand flies. The *chigger* is the larva of a mite (thus actually an arachnid, not an insect). Found in the southern United States, it lives in grass; digging into your skin, it can cause an infuriating itch.

You defend yourself against this army with physical barriers or with chemical repellents. In very buggy places, hikers wear headnets. For night protection, in addition to netted tents, there are specialized bug shelters to be had: these cost $30 to $60 and weigh from a few ounces to a tentlike couple of pounds.

Repellents, however, are the first line of defense. There is one chemical that really does the job: n,n-diethyl-meta-toluamide, known universally as DEET and found in numerous products. In recent years there has been some concern about the safety of DEET, which strips paint, dissolves plastic, and gets into your system through the skin. Considering the rivers of DEET applied each year around the world, the incidence of problems is tiny, but some caution is indicated. Buy DEET in lotion or stick form and in concentrations of 30 percent or less. New formulations are now available that last longer and are less readily absorbed into the body. Apply it to clothing, when practical, rather than to bare skin; but remember that the substance can damage rayon, acetate, spandex, and urethane waterproofing. Avoid getting it into eyes and mucous membranes; keep it off cuts, scrapes, and irritated areas; don't rub it in. If wearing both sunscreen and repellent, apply the sunscreen first. On children, DEET should be used sparingly, and in concentrations under 10 percent.

If there is a runner-up to DEET, it is oil of citronella, a lemony substance derived from an Asian grass. Some swear by it; some find it wanting. Eucalyptus oil also has its advocates. Another perennial favorite is Skin-So-Soft by Avon, a product not marketed as a repellent but found (by some) to function as one. Don't assume that products of plant origin are harmless; citronella, like DEET, can irritate sensitive tissue, and the lower concentrations are preferred.

BEES, WASPS, AND YELLOWJACKETS

Bee stings, relatively harmless to most of us, are very dangerous to some. If you have an allergy to stings, you probably know it; if you even suspect it, be sure to get a doctor's advice on how to deal with it. Desensitization is possible for some people; the injection of epinephrine is often lifesaving. Kits with preloaded push-button injectors are now available.

If there is an allergic reaction, it will be unmistakable. In a few minutes the person will feel faint and giddy. The skin will be cool and moist. In severe cases the reaction will resemble an insanely exaggerated attack of hay fever. The tissues of the throat may swell so much that breathing is cut off. There is little the first-aider can do in such a case. If you have the allergy, carry a kit and be prepared to give yourself the lifesaving injection.

If you're stung by a bee, you want to get rid of the stinger, which keeps delivering venom for a while. Just pluck it out with tweezers or your fingernails. Until 1997, the conventional wisdom was different: we were told that, to avoid forcing more poison into the skin, we should dislodge the stinger with the scrape of a knifeblade. New research, however, shows that method makes no difference. Quick removal is the thing. If you have a venom extractor (see Treating Snakebite, below), use it to get rid of injected toxin. After-sting treatments such as Sting-Eze also help.

What about the notorious "killer" or Africanized bees? Bees of this strain, recently arrived in the United States from points south, are no more venomous than other sorts, but are uniquely and dangerously inclined to attack by the swarm. It is hoped that climate will limit their territory to the southern rim of the country. If they do move north into cooler regions, they will probably live in and around buildings, not in the wild. If you should be attacked by a swarm of bees, it's a highly unpleasant experience but rarely a fatal one. Cover your eyes with your hands, leaving just a slit to see through, and run back the way you came.

The southern United States is plagued by another dangerous exotic, the fire ant. If you disturb a fire ant mound, you'll draw a mass counterattack, and every ant is capable of multiple stings. Keep your distance.

TICKS AND TICK-BORNE DISEASES

Ticks, like mosquitoes, are bloodsuckers, but they do the job slowly. Their bites are not to be taken lightly, as they can inoculate you with more or less dangerous disease-causing agents.

These unpleasant arachnids come in numerous species, colors, and sizes, up to ¼ inch long; but it is the early "nymph" stage, truly tiny and hard to spot, that is most likely to get you. Nymphs are abundant in spring and summer. They climb onto you from tall grass or other foliage close to the ground. After riding on you for some time, they find bare skin and attach themselves painlessly. Long-sleeved shirts and long pants protect you to some extent. Tucking pants into your socks helps. So do built-in elastic cuffs or slip-on gaiters. So does DEET, applied sparingly at wrists, waist, and ankles. Clothing can be sprayed with permethrin, which is not only a repellent but also a potent insecticide harmless to our species. Permanone is one of several brands of permethrin preparations.

Ticks tend to prospect for a while before staking a claim; you can often catch and kill them before they dig in. Examine your clothes every now and then for small, dark, crawling objects, and do the same for your com-

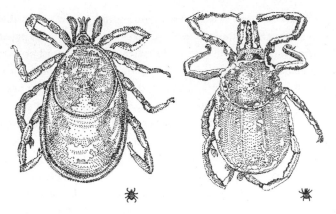

TWO TICKS THAT CARRY LYME DISEASE (MAGNIFIED 15X): DEER TICK (LEFT),
WESTERN BLACK-LEGGED TICK

panions. Light-colored fabrics make the animals easier to see. Check your
skin for ticks at least once a day, especially where clothing has been tight,
as at waist and ankles. Check also hairline and groin. On a brushy, off-trail
trip, hikers often strip before bed and inspect each others' backs. Parents
should similarly inventory children, twice a day. Very fine-toothed tick
combs, sold for use on pets, also work well on human heads of hair.

Once a tick is well attached, remove it with sharp-pointed tweezers.
Grasp it as far toward the buried head as you can. Pull straight outward
firmly and steadily until the creature, or most of it, comes out. Don't rock,
twist, jerk, or crush. It is no great cause for concern if the mouth parts stay
in your skin.

Several companies now make little specialty tools for tick removal.
One of them looks like a short nail file with a split tip. You slide the cleft
under the body of the tick, so that its neck is caught in the apex of the
groove, and apply gentle upward pressure. The animal should release its
grip before its head and body separate.

If the tick is a nymph—the tiny form that's actually most likely to
transmit Lyme disease—such devices may not serve. Instead, it's recommended that lever it off with the stiff edge of something like a credit card.

When you have extracted the tick, wash the puncture with soap and
water and watch the spot for possible infection. Apply a venom extractor
if you've got one (see below). Don't throw the extracted tick away, but

keep it as a possible aid in diagnosis if you should get sick. If it's alive, seal it in a bag or other container with a scrap of moistened toilet paper.

There is now a whole list of tick-borne diseases, the most notorious of which is Lyme disease. Lyme is known to be spread in the Northeast and upper Midwest by the deer tick, and on the West Coast by deer and Western black-legged ticks, both quite small even as adults and poppy-seed sized as nymphs. Early indicators of Lyme may be flulike symptoms and a bull's-eye rash resembling ringworm; these won't appear until several weeks after exposure. If not treated properly with antibiotics, Lyme disease can take very nasty forms, including a severe chronic arthritis. A vaccine, fortunately, is on the way. If a rash or sudden illness follows a trip, seek medical advice. Other serious tick-borne diseases are Rocky Mountain spotted fever, babesiosis, ehrlichosis, and tularemia. Scary but less dangerous is tick paralysis, a weakness that afflicts some people while ticks are attached to them but clears up when the animal is removed.

SPIDERS, SCORPIONS, AND CENTIPEDES

The one acutely dangerous spider in North America is the black widow, a name for several species in the genus *Latrodectus*. "Black" widows may also be red or brown; the famous red hourglass pattern on the abdomen may be pronounced or not. The head is small compared with the round body; front and back legs are markedly longer than those on the side. The smaller and inconspicuous male is harmless.

Many people bitten by this spider see no worse effect than swelling or

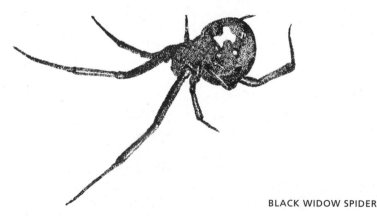

BLACK WIDOW SPIDER

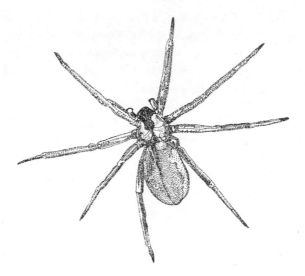

BROWN RECLUSE SPIDER

redness at the bite; others suffer painful and prolonged muscle cramps. In severe cases, hospital treatment is required. In about one case out of twenty there is danger of death; most victims are children.

Another species of concern is the brown recluse spider, also called the violin spider because of a distinctive mark on its head. The bite of the female can produce a troublesome ulcer. Of no concern at all are the tarantulas, various species found in the Southwest and as far east as the Ozarks; though large, furry, and spectacular, they have an insignificant sting.

If you're bitten by any spider, use your venom extractor on the site. Cooling the spot can reduce pain. Also catch the animal if you can. If you're sure it's a black widow, it's prudent to head for civilization. If a spider bite raises a blood blister, puncture it, drain it, and apply antibiotic ointment. If the spot is slow to heal, seek attention when you get home. With any bite, take precautions against infection. If flulike or other untoward symptoms follow a bite, seek medical advice.

Scorpions are spider relatives and sting with their tails. There are various species in North America; though most are found in deserts, scorpions occur in many environments and as far north as Oregon and Montana. All are at least mildly venomous. The dangerous one is the bark scorpion, *Centuroides exilicanda,* found only in Arizona and immediately across the border in desert California. Though some scorpions are as long as 8 inches, *Centuroides* are less than half that length; they're colored yellow to yellow-green and have long, narrow pincers. Scorpions hunt at night. It's a good idea in any region to shake out your clothes and boots in the morning, though you seldom find anything inside them. In the daytime be careful when digging in sand or lifting rocks and logs. Scorpion venom attacks the nerves; even a *Centuroides* bite is unlikely to kill a healthy adult but can threaten the very young, the old, and the allergic. If bitten by any species, apply a venom extractor.

Centipedes—many species—live under rocks and in downed wood. Some have a pretty good sting. The harmless millipedes, sometimes confused with centipedes, have two pairs of legs growing from each body joint—the centipedes, just one.

SNAKES

We have four kinds of poisonous snakes in the United States and Canada. Most important by far are the *rattlesnakes,* about thirty species, found somewhere in each of the forty-eight contiguous states and in southern Canada, but there are other types: the *copperhead* in the East; the *cottonmouth,* or *water moccasin,* in the southeastern swamps; and the *coral snake.*

Rattlesnakes, copperheads, and cottonmouths are all pit vipers. They inject through fangs a venom that attacks via the bloodstream.

The markings of rattlesnakes vary; actual rattles may or may not be

WESTERN DIAMONDBACK RATTLESNAKE, *CROTALUS ATROX*

present. The snakes seldom grow longer than 5 feet. Rattlers become scarce above 7,000 feet in the warm Southwest and aren't found much above 3,000 feet in areas near the United States–Canada border. In wet, cool regions, they prefer the drier sides of ridges, especially southern exposures.

The copperhead is found widely through the East as far north as New York State. It has, indeed, a copper-colored head, and hourglass markings along its body. The cottonmouth, or water moccasin, lives in wetlands from Virginia south, and west to central Texas. It is a thick, dark snake, up

COPPERHEAD

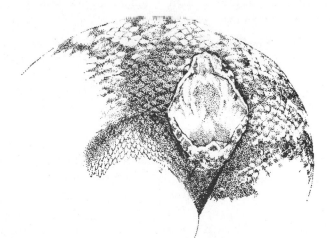

COTTONMOUTH

CORAL SNAKE

to 6 feet long, without obvious markings. Dry-footed hikers aren't likely to see it, but waders and canoeists must be aware of it.

All the pit vipers have a markedly wide head swelling from a much narrower neck. The body is heavy looking, ropy. The pupil of the eye is elliptical. Snakes not of this family, by contrast, have slender bodies merging into narrow heads with little indentation at the neck; the pupil of the eye is round.

Among those American snakes that are not pit vipers, only one is venomous: the coral snake. The coral is rather small, 2 to 4 feet long, and thin of body and head; it secretes a poison that attacks primarily the nerves. Coral snakes are handsomely marked with rings of yellow, black, and red. To distinguish a coral snake from other, harmless snakes that have red bands, remember that only coral snakes have red rings adjoining yellow:

> *Red on yellow, kill a fellow;*
> *Red on black, venom lack.*

One species is found in the southeastern United States, another in southern Arizona and New Mexico.

AVOIDING SNAKEBITE

Snakes of different species vary in their readiness to strike, but none is out to get you. Recognizing that you are far too big to eat, they don't regard you as prey. They may, however, perceive you as a threat. That's what you want to avoid.

Snakes, cold-blooded animals, are active only when it is pleasantly warm. In some regions and seasons, days are too hot for them, and they do their hunting at night. If only the morning and evening hours are temperate, snakes will be moving then. Torpid snakes, however, will still strike if stepped on.

Remember these simple precautions:

First, wear long pants and high-topped boots in snake country—and especially when you leave the trail. Heavy fabric gaiters are protective. Some people headed for snake-rich terrain make tubes of thin cardboard and tuck them around the ankles, under the trouserlegs: clumsy but effective shields.

Second, make sure you can see where you're putting your feet and hands. Be especially careful in rock scrambling. Never thrust a hand over an unseen edge to grope for a hold. If you get up at night, put on your boots and carry a flashlight.

Third, if you hear a snake rattling, stop dead still until you see where it is; then move away. Meanwhile, the snake will probably be moving away from *you*.

Fourth, never pick up an unidentified snake. A large number of bites result from this kind of provocation.

TREATING SNAKEBITE

For many years, experts in wilderness medicine recommended the "cut-and-suck" treatment for snakebite, in which the skin at the bite site was sliced and suction cups used to extract as much of the venom as possible. This treatment is now definitely out of favor. Instead of a snakebite kit, you now carry a multipurpose venom extractor, a pumplike device that can be used also on bee stings, tick sites, even mosquito bites.

If someone has been struck at by a snake, examine the spot. If there are one or two deep, widely spaced punctures—the fang marks—you know that a viper has struck. You do *not* know that it has left a dose of venom—in about half of all cases, none is injected. Don't wait to find out, however. Unlike the more drastic treatments of the past, the extractor can and should be applied immediately, the sooner the better; it will do little good after half an hour. But do not apply it to eyelids, genitals, or other areas of very sensitive skin.

Calm the injured person and put her in a restful position, keeping the bitten limb low (below the level of the heart). Use a razor (part of the kit) to shave skin if it is very hairy. Choose the suction cup that best fits the area of the bite. Pull the pump handle all the way out and place the cup on the bite site. Now press the handle in, creating a vacuum; at the end of the stroke you'll see the skin puff upwards into the tube. Leave the pump in place for 3 minutes.

When time is up, pull the handle out again, gently. Any extracted liquid will fall onto the skin; wipe it off carefully and wash the site with soap and water. If there's nothing, or just a little blood, you know that no venom was injected. Wash the suction cup as well.

The same directions apply to bites and stings by insects, spiders, and scorpions, except that the time of application is shorter: 30 to 90 seconds.

If, despite your efforts, some snake venom has made it into the person's system, the unmistakable symptom will arrive in a hurry: violent, increasing pain. The bitten area will also swell and become discolored. The victim may sweat profusely, feel nausea, and perhaps vomit (though these symptoms are sometimes caused by anxiety alone). Keep her comfortable, quiet, and cool. Place a cold pack on the bitten limb. Do not give coffee, tea, or alcohol. Depending on the amount of venom she got, your friend may be very sick or scarcely sick at all. Reassure her, watch her, and guard against shock. If symptoms have appeared, arrange an exit from the wilderness.

Meanwhile, try to identify the snake, or at least to determine whether it is a pit viper (or coral snake). Kill it, if you can safely do so, and keep the body. This may help a doctor to choose an antivenin later on. But don't handle a snake for an hour after its death: a reflexive second strike is possible.

A COUPLE OF LIZARDS

The Gila monster, found in the Southwest, is an almost harmless creature with a reputation. Massive, colorful, and up to 2 feet long, it certainly has a formidable look; it has jaws like a pit bull; and its venom can in fact be dangerous. But the monster is not in the least inclined to attack, and almost every bite on record took place when somebody picked up a captive specimen. Incidentally, the Gila monster is an endangered species and has full protection. For its sake and yours, leave it alone. Same goes for the similar Mexican beaded lizard, occasionally seen in southern Arizona.

BEARS

High on the list of worrisome wilderness animals in North America are the bears: common black bruins in most wild areas; and in the northern Rockies and Canada, the magnificent, unpredictable brown bear, or grizzly. Backpackers outside the high Arctic won't encounter the third, and most dangerous, North American bear, the polar.

The black bear, *Ursus americanus*, can in fact be almost any color in a range from black through brown to blond. It has a sleek, pointed head: think of a seal. Adult females average 140 pounds, males 220 pounds. Black bears in the eastern United States are heavier. Blacks are found in every wilderness region outside the desert; lured by backpackers' food, they have even colonized formerly unused areas above timberline.

The grizzly, or brown bear, *Ursus arctos*, is an altogether more formidable beast. (The Blackfoot Indians of Montana called it Real Bear.) A mass of muscle between its shoulders gives it an almost bisonlike appearance, and the muzzle forms an angle with the massive head: think of a chow dog. Its claws are often 4 inches long, more than double the length of black bear claws. Colors run in the same range as black bear hues, but solid black is rare. Many but not all *arctos* bears have white-tipped hairs that give them the "grizzled" look. Adult grizzlies average about 500 pounds.

Grizzlies are found throughout western Canada and Alaska, in several mountain ranges in northwest Montana, in far northern Idaho and the extreme northwestern corner of Washington State, and tenuously in the North Cascades. An isolated population lives in and around Yellowstone National Park. There is just possibly a remnant in the San Juan Mountains of southwestern Colorado. Though we think of them now as a forest species, grizzlies are naturally bears of open country and operate quite happily above, or north of, timberline.

The black bear is traditionally more nuisance than hazard. A pesky black can generally be frightened off by shouting, banging pots, even throwing rocks. The authorities recommend a policy of "mild aggression." You will often read that a mother bear with cubs is dangerous, but the record fails to confirm even this. Keep a reasonable distance, however, and never try to take food from a black bear or—even worse—*give* food to a bear.

AMERICAN BLACK BEAR, *URSUS AMERICANUS*

The grizzly is another matter. Every year, it seems, several people are mauled, even killed, in grizzly encounters. The hazard is still statistically slight, but special precautions are needed in grizzly country.

GRIZZLY BEAR PRECAUTIONS: PREPARATIONS

If you're headed for "real bear" country, do a little homework. Learn in advance to recognize both grizzlies and black bears (if both may be present) and how to tell them apart. Learn to spot bear sign: not only tracks and scat but also bitten, clawed, or abraded areas on tree trunks; crushed vegetation (at resting sites) ; and indications of rooting or grazing, like overturned rocks, demolished rotten logs, decapitated flowers. As part of your planning, contact the managing agency in the area you are visiting and get their advice about the local bears. Any traveler to grizzly territory should consult Stephen Herrero's *Bear Attacks* (see the Resources appendix).

In putting together your party, recognize that there is safety in numbers. Groups of three and four rarely get into trouble, groups of six or more virtually never—provided that they stick together and preserve the advantage. Even if your ordinary style is more spartan, plan to carry a tent that encloses you completely with opaque walls and has plenty of headroom. Binoculars, too, become basic equipment now.

Plan to do your cooking on a stove, and choose and pack your food to

BROWN OR GRIZZLY BEAR, *URSUS ARCTOS HORRIBILIS*

minimize odors. In this case, freeze-dried foods are actually preferable to those that are otherwise preserved, or fresh. Some traditional but smelly items—sardines, tuna, bacon, cheese, and the like—should simply not be carried. If you are accustomed to catching fish to supplement your larder, reconsider here: both the act of fishing and the odors of fish are somewhat dangerous in grizzly country. Bearbagging, of course, must be provided for, and practiced at home (see Chapter 18). If heading for a treeless area or a bear hotspot, purchase (or arrange to borrow) a bearproof food canister. The more cautious authorities also recommend that you carry a separate set of outer clothing to use while cooking (to be bearbagged afterwards): perhaps a spare light cotton shirt and an apron (see below).

When you get to that region, inform yourself further. Land managers in grizzly country keep track of bears, especially aggressive ones, and close trails and campgrounds accordingly. Warning signs may be placed at roadheads, and wilderness permits will be used to steer people away from problem areas. Get the official advice, and follow it to the letter. Be ready to change routes or even destinations if you must. Rent canisters now if this is recommended.

Two kinds of grizzly bear encounters account for most of the trouble: sudden, unexpected meetings, where the bear's defensive instincts are aroused; and cases where the bear knows about you, all right, but is interested in your food (in rare, extreme cases, interested in you *as* food).

Though each kind of encounter can take place around the clock and in any situation, most surprise meetings occur on the trail; most food-related problems occur in camp.

GRIZZLY BEAR PRECAUTIONS: ON THE TRAIL

The conscientious backpacker ordinarily wants to move rather quietly, but safety comes first, and in grizzly country, safety requires noise. If you suddenly appear a few yards away from one of the creatures, defensive instincts kick in and an otherwise peaceable animal may charge. Hikers in grizzly country like to make racket as they move along, conversing rather loudly with companions; singing; banging a spoon on a metal cup; clapping hands; talking to the air; blowing a whistle. Some wear bells as automatic noisemakers, though these may not be loud enough to do the job. Some favor tin cans with pebbles in them. Beside a noisy stream, or where dense trees block views and muffle sounds, be louder still. The same applies when you have wind in your face, carrying sound and scent the wrong way, back down the trail.

Don't count on the bear to do all the work of detection and avoidance. Keep your own senses sharp. Don't get lost in the rhythm of hiking. Watch for sign. Every few minutes, stop and listen—bears are too big to move quietly, especially through brush. Watch for, and if going cross-country avoid, berry patches, cow parsnip thickets, fields of glacier lilies, streams where fish are spawning, and areas where nuts litter the ground. Don't go anywhere near carrion, which may be evidenced by smell or by circling ravens and crows.

Don't let your party spread out, losing the advantage of your numbers. Children, obviously, must be kept close at hand. Make your rest stops in spots where there's a view; sit back-to-back and keep an eye on your perimeter. Don't spread lunch or other gear all around and don't shed crumbs.

If you see a bear before it has sensed you, stop your noisemaking and try to see which kind it is. Binoculars help here. If there's a grizzly cub in the picture, just leave. If a solo adult is a grizzly, look for a safe, wide detour (on the downwind side); if there's no way around, retreat or stay put until the animal has moved on.

If you see a grizzly that is already aware of you, it may soon retreat—this is in fact the most common outcome. In this case, you can continue, maybe with a cross-country detour if the beast seems to be using the formal trail; since the animal has already registered your presence and decided to avoid you, keep its sensitive nose informed by traveling *upwind* from the bear.

If the grizzly takes unwelcome interest in you, much may depend on how you react, and how you read the signs present in its behavior. A bear that just looks at you, without making noises or laying back its ears, is checking you out. If it stands up on its hind legs, it is checking you out from a higher vantage. It is appropriate to stay where you are and make conversational noises. Watch the bear, but from a corner of your eye; in the animal world, a straight-on gaze is a challenge. Reduce your apparent bulk by turning sideways or flexing your knees.

If a grizzly stands crosswise to you and puts its head down, it is suggesting—so experts say—that you back off. Do so, not too fast, while continuing to face generally toward the bear. If your retreat seems to increase its agitation, pause for a time, then try again. Just in case, keep an eye out for a tree that looks like you could climb it rapidly to a height of 30 feet or more, and work your way to its base.

The threat escalates when a bear faces you squarely, lowers and perhaps sways its head, flattens its ears, and makes sounds—moaning, huffing, or clacking of teeth. These signs may precede a mock charge or, in the worst case, a deadly serious one. All you can do is keep backing away. Never turn and run. Tossing an object like a camera toward the bear may distract it, but do not shed your pack. If you've managed to get very close to a suitable tree, climb it. Don't try to race the bear to a distant tree—you'll lose. But you may be able to gain time by dodging around trunks.

After the threat behavior may come the charge: a bluff attack if you're lucky, veering off at the last moment; a real attack if you're not. When contact seems inevitable, hit the dirt, face down, with legs slightly spread and your arms protecting your face and the back of your neck. If the bear cuffs or bites you a few times, force yourself not to resist or to cry out. If it flips you over, flip yourself back; otherwise remain still. When the attack ceases, hold this position in silence for at least 20 minutes before peeking, cautiously, to see if you've been left alone. Repeat attacks are rare.

What if the charging bear is not a grizzly but a black bear? It is probably an opportunist after food and may be deterred. Passivity is exactly the wrong approach. Yell, bang pots, blow a whistle, throw rocks. Do this for a full 60 seconds; if the animal hasn't backed off by then, treat it as dangerous and back calmly away. Never, however, drop to the ground, and if an actual attack ensues (a rarity) fight back all the way.

There is another exception to the passive-defense rule. If any bear's attack appears earnest and shows no sign of abating—if the animal seems not just to be making a point but proceeding to devour you—nothing is lost and something may be gained by fighting back as hard as you can. The same is true if any bear pursues you well up into a tree.

Since bears are more or less nocturnal, you can lower your chance of encounters in grizzly country by hiking in full daylight.

GRIZZLY BEAR PRECAUTIONS: IN CAMP

Bear strategy in camp revolves around the handling of food and other odorous substances. The precautions described throughout this book should help you avoid unpleasant encounters with either sort of bear. In grizzly country, these measures become still more exacting.

At the end of the hiking day, stop early enough to find an appropriate camp and complete your cooking and food storage in daylight. Alternatively, schedule an early dinner break on the trail a mile or more before your actual camp. The ideal site will be fairly open, with some nearby climbable trees. (Or camp in a wide open area where an approaching bear would have no cover.) Avoid campsites right next to the trail (or any obvious game trail) or next to running or standing water. Avoid also berry patches and other ursine food sources; areas with bear sign; and of course areas that show evidence of earlier raids (like scattered garbage or scat with remnants of human food in it). Also be wary of dirty camps with garbage or trash; if you can't avoid them, clean them up. You may need to light a fire to sanitize a fouled pit. If a party nearby is practicing poor bear hygiene, and can't be gently talked out of it, better just get back on the trail.

The kitchen and food-handling area should be set up 100 yards away from your sleeping spot, and downwind from it, so that odors blow away from you. Since breezes tend to blow downslope at night, beds on a slope should typically be uphill. Locate also a suitable tree for bearbagging, ideally near the kitchen, and in any case similarly far way and downwind from the bed. If lockers, wires, or elevated poles are provided, by all means use them.

Should you in fact, as some sources suggest, carry and use a special set of clothes for cooking, to be bearbagged after the meal? This idea seems to be more preached than practiced. Stephen Herrero, perhaps the most respected student of human-bear encounters, admits, "I almost never bag my clothes." But, he adds, he would do so on a visit to a place where grizzlies were known to be in the habit of scavenging human food.

After the meal, clean up scrupulously. Replace all foodstuffs in ziplock plastic bags, completely closed. Washwater and excess cooking water should be strained and the solids treated as garbage. Small quantities of washwater may be evaporated at the edge of a hot fire; large quantities can be scattered on the ground at least 100 yards away and downwind from all other camp activities. Wash yourself well.

Now for the bearbagging. What gets bagged depends, once more, on the local situation. In a bear "hot spot," you'll gather everything that has been in contact with food, including items you might not think of: stoves; clean pots and utensils; water and water containers, and maybe those cooking clothes.

Besides food, every cosmetic, skin cream, dentrifice, and medicine should be suspected as a bear attractant. So should canned food, pet food, used toilet paper if you are packing this item out, and feminine hygiene products. Some body odors may also attract the interest of bears. Wash up after sexual activity. Menstruating women need to take special care with their hygiene, though a controversial suggestion that they avoid bear country entirely during their periods has been withdrawn. Use tampons rather than pads; wrap used tampons in foil and then place in a plastic bag; clean up with moist towelettes.

In alpine or treeless regions, and wherever the local managers recommend it, you should be carrying bearproof canisters. These can also be useful in regions where all the available trees seem to be scrubby lodgepole pines. Place canisters at least 100 yards from any bedsite, downwind, and also at least 100 yards away from your kitchen. If possible, place them in brush, pile rocks on them, or suspend them over rocky faces. If trees are available in grizzly country, authorities recommend that even canisters should be bagged and hung.

Packs should ideally be hung, especially if you suspect that they are odorous. If not hung, they should be placed on ground outside your tent, empty and crumb-free, with zippers and flaps open.

Sleep in your tent, period. By all means pitch the fly, and keep as far as possible to the middle. Passing bears have been known to sniff at, paw at, or nibble on open-air sleepers, and to make investigative holes in nylon roofs. Never take a snack, or even a water bottle, to bed. Make sure there are no food fragments about. Have a flashlight at hand and, if you must get up at night, use it. The ideal bedsite will have a climbable escape tree nearby.

If you find a bear haunting your camp in the dark hours, you'd better forget about sleeping. Build and tend a fire, which discourages most invaders. If the intruder is definitely a black bear, try to drive it off by shouting and throwing things. If it's a determined grizzly, better get out of its way.

There have been cases, rare but disturbing, of campers being dragged from their tents by predatory grizzly bears and even by black bears. This is one of the cases where the victim should forget all complicated rules and fight back like mad.

In the morning, use caution when you leave your tent and when you go to retrieve your food; if a grizzly is investigating, don't interfere. If the culprit is a black bear, however, be "mildly aggressive."

You might think that snow campers could disregard grizzly bears, but that's not quite the case. The animals may emerge in late winter and spring; they move just fine over snow. Inconvenient though it is, late-season winter campers should separate cooking and sleeping areas and in general take the usual precautions.

What about weaponry? Few backpackers will have firearms, but there's something that works better: bear-deterrent sprays containing capsicum, the chemical that makes peppers hot. If charged by a bear, you lay down a cloud between the animal and you; at closer range, aim at the face. This tool is now well proven. Canisters with holsters cost $40 to $60.

All bear encounters, including benign ones, should be reported to the authorities.

OTHER LARGE-ANIMAL ATTACKS

Mountain lions, long regarded as no threat to human beings, have recently injured or killed people in several western states. Children and smallish people, especially hiking solo, are most at risk. There is safety in numbers. If a lion attacks, it will have in mind eating you, not scaring you off; your response should be to threaten, not to reassure. Do not run or crouch down. Make yourself as formidable as possible: stand tall, raise your arms and wave them slowly, or open your jacket like wide wings. If you're wearing a pack, hoist it above your shoulders. If you have kids in tow, pick up any small child, not crouching down to do so; position older youngsters behind you. Face the cat and maintain eye contact; bare your teeth; speak loudly and firmly; wave menacingly with a staff or stick; throw rocks or anything you can reach without ducking down. If possible, back slowly to higher ground or around a boulder or tree. If the cat stops moving, looks away from you, and begins ostentatiously to wash, you're making your point; reduce your own aggressive behavior to match, but keep the animal in sight and make a dignified retreat. If a mountain lion actually attacks you, shield your head and neck and fight back. It should be emphasized that lion attacks, though impressive to read about, remain exceedingly rare.

Besides lions and bears, various other sizable critters have been known to threaten, bite, gore, or trample humans from time to time. The list includes bison, elk, moose, and alligators. Surprisingly, given the stories we all read as children, it does not include wolves, a species never known to attack human beings. With mammals, a perceived threat to young is the most common trigger for trouble. For instance, moose cows, protecting unseen calves, very occasionally charge at hikers. In this situation, stand very still—moose have poor eyesight and may lose track of you. If that doesn't work, move away slowly, as you would when faced with a grizzly, talking quietly but looking to one side; seek shelter among trees. All problematic animal encounters should be reported.

We're accustomed to put ourselves in the middle of the picture: to regard other animals in the wild as elements in our experience, whether as problems, as dangers, or as entertainments. But of course it works both ways. Our presence affects them as well. A bear habituated to human food will probably wind up dead. A squirrel that grows up begging from campers may fail to master its normal foraging skills. On another note, do not handle or disturb young birds or mammals that appear to be orphaned: they probably aren't, and your interference is likely to be unwelcome if not damaging. In general, leave animals untouched, unpetted, unharassed, and photographed, if at all, from a distance with long lenses.

FIRST AID FOR ANIMAL WOUNDS

First aid for a person damaged by a bear or other wild animal is simply first aid: maintain breathing, control bleeding, protect against shock, and seek help.

Even a minor wound inflicted by an animal wild or domestic can bring three possible dangers. The first is *infection*; you fight it by ordinary care in treating the wound, and later, if they are needed, with antibiotics.

Second is *tetanus*, a dangerous but completely preventable disease. An immunization shot, plus one booster every 10 years, protects you. Every hiker should maintain this insurance.

By far the most serious of the three dangers, in the case of bite wounds only, is *rabies*. Skunks are the wild animals most likely to transmit rabies; raccoons, foxes, and bats can also carry it. Beware of any animal that acts oddly, including one that seems overfriendly.

If you are bitten by an animal that may carry rabies, try to catch it and kill it, if you safely can. The immediate treatment for the bite is simple: wash the wound thoroughly with *copious* soap and water. This will flush out many of the viruses, and if a rabies infection does occur, it will be less severe. Do not close the wound.

The next step is to get back to civilization as fast as you can. Take with you the animal's body, or at least the head. (If you can get the critter home without killing it, that's still better, but obviously difficult.) With luck, lab analysis of the animal's brain will show it not to be rabid and spare you the discomfort of the treatment. If the bite was below the neck, you have several days in which the treatment can be successfully begun. A bite on the head or neck gives you less margin.

Treatment after a bite, a series of injections, is really a matter of immunization; rabies is incurable once it is established in your system. Spelunkers, and other people who come into frequent contact with possible carrier animals, are advised to get immunized in advance; but even pre-vaccinated people must get additional shots if bitten.

HANTAVIRUS

Most diseases that pass from animals to human beings do so through a bite or puncture, made either by the infected animal itself or by an intermediary, or vector, like a tick. A notable exception is the serious respiratory disease caused by the Sin Nombre hantavirus: you can catch it just by breathing dust where its rodent hosts have lived. Deer mice in the southwestern United States are the most common vector. These creatures are found especially in pinyon-juniper woodlands, and in such protected places as old cabins, mine shafts, caves, and ruins. Stay out of such enclosures, and don't camp where you see mouse-sized burrows and droppings (resembling black grains of rice). Though rare, the respiratory disease caused by the Sin Nombre virus is no joke: about half the afflicted people die.

HUMAN PREDATORS

You can't quite overlook the risk from certain other mammals, those large bipedal ones. Crime is not much of a problem in the wilderness, but there are exceptions. As noted in Chapter 14, roadhead burglaries are not uncommon. In a very few areas, human hazards are found away from the road. Rapes are not unknown. There have been murders on the Appalachian Trail. Certain wild areas near the Mexican border may be traversed by smugglers of drugs and of illegal aliens, and by the aliens themselves. Occasionally, too, marijuana growers set up shop far back in roadless areas. If you encounter unfriendly folk in the backcountry who seem not to be just recreationists, don't confront. Keep your distance, and, if necessary, change your route. Once out in civilization, let the authorities know what you saw. Whatever your attitude toward the social issues involved, the wild places are not the stage on which they should be played out.

IRRITANT PLANTS

There are many, many plants in the wild that are more or less poisonous if eaten. Know exactly what you're doing before you eat any part of any wild plant, including, most especially, any mushroom. The only general first-aid rule for plant poisoning is to drink water and induce vomiting (but see the cautions in Chapter 26).

Much more common is another kind of toxic reaction: the brief, inconsequential sting of nettle or the unbearable itch of poison ivy and sim-

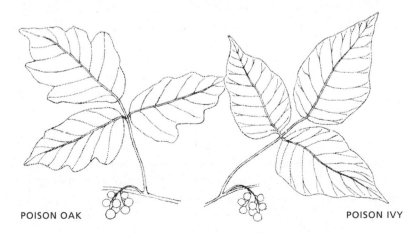

POISON OAK   POISON IVY

ilar irritant plants. Poison ivy is hardly a danger to life and limb, but it can certainly take the pleasure out of a wilderness trip or, more probably, the first week home.

There are three species of the genus *Rhus* known as poison ivy or poison oak. These bushes or vines are found over most of the United States at lower elevations. The best field mark to look for is leaves grouped in threes. Each group of three leaflets grows out at a different point along the stem: the clusters are "alternate," not "opposite." Sometimes the leaflets are hairy, sometimes smooth; their edges may be smooth, toothed, or lobed.

Poison sumac, though related to poison oak and ivy, is quite different in appearance. A shrub or small tree, it has smooth, pale-gray bark and alternate leaves divided into seven to eleven leaflets, with smooth margins and a reddish tinge. This species grows throughout the eastern United States and Canada. In the South it is a tree up to 25 feet tall, growing in swamps and river bottoms; in cooler regions it is shrubby and keeps to boggy places.

Trumpet creeper is a woody climbing vine that grows in woods and thickets throughout the eastern United States. Like the sumac, it has divided leaves, which, however, grow in opposite pairs. The leaflets are toothed at the edges.

All these species produce the same irritant, a chemical called urushiol, and cause the same miserable dermatitis. The oily sap, most plentiful in spring and summer, is the carrier.

About 2 million people each year come down with cases of poison oak and poison ivy. Sensitivities vary, but most people are allergic to some degree, or can become so without warning.

Twenty-four to 48 hours after you bruise or even brush a plant, your skin begins to itch and redden, and blisters rise. Delayed onset in some places may make it seem that the pox is spreading, but the eruption occurs only where sap contacted the skin. The problem will last for 7 to 10 days.

The best defense against urushiol-bearing plants is, obviously, to avoid contact with them. Keep an eye on the vegetation as you walk. Wear long pants and long-sleeved shirts. Hands are likely to pick up oil from clothing or boots, so try not to touch your face as you mosey along, and wash carefully before touching your genitals. If you're hiking in poison oak country with a dog, assume that the dog is "hot."

For people who can't avoid poison oak, there are protective creams. Several substances seem to intercept urushiol, binding to it before it can bond to the skin. The latest and most promising of several commercial products in this line is a formulation containing quaternium-18 bentonite, a modified clay.

Urushiol can also be washed from the skin within the first few hours. Plain water is far better than nothing, and generous rinsing in a creek can decontaminate you quite well. Soaps, detergents, abrasives, and hotter water do no added good, and scrubbing just spreads the bad stuff around. For more total removal, you need a solvent like rubbing (isopropyl) alcohol or acetone; white gas, much more likely to be in your pack, can hardly be recommended but will work in a pinch. Tecnu is a high-priced solvent found in gear stores. These substances are all more or less irritating to the skin, however, and strip it of its natural protective layer of oil. Use them with caution, and not at all if you're likely to encounter more poison oak on the way home—de-oiled skin is doubly vulnerable to urushiol.

For some people, urushiol dermatitis is really disabling. If you know you are one of these, and know you have just been exposed, head for the road. A cortisone shot, administered just after the first appearance of the rash, can spare you a week of suffering. For more typical cases, the old soothing treatment, calamine lotion, is better than nothing.

The saps of the urushiol plants are transported by anything they touch, including boots, clothes, packs, car seats, and dog fur. They stay potent for quite some time. To avoid infecting others or yourself at second hand, wash suspect items thoroughly with water or solvents.

THE PLACES & THEIR FUTURE

We are not fighting a rearguard action, we are facing a frontier. We are not slowing down a force that inevitably will destroy all the wilderness there is. We are generating another force, never to be wholly spent, that, renewed generation after generation, will be always effective in preserving wilderness. . . . We are working for a wilderness forever.

Howard Zahniser,
at the Seventh Biennial Wilderness Conference,
San Francisco, 1961

Once wilderness was nearly everywhere on our continent, the background condition of the land in North America. Then European settlement began, capturing enclaves on the eastern coast, spreading west in spots and splotches and corridors, and finally sweeping from ocean to ocean through the forty-eight contiguous states of the United States and the southern tier of Canada. Except in northern Canada and in Alaska, settled or otherwise exploited land is now the background within which undeveloped areas exist, a scattered (and still shrinking) archipelago.

Those wild areas are found mainly on land owned by government—federal, provincial, or state. They may, for instance, lie within parks, though no park is 100 percent wild. They may lie within national or provincial forests, or areas set aside for wildlife habitat; or they may lie in the broad expanses of public land known simply as crown lands (in Canada) or the public domain (in the United States). They may in addition be protected under the formal label "Wilderness," or they may not. Wilderness watchers learn to ignore the jurisdictional labels and zero in on the condition of the land: is it free of roads in fact and generally wild? Much of our wilderness is "de facto": wild in truth, but in no way shielded from future development. In some regions, more areas than not are still at risk. For more about all this, see Chapter 31.

Here's a brief overview of our archipelago of wild places, taken from east to west. (For more about boreal Canada, as well as Alaska, see the end of this chapter.) In the eastern United States, the archipelago is sparse: there are whole states that lack significant roadless areas. In the West, the wild islands are larger and often densely clustered.

EASTERN BEACH AND WETLAND WILDERNESS

Along the Atlantic and Gulf of Mexico shorelines, wilderness is not just metaphorically islanded. Here the backpacker's destinations are barrier spits and islands, the continent's sandy breastworks against surf and hurricanes, often sheltering broad zones of salt marsh and mudflat behind

WILDERNESS REGIONS OF THE EASTERN U.S. AND ADJACENT CANADA

them. Though much of the original fringe of beaches and wetlands has been profoundly altered, certain areas are still pristine. Some of the notable enclaves: Monomoy Island National Wildlife Refuge (NWR) in Massachusetts; Brigantine NWR in New Jersey; Assateague Island National Seashore and Chincoteague NWR in Maryland; Cape Lookout and Cape Hatteras National Seashores and Swanquarter NWR in North Carolina; Cape Romain NWR in South Carolina; Cumberland Island National Seashore and nearby wildlife refuges in Georgia; Cape Canaveral National Seashore on Florida's Atlantic shore; Gulf Islands National Seashore in Florida, Alabama, and Mississippi; and Padre Island National Seashore in southern Texas, with adjacent refuges.

Access to these places is often by ferry, kayak, or canoe. Once off the boat, you may find yourself sharing the long, thin territory with mountain bikes and even motor vehicles, which can drive on the firm, moist sand. Though extensive areas of the marshes are protected as formal wilderness, only a few beaches have this designation. Check in advance to find when and where you can be alone. Find out, too, what schedule the birds are on. The marshes, among the most biologically productive zones on the continent, are key habitats for species that breed in these places or stop there on long migrations: ducks and geese by the millions, herons and ibises and egrets, terns and eagles and ospreys, and hundreds of species more.

The climate of these coastlands is in general very mild, but of course it varies greatly from the semiarid southern tip of Texas to the lush shores of Florida and the hard capes of New England, where the coastal wetlands pinch out at last. Ordinarily, you will have to carry all your water. (See Coastline Hiking, in Chapter 23.)

In the flat country inland from the coast, there is another scattering of wild places. Most of them are wet: the swamps of the Gulf and Atlantic coastal plains, and of the lower Mississippi Valley, where water pauses and spreads on its way to the sea. These are not, for the most part, open marshes, but rather waterlogged forests of tupelo, bald cypress, and oak, hung with Spanish moss. Because logging was difficult in the swamps, a number of them survived more or less intact until they could be protected as wildlife refuges, parks, or Forest Service wilderness; some still await such status. Some of the better-known wild swamps are the (small) Great Swamp in New Jersey; the Great Dismal on the Virginia/North Carolina line; the Santee in North Carolina; the Congaree in South Carolina, noted for its noble cypresses; and the vast Okefenokee in southern Georgia, which contains over 350,000 acres of protected wilderness. There are clusters of swampland wilderness in national forests on the coastal plains of North Carolina, South Carolina, and northeast Florida. The west coast of Florida has a big wild block at Chasshowitzka National Wildlife Refuge. West of Tallahassee in the Florida panhandle, you'll find several good-sized wilderness areas in St. Marks National Wildlife Refuge and an adjacent national forest. The Atchafalya is Louisiana's best-known swamp, and in eastern Texas a few fragments of soggy forest in and around the Big Thicket region have been preserved.

Though some of the inland swamps are best traveled by boat, only a few are so wet as to rule out exploration on foot. Some areas have raised boardwalks; in others, old railroad beds, dikes, and "ridges" (streaks of drier ground) provide dry-footed access. Away from such routes, you must count on getting your feet wet. Swamp hikers favor boots with mesh panels and holes in the sole through which water can drain. Landmarks are scarce, and skill with map and compass is essential for cross-country travel. Some swamps are habitat for bears, alligators, and cottonmouth moccasins; of these, the alligator is the most significant hazard. In southern states, the months from November to mid-March are the best swamp-hiking season: cool and insect-free.

The greatest of all the eastern wetlands is the Everglades, the enormous marsh and wildlife paradise that occupies much of southern Florida. It's a huge, slow-moving sheet of water, flowing imperceptibly south through an endless, rustling expanse of sawgrass, varied by the occasional open channel or mangrove-wooded island. The American crocodile lives here, and the endangered Florida panther. Much of this system is now protected in Everglades National Park and the Big Cypress National Preserve, among the most valued (and embattled) natural preserves in the world. There are over a million acres of wilderness in the Everglades. Backpacking, however, is not what you go there to do.

EASTERN MOUNTAIN WILDERNESS

The Appalachians, the Ozarks, the Adirondacks—all the mountain masses of the eastern United States—are wilder today than they were half a century ago. Even the national parks in this region were repurchased from private owners after settlement and exploitation; the forests within their boundaries are largely young growth. But this reach of the continent is temperate and well watered. Here it doesn't take geological time to restore the appearance of wilderness. Hiking through primitive woods, you may be surprised and charmed to discover old roads now gone to trails, old orchards still bearing fruit, even the stone foundations of old houses.

North Carolina's Mount Mitchell, the tallest peak east of the Mississippi and south of the Arctic, is just 6,684 feet high. Considering the moderate elevations, it is easy to underestimate the ruggedness of eastern highlands. Five-thousand-foot summits may still rise the larger part of a mile from valley floors below. Along with some gentle trails, there are many that are steep and roughly surfaced, especially in the Northeast.

The eastern ranges are almost entirely wooded, mostly with hardwoods—oaks and hickories, maples and beeches, birches and basswood, and dozens of species more. When you travel under broadleaf trees in summer, you don't see out very often or very far. Under the trees, dense brush—dogwood, rhododendron, mountain laurel, wild rose—tends to confine you to the trail.In fall and winter, when the leaves are off the hardwood trees and the stems of brush are bare, cross-country travel becomes more feasible. You see out, see for miles, see where you are. Besides, in cooler weather, you'll be better dressed for bushwhacking.

With a few exceptions, eastern mountain wilderness comes in rather small pieces. On long trips, hikers may traverse several wild areas, rather than choosing a single district to explore. Indeed, they may not think of themselves as visiting wilderness areas at all. Their focus may be rather on some *extended trail*—a pedestrian route that traverses both wild lands and tame, and even crosses (by arrangement with the owners) long gaps of private land. The Appalachian Trail is the most famous of these, and the great model, but there are now a great many others.

Anywhere in the eastern mountains, you will want a tent year-round. A tarp may serve for rain and dew, but not for the insects of summer. Gear must be moisture-resistant, boots well waterproofed, sleeping bags not of unprotected down. At lower elevations in the South, where summer nights are often uncomfortably warm, you may not want a sleeping bag at all in that season, but only something on the order of a wool blanket.

You will definitely need to carry a stove. Fires are widely restricted, and in some places where they aren't, they should be.

Throughout the region, and especially along the various long trails, you find simple, three-sided shelters. Although these can be handy at times, it is best to leave them out of your plans. They are often crowded and may be littered, dirty, or vandalized. Nuisance animals—bears, skunks, raccoons—naturally congregate at these sites. In some areas, rangers now discourage the use of shelters except on day hikes and in emergencies. In others, they are available to long-trail hikers only.

THE SOUTHERN APPALACHIANS

In this highest part of the Appalachian chain, the federal government has considerable wild holdings. The most significant is Great Smoky Mountains National Park in North Carolina and Tennessee, where two roadless areas total almost half a million acres. The national forests around the park and northward to the Potomac River contain numerous smaller wild areas, some protected and some not. Notable southern Appalachian wilderness areas, containing 20,000 acres or more, are the Sipsey in Alabama, the Cohutta in Georgia, the Southern Nantahala in Georgia and North Carolina, and the Cranberry and Otter Creek in West Virginia.

This is above all forest country. Appalachian Trail hikers complain of weeks in a "green tunnel," but botanizers find endless variety in a hardwood forest of uncommon richness. Above 5,000 feet, fir and spruce appear. Summits may have "balds" of grass or heath, mostly rhododendron and mountain laurel.

Summers are warm and wet: days typically in the seventies or eighties Fahrenheit, though afternoon thunderstorms can cool things off; humidity almost always high. The hiking uniform in such conditions is the minimum: shorts, perhaps a light shirt or net undershirt, and boots. (But you need long pants where poison ivy is dense along the trail.) On the lower slopes, nights may be only a little cooler than the days.

September, October, and November, the driest and clearest months, are really the best of the hiking weather. The trails are less crowded (except at times in popular hunting areas!), the mosquito problem is past, and in cooler autumns the turning leaves can put on a good show.

In winter, snow is frequent but unpredictable. At middle elevations, rain mixes with snow and alternates with snow—it may snow at night and rain during the day. Freezing rain—glaze—is also fairly common. As anyone knows who has dealt with such conditions, they make for difficult camping. For all that, midwinter in this region is actually one of the drier times of year.

North and west of the loftiest ridges, the Appalachian highland continues as a plateau that reaches to and beyond the Ohio River in far southern Ohio, Indiana, and even Illinois. Hill country along the river in each of these states contains state parks, national forests, and some reverting-to-wild areas that are worth a visit.

NORTHEASTERN MOUNTAINS

Pennsylvania, with its low but still prominent ridges and plateaus, is a transition zone between southern and northeastern mountain landscapes. When the land rises again in New York State, the character of the mountains has changed. They are rougher, cooler, stonier; they often bear the marks of ancient glaciation, evidenced also by the many lakes at their feet.

North and east of the Mason-Dixon line, the federal government is not the major landlord. Rather, states and even private owners control the wild land. In Pennsylvania, the state-run parks and forests are extensive; in New York, they are huge. Because the voters long ago forbade logging on state land in the Catskills and Adirondacks, great tracts of forest are more or less wild; the authorities have given explicit wilderness status to about 100,000 Catskill acres and to 1 million acres, in several chunks, in the Adirondacks. In Maine, too, it is the state that is responsible for the wilderness and semiwilderness of Baxter State Park and the Allagash Waterway, together with "public reserved lands" open to various uses. In addition, several million acres of private timberlands in northern Maine remain primitive in part; these are the subject of a growing preservation campaign.

In New Hampshire and Vermont, in the White and Green Mountains, the U.S. Forest Service does control most of the public land. Even here there is an unusual setup. Much of the work of management—the trail maintenance, the staffing of backcountry shelters, even some of the planning—is done by private clubs, chief among them the Appalachian Mountain Club. Westerners may be taken aback at the relative luxuries available in some of these mountains. Besides the traditional primitive lean-tos, there's a system of eight elaborate backcountry hostels, or huts, where meals are served—reservations, of course, required.

North of the Catskills, northeastern mountains are distinctly cool. Although some summer days may be hot, warm nights are rare, and cold storms can come in at any time of year. The 4,000-to-6,000-foot peaks of the White Mountains can get snow, high winds, and subfreezing temperatures in any month of the year. Hypothermia has killed many an unprepared hiker in these hills.

Early fall in the Northeast is an excellent time for the hiker, with many crisp, clear days and wonderful color displays if you time it just right; the notorious blackflies are gone. The peaks may be white by Halloween. Winter can be disconcertingly variable. Snow campers tolerate the cold but dread the occasional warm southeasterly rainstorm followed by a shift of weather, subzero temperatures, and northwest gales. Everything gets wet and then freezes solid. Travelers go home.

The original forests of these mountains were almost entirely spruce and fir. In the few unlogged areas, they still are. Elsewhere, deciduous hardwoods have taken over. Above the zone of full-sized timber, there may be a thousand feet of dwarfed birch and mountain ash; then, as low as 5,000 feet in some sections, only tundra and stone. Everybody wants to visit these alpine islands, and managers have their work cut out in protecting them from trampling and erosion.

The Appalachians don't stop at the Canadian border. The hills and plateaus of New Brunswick, southeastern Québec, Nova Scotia, and even Newfoundland are considered part of the range. Though not lofty, these northern highlands may reach the arctic/alpine zone. National parks—Forillon in Québec; Fundy and Kouchibouguac in New Brunswick; Kejimkujik and Cape Breton Highlands in Nova Scotia; and in Newfoundland, Terra Nova and the vast and primitive Gros Morne—protect some climaxes. There is a plan to extend the Appalachian Trail to Mount Jacques Cartier on the Gaspé Peninsula of Québec.

THE OZARKS AND OUACHITAS

West of the Appalachians, on the long, gradual slope toward the Mississippi, you find little wild land in public ownership. But beyond the great river, in the knot of low mountains called the Ozarks and Ouachitas, there are quite a few spots where the original wilderness, once driven back, has been permitted to restore itself. There are national forests here, and the National Park Service has narrow, linear parks along several rivers. A couple of dozen small wilderness areas, scattered over southern Missouri, northwestern Arkansas, and far eastern Oklahoma, protect some 200,000 acres of land.

In many ways the Ozark country resembles the southern Appalachian region, to which it is geologically related. It is only a shade more continental in climate—the summer a little hotter, winters slightly less mild. Summer lacks the hot nights that can be so troublesome in the Southeast. Autumn is very pleasant. The wettest months are April, May, and June, and the driest (though by no means rainless) are December, January, and February. There's some snow, but it doesn't last. Because the high ground in these mountains tends to be rather flat and accessible to settlement, the primitive tracts are often found on steeper terrain descending ruggedly to streams. When civilization lies above, water treatment is more than ordinarily vital.

GREAT LAKES WILDERNESS

Along the United States–Canada border, from the Adirondacks to the High Plains, extends a great, flat tangle of blue lakes, bogs, potholes, and circuitous rivers. Many American landscapes bear the marks of glaciation; but in this flat expanse, where other obvious landmarks are lacking, almost every feature you see is glacial: put there by the unimaginable weight and power of the ice sheets that, not long ago in geological terms, lay over it.

The ice laid down moraines and eskers and drumlins and erratic boulders; it shoved old rivers into modern courses; it scraped some landscapes bare and covered others with rich soil. Most of all, it made lakes: the five Great Lakes and uncountable smaller ones.

The result is a handsome country: mostly gentle in topography, mostly forested with hardwoods and various conifers, and in large part well settled. But near the international boundary are blocks of government land, set aside by the two national governments, several states, and the province of Ontario, where wilderness remains, or is being allowed to return.

The U.S. National Park Service has some of the larger properties, wild at least in part, around the Great Lakes: Sleeping Bear Dunes and Pictured Rocks National Lakeshores in Michigan, Apostle Islands National Lakeshore in Wisconsin, and splendid Isle Royale National Park, a 100,000-acre archipelago in Lake Superior. In northern Wisconsin and Michigan's Upper Peninsula, there are numerous vest-pocket wilderness areas in national forests and wildlife refuges. Michigan, Wisconsin, and Minnesota have also delineated areas within their larger parks for protection as state-owned wilderness zones.

In Canada, hikers treasure the long Bruce Trail, which runs from Niagara Falls northwest along the limestone Niagara Escarpment, past metropolitan Toronto, to the end of the Bruce Peninsula in Lake Huron. Killarney Provincial Park, Ontario, holds a slice of the north shore of Huron.

Near Sault Sainte Marie are the Algoma Highlands, a rare island of old-growth pine and deciduous forest whose fate is still to be determined. On the north shore of Lake Superior, Pukaskwa National Park is in the process of establishment.

The greatest lake country wilderness lies just west of the Great Lakes, in northern Minnesota and adjacent Ontario. On the American side is the famous Boundary Waters Canoe Area Wilderness within Superior National Forest, some 800,000 acres of pines, portages, and labyrinthine waters. Adjoining the Boundary Waters are parks in two nations: small Voyageurs National Park on the American side and the million-acre Quetico Provincial Park in Canada. Together these areas make up one of the major wilderness reserves of the North American continent. Despite the emphasis on water travel, there are trails among the lakes, and backpackers do find much to explore.

The climate of the lakes country is continental—hot in summer and cold in winter—but somewhat tempered close to the shores of the Great Lakes. In the eastern part of the region, late summer is the rainiest time; to the west, on the edge of the Great Plains, the rain peak comes earlier. The bugs are gone by August. Winter comes early. The Boundary Waters area gets six months of snow cover and some of the lowest temperatures in the contiguous United States.

WILDERNESS ON THE PLAINS

The Great Plains at the center of our continent are perhaps the most profoundly altered of all our natural regions. Of the original grassland ecosystems, only a few scraps and traces are left, these largely on hilly, nonarable ground. The limited protected areas are charming, though, and have the added fascination of the rare: remnant puddles of what used to be the "sea of grass." Only a few of these sites are large enough to reward a long hiking trip, but there's a good deal here for the weekend traveler and the day hiker, visiting perhaps several areas in succession.

In western Oklahoma, Wichita Mountains National Wildlife Refuge, on an island of stony hills amid farms, is habitat for the totem animal of the Great Plains, the bison. Farther east, The Nature Conservancy has the 30,000-acre Tallgrass Prairie Preserve in the Osage Hills. In the Flint Hills of eastern Kansas, you'll find the Tallgrass Prairie National Preserve, administered by the National Park Service, and the Konza Research Natural

WILDERNESS REGIONS OF THE WESTERN U.S. AND CANADA

Area, maintained by Kansas State University. Except for Wichita Mountains NWR, these areas are open to day hiking only. Nebraska has fine small roadless tracts in its northern sandhills at Fort Niobara, Crescent Lake, and Valentine National Wildlife Refuges, and in Nebraska National Forest. Farther north in the plains belt, fantastically eroded regions called badlands interrupt the smooth ascent of the plains. In South Dakota, Badlands National Monument preserves tablelands, gulches, canyons and buttes, ramparts of colored and crumbling earth, and a couple of decent chunks of rugged, roadless prairie. One of these, the 50,000-acre Sage Creek area, is the largest designated wilderness on the plains. To the west, the Black Hills, a forested island mountain range, contain a bit of Forest Service wilderness. Theodore Roosevelt National Park in North Dakota, another badlands landscape, has smaller areas of grassy wild ground.

Near the Canadian border, lakes, rivers, and water-filled "potholes" are precious habitat for ducks, cranes, pelicans, and other birds. Several wildlife refuges here—Chase Lake and Lostwood in North Dakota, Medicine Lake and UL Bend in Montana—have wilderness units within them.

Near the western fringe of the plains, the grass grows shorter, the weather drier, and the federal holdings more extensive. Here there are many "national grasslands," terrain that was badly overgrazed in private ownership, then purchased by the government for restoration. In eastern Montana there are more than 1 million acres of rough-textured public domain land, wild in part, around the backed-up waters of Fort Peck Reservoir on the Missouri. Part of this region is managed as the Charles M. Russell Wildlife Range. Though roadless areas exist on these federal lands, none have formal protection.

On the Canadian side of the border, the record of prairie preservation is rather better. Several small, timbered mountain ranges, rising from the fields, are provincial parks: Turtle Mountain and Spruce Woods in Manitoba, Moose Mountain in Saskatchewan, Cypress Hills in Saskatchewan and Alberta. But the most significant preserve is Grasslands National Park in Saskatchewan, proclaimed in 1981 (but still in the process of creation as land is purchased from private owners). Its 350 square miles, in two chunks along the border with Montana, incorporate more relatively unaltered shortgrass prairie than all the U.S. areas combined. You'll find here such "un-Canadian" species as the prairie dog, the prairie rattlesnake, the sage grouse, and the pronghorn. You can prick yourself on a cactus.

Especially toward the north, the regional climate is rigorous. There can be a 150-degree range in temperature over the year, from 100 degrees above zero Fahrenheit to 50 or more below. In some areas, wind is all but perpetual. Early summer is the wettest time of year.

THE WILD ROCKIES

When the first far ridges of the Rocky Mountains begin to detach themselves from the horizon—when the mountain-hungry eye spots solid peaks among the deceptive clouds—the westbound traveler is approaching the first of the real wilderness strongholds of North America.

The barrier ahead is no simple line of peaks. The Rockies are many ranges, tangled, branching, offset one from another—a world of mountains, not a chain. They subside completely in central Wyoming, at the broad gap traversed by the old Oregon Trail. This opening divides the Rockies into two very different regions: the southern, or Colorado, Rockies, and the northern U.S. Rockies of northern Wyoming, Montana, and Idaho. Nothing but a line on a map separates these from the Canadian Rockies, which run another 1,000 miles north through Alberta and British Columbia.

The southern Rockies don't really get started much south of the Colorado–New Mexico border. When they do rise, they go up all the way: New Mexico has a couple of 13,000-foot peaks, and Colorado has fifty-four summits over 14,000. The wild mountain areas here are numerous and grandly scenic; often they clump together in larger complexes divided only by narrow road corridors. The Pecos Wilderness in New Mexico, the Sangre de Cristo Wilderness in southern Colorado, and the Flat Tops Wilderness in northwest Colorado each top 200,000 acres; the Weminuche Wilderness near the southeast corner of the state approaches half a million—moderately large by western standards. To the west in Utah, the granitic Uinta Mountains, though sometimes classed with the northern Rockies, feel more like Colorado than Montana. Here is the very alpine High Uintas Wilderness, as large as the Weminuche and in need of expansion to include foothill forests and glaciated basins that missed inclusion when the boundaries were first drawn.

The southern Rockies have a strong summer thunderstorm season; in the southern part of the region, more rain may fall in August than in any other month. Mountain hikers are accustomed to scuttling down off these peaks, and out of the reach of lightning, by noon at the latest.

Winter in this part of the Rockies is an inviting season, with many clear stretches between storms. Though nighttime temperatures can go far below zero, the mountain climate is, if anything, a shade milder than that of the adjacent plains. Snow is that dry, cold, luminous stuff that skiers love—and fear, for this is the snow best suited to avalanche formation. Most areas can be hiked without skis or snowshoes in late June.

In the northern Rockies, beginning in Wyoming, the peaks are somewhat lower, the forest rather lusher, and the land considerably wilder. Yellowstone National Park is the center of one great complex of primitive lands. Two hundred miles to the west, the Idaho Batholith, a granitic region around the upper Salmon and Selway Rivers, is a stronghold of Forest Service wilderness. The Rockies of northern Montana, including Glacier National Park and the national forests to the south, is a third wild core.

A million acres is land enough to fill a square about 40 miles on a side. Five individual roadless areas in these regions contain that or more. The southernmost megawilderness is centered on the southeast corner of Yellowstone and includes the Washakie and Teton Wildernesses on adjacent national forests. A second, the Absaroka–Beartooth Wilderness, adjoins the park on the north. In Idaho, two great wilderness units adjoin: the Frank Church/River of No Return, around the Middle Fork of the Salmon; and the Selway–Bitterroot adjacent to the north and separated from its neighbor by only the width of a road. In northern Montana, the fine wilderness in Glacier National Park itself is dwarfed by a national forest complex containing the Scapegoat, Bob Marshall, and Great Bear Wildernesses, adjacent to the south.

Wilderness areas on this scale have the splendor of the things within them—river gorges and fierce rapids, elk and grizzly, lakes and residual glaciers, bright forests, walls of granite and layered sedimentary stone. But most of all they have the splendor that comes simply from their size. Here, if anywhere south of the boreal forests, you can imagine yourself in the continent-spanning wilderness that was.

The hiking climate in the northern U.S. Rockies is distinctly damper and cooler than at points south. In the higher and wetter regions, the summer hiking season is July, August, and perhaps September; June is the end of one winter and October the transition to the next. Along with the usual summer thunderstorms, more substantial frontal storms may arrive from the west at almost any time. The winter wet season is long and cloudy, though not without clear windows for the well-timed trip. As everywhere in the mountainous West, local climates vary with topography. Notably, lower and east-facing slopes receive less precipitation than higher and west-facing ones.

Across the international border, the Canadian Rockies march onward toward the Arctic. One hundred and fifty miles north, a magnificent cluster of national and provincial parks—Banff, Jasper, Mount Robson, and others—blankets over 6 million acres of glaciated scenery. Despite overdevelopment here and there, several million-acre blocks remain wild. Plans are afoot for a comparable cluster at the far northern tip of the range. Westward, across the trench occupied by the upper Columbia River, lies the Columbia Mountain System (including the Selkirks, the Purcells, the Bugaboos, and many other named ranges). Here too are several national and provincial parks; the provincial government of British Columbia has plans for more.

THE COLORADO PLATEAU AND CANYON COUNTRY

From sources in Wyoming and Colorado, the tributaries of the Colorado River gather and converge. Flowing toward the Pacific, they encounter the Colorado Plateau, a great oval of highlands in Colorado, Utah, New Mexico, and Arizona. The result is a 10-thousand-mile web of precipitous canyons in rock now gray, now black, now yellow, now the famous southwestern rust or rose. Some of these gorges are gigantic, like the Grand Canyon itself, the mile-deep slot cut by the Colorado into the layered, colored rock of northern Arizona. Others are closed-in, convoluted, narrow. In the greater gorges, travel is by water; the lesser ones are footways. And above the canyons rise the mesas—isolated, flat-topped mountains, left behind in the general erosion, many of them high enough to be forested, some of them partly wild.

Rivers in canyons make possible damsites, enchanting to engineers. Several of the most exciting stretches of the Colorado and its tributaries have been flooded by government reservoirs. Even the Grand Canyon itself was almost so flooded. Much of the course of the main river is now included in parks or national recreation areas (the latter around the reservoirs); up the tributaries, the fate of large and fascinating wild areas remains to be decided. The new Grand Staircase–Escalante National Monument in southern Utah has plugged one of the major conservation gaps. The largest roadless expanse in the region—a million acres stepping down with the strata from rims to river—is contained in Grand Canyon National Park.

The southern flank of the Colorado Plateau is the long band of mountains called the Mogollon Rim, which swings across the Southwest in an east-west arc from the Rio Grande to the Colorado. Timbered, cool, incised on its south flank by dozens of canyon systems of its own, the Mogollon is prime recreation country. Several wilderness areas have been designated within the national forests here. One of these, the Gila Wilderness at the eastern tip of the rim, was the first such area ever set aside, explicitly, with formal boundaries; though it has suffered some shrinkage since, it still protects some half a million acres of red rock and pine woodland.

On the Colorado Plateau, desert and mountain climates interlock. In the canyons, April and May, cool and clear, may be the best travel months. Water is comparatively abundant then, and the thunderstorm season, with its flash flood danger, has not yet begun. When it does, be cautious about hiking a narrow, no-exit canyon, and above all don't camp in a narrows.

THE DEEP SOUTHWEST

South of the Mogollon Rim and the southern tip of the Rocky Mountains, the land subsides toward the Mexican border. Along the Rio Grande in New Mexico and Texas is the U.S. share of the binational Chihuahuan Desert. In this region, the bulk of the year's precipitation arrives during the summer growing season, which makes for a rich desert flora. The wildest corner is Big Bend National Park, in Texas, on a bight of the Rio Grande.

In southwest Arizona lies the U.S. portion of another primarily Mexican desert, the Sonoran. In this driest of the North American deserts, cacti are the big, dramatic growing things. The region contains the major cities of Tucson and Phoenix; numerous low, stark mountain ranges; and plenty of wild land. Of wilderness areas managed by the Forest Service, the Matzatzal is the largest and the Superstition probably the best known. The half-million-acre Kofa Game Range is a refuge for desert bighorn sheep. Along the Mexican border, Organ Pipe Cactus National Monument and the enormous Cabeza Prieta National Wildlife Refuge protect a magnificent desolation. A number of big chunks of desert controlled by the Bureau of Land Management have wilderness status as well. Only a few of these fascinating places get much recreational use at all.

Backpacking in these regions is the purest desert hiking; winter, and at higher elevations spring and fall, are the comfortable seasons. But between the two deserts and on their fringes, a number of mountain ranges, small in extent but high in elevation, rise like seamounts into the temperate forest zone. Such national forest wilderness areas as the Chiricahua (Arizona) and the White Mountain (New Mexico) perch on top.

THE INTERMOUNTAIN REGION

West and north of the Colorado canyonlands, between the Rockies and the Sierra-Cascade chain, lies a generally lower, generally drier region that is nonetheless rich in mountains and in mountain wilderness. Toward the northern end, Oregon's Blue Mountains run east to west across it, bridging the Rockies to the Cascades like the bar of an H. The Snake River cuts a path through this bar near the eastern end, forming wild Hells Canyon. The big Eagle Cap Wilderness is just west in Oregon, and the lava canyons of the Owyhee River, untamed but also unprotected as yet, lie nearby in Oregon and Idaho.

South of the Blue Mountains is the heart of the intermountain west, the Great Basin. Here hundreds of separate mountain masses, oriented north and south, rise from a floor of cool sagebrush steppe. Despite the diligent scrapings of miners and prospectors, most of these rugged fault-block ranges have pristine country in them, and a few wilderness areas exist on national forest land (many, many more await protection). The largest designated area, so far, is the 120,000-acre Arc Dome Wilderness in the Toiyabe Range of Nevada. Another, stranger kind of wildness is found in certain valleys, where streams that never reach the sea lay down their sediments to form the dead-flat, sterile, weirdly beautiful plains called playas. The Black Rock Desert of northwest Nevada is perhaps the most notable of these. Except in very wet years, you can walk across these expanses, keeping pace with mirages and sensing, as on a calm ocean, the curvature of the earth.

Toward the south of the intermountain region, in southern Nevada and adjacent California, the elevations are generally lower and the vegetation different. This is the Mojave Desert, its signature species a lily that looks like a cactus, the curious Joshua tree. Death Valley National Park and Joshua Tree National Preserve, both full of wilderness, are here. In the California part of the Mojave, a swarm of small wilderness areas, on land administered by the federal Bureau of Land Management, surrounds these vaster cores. Near the Mexican border, California's Anza-Borrego Desert State Park is a major holding, including state-designated wilderness zones.

In the lowest, hottest parts of the intermountain region, as in the Mojave, winter is the pleasant hiking season; spring and fall are reasonable; summer is impossibly hot. Farther north and at higher elevations, spring and fall can be delightful. From central Nevada north, summer in the valleys is merely warm; in the lofty, forested mountain masses, it is cool. Winter brings plenty of snow to the higher ranges. Most of the sparse precipitation comes in the colder months of the year.

THE PACIFIC RANGES

Along the Pacific Coast of the conterminous United States, just about all the remaining wilderness is found in mountainous country. These highlands rise in two parallel north-south lines.

Inland lies the greater mountain wall, the Sierra-Cascade chain. The southern half of this barrier is the Sierra Nevada. A single enormous fault block, it slopes gently on the west but breaks abruptly to the deserts on the east in a scarp as much as a mile high. The Cascades of northern California, Oregon, and Washington are built on a different plan. From a forested base of moderate height there rise, isolated and commanding, a dozen cones and spikes of lava: Mounts Lassen, Shasta, Jefferson, Hood, and Rainier and numerous lesser-known cousins. The Sierra and the Cascades are cool enough, and wet enough, to carry glaciers—small remnant ice fields in the Sierra, impressive icecaps on the taller volcanoes and other high points of the Cascades. The far vaster glaciers of the past gouged out Sierra granites and Cascade lavas to make the sockets of hundreds of modern lakes.

Yosemite Valley in the Sierra and Mount Rainier in the Cascades, each now the centerpiece of a national park, were among the first western places to draw preservation campaigns. Many more followed. Today a hiker traversing these ranges on the Pacific Crest Trail, the western counterpart of the Appalachian, will spend about half the trip in protected areas. These are largest and most densely clustered in the Sierra, where more than 2 million acres of contiguous wilderness form a roadless block 130 miles long, and again in the North Cascades of Washington, where several closely clustered areas encompass another 2 million acres.

Nearest the ocean are the tangled, many-ridged coastal ranges. Typically rather low in the United States, these ranges nevertheless do rise, in several places, to 8,000 feet or more. There is a constellation of classified wilderness areas within easy reach of the southern California metropolitan area. On the central California coast, the territory of the California condor, large reaches of brush and fire-tolerant forest are protected. The heavily timbered Klamath Mountains region, on the California-Oregon border, contains over 1 million acres of wilderness, half of it in the Trinity Alps; much more roadless land in the region is still vulnerable to logging. Olympic National Park near Seattle is essentially all wilderness, some 800,000 acres in extent.

The hiking season in the Pacific ranges depends on altitude and latitude. In southern California, summers are hot and dry; hikers head for the highest country then, saving lower-lying destinations for spring and fall. Some areas are closed to public use in the rainless months because of the extreme danger of fire. Only the highest peaks are forested; lower and middle slopes are covered with the complex and typically Californian brushfields called chaparral.

As you move north along either chain of mountains, the climate becomes steadily wetter and cooler, the forests greener, and the dry season gradually shorter. In the Sierra-Cascade chain (but rarely in the coastal ranges), summer thunderstorms are normal. In Oregon and Washington, serious summer rain can no longer be regarded as a surprise. The coastal side of the Olympic Mountains is the most sodden area in the forty-eight contiguous states: lavishly green below timberline and glittering with ice above. The North Cascades, inland across Puget Sound, are only a little drier. Hikers in this region, like hikers in the East, go ready for rain, and count themselves lucky if they do not get it.

This pattern is varied by the usual local factors. Both the coastal ranges and the Sierra–Cascade chain cast rain shadows: their eastern slopes are markedly drier than their western sides. And hikers on the immediate coastline learn to count on the persistent drizzle of summer fog.

Snow camping is at its best in the Sierra and southern Cascades, high enough to get lots of snow but southerly enough to enjoy clear spells between Pacific storms; farther north, such respites are rarer. All snow in the Pacific ranges is fairly wet and less ideal for skiing than the dry, loose powder of more continental ranges. It is also somewhat less prone to the formation of massive slab avalanches. There's all the more danger, though, from wet-snow avalanches, massive amorphous slumps that occur when the temperature rises.

In British Columbia, the Pacific ranges are a great reservoir of wilderness. Between the Fraser River on the south and the southern tip of the Alaska panhandle on the north, a band of high country inland from the shore is predominantly wild in fact, if not yet in name. A few preserves exist, the largest of which is Tweedsmuir National Park; many more or under discussion by the provincial government, and, if designated, would constitute a true national treasure. The alternative to protection, for all but the most alpine areas, is clearcut logging.

Recreationally, this is wild and woolly country, a temperate coastal rainforest with only the ghost, if that, of a summer dry season. Trails are few; cross-country travel, in a sort of cool jungle defended by the prickly plant called devil's club, is hard; the higher country may require technical mountaineering skills.

BOREAL CANADA

Canada, unlike the United States, is still in large part a wilderness nation. Like the United States in an earlier period, it is laboring mightily to change that situation; at the same time, it is struggling to preserve a suitable chunk of its wild heritage (see Chapter 31).

The metaphor of the archipelago of wilderness continues to apply in the southern reaches of Canada. Agriculture, logging, and mining are the norm, wildness the exception, in the maritime provinces of Nova Scotia, Prince Edward Island, and New Brunswick. The same is true along the southern margins of Québec and Ontario; and it applies in at least the southern halves of Manitoba, Saskatchewan, Alberta, and British Columbia. Much, though by no means all, of the remaining wild land in this southern tier is contained in provincial and a few national parks; some of these are mentioned above in connection with the related regions of the United States.

WILDERNESS REGIONS OF CANADA

For more northerly parts of Canada, however, and for the state of Alaska, we have to abandon the habit of thinking of wilderness islands in a sea of occupied land. Rather, the older situation prevails: developed areas are the archipelago, albeit a rapidly expanding one; wildness is the background, the matrix.

A few years ago, the frontier between the (mostly) settled and the (largely) wild lay near the southern fringe of the great coniferous boreal forest, or taiga, that arcs across the continent from Newfoundland almost to the mouths of the Yukon River. Now the Canadian taiga is everywhere invaded from the south by government-sanctioned logging and mining operations. Only above the sixtieth parallel, in the Yukon and Northwest Territories, does the old situation prevail. Canadian conservationists are working hard to preserve some significant fragments south of the sixtieth parallel, and to set limits on the scope of exploitation north of it.

Between the open prairies to the south and the boreal woods to the north lies a broad transitional zone where groves of trembling aspen mix with meadows of rough fescue, a uniquely charming Canadian landscape of which little remains wild. Riding Mountain and Prince Albert National Parks protect remnants of the original scene.

The boreal forest proper seems half woods, half water: thousands of miles of spruce and fir rather open underneath, lightened a little by aspen, birch, and willow; thousands of miles of mazy lakes and rivers. More than the rare trails, these waterways are the travel routes, traversed by watercraft in summer and in winter by over-snow vehicles, people on skis and snowshoes, and now and then a sled-dog team. Where roads have not yet penetrated, basic access is by small airplane. In western Canada, the boreal forest washes up against and in between a swarm of remote and wild mountain ranges, in northern British Columbia, the Northwest Territories, and the Yukon.

North of the great boreal forest band begins the true Arctic, the tree-less tundra region. Below a surface mat of lichens, mosses, grasses, sedges, heaths, and stunted willows lies ice, the frozen groundwater called permafrost. This never melts, unless the overlying vegetation is disturbed.

The Arctic tundra may be the most difficult terrain to travel in all North America. Trails, as such, don't exist. The ground is boggy and treacherous. You often progress by stepping from tussock to unsteady tussock of the ubiquitous cotton grass. Mosquitoes in summer make a kind of stinging smog. This is truly a wilderness for wildlife: habitat for vast herds of Arctic caribou and the wolves that prey on them, and vital breeding ground for half the birds of the Americas. Though people venture down the Arctic rivers in canoes, kayaks, and rafts, backpackers can best admire this region, and root for its preservation, from afar.

Still farther north, in parts of the Canadian Arctic Archipelago and on Greenland, lies the zone of permanent ice. Though travel here is expeditionary, the region actually sees a bit more recreational use than does the tundra to the south of it. Summers are full of cool light, with pale sunshine twenty-four hours a day around the solstice; the climate, for all its sometimes deadly rigor, is quite dry.

Canada has many great national parks in the Arctic, and is designating others as rapidly as negotiations with the aboriginal "First Nations" can be concluded. In most cases, traditional native subsistence hunting and fishing are to continue.

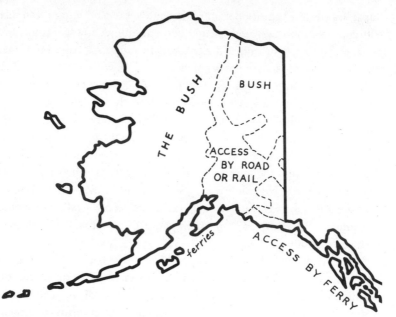

WILDERNESS REGIONS OF ALASKA

WILD ALASKA

In Alaska, the North American West, with its washboard pattern of mountains and valleys, makes a great left turn. Structures that ran north and south for thousands of miles are now oriented east and west. The several southern mountain masses of the state, including the high point of the continent at Mount McKinley, continue the general arc of the Pacific coastal ranges. The state's interior lowland, where the Yukon River flows west to the sea, is the last in a succession of intermountain troughs running all the way to Mexico. The Brooks Range in the north continues the line of the Rocky Mountains. Alaska is a continent in miniature.

At least 90 percent of the territory of the fiftieth U.S. state is in fact still roadless. Here wildness is still the matrix, the modern human imprint the exception. Well over a third of this matrix is protected in parks, wildlife refuges, and such; about 15 percent of it is actually classified as wilderness. Six of every 10 acres thus protected in the United States, to date, are in Alaska.

For recreation purposes, the empire can be subdivided in various ways. By summer climate, for instance: moderate, damp, and maritime along the southern coasts; drier and more continental in the middle; still drier and ever chillier toward the north. Or by topography: mountainous in the south, flat in the middle, mountainous again north of the Arctic Circle, leveling out once more along the Arctic Ocean. By vegetation: rainforest in the southeast, windswept grassland in the southwest, boreal forest amidships, tundra to the north. (Going up, as always, is like moving to the north: even in the southern forests, a modest climb will take you to treeline and tundra, and often onto permanent ice not far above that.)

For the traveler, though, the state's terrain is best classified by access. There are areas (in the southeast) where your trip is likely to begin with a ride on a boat; areas (around the major city, Anchorage, and north to Fairbanks and beyond) where your access can be by train or motor vehicle; and the great balance of the state, where you don't get far without a trip in a small airplane.

In southeastern Alaska, and in far northern British Columbia as well, the coast is a fretwork of islands, fjords, and headlands, with mountains banked enormously behind. Water is the only major highway. Regular ferry service takes you to towns that may adjoin wild forest or melancholy cutover land; Juneau, the state capital, has some of the most rewarding surroundings. In Glacier Bay National Park at the north, a local tour boat will drop you off anywhere. Floatplanes, though much more expensive, will get you to any southeastern Alaskan inlet you choose.

Most people are content to admire this coast from water level. A temperate jungle below treeline, a tangle of peaks and glaciers above, it doesn't exactly welcome hikers—but it rewards the ones who push their way in. There are rather few trails. Often the function of a formal path is to get you through rainforest and muskegs (peat bogs) to higher ground, tundra covered, where cross-country travel begins. There are over one hundred Forest Service cabins in the woods, mostly on shorelines, equipped with bunks and wood stoves and rentable for a few dollars a night; you don't find many purists scorning to use these.

The region's longest trail, the 33-mile Chilkoot, is more a historical artifact than a wilderness experience: in 1897–98, tens of thousands of prospectors took this rugged path across the coastal mountains from the northern port of Skagway to placer mines in the Yukon Territory in Canada.

The Alaska panhandle is almost all public land. Glacier Bay National

Park occupies its northern end, Misty Fjords National Monument its southern. Most of what lies between is Tongass National Forest. Though the Tongass contains some large wilderness areas, Congress has followed the urging of Alaska politicians and earmarked it mainly for timber production. The magnificent cover of virgin cedar, spruce, and hemlock is fraying fast.

The Alaskan regions accessible by road include some of the state's best destinations, in the Chugach, Talkeetna, and Alaska mountain ranges. Immediately outside of Anchorage is half-million-acre Chugach State Park, in Alaskan terms a mere neighborhood playground. Nearby to the southwest is the Kenai Peninsula, a compact region that blends coastal, alpine, and forest Alaska in one. The Kenai has one of the state's best trail networks and one of its most welcoming hiking climates. The peninsula is more or less blanketed with state and federal parks and the Kenai National Wildlife Refuge.

A drive south and east from Anchorage will get you to the borders of the 13-million-acre Wrangell–Saint Elias National Park and Preserve. Vast though it is, this area is only about half of a binational arc of protected lands stretching all the way to Glacier Bay and including Kluane Provincial Park in the Yukon and Tatshenshini–Alsek Wilderness Provincial Park in British Columbia. The combination is the continent's largest zone of preservation. This great complex of volcanic and sedimentary mountains holds North America's most extensive glaciers, many of its highest peaks, and wildlife including three separate herds of caribou. The Alaska–Canada Highway skirts the northern rim of the region, and another road, the access to the village of McCarthy, penetrates it deeply from the west. Small planes ferry hikers in to more remote regions, but there are peripheral hikes you can do without taking to the air. Your path will probably be an overgrown prospector's track, or a game trail.

North from Anchorage lie the granitic Talkeetna Mountains, a rather tame area by Alaskan standards but unusually well supplied with trails. Beyond in the Alaska Range looms Mount McKinley, which many prefer to call by its Athapaskan name Denali, "The Great One." The parkland around it, Denali National Park and Preserve, is actually fairly accessible. A major highway passes the east end of the park, and a road (for buses only) runs westward 90 miles along the north side of the Alaska Range. Hiking is fairly easy in the boreal forest and alpine tundra (encountered at about 2,700 feet). You have to be duly cautious about stream crossings, and about bears. A vast state park, also called Denali, abuts the national area on the southeast.

Alaska's great interior region is largely flat and largely wet. Northeast of Fairbanks, though, lies a hilly quadrant called the Tanana–Yukon Upland, very attractive for hiking. Here are the Chena River State Recreation Area, the White Mountain and Steese Mountain National Recreation Areas, the Pinnell Mountain National Recreation Trail, and the Yukon–Charley Rivers National Preserve. Developed to some extent with trails and cabins, areas like these—true wilderness to a refugee from the Lower Forty-Eight—might strike an Alaska hiker as rather tame.

North from Fairbanks the Elliott and Dalton Highways run with the Trans-Alaska Pipeline all the way to the Arctic Ocean. There is bus service, and passenger cars are allowed (but not recommended). Even in relatively civilized parts of Alaska, airplane access may be simpler, even cheaper, than travel by car. The vast residue of Alaska, known simply as "the bush," is airplane country purely. There are now scheduled flights to many villages. In addition, bush pilots and air-taxi services, their vehicles equipped with wheels or floats or skis depending on landing surfaces, can get you just about anywhere, for a price.

"Anywhere" might be the western Alaska Range and the Aleutian Peninsula, where an almost unbroken chain of parks and wildlife refuges runs southwest toward Japan. It might be one of the parks or refuges of the boreal forest interior, along the Yukon and its tributaries, north of Fairbanks. It might be the remote west coast, on the Bering Sea, where the Yukon Delta National Wildlife Refuge is the largest of several land reserves. Perhaps the most enticing destination is the Brooks Range north of the Arctic Circle. Here, Gates of the Arctic National Park, the Arctic National Wildlife Refuge, and several similar units create a wall of wilderness broken only by the Trans-Alaska Pipeline corridor. Although there are no formal trails, higher and rockier sections are relatively easy to traverse; quite a few people also hike the difficult ground of the lower-lying tundras.

Travel in "the bush," obviously, is a step beyond backpacking as we think of it in the Lower Forty-Eight or even in some parts of Alaska. You have to be well equipped, self-sufficient, and prepared for slow going and just about any kind of weather. Chartered flights take money, time, and a pretty flexible schedule—you'll be flown in, and out, when conditions permit. These challenges work to keep visitation pretty light. Vast reaches see hardly any use at all, unless by native peoples who continue to occupy their ancient lands (and strive to maintain some aspects of their ancient ways of living).

If your travels bring you near a native village, by the way, don't count on it for lodging or resupply, and seek permission if you want to linger in its neighborhood. It has its own life and business, which may or may not include catering to travelers. Inquire.

In this vast and demanding wilderness, is it really important to think about the impact of your travel on the land? Arguably, even more so than in the Lower Forty-Eight. Parts of the Alaskan bush are just now reaching the level of use at which the scars first start to appear. By the standards of the California Sierra Nevada, say, the danger signs are slight—a discernible use-trail along a stream, a bare dusting of litter. By the standards of Alaska, where people go to experience wilderness uncompromised, they are jarring. A choice lies ahead between sharply limiting use on the one hand and accommodating it, on the other, with formal trails and campsites; to which, however, the land is not well suited. Be glad it's not your choice, and seek advice from managing agencies about the practices they recommend. Unless otherwise instructed, behave as you would when traveling off-trail in any vulnerable terrain. Avoid trampling, especially repeat trampling, of any vegetation. Camp on durable surfaces, or move camp every night. Light no fires. Avoid spooking wildlife. Safeguard your food from bears. Take exquisite pains to pass invisibly.

By way of preparation for an Alaska trip, I especially recommend *Adventuring in Alaska,* by Peggy Wayburn. Drier but very useful is *Backpacking in Alaska,* by Jim DuFresne.

Some people count sheep. When I'm in need of a soothing mental exercise to go to sleep by, I sometimes count wilderness areas: list them in my mind, visualize their boundaries, imagine the landscapes within them. When I first fell into this habit, it didn't take me long to run through the roster of formally protected areas, at least. Now the list is far too long for that, and I'm thankful. My acquaintance with most of these places will never go beyond this kind of long-distance touring. That's fine with me, too. These are treasures to be enjoyed in person; to be valued from afar: and to be preserved forever—if we can.

TOWARD A
WILDERNESS FOREVER

The effort to preserve some of the wilderness of North America goes back more than one hundred and fifty years. Along the way, we've several times redefined what it is we are doing. We've tried a succession of approaches, each bolder than the last. Now we stand at the beginning of a new campaign, the boldest of them all: one that goes beyond salvaging pieces and dares to seek the restoration of whole landscapes.

ROADS TO THE WILDERNESS

In the beginning, there were the Native Americans, who lived lightly and thinly on the future territories of Canada and the United States. One can debate to what degree these peoples practiced conservation in the sense of a conscious self-restraint. Certainly it is a mistake to read back into that culture our modern preoccupation with preserving nature, a concern that arises only after we have demonstrated our ability to disrupt nature. But the fact remains that, under the native peoples' management, the natural systems of North America were largely intact. Away from the tiny zones of dense inhabitation—villages, pueblos, nomadic encampments—the land was essentially wild. Wilderness needed no recognition: it was simply the way things were.

The Europeans who arrived on these shores from Columbus onward recognized wilderness, all right. For them it was first a storehouse to be looted and then a public enemy to be subdued, a vast force to be beaten back and down. They set about to do this with great courage and ever-increasing efficiency. At the same time, and from very early days, they expressed their awe at the magnificence they were invading. Almost in advance, they were nostalgic for wildness lost.

By the middle of the nineteenth century, people were wondering aloud if certain areas of wild land should not be left more or less alone. Calls for preservation came from such writers as frontier painter George Catlin, geographer George Perkins Marsh, and philosopher Henry David Thoreau. Presently this ferment began to have results. In 1864, Yosemite

Valley in California was earmarked for preservation, initially through a grant to the state. In 1872, the Yellowstone region became the world's first national park. In 1894, the voters of New York State, appalled by the wave of deforestation sweeping over the Adirondacks, decreed that the remaining state-owned lands in the region be held unlogged, "forever wild."

Thus began what might be called the park model of wilderness protection. It aimed at preserving a few extraordinary areas, singled out for their scenery or (occasionally) their wildlife, and often compared to crown jewels. Since Yellowstone, a noble assortment of areas in the United States and Canada, and indeed around the world, has been set aside on this model. More recently, the emphasis has shifted from scenery to representation: national park systems are seen as collections, to be made as complete as possible, of a country's ecosystems and landscape types. Maintaining wilderness in the strict sense is not an automatic purpose of parks, and many roads and other visitor accommodations have been built there.

For the United States, the creation of the first national parks marked something broader: a turning away from the policy of wholesale federal land disposal. Under policies going back to the Northwest Ordinance of 1787, most new lands annexed to the country became, not only federal territory, but also federal property. This, however, was regarded as a temporary and undesirable state of affairs. Barring a few shrinking and unstable allocations to Indian tribes, the goal was to have almost every acre in state or private hands, and yielding wealth somehow.

With Yellowstone, that policy began to change. Soon timbered areas were being withdrawn from the undifferentiated public lands and entrusted to a specialist agency, the U.S. Forest Service. Some key wildlife habitats became national wildlife refuges and ranges in the care of the U.S. Fish and Wildlife Service. Much later, the remainder of the public domain—mostly in the western deserts—was acknowledged to have value in itself and taken officially off the auction block. (No one has come up with a very satisfactory label for these lands, controlled by the Bureau of Land Management; they are usually just called BLM lands or public domain lands.) Again, wilderness preservation was not the object; but continued public ownership left the possibility open.

The notion of deliberately keeping certain areas free of roads can be dated to 1919 and to two rather low-level officials of the U.S. Forest Service, Arthur Carhart and Aldo Leopold. It was Leopold who really pursued the idea, urging his superiors to establish a system of wild recreational preserves. Starting with the Gila Primitive Area in 1924, the Forest Service set a number of such zones aside. In the 1930s a more upwardly mobile federal forester, Robert Marshall, made it his personal cause to multiply this system. In 1937, Marshall became one of the top officials of the Forest Service in Washington, D.C. Under his prodding, the list of protected areas was swelling fast.

But then, less than three years after his new appointment, Bob Marshall died. So did the job he had undertaken. In the ensuing decades, little new land was protected; indeed, much land in Marshall's primitive areas was now opened to logging and other invasions. Each time this happened, disappointed conservationists looked for another style of wilderness protection, one that could be counted on to stick.

THE WILDERNESS ACT OF 1964

And so, after a decade of lobbying, came about the Wilderness Act of 1964.

The Wilderness Act is an extraordinary law. Before it descends into mechanics, and into the compromises that were necessary to its passage, it is readable, even stirring:

> It is hereby declared to be the policy of Congress to secure for the American people ... the benefits of an enduring resource of wilderness ... [a place] where the earth and its community of life are untrammeled by man, where Man himself is a visitor who does not remain.

In the act, Congress created what is called the National Wilderness Preservation System. Simply put, it is a national roster of protected wild areas on the public lands. Only Congress can place areas on that roster; only Congress can remove areas from it. The boundaries of each preserve are defined with legal precision: from this peak (for instance) down that ridge to this survey marker to that stream. Within those boundaries, wilderness is paramount. Roads may not be built; timber may not be cut; motorized vehicles may not enter. Neither may mountain bikes. (Grazing is permitted in certain areas, though, and even mining, where established claims exist.) Each such protected area is known as a "wilderness":

"wilderness" in a legal sense, "wilderness" with metes and bounds, "Wilderness" with a capital "W."

When Congress creates a wilderness, the designated area remains part of the national park, national forest, wildlife refuge, or BLM district in which it lies. The same people continue to manage and control the land. Little changes. But changes that might otherwise take place are forestalled. Strict limits are set on what the managers can do with the land— or on what they can do *to* it.

The new wilderness roster started with a relative handful of areas inherited from the old Forest Service program. But it was open ended. The new law required not only the Forest Service but also the Park Service and the Fish and Wildlife Service to comb through their territories and recommend further roadless regions for the congressional imprimatur. (The fourth principal land agency, the Bureau of Land Management, was brought under the same mandate in 1976.) Several rounds of such inventories have occurred since 1964. And ever since the Wilderness Act was passed, local debates about the future of wild land have tended to be kicked up to Congress for their ultimate resolution.

Each case is something of a fight, of course. There are always people who want the largest possible amount of land placed in the formal wilderness system; there are always people who want the smallest possible allocation. Among the natural opponents of wilderness are the timber industry; the mining industry; the off-road-vehicle lobby; dam builders and power companies; chambers of commerce and local governments in rural parts of the Far West; and the aggressive pro-development lobby that calls itself the Wise Use movement. Speaking for maximum wilderness are the various conservation groups, local and national, and the people they represent. In the end it always comes down to a simple test of public support: which side can pile up the most mail on the legislators' desks.

By the record, it seems fair to say that the pro-wilderness public is the larger. It may take time, but once a proposed wilderness begins to be seriously considered by Congress, the area almost always makes it into the system. Though the boundaries are usually settled by compromise, the compromises tend to be more generous than miserly.

Along the way the wilderness project has widened its focus. At the beginning, most of the protected areas were alpine, recreationally attractive, and relatively uncontroversial. But gradually more varied lands—deserts and lowland forests, swamps and marshes—began to find their way into the system. There was a sharp debate as to whether or not to accept areas, especially in the eastern United States, that had recovered from past logging. (The eventual answer was yes.) Along the way, it began to be understood that wilderness was only incidentally a type of recreation land: that the goal was more fundamentally the preservation of the healthy, living fabric of the natural world.

With each new round of inventories, too, it became evident that there was considerably more roadless acreage left than we had thought. To the frustration of people who didn't like the idea of wilderness in the first place, advocates kept raising their sights. At first, they thought 2 or 3 percent of the area of the United States might wind up in the wilderness system; a few years later, they were thinking in terms of a tenth—a tithe, as the eminent conservationist David Brower put it.

How large in fact could the wilderness system envisioned in 1964—based on the preservation of parts of the existing, shrinking stock of roadless areas—actually become?

The United States is a big country. Setting Alaska aside for the moment, we have, in the other forty-nine states, about 1.9 billion acres of land—about 3 million square miles. About one-sixth of that land is owned by the federal government.

Adding up the inventories made by the land agencies, we find that at least 120 million acres is still roadless and undeveloped. That sounds impressive, and it is. But compared with the total acreage of those forty-nine states, it's not quite so imposing—something under 7 percent of all the land, well under Brower's tithe.

By 1997, about 50 million acres in the non-Alaskan states had actually been placed in the federal wilderness system. That's an area about half the size of California—still less than half of the potential in these states. Many a sharp battle remains to be fought. The biggest potential additions to the system now lie in the Rocky Mountain and intermountain states of Nevada, Utah, Idaho, and Montana. And they lie, not in the national forests, parks, or wildlife refuges, but in the largely arid holdings of the Bureau of Land Management. The desert, for all its fascination and beauty, is always the last landscape to be appreciated.

Meanwhile, however, the game has continued to change.

THE FIGHT FOR WILD ALASKA

When the forty-ninth state was admitted to the union in 1959, nearly its entire area was federal land. As part of statehood, Alaska was due to receive a large grant of property. But here something new intervened: the indigenous peoples of the region, left out of the initial calculations in the best traditional manner, asserted through the courts their own land claims. The situation froze.

By the time it unfroze, in the late 1970s, the time was right for a grand allocation of public domain lands in Alaska—not only to the state, and not only to what became a set of native corporations, but also to the federal conservation systems on a scale never seen before. The American conservation movement realized that it had an opportunity that would never come again: the "last great first chance," as the slogan went, to preserve landscapes and wildlife wholesale.

The wilderness areas of the lower forty-eight states, for all their grandeur, are the uneaten scraps at a great resource consumption banquet. They contain more heights than lowlands, more rugged ground than flat, more deserts and tundras than forests and fertile soils. And in truth they are rather small. Though some wilderness areas bulk pretty large on the map of a national forest, very few of them look like much on the map of a state. In the United States south of Canada, you will be hard put to find a spot more than 20 miles from a road.

You will also be hard put to find a spot where all the plant and animal species present a hundred years ago are still around. This is especially true of the keystone predators, animals like the wolf and the grizzly bear.

Henry David Thoreau, writing of New England in the 1840s, was already troubled by this impoverishment. "Is it not a maimed and imperfect nature I am conversing with?" he asks in *Walden*. And he adds longingly: "I want to know an entire heaven and an entire earth."

With Alaska, the United States had its great opportunity to preserve "an entire heaven and an entire earth": to secure—in single, unbroken, protected regions—natural units as vast as the whole watershed of a major river, or a mountain range from plain to peak, or the entire range of a migratory caribou herd. With a tremendous spasm of energy, on the eve of the conservative "Reagan Revolution" that would have doomed the effort, the challenge was met. In the Alaska National Interest Conservation

Lands Act of 1980, the national legislature established parks and refuges and wilderness areas on a scale never seen before, and sufficient not only to safeguard scenery or recreation, but also to honor biological realities.

All is not well in Alaska. When it comes to formal wilderness classification, much land was left out of the system that should someday be in. In the Tongass National Forest, Congress has imposed the will of the timber industry on a temperate rainforest of planetary significance. Oil drilling is a perennial possibility in the Arctic National Wildlife Refuge in the Brooks Range, and will only be foreclosed when the land finally gets wilderness as well as refuge status. The expanded state, private, and Native corporation lands—sometimes constituting inholdings in the new federal preserves—are subject to all sorts of management. It will be a long time before the work of 1980 can be consolidated, let alone added to.

For all that, the outcome in Alaska is one to which the rest of the country, indeed the rest of the world, can only look in awe.

BAD NEWS FROM BIOLOGY

In the years following the Alaska battle, there was a new recognition of the biological inadequacy of the system of land reserves in the rest of the United States.

Many animals, especially large mammals that rove, need extensive wild country for their survival. It is not coincidental that grizzly bears remain only in the wildest corners of the Lower Forty-Eight. Animal and plant species also need to be able to shift their ranges in response to changes in the environment—for instance, a series of warmer or colder years, or a vegetation shift due to natural succession. In addition, different local populations of a species need to be in contact to permit interbreeding, and to allow replacements to filter in if one local group is lost to an event like a forest fire.

Biologists studying oceanic islands have long noted the correlation between size and biotic wealth: the smaller the area of an island, the lower the count of species it supports. They have pointed out the troubling analogy: by our wholesale alteration of landscapes, we have made many wildlife habitats on the U.S. mainland into islands of a sort, surrounded by oceans not of water but of altered, unusable land. Most of the islands have long since lost keystone species. The southern Rockies have no wolves; the Sierra Nevada, for all its grandeur, no grizzly bears. Between

1920 and 1976, thirteen mammal species disappeared from Mount Rainier National Park. Some other islands still support nearly their full complement of plants and animals. But can they continue to do so as time passes and the accidents of life, both natural and imposed by human activity, multiply?

The by now almost undeniable process of global warming—the great climate change induced by deforestation and the burning of fossil fuels—can only add to the risk of extinction. If the last population of a certain plant of the tundra zone clings to the uppermost acres of a chilly peak, what will save it when the peak gets warmer and the forest closes in? How can a beleaguered species retreat to the cooler north when the way is blocked by a settled valley and a superhighway?

In 1960, at one of the conferences that generated the push for the Wilderness Act, the Wilderness Society's Howard Zahniser challenged his listeners to think in the very long term: "We are working for a wilderness forever." In the United States, with the Wilderness Act, we thought we had achieved that permanence. But by the 1980s we knew that mere legislated boundaries are not enough to make "a wilderness forever"—not if wilderness means something more than roadless recreation land. Most of the pieces of land we have protected, however beautiful and valued, are too small, or too far apart, or both, to make sense as biological reserves. And, of course, whole ecosystems and landscapes are not represented at all.

CORES AND CORRIDORS: A DREAM OF RESTORATION

In the 1980s, alarmed by the prospect of species extinction on a scale not seen since the end of the dinosaurs, biologists proclaimed a new specialty called conservation biology. Increasingly, too, they began to speak out about policy. Studying the situation in the Cascade Mountains and elsewhere, they recommended that federal land be managed in a systematic way to preserve habitat, maintaining vital linkages.

This way of thinking cast a new light on roadless lands whose fate was still to be decided. Take the Klamath Mountains region of northwest California and adjacent Oregon, habitat for old-growth-dependent species like the spotted owl, the fisher, and the rare Humboldt marten (and also a planetary hotspot of botanical diversity). Here there are five important roadless areas, containing altogether about 1.5 million acres and more than a quarter of the old-growth forest remaining in the Pacific Northwest; a somewhat smaller classified wilderness area exists at the center of each. The roadless areas almost touch, creating corridors for species movement; the wilderness area boundaries stand well apart. If the connecting corridors are logged, as perennially planned, the biotic value of the entire complex will shrink disproportionately. In 1989, the California Wilderness Coalition urged that these corridors be protected, citing biological rather than recreational grounds. Although the Forest Service has so far resisted this plan, the corridors so far remain substantially unlogged.

The Klamath proposal was the first of many. From coast to coast, the goals and arguments of wilderness defenders were shifting. Advocates sought advice from scientists; sometimes they were the same people. They learned to think less in terms of single wilderness areas, important though these will always remain, and more in terms of clusters, connections, specific wildlife needs: a wilderness *system*, not in the merely formal sense of a list of areas, but in the practical sense of a web of interrelated lands.

In other parts of the United States, of course, the process of habitat fragmentation has gone vastly further than in the Klamath Mountains. In many regions, connections cannot simply be preserved; they would have to be restored. Among other things, restoration might require buying a great deal of land from private owners and closing lesser, or even significant, roads.

And what about the vast areas of the country where not even islands of wild land remain?

In 1992, an assortment of biologically oriented conservation veterans set out the boldest vision yet: the North American Wilderness Recovery Project (also called the Wildlands Project). A continental dream of biotic richness restored, the project sketches a network of protected areas threading through every state and region. The system would be anchored by large, strictly protected core reserves, often based on existing wilderness and parks. These cores would be linked by narrower corridors, not necessarily pristine but sufficiently unaltered to permit the passage of moving animals and slowly shifting plant populations. Around the cores and corridors would lie buffer zones, in economic use but not too densely roaded and free of activities that would compromise the more strictly protected lands within.

The initial Wildlands Project manifesto offered pilot plans for the state of Florida, for the Blue Ridge region of the southern Appalachians, for the Colorado Rockies, and—most ambitious of all—for the northern Rockies of the United States, a region where past preservation victories provide a good foundation. The sketch plan shows core areas around Yellowstone; in the Glacier National Park–Bob Marshall Wilderness region near the Canadian border; and in central Idaho, where vast forest wilderness areas exist. Two more core areas would be created in the Hells Canyon region of Idaho and Oregon and in the Cabinet Mountains–Yaak Valley area of western Montana, where Canada's wild Columbia Mountains nudge south of the border. Primitive habitat corridors, mostly along mountain ridges, would interlink these cores.

It isn't hard to visualize such a system for a region like the northern Rockies (though political enactment is another matter). It's quite something else to imagine it on a national scale. The obstacles are formidable and obvious. To build such a reserve system would require a shrinking-back of industrial forestry. It would require a great reduction in wildland grazing and the retirement of much marginal farmland. It would require the closure of numerous roads—even the bridging, somehow, of interstate highways. It is also inconceivable without the cooperation of the owners of millions of acres of private land.

Obviously, a continental reserve system is the project of generations, maybe of centuries. It cannot, like the Alaska National Interest Conservation Lands Act of 1980, be rammed through. The originators envision a long period of transition while we all get used to the idea. They foresee many compromises along the way, not in the goal but in the timing and details. They don't use the conventional heated rhetoric of "now or never."

Even in the very short term and the very small scale, however, the system idea reorganizes our thinking. It shifts attention from single wilderness areas to wilderness regions, wilderness sequences, wilderness constellations. It may suggest which fights deserve most energy. It puts a new emphasis on the restoration of less-than-wild landscapes. And it provides a galvanizing, almost painful hope: for a future in which we are not (as Zahniser said) merely slowing down the forces of degradation, or even stopping them at certain lines, but beginning, here and there, to roll them back.

CANADA'S GREAT OPPORTUNITY

In Canada, the story of wilderness preservation has unfolded rather differently.

Here, too, it begins with parks. Banff National Park, in the Canadian Rockies, dates to 1885, and it has many impressive peers. But soon the paths of the two nations diverge. In the United States, the first park set-asides started a trend toward keeping all the western public lands in federal ownership. Canada, by contrast, had already ceded its public domain lands, known as crown lands, to the provinces. Thus public land policy south of the sixtieth parallel has been chiefly the affair of the ten provincial governments. Their approaches have varied as much as might those of ten different nations.

North of the sixtieth parallel, where federally administered territories remain, less has changed; but even here land allocation is no longer accomplished, as often in the United States, by fiat. The Canadian central government just doesn't make major decisions here without the consent of territorial officials and of the Native groups that it recognizes as First Nations.

Given this institutional setup, the idea of a unified system of wilderness preserves, so central in the United States, could not develop in Canada. Rather, the park model has continued to prevail, in its second, more sophisticated form: parks as a representative sample of natural regions rather than merely as scenic jewels. National parks are still being designated, mostly in the territories north of the sixtieth parallel, occasionally also in the southern provinces, in every case as products of elaborate intergovernment negotiation.

The great majority of Canada's parks, however, are creations of the provinces alone, and a varied lot they are. Some provincial parks are largely wild preserves that equal in scope and grandeur anything found in the United States; others are not true parks at all but are rather akin to U.S. national forests—managed for timber harvest and all sorts of other uses and containing, at best, limited wild zones. At this writing, British Columbia is doing the best job of park building, both in quantity and in quality. The prairie province of Manitoba, where park status means next to nothing, is a notorious laggard. Conservationists and the federal government are encouraging the work through a high-level, low-pressure

effort called the Endangered Spaces Campaign. Outside the parks, exploitation continues at a dizzying pace. As a 1997 federal report put it,
"Little land exists now in Canada that does not have some kind of interest or commitment for uses such as oil and gas development, mining,
hydro-electricity, forestry, agriculture, and private recreation."

Mixed though the record is, Canada has opportunities still that the
United States may envy. It has enormous amounts of land in government
ownership, and it has truly vast tracts of de facto wilderness, especially in
the Yukon Territory, the Northwest Territories, and the soon-to-desig-
nated northeastern territory Nunavat. The door is still wide open to developing the kind of reserve system envisioned by the Wildlands Project.
Already there is talk on both sides of the international border of a chain
of linked reserves running up the line of the Rockies from Yellowstone
country to the Yukon, and another sequence linking the New York State
Forest Preserve in the Adirondacks with Alonquin Provincial Park in
Québec.

THE MANAGEMENT CHALLENGE

Meanwhile, in the old core wilderness areas—and wherever wild land is
subject to recreational use—we face the more traditional question: How
can we enjoy these places without causing them to deteriorate either biologically or esthetically? That is, without making them less wild, either in
function, or in feel?

It is easy to exaggerate the problem. We are not yet truly in danger of
"loving the wilderness to death"—not much of it anyway. Some places
look and seem wilder today than they did thirty or even sixty years ago.
But if there is no longer a crisis, as there seemed to be in the 1970s, there
is a challenge constantly renewed. How shall we act to maintain what has
so nourished us, and maintain it not for a handful of years, not for a generation or two, but over centuries—a wilderness experience forever?

There is a whole science now of wilderness management. It concerns
such matters as the reintroduction of fire to natural systems that cannot
be healthy without it and the fending-off of exotic plant and animal
species that increasingly threaten to displace native ones. Most of all,
though, wilderness management has to do with us, the tourists, the visitors. It involves the building of facilities—starting with trails—to handle
heavier use than the land could take without them. It involves education.

It involves managing access, as in steering people to lesser-used areas (a controversial idea) or deliberately concentrating them in more heavily used ones (ditto). And it may involve quotas, formal limits on the number of people allowed in particular places at particular times.

Out of the complexities, two simple facts emerge. First, our own behavior, person by person and group by group, is key. The more intelligent responsibility we take for walking softly in the wilderness, the less reason (or excuse) the managers will have for heavy-handed actions. Second, recreationally as well as biologically, bigger wilderness is better. A small, attractive alpine area, with good road access, is naturally going to come under great pressure. A large, forested wilderness, with high country nestled perhaps two days' march within it, is far less likely to be overrun—unless, of course, as in Alaska, access is permitted by plane.

So the problem of *managing* wilderness is in no way separate from the problem of *preserving* wilderness. The more we have, the easier it is to manage; the more the supply diminishes, the greater the manager's difficulties become. For eminently selfish reasons, we should insist on a generous wilderness, not a narrow, cramped, and superregulated one.

WHAT YOU CAN DO

If you've enjoyed the wilderness that is and would like to cast your vote for a "wilderness forever," there's no end to the ways you can do so.

One excellent and easy thing to do is to take a few notes. Wilderness managers and interested conservationists are far too few to keep track of the state of millions of acres of land. Backpackers can be their eyes and ears. Is a stretch of trail eroding? Are illegal vehicles crossing the wilderness boundary? Is livestock grazing where it shouldn't? Are exotic plant species—like purple loosestrife in many western areas—on the march? Armed with a camera, and maybe a little knowledge picked up at a ranger station, we can further document such problems.

A second simple thing to do is to write a letter, just one per trip. Every time I come out of a wilderness area, I like to send a note to the local staff of the managing agency. If nothing else, I compliment them on the beauty of the place and on their management of it (even if that management is merely inadvertent neglect). I thank them especially for any assistance given. I report any concerns. And if the area is one whose fate has yet to be decided, I ask to be on a mailing list to learn of future plans.

If you visit an area that is not yet in a wilderness or equivalent protected zone, your written witness could prove very important. It can be vital, when push comes to shove, to demonstrate that specific people have stated concern for specific places, based on documented visits: that they visited Indigo Creek in May, or Silver Prairie in July, or King Lear Peak in September, and loved it there. Keep copies of such letters.

Not sure where to write? Get the address if you stop off at a local agency office—for instance, to pick up a wilderness permit. If you're using an agency map, you may also find an address on that. If you're missing the address, you can contact the regional or central office of the appropriate bureaucracy—see Resources appendix.

Beyond the simple letter, of course, lies a world of involvement, if you want to enter it.

> ➡ *Write your elected representatives.* In the United States, where the federal government has the largest role in public land management, that means your representative and your state's two senators, as well as the president and his or her top staff. In the less centralized Canadian system, your first letter, at least, should go to your member of parliament on the provincial level. Tell them of your interest in wilderness in general and in such efforts as the North American Wilderness Recovery Project and Canada's Endangered Spaces campaign. If you've written to an agency regarding a particular area, send your legislators a copy of that letter, too. You may not get a very promising response, but don't let that bother you—politicians notice, though they may not read, their mail. (To reach a U.S. senator, write Honorable X, Washington, DC 20510; a representative is Honorable Y, Washington, DC 20515.) Phone calls and electronic mail, though better than nothing, don't carry the same weight.
>
> ➡ *Hook up with an environmental organization* that is interested in the same issues you are. If you don't have contacts in this direction, the central offices of the Sierra Club and the Wilderness Society can help; so can the Canadian Parks and Wilderness Society; so can some gear stores. A few addresses are found in the Resources appendix of this book. In a number of

states and provinces, there are regional wilderness groups that follow issues jurisdiction-wide. Very local groups of wilderness advocates may concentrate on some single area. (You might contact such a group when planning a trip to its backyard.) Joining any of these organizations, for a few dollars, can be worthwhile. Hooked into a grapevine, receiving current information, you know, at a minimum, to whom your letters should go, and when, in order to get the greatest possible effect.

- *Locate a trails group.* In addition to the many organizations working to protect wild areas as such, many more exist to promote and to help maintain recreational trails. Some concentrate on the long, glamorous paths like the Appalachian and its numerous progeny; others tend to the local trail networks where most of the day-to-day hiking gets done, and where the need is particularly great. In some parts of the United States, private organizations do as much to care for the land as do the government agencies that are in overall charge. Since the national governments seem to be spending less and less on wildland recreation, such partnerships are gaining in importance everywhere.

Every conceivable kind of work is waiting somewhere to be done: exploring unprotected areas, bucking loads up trails, monitoring timber sales and mining claims, censusing species of concern, attending lengthy hearings, combing through government documents, and much, much more. You'll like the people you meet in these endeavors.

But please don't be scared off: it isn't necessary to go beyond the almost effortless project of writing the occasional letter. And if a decent proportion of today's wilderness users did speak up to just that degree, their common voice would be very loud indeed.

There is more than a little satisfaction in doing something, however slight, to protect the future of a place you have enjoyed. It is as though you had paid a small and proper fee for the use of the land. If there is a tiny, unavoidable impact on the wilderness whenever a hiker goes into it, the hiker's letter written after the trip can more than cancel out that debt.

Appendix   RESOURCES

Here are some starting points for your exploration of the wilderness of information about wilderness: a list of citizen organizations concerned with wild land; lists of government agencies in the United States and Canada that manage it; information on ordering maps; a list of publications mentioned in the text; a selection of information sources accessible via computer; a (very small) selection of equipment makers and sellers; and the phone numbers of a couple of shuttle bus services mentioned in the book. Fax numbers, electronic-mail addresses, and Internet websites are provided as available.

CONSERVATION AND WILDERNESS TRAVEL ORGANIZATIONS

American Hiking Society
P.O. Box 20160
Washington, DC 20041
Phone: 301-565-6704
Fax: 301-565-6714
E-mail: AMHIKER@aol.com
America Online, keyword AHS; Internet: www.orca.org/ahs

American Trails
P.O. Box 11046
Prescott, AZ 86304
Phone: (520) 632-1140
Fax: (520) 632-1147
Email: AmTrails@lankaster.com
Internet: www.outdoorlink.com/amtrails/

Appalachian Mountain Club
5 Joy Street
Boston, MA 02108
Phone: 617-523-0636
Fax: 617-523-0722
Internet: www.outdoors.org

Appalachian Trail Conference
P.O. Box 807
Harpers Ferry, WV 25425
Phone: 304-535-6331
E-mail: info@atconf.org
Internet: www.atconf.org

Canadian Nature Federation
1 Nicholas Street, Suite 606
Ottawa, ONT K1N 7B7
Phone: 613-562-3447
Fax: 613-562-3371
E-mail: CNF@cnf.ca
Internet: www.magma.ca/~cnfgen

Canadian Parks and Wilderness
  Society
401 Richmond Street W, Suite 380
Toronto, ONT M5V 3A8
Phone: (800)333-9453
Fax: (416) 979-3155
E-mail: cpaws@icomm.ca
Internet: www.cpaws.org

Federation of Western Outdoor Clubs
512 Boylston Avenue E, Suite 106
Seattle, WA 98102
Phone: 206-322-3041

Leave No Trace
P.O. Box 997
Boulder, CO 80306
Phone: 800-332-4100
Fax: 303-444-3284
E-mail: LNT@Nols.edu
Internet: www.lnt.org

The Mountaineers
300 Third Avenue W
Seattle, WA 98119
Phone: (206) 284-6310
Fax: 206-284-4977
E-mail: clubmail@mountaineers.org
Internet: www.mountaineers.org

National Audubon Society
700 Broadway
New York, NY 10003
Phone: 212-979-3000
Fax: 212 979 3188
E-mail: webmaster@list.audubon.org
Internet: www.audubon.org

The Nature Conservancy
1815 N. Lynn Street
Arlington, VA 22209
Phone: 703-841-5300
703-841-1283
Internet: www.tnc.org

Sierra Club
85 Second Street, Second Floor
San Francisco, CA 94105
Phone: 415-977-5500
Fax: 415-977-5799
E-mail: information@sierraclub.org
Internet: www.sierraclub.org
Newsgroup: alt.org.sierra-club

The Wilderness Education
   Association
Department of Natural Resources
   Recreation and Tourism
Colorado State University
Fort Collins, CO 80523
Phone: 970-223-6252
E-mail: wea@lamar.colostate.edu
Internet: www.prairienet.org/~inewby
   /WEA/WEAHomePage.html

The Wilderness Society
900 Seventeenth Street NW
Washington, DC 20006
Phone: 202-833-2300
Fax: 202-429-3957
E-mail: tws@tws.org
Internet: www.wilderness.org

The Wildlands Project
1955 W. Grant Road, Suite 148A
Tucson, AZ 85745
Phone: 520-884-0875
Fax: 520-884-0962
E-mail: wildland@waonline.com
Internet: www.wild-lands.org

U.S. FEDERAL AND SELECTED STATE AGENCIES THAT MANAGE WILDERNESS LAND

BUREAU OF LAND MANAGEMENT

Washington, D.C.
Bureau of Land Management
1849 C Street, Room 504-LS
Washington, DC 20240
Phone: 202-452-5125
E-mail: woinfo@wo.blm.gov
Internet: www.blm.gov

Alaska
Bureau of Land Management
222 W. Seventh Avenue, Suite 13
Anchorage, AK 99513
Phone: 907-271-5960
Internet: www.ak.blm.gov

Alaska Public Lands Information
  Center
605 West Fourth Avenue, Suite 105
Anchorage, Alaska 99501
Phone: 907-271-2737
Internet: www.nps.gov/aplic

Arizona
Bureau of Land Management
Arizona Public Lands Information
  Center
222 N. Central Avenue
Phoenix AZ 85004
Phone: 602-417-9200
E-mail: azasouweb@az.blm.gov
azInternet: www.az.blm.gov

California
Bureau of Land Management
2135 Butano Drive
Sacramento, CA 95825
Phone: 916-978-4400
E-mail: gcatledg@ca.blm.gov
Internet: www.ca.blm.gov\caso

Colorado
Bureau of Land Management
2850 Youngfield Street
Lakewood, CO 80215
Phone: 303-239-3600
Fax: 303-239-3933
Internet: www.co.blm.gov

Eastern States
7450 Boston Boulevard
Springfield, VA 22153
Phone: 703-440-1600
www-a.blm.gov/eso

Idaho
Bureau of Land Management
BLM Idaho State Office
1387 South Vinnell Way
Boise, Idaho 83709
Phone: (208) 373-4000
E-mail: klong@id.blm.gov
Internet: www.id.blm.gov

Montana, North and South Dakota
Bureau of Land Management
222 N. Thirty-second Street
P.O. Box 36800
Billings, Montana 59107
Phone: 406-255-2885
Fax: 406-255-2762
E-mail: mtinfo@mt.blm.gov
Internet: www.mt.blm.gov

Nevada
Bureau of Land Management
850 Harvard Way
P.O. Box 12000
Reno, NV 89520
Phone: 702-785-6400
Fax: 702-785-6411
Internet: www.nv.blm.gov

New Mexico, Oklahoma, Kansas, and Texas
Bureau of Land Management
1474 Rodeo Road
P.O. Box 27115
Santa Fe, NM 87502-0115
(87505 for street)
Phone: 505-438-7400
E-mail: ratkinso@nmo151wp.
nmso.nm.blm.gov
Internet: www.nm.blm.gov

Oregon and Washington
Bureau of Land Management
1515 Southwest Fifth
P.O. Box 2965
Portland, OR 97208
Phone: 503-952-6001
Fax: 503-952-6308
E-mail: or912mb@or.blm.gov
Internet: www.or.blm.gov

Utah
Bureau of Land Management
324 S. State Street
P.O. Box 45155
Salt Lake City, UT 84145
Phone: 801-539-4001
Internet: www.blm.gov/utah

Wyoming
Bureau of Land Management
5353 Yellowstone
P.O. Box 1828
Cheyenne, WY 82003
Phone: 307-775-6256
Internet: www.wy.blm.gov

NATIONAL PARK SERVICE

Washington, D.C.
National Park Service
1849 C Street NW
Washington, DC 20240
Phone: (202) 208-6843
Internet: www.nps.gov

Alaska Region
National Park Service
2525 Gambell St. Room 107
Anchorage, AK 99503
Phone: 907-257-2574
Anchorage, AK 99503

Alaska Public Lands Information
Center
605 West Fourth Avenue, Suite 105
Anchorage, Alaska 99501
Phone: 907-271-2737
Internet: www.nps.gov/aplic

Intermountain Region (Ariz., Colo., Mont., N.Mex., Okla., Tex., Utah, Wyo.)
National Park Service
12795 Alameda Pkwy
Denver, CO 80225
Phone: 303-969-2500

Midwest Region (Ark., Ill., Ind. Iowa, Kans., Mich., Minn., Mo., Nebr., N.Dak., Ohio, S.Dak., Wis.)
National Park Service
1709 Jackson Street
Omaha, NE 68102
Phone: 402-221-3456

Northeast Region (Conn., Del., Maine, Md., Mass., N.H., N.J., N.Y., Pa., R.I., Vt., Va., W.Va.)
U.S. Custom House
200 Chestnut St. Rm.322
Philadephia, PA 19106
Phone: (215) 597-4971

Southeast Region (Ala., Fla., Ga., Ky., Miss., N.C., S.C., Tenn.)
National Park Service
100 Alabama Street SW
1924 Building
Atlanta, GA 30303
Phone: 404-331-5711

Pacific West Region (Calif., Hawaii, Idaho, Nev., Ore., Wash.)
National Park Service
600 Harrison Street, Suite 600
San Francisco, CA 94101
415-556-0560

U.S. FISH AND WILDLIFE SERVICE

Washington, D.C.
U.S. Fish and Wildlife Service
Department of the Interior
Interior Building
1849 C Street NW
Washington, DC 20240
Phone: 202-208-7535
Fax: 202-208-7407
E-mail: Web_Reply@mail.fws.gov
Internet: www.fws.gov

Alaska Regional Office
U.S. Fish and Wildlife Service
1011 E. Tudor Road Room 229
Anchorage, AK 99503
Phone: 907-786-3309
Fax: 907-786-3652
E-mail: stephen_hanson@mail.
fws.gov

Alaska Public Lands Information
Center
605 West Fourth Avenue, Suite 105
Anchorage, Alaska 99501
Phone: 907-271-2737
Internet: www.nps.gov/aplic

Great Lakes–Big Rivers Regional Office (Ill., Ind., Iowa, Mich., Minn., Mo., Ohio, Wis.)
U.S. Fish and Wildlife Service
BHW Federal Building, 1 Federal Dr.
Fort Snelling, MN 55111
Phone: 612-725-3519
Fax: 612-725-3583
E-mail: r3_pao@mail.fws.gov
Internet: www.fws.gov/~r3pao

Mountain-Prairie Regional Office (Colo., Kans., Mont., N.Dak., Nebr., S.Dak., Utah, Wyo.)
U.S. Fish and Wildlife Service
134 Union Boulevard
P.O. Box 25486
Denver, CO 80225
Phone: 303-236-7905
Fax: 303-236-3815
E-mail: diane_katzenberger@fws.gov
Internet: www.r6.fws.gov

Northeast Regional Office (Va., W.Va., Pa. and states to the northeast)
U.S. Fish and Wildlife Service
300 Westgate Center Drive
Hadley, MA 01035
Phone: 413-253-8200
E-mail: john_eaton@fws.gov
Internet: www.fws.gov/~r5fws

Pacific Regional Office (Calif., Hawaii and Pacific Islands, Idaho, Nev., Ore., Wash.)
U.S. Fish and Wildlife Service
Eastside Federal Complex
911 N.E. Eleventh Avenue
Portland, OR 97232
Phone: 503-231-6121
Internet: www.r1.fws.gov

Southeast Regional Office (Ala., Ark., Fla., Ga., Ky., La., Miss., N.C., S.C., Tenn., Puerto Rico, U.S. Virgin Islands)
1875 Century Boulevard
Atlanta, GA 30345
Phone: 404-679-7289
E-mail: barbara_orisich@fws.gov
Internet: www.fws.gov/~r4eao

Southwest Regional Office (Ariz., N.M., Okla., Tex.)
U.S. Fish and Wildlife Service
500 Gold Avenue SW, Suite 3018
Albuquerque, NM 87102
Phone: 505-248-6911
Fax: 505-248-6915
sturgeon.irm1.r2.fws.gov

U.S. FOREST SERVICE

Washington, D.C.
U.S. Forest Service
P.O. Box 96090
Washington, DC 20090
Phone: 202-205-1760
Fax: 202-205-1610
E-mail: /s=pao/ou1=wo1b@mhs-fswa.attmail.com
Internet: www.fs.fed.us

Alaska Region
U.S. Forest Service
Federal Office Building
709 W. 9th Street
P.O. Box 21628
Juneau, AK 99802
Phone: 907-586-8751
Fax: 907-586-7928
Internet: www.fs.fed.us/intro/
  directory/rg-10.htm

Alaska Public Lands Information Ctr.
605 West Fourth Avenue, Suite 105
Anchorage, Alaska 99501
Phone: 907-271-2737
Internet: www.nps.gov/aplic

Pacific Southwest Region (Calif., Hawaii, Guam and Pacific Islands)
U.S. Forest Service
630 Sansome Street
San Francisco, CA 94111
Phone: 415-705-2874
Internet: www.fs.fed.us/intro/
  directory/rg-5.htm

Eastern Region (Ill., Ind., Maine, Mich., Minn., Mo., Ohio, Pa., N.H., Vt., W.Va., Wis.)
U.S. Forest Service
310 W. Wisconsin Avenue, Suite 500
Milwaukee, WI 53203
Phone: 414-297-3693
Internet: www.fs.fed.us/intro/
  directory/rg-9.htm

Intermountain Region (eastern Calif., southern Idaho, Nev., Utah, western Wyo.)
U.S. Forest Service
Federal Office Building
324 Twenty-fifth Street
Ogden, UT 84401
Phone: 801-625-5605
Fax: 801-625-5127
Internet: www.fs.fed.us/intro/
  directoryrg-4.htm

Northern Region (Mont., northern Idaho, N.Dak., northwest S.Dak)
U.S. Forest Service
Federal Building
P.O. Box 7669
Missoula, MT 59807
Phone: 406-329-3511
Fax: 406-329-3347
Internet: www.fs.fed.us/intro/
  directory/rg-1.htm

Pacific Northwest Region (Ore., Wash)
U.S. Forest Service
333 S.W. First Avenue
P.O. Box 3623
Portland, OR 97208
Phone: 503-808-2971
Fax: 503-808-2229
Internet: www.fs.fed.us/intro/
  directory/rg-6.htm

*Rocky Mountain Region (Colo., Wyo.
east of Continental Divide, S.Dak.,
Nebr., Kans.)*
U.S. Forest Service
P.O. Box 25127
Lakewood, CO 80225
Phone: 303-275-5350
Internet: www.fs.fed.us/intro/
directory/rg-2.htm

*Southern Region (Ala., Ark. Fla., Ga.,
Ky., La., Miss., N.C., S.C., Okla.,
Tenn., Va., Tex., Puerto Rico, Virgin
Islands)*
U.S. Forest Service
1720 Peachtree Road NW, Suite 154
Atlanta, GA 30367
Phone: 404-347-2384
Internet: www.fs.fed.us/intro/
directory/rg-8.htm

Southwestern Region (Ariz., N.Mex.)
U.S. Forest Service
Federal Building
517 Gold Avenue SW
Albuquerque, NM 87102
Phone: 505-842-3292
Internet: www.fs.fed.us/intro/
directory/rg-3.htm

STATE AGENCIES

Alaska Department of Natural
Resources
Division of Parks and Outdoor Recre-
ation
Frontier Building
3601 C Street, Suite 200
Anchorage, AK 99503
Phone: 907-269-8400
Fax: (907) 269-8901
E-mail: pic@dnr.state.ak.us
Internet: www.dnr.state.ak.us

Alaska Public Lands Information
Center
605 West Fourth Avenue, Suite 105
Anchorage, Alaska 99501
Phone: 907-271-2737
Internet: www.nps.gov/aplic

California Department of Parks and
Recreation
1416 Ninth Street
Sacramento, CA 95814
Phone: 916-653-6995
Internet: www.ceres.ca.gov/parks

Maine Bureau of Parks and Lands
22 State House Station
Augusta, ME 04330
Phone: 207-287-3821
Internet: www.state.me.us/doc/
prkslnds/prkslnds.htm#parks

Baxter Park Authority
64 Balsam Drive
Millinocket, ME 04462
Phone: (207) 723-5140)

Michigan Department of Natural
Resources
P.O. Box 30028
Lansing, MI 48909
Internet: www.dnr.state.mi.us
Parks and Recreation Division
P.O. Box 30257
Lansing, MI 48909
Phone: 517-373-9900

Forest Management Division
P.O. Box 30452
Lansing, MI 48909
Phone: 517-373-4175
E-mail: fullerm@dnr.state.mi.us

Minnesota Department of Natural Resources
Division of Parks and Recreation
500 Lafayette Road
Saint Paul, MN 55155
Phone: 612-296-6157
Internet: www.dnr.state.mn.us

New York Department of Environmental Conservation
Bureau of Public Lands
50 Wolf Road, Suite 438
Albany, NY 12233
Phone: 518-457-7433
Internet: www.dec.state.ny.us

Pennsylvania Department of Conservation and Natural Resources
Bureau of State Parks
P.O. Box 8551
Harrisburg, PA 17105
Phone: 717-787-6640, 800-637-2757
E-mail: enved.sp@a1.dcnr.state.pa.us
Internet: www.dcnr.state.pa.us

Bureau of Forestry
P.O. Box 8552
Harrisburg, PA 17105
Phone: 717-787-2703

Wisconsin Department of Natural Resources
Bureau of Parks and Recreation
P.O. Box 7921
Madison, WI 53707
Phone: 608-266-2181
E-mail: wiparks@dnr.state.wi.us
Internet: www.dnr.state.wi.us

CANADIAN FEDERAL AND PROVINCIAL AGENCIES
THAT MANAGE WILDERNESS LAND

Parks Canada
Department of Canadian Heritage
25 Eddy Street
Hull, QU K1A 0M5
Phone: 819-997-0055
E-Mail: parks_webmaster@pch.gc.ca
Internet: parkscanada.pch.gc.ca/
parks/main_e.htm

Alberta Department of Environ-
mental Protection
Division of Recreation and Protected
Areas
Second Floor, Oxbridge Place
9820-106 Street
Edmonton, AB T5K 2J6
Phone: 403-427-7009
Fax: 403-427-5980
E-mail: infocent@env.gov.ab.ca
Internet: www.gov.ab.ca:80/~env/
parks.html

British Columbia Ministry of
Environment, Lands and Parks
2d Floor, 800 Johnson Street
Victoria, BC V8V 1X4
Phone: 250-387-5002
Internet: www.env.gov.bc.ca

Manitoba Natural Resources
P.O. Box 22
200 Saulteaux Crescent
Winnipeg, Manitoba R3J 3W3
Phone: 800 214 6497
Internet: www.gov.mb.ca/natres/
index.html

New Brunswick
Internet: www.gov.nb.ca
Department of Natural Resources and
Energy
P.O. Box 6000
Fredericton, NB E3B 5H1
Phone: 506-453-2730
Fax: 506-457-4881

Department of Economic
Development and Tourism
P.O. Box 12345
Woodstock NB E0J 2B0
Phone: 800-561-0123

Newfoundland Department of
Tourism, Culture and Recreation
P.O. Box 8700
St John's, NF A1B 4J6
Phone: 709-729-2424
Fax: 709-729-1100
E-mail : info@gov.nf.ca
hcumming@tourism.gov.nf.ca
Internet: www.gov.nf.ca

Northwest Territories Department of
Resources, Wildlife and Economic
Development, Parks and Tourism
Division
Scotia Centre, Box 21
600 5102 Fiftieth Avenue
Yellowknife, NT X1A 3S8
Phone: 800-661-0788, 403-873-7903
Fax: 403-873-0163
Internet: www.gov.nt.ca

Nova Scotia Department of Natural
  Resources
P.O. Box 698
Halifax, NS B3J 2T9
Phone: 902-424-5935
Fax: 902-424-7735
Internet: www.gov.ns.ca

Ontario Ministry of Natural
  Resources
300 Water Street
P.O. Box 7000
Peterborough, ONT K9J 8MJ
Phone: 705-314-2000
Fax: 705:755-1701
Internet: www.gov.on.ca

Québec Department of Environment
  and Wildlife
675, boulevard René-Lévesque Est
Édifice Marie-Guyart, r.-d.-c.
Québec, QU G1R 5V7
Phone: 800-561-1616, 418-521-3830
Fax: (418) 646-5974
E-mail: info@mef.gouv.qc.ca
Internet: www.gouv.qc.ca/minorg/
  indexa.htm

Saskatchewan Environment and Re-
  source Management
3211 Albert Street
Regina, SAS S4S 5W6
Phone: 306-787-2700
E-mail: inquiry.centre.serm@sk.
  sympatico.ca
Internet: www.gov.sk.ca/govt/environ

Yukon Territory Department of
  Renewable Resources
P.O. Box 2703
Whitehorse, YT Y1A 2C6
Phone: 403-667-5261
Fax: 403-393-6223

MAPS

UNITED STATES

U.S. Geological Survey (USGS) topographical maps may be purchased over the counter at USGS Earth Science Information Centers in several cities: Anchorage, Alaska; Denver, Colo.; Menlo Park, Calif.; Reston, Va; Rolla, Mo.; Salt Lake City, Utah; Sioux Falls, S.D.; Spokane, Wash.; and Washington, D.C. You can also obtain topo maps from many gear stores and commercial map dealers, or you can order them from USGS at the address below.

Current price for all sheets is $4.00, plus a handling charge of $3.50 per order. To get started, order free state catalogs (lists) and indexes (sheet location charts) from USGS at 800-872-6277 (800-USA-MAPS). Also request the brochure *Topographic Map Symbols*.

Map Distribution
U.S. Geological Survey
P.O. Box 25286, Federal Center
Denver, CO 80225

Phone: 800-872-6277
Fax: 303-202-4693
Internet: www.usgs.gov

Topographic maps for the United States are also available on CD-ROM disks (see Chapter 16) from the USGS and private suppliers, including:

Earth Visions
655 Portsmouth Avenue
Greenland, NH 03840
Phone: 800-627-7236
Internet: www.earthvisions.com

Wildflower Productions
375 Alabama Street, Suite 230
San Francisco, CA 94110
Phone: 415-558-8700
Fax: 415-558-9700
E-mail: info@topo.com
Internet: www.topo.com

CANADA

Canadian topographical maps are available from the Canada Map Office in Ottawa and at many stores. From the United States, the best procedure is to contact Ottawa to request free indexes (three cover the entire nation) and then to place an order by phone, using a credit card; the day's exchange rate between U.S. and Canadian dollars will apply.

Natural Resources Canada
Canada Map Office
130 Bentley Avenue
Nepean, ONT K1A OE9

Phone: 800-465-6277
Fax: 899-771-6277
E-mail: info@GeoCan.NRCan.gc.ca

PUBLICATIONS MENTIONED IN THE TEXT

Adventuring in Alaska
Peggy Wayburn
San Francisco: Sierra Club Books,
1998

Backpacker Magazine
33 E. Minor Street
Emmaus, PA 18098
America Online, keyword Backpacker;
Internet: www.gearfinder.com

Backpacking in Alaska
Jim DuFresne
Hawthorn, Victoria, Australia: Lonely
Planet, 1995

*Bear Attacks: Their Causes and
Avoidance*
Stephen Herrero
New York: Lyons & Burford, 1985

Composition of Foods
Agriculture Handbook #8
U.S. Government Printing Office
Washington, DC 20401
Phone: 202-512-1800
Fax: 202-512-2250
Internet: www.access.gpo.gov

The Essential Outdoor Gear Manual
Annie Getchell
Blue Ridge Summit, PA: Ragged
Mountain Press, 1995
Phone: 800-233-1128
Fax: 800-932-0183

Magnetic Declination Chart
Geomatics Canada, Canada Map
Office
130 Bentley Avenue
Nepean, ONT K1A OE9
Phone: 800-465-6277
Fax: 899-771-6277
E-mail: info@GeoCan.NRCan.gc.ca

Magnetic Field/Declination U.S.
Map Distribution
U.S. Geological Survey
P.O. Box 25286, Federal Center
Denver, CO 80225
Phone: 800-872-6277
Internet: www.usgs.gov

Medicine for Mountaineering, 4th ed.
James A. Wilkerson, editor
Seattle: The Mountaineers Books, 1992

*Mountaineering: The Freedom of the
Hills*, 6th ed.
Don Graydon and Kurt Hanson,
editors
Seattle: The Mountaineers Books, 1997

Outside Magazine
P.O. Box 54729
Boulder, CO 80322
800-678-1131
Internet: www.outside.starwave.com

*The Pacific Crest Trail Hiker's
Handbook*, 2d ed.
Ray Jardine
AdventureLore Press, 1996
P.O. Box 804
LaPine, OR 97739

*The Pocket Doctor: Your Ticket to Good
Health While Traveling*, 2d ed.
Stephen Bezruchka
Seattle: The Mountaineers Books, 1992

SELECTED ON-LINE INFORMATION SOURCES

To get at these Internet information sources, you need at least a 386 PC computer running Windows or OS2; Macintosh users will need system 6.0.5 or higher. Your modem—the device that turns computer information into pulses that can travel on the phone lines—must have a speed of 9,600 bits per second (bps) or preferably higher. You also need an intermediary service (with a far bigger computer than you have) to tap into the Internet. There are several such "Internet service providers" in almost any locality. You can also get access through national networks such as America Online or Prodigy, which offer Internet connections along with specially packaged materials of their own. The monthly cost of Internet access ranges from about $10 to $25.

Two likely kinds of places to visit are "newsgroups," basically bulletin boards where you can post your messages and read those posted by others; and "websites," which provide information to you in words and pictures, with limited opportunity to answer back. Related websites often have built-in "hot links" you click on to jump swiftly from one to another.

Internet technology is changing rapidly, the specific Internet offerings faster still. Here are a few good ones at this writing:

WEBSITES

Adventure Sports
Internet: www.adventuresports.com
A good general starting point.

Appalachian Trail
Internet: www.fred.net/kathy/at.html
Information about the trail.

Backpacker's Basecamp
Internet: www.bpbasecamp.com
Virtual magazine, with discussions, gear guide, destinations, and so forth.

Backcountry
io.datasys.swri.edu/Overview.html
Another multifaceted site.

Backcountry Toilet
Internet: www.uvm.edu/~plachape/toilets.html
Wilderness sanitation and related topics.

Gearfinder
Internet: www.gearfinder.com
Searchable tables showing currently available backpacks, boots, sleeping gear, stoves, and tents.

Great Outdoor Recreation Pages (GORP)
Internet: www.gorp.com
Starting place for information on varied outdoor activities.

Leave No Trace Program, National Outdoor Leadership School
Internet: www.lnt.org
Information on recommended practices.

NEWSGROUPS

Participate by (free) subscription.
alt.org.sierra-club

rec.backcountry

EQUIPMENT SOURCES

There are hundreds of gear makers and major suppliers. This short selection makes no claim to be fair. I have chosen a few outfits that are large, prominent, historic or in some sense leaders in the field. Many of these firms publish interesting and informative catalogs.

Columbia Sportswear Company
6600 N. Baltimore
Portland, OR 97203
Phone: 800-622-6953
Internet: www.columbia.com

Dana Design
333 Simmental Way
Bozeman, MT 59715
Phone: 406-587-4188

Danner
LaCrosse Footwear, Inc.
1319 St. Andrew Street
LaCrosse, WI 54603
Phone: 800-345-0430
Internet: www.danner.com

Eastern Mountain Sports
1 Vose Farm Road
Peterborough, NH 03458
Phone: 888-463-6367
Internet: www.emsonline.com

Eureka Tent
See Johnson Worldwide Associates

Fabiano Shoe Company
850 Summer Street
South Boston, MA 02127
Phone: 617-268-5625
Internet: www.Fabiano.com

Garcia Machine
14097 Avenue, Suite 272
Visalia, CA 93292
Phone: 209-732-3785

Gerry Sportswear
1051 First Street S
Seattle, WA 98134
Phone: 206-623-4194

Helly-Hansen
P.O. Box 97031
Redmond, WA 98073
Phone: 800-635-9595
Internet: www.hellyhansen.com

Hi-Tec Sports USA, Inc.
4801 Stoddard Road
Modesto, CA 95356
Phone: 800-521-1698
Fax: 209-545-2543
Internet: www.hi-tec.com/boots

Johnson Worldwide Associates
(Camp Trails, Eureka, Silva)
P.O. Box 966
Binghamton, NY 13902
Phone: 800-572-8822
Internet: www.jwa.com

Kelty Pack, Inc.
6235 Lookout Road
Boulder, CO 80301
Phone: 800-423-2320
E-mail: supertioga@aol.com
Internet: www.kelty.com

L.L. Bean
Freeport, ME 04033
Phone: 800-221-4221
Internet: www.llbean.com

Lowe Alpine Systems
P.O. Box 1449
Broomfield, CO 80038
Phone: 303-465-0522
Internet: www.lowealpine.com

Madden Mountaineering
2400 Central Avenue
Boulder, CO 80301
Phone: 303-442-5828
Fax: 303-442-5846

Marmot Mountain Ltd.
2321 Circadian Way
Santa Rosa, CA 95407
Phone: 707-541-2166, ext. 701;
   or 707-544-4590
Fax: 707-544-1344
E-mail: info@marmot.com
Internet: www.Marmot.com

Moss Tents
P.O. Box 577
Camden, ME 04843
Phone: 800-859-5322

Mountain Equipment Coop
1655 W. Third Avenue
Vancouver, BC V6J 1K1
Phone: 800-663-2667
Fax: 604-731-6483
Internet: www.mec.ca

Mountain Gear
2002 N. Division
Spane, WA 99207
Phone: 800-829-2009
Internet: www.mgear.com

Mountain Hard Wear
950 Gilman Street
Berkeley, CA 94710
Phone: 510-559-6700
Internet: www.mountainhardwear.
  com

Mountain Safety Research
P.O. Box 24547
Seattle, WA 98124
Phone: 800-877-9677
Fax: 206-224-6492
Internet: www.msrcorp.com

Mountainsmith
18301 W. Colfax Avenue
Golden, CO 80401
Phone: 888-687-6484
Fax: 303-278-7739

The North Face
2013 Farallon Drive
San Leandro, CA 94577
Phone: 800-719-6678 (USA)
   or 800-215-2962 (Canada)

Optimus: A&H Enterprises
1582 Parkway Loop, Suite G
Tustin, CA 92780
Phone: 714-258-2525
Fax: 714-258-7077
E-mail: Ahoptimus@aol.com

Outbound Products
8585 Fraser Street
Vancouver, BC V5X 3Y1
Phone: 604-321-5464
Fax: 604-321-8525

Outdoor Research
2203 First Avenue S
Seattle, WA 98134
Phone: 888-467-4327
Internet: www.orgear.com

Patagonia, Inc.
P.O. Box 32050
Reno, NV 89533
800-638-6464
Internet: www.patgagonia.com

Peak 1
3600 North Hydraulic
Wichita, KS 67219
Phone: 800-835-3278

Polar Equipment
12881 Foothill Lane
Saratoga, CA 95070
Phone: 408-867-4576

Recreational Equipment, Inc. (REI)
P.O. Box 1938
Sumner, WA 98390-0800
Phone: 800-828-5533
Internet: www.rei.com

Royal Robbins
1314 Coldwell Avenue
Modesto, CA 95350
Phone: 800-587-9044 (USA)
   or 800-672-3158 (Canada)
Internet: www.royalrobbins.com

Sherpa Snowshoes
444 South Pine Street
Burlington, WI 53105
Phone: 800-621-2277

Sierra Designs
1255 Powell Street
Emeryville, CA 94608
Phone: 800-635-0461

Sierra Trading Post
5025 Campstool Road
Cheyenne, WY 82007
Phone: 800-713-4534
Fax: 800-378-8946

Silva Compass
See Johnson Worldwide Associates

Stephenson's Warmlite Equipment
22 Hook Road
RD 4, Box 145
Gilford, NH 03246

Sun Precautions
2815 Wetmore Avenue
Everett, WA 98210I
Phone: 800-882-7860
E-mail: spf30plus@aol.com

Suunto USA
2151 Las Palmas Drive, Suite G
Carlsbad, CA 92009
Phone: 800-543-9124
Internet: www.suunto.fi

Terramar Sports Worldwide, Ltd.
10 Midland Avenue
Port Chester, NY 10573
Phone: 800-468-7455
E-mail: terramar25@aol.com

Tough Traveler Kidsystems
1012 State Street
Schenectady, NY 12307
Phone: 800-468-6844
Fax: 518-377-5434

Vasque
314 Main Street
Red Wing, MN 55066
Phone: 612-388-8211
Fax: 612-388-7415

Vibram Fix By Mail
Phone: 800-842-7267

Western Mountaineering
1025 S. Fifth Street
San Jose, CA 95112
Phone: 408-287-8944
Fax: 408-287-8946

Wiggy's, Inc.
P.O. Box 2124
Grand Junction, CO 81502
Phone: 970-241-6465
Fax: 970-241-5921

ZZ Manufacturing, Inc.
1520A Industrial Park Street
Covina, CA 91722
Phone: 800-594-9046
Fax: 626-332-7947
E-mail: zzmfg@fia.net
Internet: www.gorp.com/zzstove

TRANSPORTATION SERVICES MENTIONED IN THE TEXT

Country Corners (Sierra Nevada)
674 Keough Street
Bishop, CA 93514
Phone: 760-872-4411

Transcanyon Shuttle
P.O. Box 348
Grand Canyon, AK 86023
Phone: 520-638-2820

INDEX